DATE DUE

MAR 2 7 1995	
APR 1 0 1995	

BRODART   Cat. No. 23-221

RUSSIAN SEAPOWER AND 'THE EASTERN QUESTION', 1827–41

RUSSIAN SEAPOWER AND 'THE EASTERN QUESTION' 1827–41

John C. K. Daly

Assistant Professor of Russian and Naval History
Kansas State University

Naval Institute Press
Annapolis, Maryland

First published 1991

Published and distributed in the United States
of America by the Naval Institute Press,
Annapolis, Maryland 21402

Library of Congress Catalog Card No. 90–62893

ISBN 1–55750–726–0

Printed in Hong Kong

To Mary Kennedy Daly, for everything.
To Celia Pesce, who helped me to remember the things I forgot.
To Maria Clara Florence Daly, who helped me to learn things that I never knew.

Contents

Preface

'Any ruler with an army has one hand, but he who also has a fleet
has two hands...'.

Peter the Great, *Ustav morskoi*
(Saint Petersburg, 1720, p. 1)

'It is then particularly in the field of naval strategy that the teachings
of the past have a value which is no degree lessened.'

Alfred Thayer Mahan,
The Influence of Seapower upon History (p. 9)

This work attempts to delineate the activities, abilities, matériel and
personnel of the Russian Black Sea Fleet during the years 1827–41 in
relation to the abilities and activities of the other Mediterranean naval
powers within the larger context of the 'Eastern Question.' The subject
is both worthwhile and largely unknown. During the one-hundred-
and-forty-year gradual decline of the Ottoman Empire from the Treaty
of Passarowitz to the Crimean War, Russian seapower in the Black
Sea emerged from obscurity to parity with the Ottoman naval forces.
The maritime balance of power between Russia and the Ottoman
Empire became the crucial pivot upon which Russian foreign policy
towards Turkey revolved during the post-Napoleonic, pre-Crimean
period. Due to the fact that this was unstated and implicit, the topic
has received surprisingly little attention in studies of the 'Eastern
Question' over the years.

There are a number of reasons for this obscurity. First and
foremost, perhaps, is the fact that 'naval science' emerged only late
in the nineteenth century with the epochal studies of Mahan and
Colomb. Both writers largely concentrated their focus on the glorious
history of the Royal Navy; other countries and their nautical abilities
were measured by this glittering yardstick, not only by British, but
frequently by foreign historians evaluating their own countries'

histories. For many, the years following Trafalgar are largely a wasteland, until they are aroused from their torpor by Tsushima. While naval history has increasingly evolved as a historical discipline in its own right, many historians have to a certain extent used the Royal Navy's performance to evaluate their own countries' endeavours, downplaying the obvious fact that national needs dictate differing perceptions and policies.

This blue-water myopia was not solely restricted to admirers of the Royal Navy. Admiral Sergei Georgievich Gorshkov was frequently referred to as a 'Russian Mahan'; in his *Morskaia moshch' gosudarstva* he dismisses the entire Russian naval effort in the period under consideration here in one pithy sentence, noting 'the ships almost never went to sea'.

This problem of interpretation is exacerbated when one considers the 'Eastern Question'; linguistic complexities unite with problems of access to sources to make such a study dauntingly difficult.

With the exception of Navarino, the period under consideration contains no major fleet actions. When Russian participation at Navarino is mentioned in the West, it is almost as an aside. Such a dismissal is unfair, however, as the period 1827–41 contains a number of events of interest, altering the traditional Mediterranean 'balance of power', beginning with the battle of Navarino, which assured the eventual freedom of Greece. In 1830, a French naval operation captured Algiers, putting an end to a nest of corsairs that had preyed on Mediterranean commerce for centuries.

To find the antecedents of the period 1827–41, we must consider Russo-Turkish relations from the time of Peter the Great. Peter is regarded as the 'father' of the Russian navy, and his successful capture of Azov from the Turks presaged an eventual Russian breakthrough to the shores of the Black Sea itself. Peter's galley fleet, built at Voronezh on the lower Don, may be regarded as the direct forerunner of the Black Sea Fleet. Although Peter had to return his hard-won gains after the Prut Treaty in 1711, the pattern was set for future Russo-Turkish relations; seapower could provide the decisive edge in warring with the Turks.

Peter's successors unfortunately lacked his dynamism, and his navy was allowed to decline. Russian maritime fortunes were to recover with the accession of Catherine the Great to the throne in 1768. Catherine immediately set about reviving the navy as a tool of Russian foreign policy, and her reign scored notable successes; the most brilliant was the burning of the Turkish fleet at Çesme in 1770, a battle which destroyed more line ships than Trafalgar. Catherine had only her Baltic squadron to use in her battles, as Russia was still barred from the Black Sea by the Turks. In order to fight the Turks, Catherine sent a squadron from the Baltic to the Mediterranean.

The appearance of Orlov's squadron in the Mediterranean opened a new phase for Russia's struggle to control the Black Sea; indeed, control of the Black Sea could only be decisively achieved in the Mediterranean. The strategic importance of 'command of the sea' in the Mediterranean has long been noted; as Mahan has observed, 'Circumstances have caused the Mediterranean Sea to play a greater part in the history of the world, both in a commercial and in a military point of view, than any other sheer of water of the same size.'

Çesme provides a useful illustration of inherent weaknesses in Russia's navy that would persist until the Nicholaeven navy and beyond. First, Orlov's squadron contained a fair number of foreign officers; there were simply not enough Russian officers with sufficient skill to man all the ships. The supreme commander of the squadron, Admiral Elphinston, was British. By the time of Tsar Nicholas I, the need for foreign officers had been alleviated, but there were still significant shortages in the officer corps of highly-trained personnel. Many Russian officers served as volunteers in the Royal Navy, in order to participate in its 'blue-water' training, which the Russian navy could only provide in limited amounts.

Orlov's squadron was in the Mediterranean entirely due to the good offices of the British. The squadron had stopped in Britain on its way to the Mediterranean, and after arriving in the Mediterranean, used Royal Navy facilities at Malta. Following the Çesme victory, Russian seapower dominated the Mediterranean, and was instrumental in forcing the Ottoman Empire to sign the Küçük Kaynarca Treaty in 1774. The treaty was interpreted as giving Russia a protectorate over Orthodox subjects of the Porte, the first time that Russia had achieved such a dominant position in Constantinople.

Russia's hold on the northern Black Sea littoral was tightened with her annexation of the Crimea in 1783; with the founding of Sevastopol in the same year, the stage was set for Russia to be able to increase her maritime pressure on the Ottoman Empire from the north.

Russian seapower in the Mediterranean had been entirely artificial, dependent on the good grace of a Mediterranean littoral power. Such support could be withdrawn if circumstances changed. The fragility of Russian seapower in this context is graphically illustrated by Admiral Seniavin's experiences in 1807.

The turmoil of the Napoleonic Wars did not spare either Russia or the Ottoman Empire. Catherine allied herself with Britain from the beginning, and this policy was initially continued by her successor, Paul; ships from the Baltic Fleet cooperated with the Royal Navy in a two-year blockade of the Dutch coast, 1799–1801.

The conflict produced a more unusual alliance between Russia and the Ottoman Empire; during 1798–1805, ships of the Black Sea Fleet passed the Bosphorus and Dardanelles (hereafter generally referred to collectively as the 'Straits') and operated in conjunction with the Ottoman and Royal Navies. Their most notable success was the amphibious operation under Admiral Ushakov which captured Corfu in 1799. For the first time, the Turks had permitted foreign warships to pass the Straits.

This arrangement was changed by the Treaty of Tilsit, signed by Napoleon and Emperor Alexander in 1805. Russia now became an enemy of both Great Britain and Turkey. Bereft of logistical support from the Black Sea with the Turkish closure of the Straits, Admiral Seniavin's squadron was hounded into neutral ports by the Royal Navy and interned. Russian vulnerability in the Mediterranean was strikingly illustrated by the incident. Britain now attempted to use her maritime might to detach the Ottoman Empire from French influence; in 1807, a squadron under Admiral Duckworth forced the Straits, entered the Sea of Marmora, and attempted to cow the Turks into submission. Duckworth hesitated to press home his advantage, the Turks improvised hasty defences for Constantinople, and the British were forced to retreat to the Mediterranean. Two years later Britain concluded a treaty with the Ottoman Empire which recognised as an 'ancient right' their sovereignity over the Straits. The situation remained largely static until peace settled again on Europe in 1815.

Russia's Patriotic War against Napoleon brought home in striking fashion to St Petersburg the limits to her maritime pretensions. Napoleon had been driven from Russia by army operations, not by seapower. British maritime superiority as exemplified by both Nelson's operation against Copenhagen in 1801 and by Duckworth's expedition had shown that the best Russia could hope for was a *regional* influence within the relatively narrow confines of her adjacent seas; one, limited by the Danish Sound, the other by the Straits. Any attempt to operate further afield could be checked by the Royal Navy. A British squadron based in the Channel could block any Russian advance from the Baltic into the North Sea, while any Russian drive from the Black Sea could meet Royal Navy resistance based on either Gibraltar or Malta.

Therefore, to compete on a 'blue-water' scale with either Britain or France was plainly beyond Russian capabilities; the geostrategic realities of her situation made a more limited ambition a necessity. Geography had made Mahan's principle of 'fleet unity' an impossibility for her widely-separated Black Sea and Baltic fleets, and resources were insufficient to field two fleets co-equal to potential regional adversaries.

The goal which Russia found herself striving for by default was regional parity, while simultaneously attempting to limit outside influence in those areas. This was the direction of post-Napoleonic, pre-Crimean Russian naval policy in the Black Sea. The question was a pressing one for Russia, as the Napoleonic Wars had generated further strains on the old regional balances of power. Nowhere were these stresses more evident than in the Ottoman Empire.

The major difference of opinion on the diagnosis of the 'Sick Man of Europe' was whether he was merely critical or terminal. Uprisings in the Ottoman Empire were becoming both more frequent and more successful; whether initiated by ambition or nationalism, Constantinople was finding it increasingly hard to cope with the problems in its outlying regions. Servia acquired a limited autonomy during this period, but a more potent threat was growing in Egypt, where the capable Mehmet Ali was biding his time while building a westernised military machine that he would eventually use in a bid for autonomy.

Mehmet Ali was an Albanian coffeehouse proprietor who ended up in Egypt prior to Napoleon's invasion. He had seen the effectiveness of Napoleon's Western military technology when it routed the Mamlukes in 1798, and once he consolidated his power, began to import it wholesale. Mehmet was acclaimed governor in 1805, and ruled until 1845. Mehmet wiped out the Mamluke threat to his own power in 1811; he raised a capable general in his son Ibrahim, who won his spurs (and the Sultan's gratitude) in a campaign in Arabia against the Wahabbis in the following year, and again in 1818–20. The Sultan would increasingly come to rely on this westernised force to clear up the Empire's hot spots; when the Greek revolt broke out in 1821, Turkish failure to subdue it would eventually engage both European public opinion and Mehmet's forces.

Post-Napoleonic Europe attempted to re-establish political legitimacy as a bulwark against renewed outbreaks of revolution. While the Turks were not represented at the Congress of Vienna, the Sultan was vaguely perceived as the 'legitimate' sovereign in his respective sphere of influence. This perception was tempered by two criteria; one, to prevent the unbridled spread of revolutionary tendencies, and two, an unstated, but powerful assumption that no dissolution of the Ottoman Empire would result in an even division of its remains by the major European powers. The Greek revolt threatened to upset this *de facto* equilibrium. As the Turks proved unequal to the task of subduing their rebellious subjects, they turned to increasingly cruel measures, which in turn, focused European attention on the unhappy land. The spectacle of Muslims massacring Christians aroused public opinion; in Russia, this awareness was heightened by recognition that the Greeks were fellow Orthodox Christians. Europe was hesitantly dragged into intervention; the pressure to do so increased when Sultan Mahmut II turned to his efficient vassal, Mehmet Ali. Troops under Ibrahim laid waste to the hapless Greeks; with the addition of Mehmet's navy attacking the Greek Aegean strongholds, it looked as if Greece might succumb. As the rest of Europe prevaricated, Tsar Alexander slowly moved, against his Holy Alliance principles, towards unilateral intervention if need be. The Greek revolt was robbed of his aid by his death in December 1825.

The subsequent accession of Tsar Nicholas further altered the picture. Having ascended the throne accompanied by the Decembrist revolt, he had little sympathy for 'revolutionarists'. His character was different from his dead brother's: where Alexander could be subtle and devious, Nicholas prided himself on his military forthrightness. He preferred to solve the Greek revolt in concert with the other European powers, but would act unilaterally if need be. While Russia had grievances against the Ottoman Empire, he would settle them separately from the 'Greek Question' if he could. His navy was to make the largest single contribution to slicing the Grecian Gordian knot, and the problems that flowed from its severing.

Every work dealing with Russia and the Middle East in the nineteenth century must run against the multitudes of languages and cultures that make consistency in spelling almost impossible. Spellings have largely followed modern usage except for well-known exceptions–thus it is that St Petersburg is preferred to Sanktpetrburg. Personal names devolve largely on who's paying the wages–Count Heyden, a Dutchman in Russian service for our purposes becomes Geiden, while Muhammad Ali, an Albanian freebooter who aspired to the rule of a Greater Egypt is known by his Turkish monniker, Mehmet Ali. Place names are also subject to this rule of propriety; while I realise that such an arrangement is imperfect at best, I can only offer the Turkish proverb, 'İt ürür, kervan yürür.'

All Russian dates have been altered to fit the Gregorian calendar in use in Western Europe at the time; the Russian 'Old Style' form of reckoning, based on the Julian calendar, was twelve days behind the system used in Western Europe in the nineteenth century. In preference to confusing the reader, these dates have been made current with the Western European/American usage.

The most pleasant part of writing a book is acknowledging the many kindnesses that made it possible. This work is a truncated and heavily revised thesis presented to the School of Slavonic and East European Studies, London University in 1986; as such, credit should be fairly distributed. My family was constantly supportive throughout my academic apprenticeship, and I owe them a debt that can never be repaid. Professors Hugh Seton-Watson, James Brewer and Robert Welter Daly provided the intellectual stimulus and energy to launch me on this endeavour. At the School of Slavonic and East European Studies, I must mention the constant interest of Professor Michael Branch, without whom this would not have been completed. Other stalwarts at SSEES include Drs William Ryan and J. E. O. Screen, for criticism and encouragement. I might also mention Professors Geoffrey Hosking, Derek Spring and Evan Mawdsley for maintaining a constant oversight on a project that frequently threatened to run off the rails. A three-month scholarship from the Finnish government allowed me to use the University of Helsinki's magnificent library, while a Caird Fellowship from the National Maritime Museum provided an entrée into the incomparable riches of Greenwich.

Yeoman service and encouragement was also provided by the University College Computer Centre–in particular, I must mention David Guppy (twice), Henry Tillotson and Jeremy Perron for efforts far beyond the duties of advising and friendship. Tira Shubart initially provided this project with a home, Peter Thwaite helped with the reproduction of this work, and Celia Pesce provided both superb proof-reading skills and pass interference to a baby who wanted 'more beeps' from Daddy's word processor. James Russell, Richard Penniman, Arthur J. Guinness and Ray Charles all provided support through the trying time of revising this manuscript. Finally, last but certainly not least, I must record my gratitude to my colleagues in the History Department of Kansas State University, for providing both a warm welcome and a Little House on the Prairie. Professors John

McCulloh and Marion Gray greatly contributed to the success of this work, and it is a pleasure to record my gratitude.

Needless to say, in the absence of any other guilty parties, all mistakes are my own.

Manhattan and London   JOHN C. K. DALY

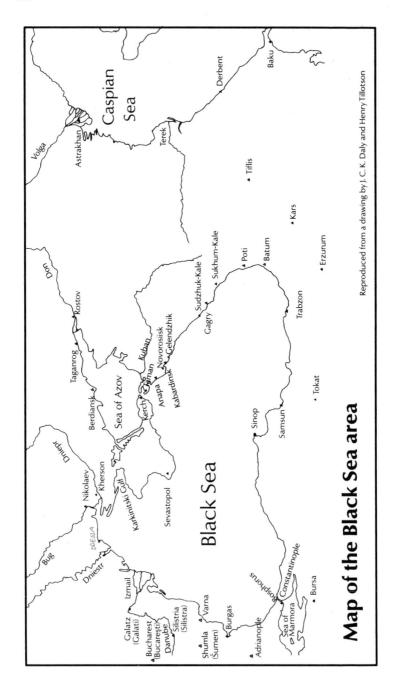

Map of the Black Sea area

Reproduced from a drawing by J. C. K. Daly and Henry Tillotson

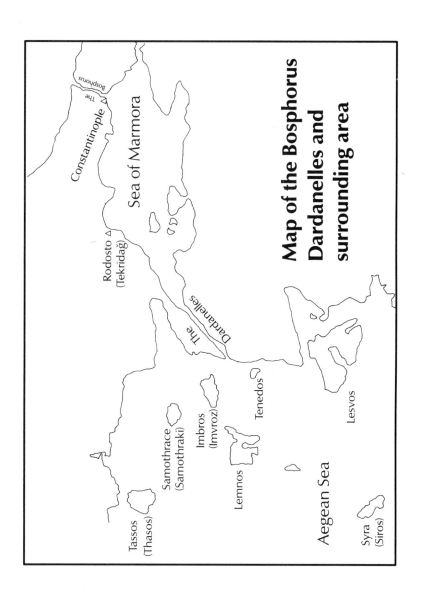

Map of the Bosphorus Dardanelles and surrounding area

The Bosphorus

The

Constantinople

Sea of Marmora

Rodosto
(Tekridağ)

The Dardanelles

Tenedos

Samothrace
(Samothraki)

Imbros
(Imvroz)

Lemnos

Lesvos

Tassos
(Thasos)

Aegean Sea

Syra
(Siros)

1 The Greek Revolt and Tsar Nicholas's First Turkish War

On the evening of 22 June 1827, after an Imperial review, a squadron of nine line ships, eight frigates, two corvettes and a brig of the Russian Baltic Fleet weighed anchor from Kronstadt and headed west.[1] Vice-Admiral Dmitri Nikolaevich Seniavin, one of Russia's most experienced naval officers, was in command.[2] Commanding the flagship *Azov*-74 was Captain Mikhail Petrovich Lazarev, future commander of the Black Sea Fleet;[3] among the junior officers were Lieutenant Pavel Stepanovich Nakhimov, midshipmen Vladimir Ivanovich Istomin and Vladimir Alekseivich Kornilov, and gardemarin Grigorii Ivanovich Butakov, future defenders of Sevastopol during the Crimean War. The ships were new, most having been built during the previous three years at the Archangel, Kronstadt, and St Petersburg Admiralty wharves.[4] The *Azov*-74 had been built at Archangel in 1826 under the personal supervision of Lazarev.[5] The squadron's immediate destination was Portsmouth, where further orders would be waiting, a result of discussions in London between Russian, French, and British representatives on how best to achieve a solution to the Greek insurrection, a running sore that European diplomacy could no longer ignore.

Seniavin's orders emphasised the value of the expedition as an extended blue-water training cruise – Seniavin was to take every opportunity to exercise his ships in manoeuvres and gunnery, while maintaining 'strict military discipline for the necessary perfection of all aspects of naval service.'[6] Stops in Reval and Sveaborg were limited to a maximum of three days in each. If while in Portsmouth orders were not received, then Seniavin was to sail to Brest, remain there several days, and then return to Kronstadt. The orders ended with an exhortation to maintain proper dress, 'especially the officers'.

Seniavin also received orders from the Ministry of Foreign Affairs. These dealt in detail with Seniavin's future relations with Prince Aleksandr Khristoforovich Lieven, the Russian ambassador to Britain, should the London negotiations prove successful. In consultation with Lieven, Seniavin was to detach a squadron of four line, four frigates and two brigs, to proceed to the Mediterranean under Rear-Admiral Login Petrovich Geiden. These were to protect Russian shipping from pirates, while maintaining a strict neutrality in the Turkish–Greek dispute. All Russian shipping was to be tightly convoyed. Russian merchantmen were to be forbidden to carry supplies, trade, or combatants for either side. Pirates were to be treated only to those considerations allowed them by international law.[7] Geiden was to coordinate his activities with the other European navies, and to preserve 'friendly relations'. The squadron would receive future orders directly from Lieven, acting in his capacity as a member of any Allied mediating body that might result from the London discussions.

The reappearance of Russian seapower in the Mediterranean after a twenty-year absence was a direct response to the Greek revolt, and the Sultan's subsequent inability to subdue it. In the six years following the outbreak of the rebellion in 1821, Sultan Mahmut II's armies and navy had been unable to achieve victory. Ali Pasha of Ioannina's revolt in 1819–22 and Mahmut's purge of the Janissaries in June 1826 had left the Ottoman army weakened and disorganised, while the loss of the Aegean islands deprived the Turkish navy of its finest reserve of sailors. In desperation, Sultan Mahmut turned to his Egyptian viceroy, Mehmet Ali.

Mehmet's army and navy were the most modern and westernised Muslim forces in the Middle East. An army under his son, Ibrahim, had earlier proved its worth to the Sultan by recapturing Mecca and Medina in 1822 from the Wahhabis. Mehmet had been importing European technology and training on a far greater scale than the Porte – his first mission of students sent to Europe in 1826 numbered forty-four members.[8] Among the European officers attracted by his high salaries were the Frenchmen Sève, Cérisy, Besson, Rey, Perrier, and Vassière.[9] Mehmet had warships built in Marseilles, Leghorn, Venice, and America.[10] Mahmut now decided to use these westernised forces to smother the Greek revolt, hoping in the process to weaken his ambitious viceroy as well.

Ibrahim's troops landed at Modon in February 1825 and quickly recaptured most of the Peloponnesus; two weeks before Seniavin set sail, Athens had fallen. Only the Aegean islands remained as real centres of resistance. As the military position of the Greeks deteriorated, so did their naval resistance. Greek seapower had played an important role in the early stages of the insurrection, but could do little of value against Mehmet's forces; the last large-scale action had been fought in September 1826 off Mitilini, where fifty Greek and twenty-four Turkish vessels had been engaged. The indecisive clash resulted only in the loss of two Greek fireships.[11] Regionalism, financial and provisioning problems, and the temptation of piracy masquerading as privateering had all lessened the disciplined effectiveness of the Greeks. Lettres of marque issued by the provisional Greek government were broadly interpreted by their holders; neutrals came under increasing attack. In April 1826 alone seven Russian merchantmen had been plundered.[12] This piracy was coming to paralyse Levantine trade, and there were no effective European naval forces in the area to check it.

Greek privateers were not the only Mediterranean 'morskie razboiniky' (pirates) troubling Russian shipping. Russia had never negotiated directly with the Barbary States, unlike the other European powers; relations had been conducted under the premise that the North African littoral was under direct Turkish suzerainity. Under Article VII of the 1812 Bucharest Treaty, the Porte was directly responsible for all attacks on Russian shipping made by the Barbary States, and was to secure the return of people and property as well as paying reparations. Article VII of the Akkerman Convention of October 1826 had reaffirmed these responsibilities, but despite these agreements, attacks were increasing in scope and intensity.

The Akkerman Convention was signed between Russia and Turkey on 7 October 1826. Mahmut regarded it only as a stalling device; his purge of the Janissaries in June had left him in no condition for an immediate war with Russia. For Nicholas, embroiled in a nasty border dispute with Persia since June, the Convention freed him from the possibility of having to divide his forces in the Caucasus in order to fight a two-front Asian war. Expediency triumphed over irritation, though only for the moment.

Further to the east, French exasperation with their southern Mediterranean neighbours' piratical activity was not so easily assuaged, and led them to consider a blockade. The projected French blockade of Algiers suggested to Tsar Nicholas the possibility of Geiden's squadron being used to help eradicate the freebooting states;

on 15 June 1827 Count Karl Nesselrode, the Russian Foreign Minister, instructed Lieven to broach the subject at a suitable time.[13] When Lieven raised the issue Prime Minister George Canning was evasive, commenting that it would be best first to observe the outcome of the French–Algerian dispute. As the proposal had little hope of British support, it was subsequently shelved.[14]

Attention to the 'Greek Question' and the revival of Russian naval power were both high priorities of the young Tsar. A 'Committee of Survey of the Fleet' had been established almost immediately after Nicholas had succeeded his brother Alexander in 1825. Nicholas stated, 'It is necessary for Russia to be third in naval strength after England and France, and it is necessary that it be stronger than an alliance of the second-rate naval powers...'.[15] While the Baltic Fleet was to be the primary beneficiary of increased governmental spending, the Black Sea Fleet was not to be neglected in this build-up. Its projected strength was to be fourteen line ships, six frigates, seven steam frigates and one-hundred-and-fifty-four smaller ships.[16]

> This number of ships will, on the one hand, not [unduly] burden the government as regards maintenance, and on the other, will be quite sufficient for the defence of our ports and borders, but also for offensive operations in the event of their being necessary....[17]

A Mediterranean-based squadron would prove a very useful auxiliary to the projected Russian Black Sea Fleet build-up in the event of any future conflict with the Ottoman Empire. Given the closure of the Straits to foreign warships, any such Russian naval aid sent to the Mediterranean would have to come from the Baltic.

It was an increased British awareness of the Tsar's inclination to act unilaterally if need be that persuaded Canning to push further the cooperation outlined by the Protocol of St Petersburg that Wellington had concluded in April 1826, during his mission to congratulate the new Tsar on his accession. For Canning, unilateral Russian action was a hazard to be avoided at all costs; an alliance would allow him to direct Russian efforts into more productive channels, lessening the risk of unilateral Russian action. By late March, Canning and Lieven had agreed upon the final draft, more than seven weeks before it was approved by the Cabinet. For Russia, this cooperation meant that her squadron would operate in the Mediterranean by grace of the British.

Seniavin departed Reval on 29 June; a storm slowed progress towards Copenhagen and damaged several of the ships.[18] The Danish capital was reached on 19 July; five days were spent in repairs and provisioning.[19] In the North Sea foul weather and contrary winds again delayed their journey; the Channel was attained on 6 August, and two days later the squadron arrived in Portsmouth, having picked up the necessary pilots off Deal.[20]

Rear-Admiral Geiden's instructions awaited him. Accompanying the orders was a copy of the projected alliance. Should the Porte refuse to accept mediation, then the Allies would interpose their navies between the belligerents. Lieven had suggested that a blockade of the Straits would most effectively achieve the Allies' purpose; such a blockade could be augmented from the Bosphorus by the Black Sea Fleet. To avoid misunderstandings, Geiden was to place himself under the most senior of his colleagues. He was also to remain on good terms with the commander of the Austrian Mediterranean naval forces; further orders would await him at Messina.[21]

On 11 August Lieven arrived in Portsmouth to confer with Seniavin and Geiden. The London discussions had resulted in the 7 July Treaty, whereby France, England, and Russia offered their mediation. While the Greeks had accepted the offer, the Turks had rejected it. Further orders were to be sent to Allied naval commanders in the Levant, clarifying the general instructions laid down in the Secret Article of the Treaty:

> in the contemplated case of the refusal of the Porte to admit the mediation, and to consent to an armistice, you will then have, on the one hand, to enter into friendly relations with the Greeks; on the other, to intercept any expedition by sea, of men, arms, &c. destined against Greece, and coming from either Turkey, or from Africa in general.[22]

The Secret Article put the Allies in the position of enforcing the Treaty two weeks after its submission to both sides; as this was assumed to be about mid-September, Geiden was ordered to complete his provisioning as soon as possible and continue to the Aegean, while Seniavin was to return to Kronstadt with the remaining ships.[23] Geiden's warships were accorded top priority for repairs.[24] Charts of the Channel, Atlantic and Mediterranean were obtained, and Russian officers toured Portsmouth's dockyard.[25] Seniavin provided Geiden with orders which further propounded the idea of the expedition as an invaluable training exercise in waters rarely visited by Russian warships: 'this long voyage...gives you the opportunity to lead the squadron...consisting for the most part of inexperienced people, to the necessary perfection in all aspects of naval skill...'.[26] Attention was particularly directed to extensive gunnery drill, 'because the sailors are weak in this field, and artillery decides victory'.

Geiden also received further instructions from Lieven. Upon his arrival in the Levant, Geiden was to instruct all Russian merchantmen to observe strict neutrality. They were also to observe all 'active, existing' blockades. Ships fulfilling these requirements and sailing under convoy were not to be searched by the belligerents; any such attempts were to be met 'with force'. Ships not under convoy that were seized were to be petitioned for as if they had been; compensation was to be demanded for losses.[27]

On 20 August Geiden hoisted his flag on the *Azov*-74 and led his squadron of four line, four frigates, and a corvette out of Spithead.[28] A week later the ships were off Mondego Bay, and on 2 September they passed Gibraltar.[29] Seniavin sailed from Portsmouth four days after Geiden, and reached Kronstadt the second week in September.[30]

As Geiden made his way eastwards, Vice-Admiral Sir Edward Codrington, commander of the British naval forces in the eastern Mediterranean, pondered his options. Since arriving in the Mediterranean in February 1827, he had watched the Egyptian devastation of Greece with growing revulsion:

> I have never felt a wish to see another war until now, and I really think it might prove a more humane way of settling affairs here than any other. One strong coercion would place the Porte at our mercy, and we then settle the whole matter as we choose, and take Candia [Crete] ourselves into the bargain, a consummation, in my opinion, devoutly to be wished.[31]

Codrington left Malta for the Aegean in mid-June; for dealing with the light, swift Greek pirate boats, he had a boat from every ship equipped with a carronade.[32] In addition to pirates and privateers, his relations with the Greek government were hampered by the fact that the Greek navy was under the command of Lord Thomas Cochrane, an energetic Royal Navy officer on half-pay whose activities, in Codrington's opinion, far exceeded his belligerent rights.

Codrington's immediate concern was the massive expedition which was fitting out in Alexandria to support Ibrahim. Ships under the Kapudan Pasha Tahir from Constantinople were to ferry supplies to Ibrahim in Patrai, there to be joined by the Alexandrian contingent. After supplying Ibrahim, troops would be embarked, and the combined forces used for an attack on Idhra, the centre of Greek naval resistance, after which it was felt the revolt would collapse. Mehmet would then be in a superb bargaining position with Constantinople regarding his aspirations towards the Syrian pashaliks. Despite Mehmet's manifest ambitions, Egyptian aid was essential if the revolt was to be successfully suppressed. Turkish resources alone were not up to such a task; a British officer in Constantinople observed,

> I cannot comprehend how the Turks manage with such materials as they possess, since the loss of their maritime population, to man and equip their vessels of war, and still less how they can possibly find officers capable of taking charge of them....[33]

Tahir had one line ship, eight frigates, fourteen corvettes and brigs; sailing in late May, they reached Patrai without incident on 4 June.[34]

Mehmet's energetic preparations afforded a striking contrast to Turkish torpor; the Alexandria Arsenal was a beehive of activity. Counting the Turkish contingent in harbour, the dockyard was involved in preparing three line ships, twenty-four frigates, thirty-eight corvettes, eighteen brigs, and six schooners, a formidable force of eighty-nine sail.[35] Many Egyptian ships were new; on 19 July a new corvette that Mehmet had ordered in Marseilles arrived.[36] French officers manned several ships.[37]

The importance of preventing this armada from sailing was not lost on London; a week after the July 7 Treaty was signed, Colonel Craddock was sent to Alexandria with orders 'to secure the neutrality of the Pasha of Egypt in the struggle still going on betwixt the Turks and the Greeks...'.[38] Mehmet came under increasing pressure to sail, as Sultan Mahmut sent messenger after messenger to demand that Mehmet launch the expedition.[39] Mehmet himself was nervous of the possibility of a blockade of Alexandria, which would maroon Ibrahim in Greece.[40] In addition, there was the danger of an attack by the Greeks on the expedition while it was still in harbour. On 15 June Cochrane had led a frigate, corvette, fourteen brigs and eight fireships in an attack on Alexandria. Codrington, who had been angered by Cochrane's irregular blockade of Patrai, felt that the attack could only force Mehmet's hand, and bitterly remarked, 'The Greeks may thank Lord Cochrane for having forced the Pasha of Alexandria to have his fleet ready when he would have willingly delayed it.'[41]

Mehmet procrastinated, but finally bowed to the inevitable, and sent out the main contingent of forty-seven warships and transports with 4000 troops on 5 August, three days before Craddock arrived.[42] After the fleet had sailed, Mehmet said, 'now a great load is off my mind, and the rest depends on God!'[43]

Craddock's first interview with Mehmet was on 16 August, by which time the rest of the ships had sailed. When Craddock pointed out the hardship that the Greek war had caused Egypt, Mehmet replied that the difficulties had been caused by two years 'bad Nile', and added, 'The Greek war has been of the greatest service to me, and I look upon the present state of affairs as by no means a bad one.'[44] Henry Salt, the British consul, believed that Mehmet felt in a strong position to ask the Porte for the Syrian pashaliks; Craddock believed that Mehmet found the conflict a heaven-sent opportunity for building a fleet and army that he would ultimately use to gain complete independence, taking the Syrian pashaliks in the bargain.

Three days later Mehmet told Craddock to have the Allied admirals send a joint letter to Ibrahim forbidding him to attack Idhra; Mehmet would also send secret instructions ordering him to comply with the Allies' demands. Mehmet recognised the possibility of conflict, but in view of the potential rewards he considered the risk justified:

> If I were to remain by the Grand Signior on this occasion, I might, it is true, lose my fleet, but I should be certain to gain Syria and Damascus. Whom else has he to lean on; he would be obliged to give me my own terms.[45]

The next day Mehmet again urged a similar course of action. The following day Craddock left for Smyrna. Mehmet's loyalty to the Sultan at this point was purely opportunistic; while he had received the pashalik of Crete in March as a reward, his desire for Syria was such that Salt felt he would risk an open rupture with Constantinople by withdrawing Ibrahim if Mahmut was not prepared to cede it.[46]

Codrington received news of the July 7 Treaty but no specific orders, on 17 July while at Spetsai.[47] After discussions with Greek leaders at Navplion, he sailed to Smyrna, where he consulted with Admiral De Rigny, commander of the French Levantine squadron.[48] De Rigny felt that Mahmut would initially resist Allied proposals, but that a 'certain number of guns would produce submission.'[49]

On 7 August the admirals' directions and the Treaty arrived from London; Codrington was to receive additional orders from Stratford Canning, British ambassador at Constantinople.[50] Codrington also received news that a Russian squadron would join him; he was not pleased by the prospect.[51] After sailing to Navplion on 17 August and informing the Greeks of the impending offer of mediation, Codrington sailed to Urla for reinforcements, while De Rigny made for Milos. The Allied ambassadors now offered their mediation to the Porte, which was promptly refused. Upon learning of this, Codrington again went to Navplion and on 3 September presented the same offer to the Greeks, which was accepted.[52] The Treaty had come into force on 1 September, two weeks after its presentation to the Turks. Several days later Codrington received Canning's authorisation to enforce the armistice laid down in the Treaty by using 'cannon-shot' if necessary.[53]

In compliance with his new orders, Codrington moved to intercept the Egyptian fleet. Reports placed it at Soudhas Bay in Crete, with Idhra as its immediate destination.[54] Codrington sailed from Aiyina to Idhra; however, the Egyptians took a different course. After leaving Alexandria, the Egyptians watered at Marmoris during 17–18 August; they then sailed westward, and reached Cape Bassatin on the Barbary coast on 21 August, where they were delayed several days by contrary winds.[55] The fleet then headed north, and reached Navarino on 7–8 September. When Codrington learned of this, he headed west, and was before the port on 10 September.[56]

Codrington issued orders to his officers to disrupt attempts by either side to break the *de facto* armistice, but he was in a weak position, and he knew it. De Rigny was still apparently at Milos, and the French along with the Russians would be essential to provide the numerical parity necessary to enforce the Treaty.[57] Orders were orders, however, and Codrington with his five ships now attempted to blockade nearly one hundred Muslim ships in the harbour. He wrote to the Turkish admiral in charge of the fleet,

> ...it is my duty to apprize you, that although it is my earnest desire to bring about a cessation of this cruel warfare by persuasion, I am ordered to proceed to the greatest extremity rather than relinquish the object on which the Allied Powers have determined. If any one shot should be fired at the British flag on this occasion, it will be fatal to the Ottoman fleet.[58]

Two days later, a section of the Muslim fleet attempted to sail. De Rigny's timely appearance on the horizon changed the situation; on 23 September De Rigny entered Navarino, and after an interview with Ibrahim, the ships were recalled. A conference between the two admirals and Ibrahim on 25 September resulted in a truce whereby Ibrahim would remain at Navarino until further orders were received from Constantinople and Alexandria.[59] De Rigny and Codrington now retired, leaving behind a token observation force; the French sailed for Milos, while Codrington headed northwards to Zakinthos.

Debate continued in London on the force needed to coerce the Sultan. Though Canning had died on 8 August, the new government under Lord Goderich largely continued the policies of its predecessor. At a second Treaty conference on 10 September Lieven again suggested a Dardanelles blockade which would cover all ships carrying munitions or provisions, starving out Constantinople should Mahmut refuse an armistice. As before, the Black Sea Fleet would supplement the blockade from the Euxine as soon as conditions would allow.[60] The British Foreign Minister, Lord Dudley, sidestepped the issue by observing that since the Allies were making their first overtures, it would be best to wait for a response before acting on Lieven's suggestions. At the third conference a week later Dudley again urged patience, though by now the Sultan's refusal had become known.[61] At the fourth conference on 15 October Lieven again raised the subject of blockade; this time Dudley agreed to the half-measure of sending expanded instructions to the admirals.

The new instructions ordered Codrington to intercept all Turkish and Egyptian warships or merchantmen bound for the Greek mainland or islands. It was also open to Codrington to deploy forces 'off Constantinople or Alexandria.'[62] The admirals were to hold open 'every inducement' to Ibrahim to withdraw, and in no case to allow the armada to sail empty. Neutrals were to be intercepted only if sailing under convoy of Turkish or Egyptian warships. The orders were soon superseded by events.

Codrington wrote to Geiden at Malta, informing him of the truce with Ibrahim. Codrington estimated that replies from Constantinople and Alexandria would arrive around 14 October, and suggested that Geiden join him and De Rigny off Navarino on 10 October to give the Egyptians ocular proof of Allied intentions.[63]

Geiden was struggling against adverse weather and winds since entering the Mediterranean, however, and only made Palermo on 22 September. There he received orders to continue to Greece as quickly as possible.[64] Geiden sent Consul Iulenets ahead to Messina to prepare supplies and a pilot for the Aegean; further orders would be awaiting there.

Provisioning in Palermo took longer than expected; port officials were afraid of angering the Turks, and imposed restrictions on the number of Russian ships that could be in harbour at any one time. Geiden sailed on 30 September, and made Messina a week later. The squadron picked up pilots and set off the same day for Zakinthos, while Geiden sent the frigate *Konstantin*-44 to Malta to inform Codrington of his arrival.[65]

'Off Navarino events had reached an impasse. Cochrane had attacked and destroyed a Turkish squadron in the Gulf of Corinth off Salona on 29 September. Ibrahim regarded the truce as binding on both sides, and had protested to the admirals; they did nothing. Now that their forces had retired, Ibrahim decided to send some ships to deal with Cochrane's renegades. On 1 October a squadron again left harbour, and was joined the next day by another detachment. Codrington hurried south, and threatened imminent destruction if they did not turn back; the threat proved sufficient, and the task force returned to Navarino on 7 – 8 October.[66] Codrington felt that Ibrahim had broken his word, '...and I will not trust the word of honour of him or any chief under his command.[67] The following evening HMS *Alacrity*-10 reported having sighted Geiden earlier that day west of Corfu.[68] The two squadrons united off Zakinthos two days later.

Geiden and his ships impressed Codrington, and he wrote a favourable report to Canning.[69] De Rigny rejoined them on 16 October, and the three discussed their position. The next day the frigate HMS *Dartmouth*-42 carried a joint letter into Navarino for Ibrahim, which his staff refused to accept, professing not to know his exact whereabouts. De Rigny sent a letter to the French officers serving aboard the Muslim ships, warning them of the possibility of conflict, and strongly urging them to leave.

On 18 October the admirals held a council of war. HMS *Dartmouth*-42 had brought out detailed intelligence on the strength and positions of the Muslim ships.[70] The difficulties of a winter blockade were discussed, along with the possibility of the combined fleets entering Navarino to force Ibrahim to resume negotiations.[71] The admirals agreed that they would enter the harbour next day and attempt to renew discussions.[72]

Codrington used his information from HMS *Dartmouth*'s reconnaissance to draw up his deployments.[73] The Turkish and Egyptian ships were anchored in a ragged horseshoe; the British would take the southern inside crescent, the Russians the centre, and the French the northern side. Light winds prevented the Allies from entering the next day;[74] the first British ships passed into Navarino in the early afternoon of 20 October. The Russians cleared for action at 12:30, and Geiden gave the Azov's crew a rousing speech about duty to God, Tsar, and Country.[75]

The Russians were last to enter the anchorage, and while they were still outside the battle began, when the nervous Turks opened fire on a boat from HMS *Talbot*-28 that had been sent to remove a nearby fireship threatening the British vessels.[76] As a result, the Russians had to pass the artillery fire of the Turkish fort at the entrance, a formidable position which mounted one hundred twenty-five cannon.[77] The battle was well underway when the *Azov* at the van of the Russian line reached her appointed position. Intense fighting raged over the next four hours.[78] At one point the *Azov*-74 was battling simultaneously five enemy ships.[79] As the Turkish and Egyptian ships became heavily damaged, many were subsequently blown up by their commanders; during the battle, two line ships and a frigate surrendered to the Allies, while a line ship and eleven frigates were blown up.[80] The Allied crews remained at their guns all night on guard against further hostile action and possible fireship attacks. During the night, a Turkish frigate converted into a fireship anchored near the *Gangut*-84; Captain Avinov led a boarding party which captured the ship, killing the Turks with the fuses still in their hands.[81]

The battle completely crippled the Turco-Egyptian armada as an effective fighting force:

> Out of a fleet composed of sixty men of war, there remains only one frigate (dismasted), and fifteen smaller vessels in a state ever to put to sea again.[82]

Muslim casualties were estimated at six to seven thousand men. The destruction was thorough enough for the commander of the *Iezekiil*-74 to note in the ship's log, 'by 6 p.m. not one enemy ship was still anchored in its earlier position. And the roadstead of Navarino Bay was illuminated by continuous explosions and the burning Turkish ships. . .'.[83]

Allied losses were also substantial – British dead numbered seventy, with one hundred eighty-four wounded; the French lost forty-three dead and one hundred forty-four wounded, while the Russian lost fifty-nine killed and one hundred thirty-nine wounded.[84] The next day all prisoners taken in battle by the Allies were set free. The Turks continued to fire their damaged vessels; the *Aleksandr Nevskii*-74 dismasted and scuttled a Turkish frigate which had surrendered the day before.[85]

With the Turco–Egyptian maritime threat now nullified, the Allied admirals turned their attention to the Greek privateers and pirates.[86]

A joint letter to the Greek government warned that piracy under the guise of governmental lettres of marque would no longer be tolerated, with Allied ships no longer recognising such papers issued by the Greek government. Any ships carrying such papers outside the areas declared in regular blockade by the Greek government would be arrested. The despatch ended with a sombre warning that the same fate which befell the Turkish–Egyptian fleet at Navarino could be inflicted on Greek naval forces should such irregularities continue unabated.[87]

The Allies remained in Navarino until 26 October; the more severely damaged French warships made for Toulon, while Codrington and the Russians headed for Malta. The British arrived in Valetta on 3 November, the Russians five days later. Codrington ordered that the Russians be put on the same footing as the British as regarded repairs, and that the usual surcharges be waived.[88] In view of the large number of wounded, the twenty-five-day normal quarantine period was reduced to fifteen, and counted from the day that the ships left Navarino, rather than their arrival at Malta, which allowed the Russians to land their wounded the day after their arrival.[89]

Damage to Allied ships had been heavy. Codrington sent the line ships HMS *Albion*-74, HMS *Asia*-84, and HMS *Genoa*-74 to England for repairs.[90] The Russians had also suffered severely. The *Azov*-74 had been especially battered, having one hundred and fifty-three shot in her hull, seven of which had pierced below the water-line.[91] Repairs to the *Azov*-74 were not fully completed until March 1828.[92] The other Russian line ships had been injured as well; their hulls were badly damaged as well as masts and rigging, especially *Gangut*-84 and *Iezekiil*-74.[93] The Russian frigates were not so badly damaged.

In addition to Royal Navy resources, Russian ships were also repaired at the shipyards of G. Germain, a wealthy private Maltese shipbuilder.[94] By March, Geiden's bill for repairs and supplies totalled more than £6950.[95]

On 2 November a battered corvette five days out from the Morea limped into Alexandria, bringing despatches about Navarino. Mehmet had earlier observed that conflict was probably inevitable, but that it would be minor; 'Yes, it must be so – there will be a naval engagement, but it will be trifling – your admiral will sink three or four of our ships, the others will turn back, and the affair will end.'[96] Upon hearing of the extent of the destruction, Mehmet angrily remarked, 'I told them what would be the consequence! Did they think they were dealing with Greeks?'[97] The Viceroy immediately sent for Barker and D'Oysonville, commander of the sole Allied warship in port, and stated that regardless of the battle and possible developments, all Europeans and their property would be safe.[98]

Navarino provided Mehmet with an expensive but plausible exit from both the Greek conflict and the imminent war. Mehmet would subsequently argue that he had only bowed to the greater Allied naval presence. In reality, his losses were not so severe; of the three Egyptian frigates and corvettes lost in the battle, two of the frigates had been considered for scrapping.[99] While waiting for the remains of his fleet to return, Mehmet busied himself by continuing work on Alexandria's shore fortifications, another development of great value in any possible future attempts at independence.[100]

Sultan Mahmut was less understanding than Mehmet about the loss of his ships. News of the battle had reached Constantinople on the same day as Alexandria. The Reis Efendi subsequently told the Allied ambassadors that the battle had effectively nullified all existing treaties; relations could be patched up only if the Allies would quit interfering in Greece, pay an indemnity, and provide 'satisfaction'. The ambassadors replied that since the Turks had been the aggressors at Navarino, the Allies had only responded to provocation.[101] The Porte then blocked all communications of the representatives, and placed an embargo on Allied shipping through the Straits. Active preparations began for war.[102] In Constantinople, a warehouse was looted of 6000 muskets by a crowd.[103] The Outer Castles at the mouth of the Straits and fortifications on Tenedos were augmented and improved.[104]

After fruitless attempts to renew negotiations, the French and British ambassadors, Guilleminot and Canning, left Constantinople. The Russian ambassador, Ribeaupierre, had hoped to go to Odessa, but adverse winds delayed his transport at Büyükdere, so on 17 December he passed the Straits and rejoined his colleagues.[105]

The consequences of Navarino were not immediately appreciated in Europe. While the immediate beneficiaries of the battle were the Greeks, that government's view of the engagement was ambivalent. Capodistrias had originally seen the Allied presence as an important factor in legitimising the Greek insurrection in Turkish eyes, tangible proof that the Allies considered the Greek uprising as valid.[106] When informed of the battle, Capodistrias had mixed feelings; he termed the engagement 'brilliant', but felt that initial results had been disappointing.[107] Soon he was convinced that the battle had been unnecessary, and that Ibrahim's evacuation could have been assisted in a less spectacular, but more useful manner.[108]

The response of the French and British governments to the battle was acute embarrassment. The Treaty talks in London had made no headway since mid-October. News of the admirals' 'grapeshot' diplomacy reached London on 12 November; five days later Lord Dudley sent to the Admiralty a list of questions regarding Codrington's performance.[109] The gap between Foreign Office theory and Codrington's practice was clear; Codrington was to become a scapegoat for resolving the Greek question in an embarrassingly direct manner. Lord Bathurst, Lord President of the Council, stated the official view of Codrington's abilities:

> When Lord Melville appointed Sir Edward Codrington to the command in the Mediterranean (by the suggestion of Sir George Cockburn) I told him that I was afraid he might be hasty, though a gallant and excellent officer.[110]

What the government earlier thought the eventual course of action an officer whose nickname was 'Go it Ned' would have chosen is less clear.

Navarino had its effects on the subsequent Greek policy of the Allies; at the next Treaty meeting on 12 December, Dudley wanted to limit Allied involvement in a possible war with Turkey in such a way that Russian independent action would be severely proscribed: 'the sole object of the war into which they would find themselves drawn, would still be that which they originally attempted to accomplish by means of negotiation.'[111] The Protocol issued after the meeting stated that in event of war, the Allies renounced all 'exclusive gains' of any sort. Opinions of Codrington and De Rigny about following up the tactical advantages conferred by Navarino with a strict blockade were ignored, though both the French and Russian representatives supported the idea.[112]

In January 1828 Goderich's government was succeeded by one headed by the Duke of Wellington, who was much less inclined than his predecessor to ally himself with the Russians to settle the Greek imbroglio. The King's Speech of 29 January 1828 described Navarino as an 'untoward event' with an 'ancient ally.'[113] The policy of Wellington's government was clear – further naval or military commitments by Britain were to be avoided, while current commitments were to be maintained at as low a level as possible. A similar aversion towards further decisive joint action also arose in Paris.

In St Petersburg, in contrast to Paris and London, news of the battle was joyously received: 'the battle had dispersed the illusions which the

Porte had entertained on the character of the agreement between us...'.[114] Nicholas 'approved completely' of the battle.[115] For his service at Navarino, Geiden was promoted to Vice-Admiral; his flag-captain and chief of staff Lazarev was made a Rear-Admiral.[116] Nicholas sent to Vice-Admiral Codrington a St George 2nd class, one rank higher than Geiden himself received. Aware of the damage sustained by the British squadron, the Tsar generously offered one of his ships to Codrington as a flagship, which would be 'un véritable honneur pour la marine Russe' if accepted.[117]

More practical if less glorious were the reinforcements sent to Geiden. On 14 December the brigs *Okhta*-20 and *Userdie*-20 arrived at Malta from Naples; four days later they were joined by the brigs *Revel*-18 and *Akhilles*-16, bringing the total Russian Mediterranean force to four line ships, four frigates, eight brigs and a corvette.[118]

Turkish vengeance meanwhile continued along increasingly anti-Russian lines; on 20 December Mahmut published a Hattışerif which denounced the Akkerman Convention as a ploy to gain time. It also stated the Greek insurrection was covertly fuelled by Russian assistance. The lack of success of the Ottoman navy was explained: 'our fleet could not be of any use, because of the disorder which has so long prevailed in our Admiralty, which is the cause of this affair having continued for so long.'[119]

All Muslims were exhorted to arm in preparation for war. Shortly before his departure from Constantinople, Ribeaupierre wrote of the increasing harassment of Russian citizens there. All trade through the Bosphorus had been halted, with captains being forced to sell their cargoes at arbitrary prices, one-third of which was paid in cash. All Russians had to register with the authorities in Galata, while their residences were searched for guns and powder.[120]

News of Navarino had arrived in Sevastopol as the Black Sea Fleet was preparing to move into winter quarters – ships were being laid up and partly disarmed for repairs. Orders now arrived to keep those ships in full readiness which might be needed during the winter.[121] Admiral Aleksei Samuilovich Greig, commander of the Black Sea Fleet, sent the brigs *Pegas*-18 and *Ganimed*-18 to the Bosphorus to reconnoitre.[122] Two transports for Ribeaupierre were sent to Constantinople. A million rubles were assigned for putting the Fleet on an immediate war footing. Pontoons and gunboats were built for the projected Danubian campaign. Sevastopol was put in a state of alert, while ships sailing to the Georgian coast were ordered to be prepared for possible attacks.[123]

Further south, on 27 and 28 December the remnants of the Muslim fleet limped back into Alexandria. Of the forty-five ships, the four remaining frigates and four of the corvettes had been severely damaged; the transports that had survived were relatively intact.[124] Aboard were 2000 sick and wounded, along with six hundred 'unfortunate Greek Christians' who were sold off in the slave market. Before leaving Navarino, the ships had been hastily repaired; many of the shot-holes in the hulls had been merely covered with canvas.[125] Repairs began immediately, and work continued on Alexandria's fortifications.[126]

Mehmet now came under increasing pressure. Sultan Mahmut realised that the Egyptians could be of crucial importance in the imminent war, and sent messenger after messenger to tempt Mehmet with the provisional offer of the Syrian pashaliks for his assistance.[127]

Wellington's Foreign Minister saw a similar role for Mehmet, and felt his aid or neutrality would be concrete proof of his true loyalty to his sovereign. Despite the presence of Geiden's squadron, Aberdeen considered the evacuation of Greece by the Egyptians feasible even during a state of war.[128]

Russia efforts were directed towards persuading Mehmet to remain neutral. Geiden now wrote to the Russian consul in Egypt outlining Russian objectives in Greece – apart from enforcing the July 7 Treaty, Russia had no hostile designs against either Egypt or Turkey.[129] Within the next month Geiden again wrote to Pezzoni several times to repeat these assurances to the Egyptian ruler.

These efforts were tinged with self-interest; since the closure of the Straits, grain supplies were no longer available from the Black Sea, and Geiden had to negotiate in Alexandria for several cargoes of rice for his ships.[130] For his part, Mehmet was pleased to hear of Russia's good intentions, but 'il suivit en tout et partout les ordres du Grand Seigneur.'[131]

These informal arrangements were strained by 'major' issues, however; on 19 January 1828 Geiden received new orders to consider relations with the Ottoman Empire as 'definitely broken,' though he was to still act jointly with the French and British. Should rumours. prove accurate regarding a forcing of the Straits by Codrington, then Geiden was to proceed 'side by side' with the British ships.[132]

Wellington's government continued to decline any joint action along the lines proposed by Russia. For his part, Nicholas was determined to settle his differences with the Ottoman Empire as well as supporting the Greeks, alone if need be. Nesselrode wrote to Lieven that 'l'Empereur est decidé à munir cette guerre avec toute l'activité que vous le connaissez.'[133] Nesselrode viewed the Hattışerif as positive insofar as it further proved Turkish bellicosity.[134] Lieven was to press for Allied action to include a Russian occupation of the Principalities, in addition to blockade and naval demonstrations off both Constantinople and Alexandria.[135] Dudley again sidestepped the Russian proposals, however, and agreed only to send modified instructions to the admirals to supersede those of 15 October 1827.

The new orders, 'which, though their form has been agreed upon, are not to be considered as definitively settled', none the less represented an advance towards the Russian views of pressuring the Turks to accept Allied mediation. A blockade was to be conducted from the Gulf of Volos in the east to the mouth of the Aspropotamus in the west. Cruisers were to be sent off the Straits and Alexandria for intercepting Ibrahim's communications.[136] Piracy was still a major issue; the admirals were to urge the Greek government to furnish them with a list of their warships and provide each with a commission. All armed vessels without documents were to be seized. Greek warships were to be allowed both to participate in the blockade and join the piracy patrols.

Skirmishing continued in the Mediterranean; on 31 January a force under Captain Hamilton attacked and destroyed a particularly noxious nest of pirates at Grabousa, on the northwestern Cretan coast.[137] Geiden's ships were similarly forceful – when a vessel fired on boats from a Russian cruiser, the Russians replied with a broadside that killed thirty men on the renegade craft.[138]

Codrington now felt from London a severe lack of confidence in his command; he had first received queries about Navarino in early December. His subsequent observations on the value of extensive blockades were ignored, while in March he even received a query about the feasibility of reducing the number of ships on the Mediterranean station.[139] The increasing pressure along with a lack of precise orders nettled him, and he now remained at Malta, leaving Geiden in a semi-independent position of authority in Greek waters. Codrington wrote, 'I do not like to show myself in the Levant until I can take decisive measures of some sort. Explain this to Count Capodistrias.'[140]

Russia and Turkey inexorably drifted into war; the Russian declaration of war was issued on 26 April 1828. Among the causes listed was the Porte's violation of Russian trade through the Straits as recently reaffirmed in the Akkerman Convention. Twelve days later,

General Rot at the head of the Second Army crossed the Prut and occupied the Principalities without incident; the Russian crossing of the Danube at Satunovo began on 8 June.

The war made Geiden's relations with Codrington and De Rigny increasingly difficult. In early April he received orders to continue under Codrington, but the latter's self-imposed Maltese exile made close cooperation difficult. Geiden at Capodistrias's invitation subsequently chose Poros as his main base of operations, and began to transfer his ships there, leaving at Malta those only still under repair.[141] Before leaving Malta, Geiden had the pleasure of presenting the St George flag to the *Azov*-74 for her distinguished performance at Navarino, the first ship in Russian history to be so honoured.[142]

Despite the conflict with the Ottoman Empire, Nicholas wished to maintain his hard-won Anglo-French alliance, even if it seriously reduced the effectiveness of his military forces. Geiden's new orders charged him 'provisionally' to exercise belligerent rights, but with the 'greatest moderation.' For guidance on neutrality, he was to follow the 1801 Convention signed with Britain. Geiden was to ensure that independent action did not adversely affect his dealings with either Codrington or De Rigny; Lieven was empowered to halt any actions which might prove detrimental to Treaty relations.[143]

Mehmet had also been preparing for war's uncertainties. As he believed a blockade of Alexandria to be only a matter of time, he stockpiled strategic materials. On 11 April he sent a convoy of nine transports and three brigs to cut ship-timber at Finike on the Karamanian coast of Anatolia.[144] He imported copper from the Turkish mines at Tokat and had machines brought from England for laminating copper plate for the hulls of his ships.[145] Coastal defence work also continued; the positions ranged from the Arab tower west of Alexandria to el-Arish on the edge of the Gaza strip; the pretext given to Constantinople was that the works were designed to keep out the plague from Syria.[146]

In April an Algerian frigate and corvette which had evaded the French blockade of Algiers came into Alexandria. Mehmet had both immediately disarmed. The ships provided a useful excuse; when pressed by the Porte to send ships and money, he replied that the French blockade of Algeria made it too risky, as any sending of the ships might extend it to Egypt.[147]

Such ingenuousness belied the actual state of available Egyptian forces, however; by early May 1828 the Arsenal had been able to repair the ships damaged at Navarino to the point where sixteen warships were seaworthy.[148] The self-sufficiency of the Alexandrian Arsenal was underlined by the launching of a 28-gun corvette.[149]

The first strain on Mehmet's and Geiden's tacit truce was not long in coming. On 2 May the *Iezekiil*-74 fell in with an Egyptian corvette while cruising near Modon. A short action ended in the corvette's capture; the ship was taken to Aiyina to await a decision on whether or not it was a war prize.[150] Geiden described his trophy:

almost new, with a long gun-deck of 123 feet, built from the best oak, and the hull copper-sheathed, so that with the necessary care the corvette would be able to serve up to twenty-five more years. The artillery on her is of the best...on English lines.[151]

The ship had been at Navarino, and its sails and masts were still badly damaged. In addition, it was infested with 'peculiar Egyptian cockroaches...white, grey and red rats...mice...and other various creatures'.

The corvette arrived at Malta on 28 June; however, repairs and modifications were so extensive that she did not join the Russian squadron at Poros until mid-March 1829.[152] The Mediterranean remained a largely passive war zone for the rest of the year; the major battle areas were Bulgaria and Anatolia.

Russian army operations had originally been planned to be independent of any naval operations undertaken by the Black Sea Fleet. The Russian operational strategic plan had been drawn up in 1827 by General Ivan Ivanovich Dibich, a modified version of one he had presented in 1821 to Tsar Alexander I.[153] Dibich envisaged a one-year campaign; in April and May, the Danube would be crossed; the Balkans would be crossed in June, with a march on Constantinople in the middle of September. The plan made no provisions for the Asiatic theatre, nor for the use of the Black Sea Fleet in combined operations. The opportunities presented by Navarino and the presence of a Russian squadron in the Mediterranean would combine with the unexpectedly stiff Turkish resistance to alter this operational pattern, especially in 1829.

Turkish war plans were strictly defensive. The Danubian fortresses were the first major Turkish line of defence; the Principalities themselves were considered indefensible. Advantage had been taken of the late start of the campaigning season to reinforce the Danubian garrisons.[154] Moltke estimated that Mahmut could field nearly 170 000 troops; 80 000 regular soldiers and cavalry and 90 000 irregulars.[155]

Sheer numbers, however, could not compensate for the haemorrhage created by Mahmut's suppression of the Janissaries two years previously. The few available Nizam-ı-Cedit troops, trained in European methods, were still raw compared to the troops under Generals Dibich and Paskevich, commander of Russian forces on the eastern Anatolian front. In Constantinople, the Janissaries were still strong enough and sufficiently discontented to force Mahmut to retain 30 000 troops in the Bosphorus castles to deal with possible disturbances.

Mahmut's navy was similarly depleted. Navarino had destroyed not only ships, but the flower of the Ottoman naval officer corps and sailors, as the Kapudan Pasha ruefully admitted to a British naval officer.[156] The Tersane-i Amire (Arsenal) could muster seventeen dilapidated ships; these were kept in the Straits, while fireships were prepared in both the Bosphorus and Dardanelles to deal with imprudent Russian invaders.[157]

The vaunted Bosphorus and Dardanelles castles epitomised the Empire's martial lassitude. The Dardanelles represented a formidable natural obstacle in itself; a five-knot southern current passed along its fifty-mile length between shores that narrowed at several points to less than a half-mile. Southern winds predominated for more than nine months a year; sailing vessels attempting a northward passage could be delayed for weeks.[158]

The European Dardanelles shore had eight fortified sites, and the Asian shore five.[159] Only the Hacı Omer battery was constructed according to current European defence concepts; the other forts without exception were badly situated, poorly constructed, and indifferently armed.[160] Gun calibres ranged from three to eight hundred pounds.[161] The large bronze cannon impressed visitors, but were extremely unwieldy and difficult to use. The gunners were little better than their ordnance – in 1827, the castles fired nearly one hundred rounds at a Russian merchantmen fleeing downstream. Three or four shots hit the ship, while a fortnight was spent repairing the damage the forts inflicted on each other.[162]

The Bosphorus works were also paper tigers. The nineteen positions ranged in age from the late fourteenth century to the Napoleonic wars; they all shared the Dardanellian flaws of poor positioning, weak construction, mismatched weaponry and ammunition, inefficient personnel, and dominating nearby heights.[163]

Against these defences Admiral Greig could bring a powerful fleet of nine line ships, five frigates, six brigs, nineteen smaller ships, and seventeen transports.[164] Following the outbreak of hostilities, supply ships were scraped up in Odessa, Kherson, Sevastopol, Feodosiia, and Taganrog, eventually numbering about one hundred and eighty.[165] These ships immediately proved their worth, as the Second Army operating in the Principalities was heavily dependent on seaborne supplies. Nicholas wrote to Greig,

> I agree *to all* that you propose, but for God's sake consider above all your means of supplying provisions to Kavarna, without which we will starve to death at Shumla.'[166]

In the absence of a significant Ottoman naval presence, the Black Sea Fleet operated in conjunction with army manoeuvres. In contrast to the initial operational plan, Nicholas envisaged a two-front gradual war, which would have the twofold advantage of allowing the use of a minimal number of troops, as well as allowing the conflict to be broken off at any stage when the Porte might surrender. A massive fleet attack on the Bosphorus and Constantinople was ruled out. Greig's forces were subsequently used to reduce shore fortifications and fought no large actions with the Turkish fleet, which remained in Büyükdere.

Greig's first objective was the capture of Anapa, on the eastern Black Sea coast south of Kerch. The fort had been an important point of contact for the Turks to supply their co-religionists in Georgia with munitions and supplies for their guerilla war against Russia. The roadstead was completely open, and relatively shallow; strong offshore winds made it an extremely difficult place for ships to work their way close inshore.[167]

Greig's squadron of eleven ships left Sevastopol on 3 May; delayed by adverse winds, they did not reach Anapa until 14 May. The attack had originally been planned to coincide with the Russian crossing of the Prut.[168] The next day the ships landed four Black Sea Cossack regiments, six companies of the Taman garrison regiment, and twenty light cannon. The troops dug in north of the fortress. During the next three days the weather was unsettled, and the troops were harassed by sorties of the garrison and attacks from the mountaineers. On 18 May the weather improved, and Prince Aleksandr Sergeevich Menshikov, Chief of the Main Naval Staff, landed to direct operations.[169]

Two regiments and eight field artillery were also ferried ashore. The Fleet began a daily bombardment, but the larger ships were unable to participate due to the shallows.

The Turks attempted to send reinforcements; on 20 May Greig's cruisers intercepted four transports with a thousand troops that had been sent out from Trabzon. Three were captured with nine hundred troops; the fourth was attacked and destroyed while unloading in a small bay near Sudzhuk-Kale.[170] On 24 May the mountaineers tried to attack the rear of the Russian position, but were unsuccessful. Two hundred armed sailors were landed to reinforce the infantry, as the mountaineers alone numbered three to four thousand men.[171] The final attack came on 9 June, but the Russians repulsed the assault. The passive blockade achieved the surrender of the Anapa garrison three days later. Among the prizes were a 4000-man garrison and eighty-five cannon.[172] The mountaineers had inflicted unexpected losses on the crews of gunboats working close in to the fortress; in order to protect the crews, Greig had the boats fitted with heavy wooden bulwarks covering their prows when the squadron returned to Sevastopol.[173]

The Fleet's next task was the capture of Varna, on the opposite coast of the Black Sea. The fort commanded one of the best roadsteads on the entire Black Sea coast; it covered the communications of Constantinople with Šumen, the main Turkish garrison position north of the Balkans. Possession of Varna would allow the Russians an advanced supply base for their troops besieging Šumen while simultaneously cutting Turkish supply lines.

A maritime attack on the fortress presented problems; while the roadstead was closed to northeast winds, it was too shallow to allow line ships to approach closer than a mile.[174] The south of the fort was protected by swamps, while immediately to the west was Lake Debno. A reconnaissance force was before the citadel on 14 July, but was too weak to interfere with 10 000 reinforcements that entered Varna two days later.[175]

On 28 July a squadron of eight line ships, five frigates, and thirteen smaller ships reached Kavarna, and landed the third division of the Seventh Brigade, troops that had participated in the Anapa campaign. The Russians now attempted to complete their blockade of the fort, though Menshikov's 10 000 troops faced nearly 27 000 Turks. Greig's ships began a desultory daily bombardment; additional sailors and artillery from the Fleet were landed for use in the redoubts.[176] Small armed rowing craft were launched on Lake Debno west of the fortress to prevent reinforcements from slipping across.[177] The evening of 8 August Captain Melikhov led Fleet rowing craft in an attack that captured the fortress's entire detachment of thirteen small vessels.[178]

During the rest of August, the encirclement of the fortress slowly continued.

On 8 September Tsar Nicholas arrived from Odessa. The siege was his first real participation in the glorious business of commanding troops in battle. He set up his headquarters on the *Parizh*-110, and set about interfering in the siege with great relish.[179] The following day the Kapudan Pasha boarded the *Parizh*-110 for a day of negotiations, but the talks were unsuccessful; the siege was resumed, and plans were made for storming the fortress.[180] On 28 September a heavy counter-attack was made by the troops in the citadel as well as by some of Omer Vrioni's soldiers, but the attempt was repulsed with heavy Turkish losses. On 7 October an attempt by the Russians to storm the works failed after heavy fighting. More negotiations followed, and the place finally surrendered on 11 October.

The capitulation produced 9000 prisoners and 291 guns, along with a large quantity of military supplies. Nicholas and his suite left Varna three days later and sailed to Odessa. On 26 October, Greig's ships returned to Sevastopol. The warships were repaired and winterised. Four small ships were readied to cruise the Bosphorus under Rear-Admiral Mikhail Nikolaevich Kumani for reconnaissance purposes.[181] Greig informed Nicholas that the Fleet would not be completely ready to resume operations until 1 March, but that it was unlikely that the Turks would attempt anything before then.

The southern Russian flank by this time was secured; in the Mediterranean, the 'Allied' issue of Egyptian intervention in Greece had since been resolved. Codrington finally had received clarification of his orders, and by 19 May was off Navarino. Four days later he wrote to Ibrahim that a blockade of all Morea ports in either Egyptian or Turkish possession was coming into effect, warning him that resorting to devastation would make his case more difficult.[182] The blockade was to cover all vessels, 'even down to boats.'[183] The effects were immediate; on 16 June a sloop and transport returned to Alexandria with four dead and many wounded after attempting to break the blockade.[184]

On 21 June Codrington received news that Lord Aberdeen had requested his recall, and now sought to secure Ibrahim's evacuation before his successor arrived. On 9 July the blockade was extended to cover Alexandria, as Mehmet had long feared that it would be. Neutrals were exempt, but warned against proceeding to Crete or to any part of Greece under blockade.[185] Codrington sent expanded instructions to Commodore Campbell off Alexandria. Should

Mehmet's forces be observed putting to sea, the blockaders were to be withdrawn, leaving only reconnaissance vessels. Once the Egyptian fleet was fully cleared from port, it could be forced to Navarino to embark Ibrahim.[186]

Codrington now sailed to Alexandria to confer directly with Mehmet; arriving on 1 August 1828, he concluded an agreement eight days later providing for the withdrawal of all Egyptian forces from Greece. Garrisons totalling 1200 men were to be allowed in the Morea. Codrington asked Geiden (whose ships had not been in the Alexandria blockade) not to interfere with the evacuation, and he agreed.[187]

Mehmet had been cautiously realigning his relations with the Russians; on 26 July Pezzoni was informed that Russian merchantmen in Egyptian waters had a 20–30 day period of grace, after which any ship flying Russian colours would be arrested.[188] Of the four Russian ships in Alexandria, three raised the Tuscan flag, and one the Spanish.

At the 19 July London Treaty conference it had been decided to send French troops to the Morea; on 30 August, 14 000 troops under General Maison landed at Petolidi in the Gulf of Corinth. A week later a convention was signed with Ibrahim regarding the details of the evacuation. On 10 September the embarkation began; the first contingent of 5000 troops with horses, and baggage set sail on 16 September.[189] The French offer of thirty transports was accepted for the second division; loading began on 26 September and the division sailed five days later. Ibrahim left on 4 October. The *de facto* naval armistice inaugurated by Navarino had now fully blossomed.

Sixteen days after Ibrahim quit the Morea, the *Fershampenuaz*-74 under Rear-Admiral Petr Ivanovich Rikord arrived at Malta.[190] During the next three weeks the remainder of his squadron of three line and three frigates arrived from Plymouth.[191] Rikord's ships were to be used in a Dardanelles blockade. Russia's Mediterranean naval strength was now impressive, but continued to be used in an extremely cautious manner.

Before the outbreak of war, Nesselrode had instructed Lieven to attempt to reconcile the British government to the limited Russian intentions in the event of war with the Ottoman empire.[192] Vice-Admiral Geiden had been 'provisionally' instructed to exercise belligerent rights following a declaration of war, but Prince Lieven had laid these aside at the 15 June 1827 conference.[193] Tsar Nicholas did not regard this as permanently restrictive, but rather as a conciliatory act initially designed to prove the sincerity of his commitment to the July 7 Treaty. In a long interview with the British ambassador Lord Heytesbury in Odessa on 10 August 1828 Nicholas had said, 'What can Russia gain by the destruction of the Ottoman Throne? All I ask is to be judged by my conduct, and not to be made the victim of suspicion.'

Should Turkish obstinacy continue, Geiden might be sent expanded orders;

> I shall then be driven to more decisive measures, and I shall want my fleet, not for the purpose which common fame would attribute to me, of bombarding or capturing Constantinople, but of doing what was once determined the combined Squadrons should jointly do, namely blockading the Dardanelles and starving the Turks into submission.[194]

Aberdeen believed Nicholas to have much more extensive ambitions;

> in the event of any territorial aggrandisement, or [as] has been obscurely hinted in the Russian official press, an intention to retain possession of the fortresses on the Bosphorus, you will adopt the gravest tone of remonstrance consistently with abstaining from all language of menace, and you will write... without delay for further instructions....[195]

Heytesbury thought that Russian demands would probably be limited to the retention of Anapa and Poti, along with an indemnity, which could be paid in either cash or material.[196]

At the 30 September Treaty conference Lieven officially informed Aberdeen of Russian intentions to resume belligerent rights in the Mediterranean. Nesselrode had earlier sent to Lieven a detailed despatch listing possible situations where Geiden would be forced to reply to Turkish or Egyptian aggression.[197] The campaigning in the Principalities and eastern Anatolia had been much more difficult than Dibich's optimistic projections; according to his timetable, Russian troops by September were to be marching on Constantinople, when in reality they had not yet crossed the Balkans. In such a situation, Geiden's forces were simply too valuable to be kept from action forever, and Nicholas began to contemplate their use. With Ibrahim's forces now returned to Egypt, there was a distinct possibility of Egyptian troops being transferred to the Danubian or Anatolian fronts, an action that Geiden's forces could prevent.

Aberdeen grudgingly acknowledged that Nicholas had a 'perfect right to assume these rights...';[198] privately he found Lieven's explanations 'beneath contempt.'[199] Aberdeen threatened that the Royal Navy would be forced to decline cooperating with Geiden if the blockade was carried through.[200]

Threats were not successful, and Aberdeen now moved to limit the blockade's effects on British shipping. He wrote to Lord Heytesbury to obtain immunity from the blockade for all British shipping clearing for Constantinople up to 1 October; a second communiqué advanced the date to 31 October 1828.[201] Should the Russians refuse, Heytesbury was to state that reinforcements would be sent to the Mediterranean to protect British commerce. Orders were sent to Vice-Admiral Sir Pulteney Malcolm, Codrington's successor, to disassociate himself from Geiden if the blockade was established.[202] Malcolm was also to lift the Cretan blockade as soon as Ibrahim's evacuation of the island was complete.

On 18 October 1828 Geiden informed Malcolm that he was sending Rikord with two line and two frigates to establish a Dardanelles blockade.[203] The only neutrals to be stopped were those carrying contraband or food for Constantinople; similarly, outward-bound neutrals were to be allowed freely to repass the Dardanelles, providing they were not carrying troops or munitions. Geiden declared that Rikord's blockade in no way affected his dealings with the Allies.

On 17 November Malcolm received instructions to disassociate from Geiden in the event of a Straits blockade. Geiden's squadron was still considered 'that of a friendly power, engaged in warlike operations with respect to which His Majesty is neutral.'[204] British Maltese facilities were still available to Geiden's ships; the demands made on Valetta naval stocks by the Russians were becoming so severe that the Commissioner now wrote to the Admiralty,

> ...I suggest the propriety of some communication...to ascertain how far it is intended to afford the facilities of refitment and supply to the Russian ships, as at present their wants and facility of supplying them are nearly equivalent to those of our own squadron.[205]

Rikord's blockading squadron took up its station on 14 November. He anchored in an open roadstead off Tenedos, battling winter storms; cruisers were also sent off Imroz, Limnos, and Mitilini.[206] Towards the end of December Rikord sent the *Fershampenuaz*-74 back to Geiden, and maintained the blockade with the *Emmanuil*-64, *Mariia*-44 and *Olga*-44.[207] The remaining Turkish ships were not so few so as to be dismissed; one writer numbered them as eight line ships, 'some' frigates, five corvettes and three brigs, for a total of nearly 1000 guns.[208]

Geiden also turned his attention towards Egypt. Mahmut had increased his demands on Mehmet – besides the return of his fleet, he wanted 24 000 troops under Ibrahim's command and three to four thousand sailors.[209] Dozens of grainships were readying in Alexandria for Constantinople.[210] On 14 January 1829 Malcolm recalled the Allied cruisers blockading Crete, which left the island open to Mehmet's forces.[211] Two weeks later Geiden established a cruiser between Budrum and Crete, in order to prevent reinforcements being sent to the island; he wrote to Malcolm that he would withdraw the ship when Allied forces again resumed the blockade.[212] The imminent possibility of Egyptian intervention caused Geiden to send to Rikord the line ships *Azov*-74, *Tsar Konstantin*-74, *Kniaz Vladimir*-74, *Velikii Kniaz Mikhail*-74, *Aleksandr Nevskii*-74, frigates *Aleksandra*-44, *Konstantin*-44, *Kniagina Lovich*-44, and *Navarin*-20, *Userdie*-20, *Telemak*-20, and *Akhilles*-16.[213]

On 9 February the *Tsar* Konstantin-74 captured an Egyptian corvette and brig off Crete.[214] On 26 February Geiden informed Mehmet that he was blockading Rhodes, Crete, and Alexandria.[215] Geiden believed that Mehmet had given orders for his navy to attack the Russian blockades, in order to open a supply line to Constantinople.[216] Geiden felt that a close blockade of Mehmet would be a wise preventive measure.

In Constantinople it was the winter of Mahmut's discontent. His Straits were blockaded, and he was unable to draw upon the resources of his North African provinces. Attempts to secure a military alliance with Persia were unsuccessful, and the Allied ambassadors were resisting offers to return and negotiate separately on the 'Greek Question.'[217] Turkish efforts were directed towards re-equipping the fleet and armies for the upcoming campaign.

In early February the Black Sea Fleet took the initiative from the army and mounted operations against Sizepol, a harbour on the southwestern coast of the Balkans. Its strategic importance was not lost on Heytesbury;

under the guns of this fortress may be landed without the slightest difficulty...troops, and should such an embarkation take place, and to any amount, the whole position of the Balkans becomes turned, and relatively useless.[218]

General Rot believed that thirty to forty thousand troops could be landed there.[219] Russian cruisers had discovered while interrogating merchantmen that Sizepol was relatively lightly defended. On 27 February 1829 three line ships, two frigates, three gunboats, and two freight vessels carrying eleven hundred men appeared off the port. A surrender offer was rejected, and cannon fire exchanged. The next day five hundred men were landed, and the position captured without difficulty.[220] Sixteen hundred men were captured, along with a large supply of military stores.[221] The importance of defending the harbour against a possible Turkish counter-attack led Admiral Greig to refuse a request by General Paskevich for a naval demonstration off Samsun, which would have divided the Fleet's forces at a critical point.[222] Paskevich's front was far enough inland that the Black Sea Fleet had little immediate bearing on his campaigns; the passive effect of Russian naval superiority was to deny Mahmut the ability to reinforce Trabzon by sea. By July Paskevich in conjunction with the Fleet had captured Poti, which would prove a useful point if an attack was made on Trabzon.[223]

Greig now transferred his squadron to Sizepol. From there he sent cruisers along the Anatolian coast, and had several frigates constantly off the Bosphorus. On 25 April he received a report that the Turkish fleet had put to sea. Greig took the line ships *Parizh*-100, *Imperator Frantz*-100, *Imperatritsa Mariia*-84, *Chesme*-84, *Nord Adler*-74, the frigate *Flora*-44 and *Ganimed*-18 brig and attempted to intercept the Turks. The Ottoman fleet retired into the Bosphorus before the Russians could find it.

The loss of Sizepol was recognised in Constantinople as a serious setback, and the Turkish fleet subsequently made five sorties, the last being 12–16 June. The cruises were of short duration with no clearcut objectives, and little was accomplished.[224] On 23 May, however, the Turkish fleet overtook and captured the *Rafaiil*-44 frigate, which surrendered without firing a shot. When Nicholas heard of this disgrace, he ordered the ship burned if it ever again came into Russian hands.[225] He was sufficiently angered by his officers' cowardice that when Captain Stroinikov and his comrades were subsequently returned to Russia during a prisoner-exchange, they were immediately court-martialled and broken to the ranks; Nicholas specifically forbade Stroinikov to marry, in order that his shameful example would not be perpetuated in future generations.[226] Three days after the *Rafaiil's* capture occurred an event remarkable enough to assuage the Black Sea Fleet's wounded pride. The frigates *Shtandart*-44, *Orfei*-20 and brig *Merkurii*-20 were cruising off the Bosphorus when they spotted the remains of the entire Turkish fleet setting sail. The Russian ships sailed for Sinop to inform the squadron there under Captain Skal'kovskii. The *Merkurii*-20 was the slowest sailer, and dropped behind to be overtaken by two Turkish line ships, one mounting 74 guns, and the other 110 guns. A war council called by Lieutenant Aleksandr Ivanovich Kazarskii, commander of the vessel, decided to fight to the last; a loaded pistol would be left on the powder magazines, and the last surviving officer would use it to blow up the ship rather than surrender.

During a two-hour skirmish, the Russians managed to disable their opponents sufficiently to be able to escape. The cost to the gallant brig was four dead, six wounded, and twenty-two shot in the hull of the ship, one hundred and thirty-three shot holes in the sails, and one hundred and forty-eight shot in the rigging.[227]

In less dramatic but more useful contributions, Geiden and Rikord now expanded their field of operations. On 28 March 1829 the Dardanelles blockade was enlarged to include the Gulfs of Saros, Edremit, Contessa, and Enez.[228] The pressure on Mehmet to commit his forces was increasing. Throughout April and May couriers flowed into Alexandria with demands for ships and troops.[229] In the Mediterranean Geiden now had seven line ships, eight frigates, two corvettes and five brigs, which allowed him to cover successfully a wide area as well as providing Mehmet with a plausible excuse that he was unable to send his forces.[230]

Geiden's expanded blockade provoked new protests. Aberdeen took up the matter with Lieven and ordered Heytesbury to discuss it with the Tsar.[231] Aberdeen hoped that such pressure would result in the blockade extensions being abandoned. Nesselrode was well aware that the expanded blockade would cause a storm in England, and instructed Lieven 'to accede in the Mediterranean all the concessions that England might want.'

He further defined Lieven's options;

among the blockades of which news torments the English Cabinet, there is one which we want to maintain permanently, and if you are able to save it, you will perform a service of which the Emperor will be profoundly grateful. All the correspondence from this area informs us incessantly of provisions assembled by the Turkish troops around Adrianople area, received via the Maritza, which flows into the Gulf of Enez. It is important to us now to close this point of theirs. Resist renouncing this blockade to the very last.[232]

Russia now compromised; on 13 June Lieven instructed Geiden that he was to lift the blockades of Edremit, Contessa, and Enez, and suspend the Crete and Rhodes patrols.[233] Three days later Aberdeen reported that these blockades had been lifted, but that the Dardanelles and Saros blockades remained in effect.[234] On 11 July Vice-Admiral Malcolm received the notification from the Admiralty, which was confirmed two weeks later by a despatch from Geiden.[235]

The Russian blockades had produced results; shortages of bread had become so severe in Constantinople that sentries were posted at the bakeries; supplies were first sent directly to the front.[236] One hundred and fifty Egyptian ships loaded with grain waited at Smyrna for the lifting of the blockade.[237] Unlike their operations in the Black Sea, the Turks made no sorties against Geiden; resistance was limited to the preparation of fireships, kept moored upstream from the Outer Castles.[238] The blockade reduced the supply of food so far that a traveller in the Marmora region wrote, 'I was informed of the scarcity of bread, and that it had risen to so high a price that the poor natives were in a state approaching starvation....'.[239]

The British ambassador returned to Constantinople on 20 June. Despite the weakening Turkish position on the Danube, the capital was still calm: 'The complacency with which . . . the campaign . . . [is] viewed, and the confidence in their own means of defence, with which the Turks are filled, is quite extraordinary.'[240] Gordon reported that an armistice offer had been made to the Grand Vizier's camp at Provadiya eight days previously, but had been rejected.[241]

Events in the Principalities now began to gather momentum. Dibich's victories at Klucheva and Silistra had freed his forces to pass the Balkans. His intelligence indicated that the mountains were lightly defended. Leaving a screening force before Šumen, the first Russian troops entered the Balkans on 6 July; five days later all the troops had passed.[242] The next day Russian forces captured Burgas, a coastal town, and opened communications with the Black Sea Fleet. The combined forces now began a rapid push through Thrace.

Heytesbury reported the probable Russian conditions for peace. According to his 'good sources', demands would include free navigation on the Black Sea for all commercial shipping of all nations and an indemnity, set against Russian retention of Anapa and Poti, with the remainder of the payment to be in ship-timber.[243] The demands were basically the same as those presented the previous year.

The Russian appearance south of the Balkans stunned and completely demoralised the Turks. Gordon reported that Constantinople was resigned to a Russian victory; in a desperate search for troops, Ottoman regiments were being filled with sixteen-year-olds.[244] Greig's ships continued their amphibious assaults almost unopposed, and captured Messemvriia, Akhiollo, Vasiliko, and Iğneada.[245] On 8 August, Dibich captured Adrianople and the way was clear for a Russian drive on Constantinople. Geiden was ordered to join Rikord off the Dardanelles and await further orders.[246] Janissaries in Constantinople began to agitate discontented elements, seeing in a Russian victory their chance to regain power. Hamit Ağa, commander of the Bosphorus forts, was executed on 25 August for his part in a coup plot.[247] Even Gordon now saw a Russian occupation as probable;

> It is certain that so heartbroken are the Turks, that if the Russians appeared with 10 000 men upon the heights above the capital, they might enter the next day, as at Adrianople by capitulation, and in ten days more they might be the masters on both sides of the Hellespont, from Tenedos to the Black Sea.[248]

In St Petersburg, discussions were taking place about the future policy of Russia towards Turkey. Reports received there had indicated the complete collapse of Turkish resistance.[249] Nicholas convened a conference of high-ranking officials, who presented a protocol that was to become the basis of future relations for the remainder of Nicholas's reign. It concluded that a weak Turkey was preferable to the complete disintegration of the Ottoman Empire.[250]

The deliberations and decisions of Nicholas's Secret Committee remained a closely-guarded secret. Even Price Lieven was not directly informed of the Secret Committee's decisions: Nesselrode sent him a long despatch paraphrasing the major governmental considerations for moderation in what became the Adrianople Treaty.

> The idea of chasing the Turks from Europe, of re-establishing at St. Sophia the cult of the True God, is certainly very beautiful, and, if realised, it would have us all live in history; but what would it gain Russia? Glory, undoubtedly, but at the same time, the loss of all the

real advantages of a neighbouring state distracted by a series of fortunate wars; of inevitable disputes with the principal European powers, with what would be their acceptance of the moment; and perhaps a general war at the end.[251]

On the subject of the 'limited war',

> it was not an exaggerated generosity that kept us from demanding advantages, but the closely-held conviction that for us to require these would soon prove more disadvantageous than beneficial...'.

Heytesbury was not informed of the decisions of the Secret Committee, but he nonetheless accurately summed up the prevailing mood of the government:

> From all that has occurred during the present war, the Russian Government has acquired the clearest conviction that under the present circumstances of the world, the conquest of Turkey is impossible. That the attempt would be followed by a war with the whole of Europe which it would be impossible for Russia to sustain.[252]

It was still not clear how much longer the Turks would prevaricate about a peace agreement. Plans were made for the encirclement of Constantinople, if necessary. Greig prepared fireships for dealing with the Turkish fleet moored at Büyükdere.[253] The Russians now held a front stretching from Midye on the Black Sea coast to Enez on the Mediterranean, where communications were opened with Geiden on 6 September.[254] Dibich wrote to Geiden that should future operations be taken against Constantinople, then his naval forces would be under direct army command.[255]

Nicholas was well aware that the growing concentration of Anglo-French naval forces in Smyrna might be used by his erstwhile 'Allies' to contest any peace agreement that they felt was overly onerous. Turkish procrastination nevertheless had exhausted Nicholas's patience, and in the event of further resistance, he had sent to Dibich detailed instructions regarding his projected operations against Constantinople.

> I approve of all your dispositions; but regarding this, in such a situation, should the negotiations be broken off, you will send a body of troops to the Dardanelles, for us to be certain, that 'unwanted guests' do not appear there to interfere and harm our

concerns . . . finally, if while at the Dardanelles, *your position is to refuse entry to all other fleets, besides our own.* If you are forced – *you reply with gunfire. But God save us from this!*[256]

An order of 26 September was even more succinct; 'Ainsi donc si tout est fini revenez; si non *vpered* ["forward"]'.[257] Even at this late stage, the plan was to surround and seal off Constantinople by land and sea, rather than to use direct force to overwhelm it.[258]

The evening of 9 September Guilleminot and Gordon had an audience with the Sultan. The situation appeared grave enough to offer to order the British and French squadrons up the Dardanelles into the Sea of Marmora. The offer was supposedly for the protection of 'all persons of any nation' in case disorders broke out in the city; in a confidential communiqué the next day, Gordon expanded on the theme:

> the presence of His Majesty's fleet would serve the double purpose of encouraging the Sultan and upholding his cause, and of producing great caution if not delay in the advance of the Russian army. I need not point out in what way the presence of a British force, commanding as it certainly would do, the entire navigation of the Black Sea, might completely change the fortunes of the day....[259]

Mahmut had realised the inevitable, however, and on 14 September concluded the Adrianople Treaty with Dibich. Two days after the signature of the peace treaty Greig received notification of it; Geiden received the Sultan's ratifications of the Treaty on 30 September and wrote to Malcolm the same day, announcing the immediate lifting of all blockades.[260]

2 The Adrianople Peace and the Growth of Russian Black Sea Trade

'No nation in the world, not England herself, possesses the natural facilities for acquiring maritime strength in greater abundance than Turkey – but never were such advantages turned to less account. What a contrast does the indefatigable vigilance of Mehemed Ali present.'[1]

'The naval power of Russia may appear to be a mere chimerical apprehension, but on examination it will be found that there is no Government in Europe which can collect within her own regions, and dominions, such material of every kind required for ship-building, or which has such facilities for transporting it with little labour and cost to her arsenals and ports.'

Sir Robert Wilson, 5 October 1829[2]

When we reflect on her admirable geographical position, the singular aptitude of her people for commercial pursuits, the principles of improvement and increase in her provinces, and which have a wider field for their development than any other country, excepting, perhaps, the United States of America; when we consider her magnificent inland navigation, connected by an admirable system of canals in every part, and her various inland seas, which, presenting every variety of coast and depth of coast afford such fine nurseries for seamen; we may safely conclude that Russia is destined to occupy, at some no very distant period, the first place among the maritime and commercial powers on the globe.[3]

The Adrianople Treaty was signed at a fortunate time for both Russia and Turkey. As late as mid-August, Turkish prevarication mystified

35

St Petersburg, with Nesselrode observing, 'It is . . . extremely difficult to know why the Sultan, currently threatened at the heart of his power in Europe, as well as Asia, has not become more tractable.'[4] In Adrianople itself, former Janissaries approached Russian troops, gave them a secret sign, and requested aid to help them take their revenge.[5] Rumours were rife in the Turkish capital; a British officer at Tarabya reported that the Russians had reached the Sea of Marmora, while Dibich's main forces were within a twenty-hour march of Constantinople.[6] The British ambassador numbered Dibich's troops at 40 000, with 25 000 reinforcements expected daily.[7]

The reality of the Russian threat was somewhat different. Dibich's forces actually numbered less than 20 000, while of these illness had incapacitated at least 9000.[8] Gordon's estimate of 40 000 troops in Adrianople was barely short of the total number of Russians in Rumelia and the Balkans.[9] Against Dibich's troops in Rumelia, however, the Sultan could field less than 8000 soldiers.[10]

The real threats to the Russians came more from European intervention and disease. At least one Russian staff officer nervously contemplated wintering in Adrianople while a hostile Europe prepared to intervene by both land and sea.[11] The Allied squadrons had assembled at Mavri by the time the Treaty was signed; in addition to the French, Russian and British ships were a Dutch frigate and Austrian schooner and frigate, a total of forty warships.[12] Admiral De Rigny felt the French and British ships should have been used to force the Turks to earlier negotiations, which would have allowed them to influence the peace talks:

> Of what use are these machines with 80 guns which cost so much money and require thirty fathoms of water? On what capitals can they be brought to bear? On Naples and Constantinople. It is there that you should make use of them.[13]

The Allied warships impressed St Petersburg, if not the Turks. The Russian ambassador in Paris complained to Polignac, 'with an energy which he cannot think a Russian agent would venture to betray if not supported by a positive instruction to that effect.'[14] No action occurred, however, and Geiden subsequently withdrew his ships from the Dardanelles, first to Smyrna, and then to Poros.[15]

Paskevich's army was similarly extended. After the capture of Erzurum the Russians were operating nearly one hundred miles from the coast, too far for the Black Sea Fleet to provision them effectively.[16] The Russian Black Sea naval blockade had not been impenetrable – in mid-September, seven cannon had been sent by sea to Trabzon, where the Serasker could still field 30 000 troops.[17]

For merchants deprived of Black Sea trade for nearly two years, the possibility of renewal caused 150 ships from various countries to assemble off the Dardanelles.[18] News of Dibich's treaty was received in London on 20 September, causing a rise in the price of City public funds, as well as Russian stocks; the Stock Exchange remained open, even though it was a Sunday.[19]

Admiral Greig received news of the Treaty on 16 September; the next day he issued orders to the Fleet to cease hostilities, while the *Merkurii*-20 and *Ganimed*-18 were despatched to inform Russian cruisers along the Anatolian and Georgian coasts.[20]

General Dibich was uncertain of Turkish intentions despite the Treaty, however, and after a number of potentially hostile troop movements, wrote to Greig asking him to keep the Fleet in readiness for possible offensive actions within the Bosphorus itself. Greig replied that the Fleet was already deployed, with two ships sent back to Russia; the remainder would be kept ready. The imminent onset of annual autumnal Black Sea storms might render amphibious assaults on the Bosphorus difficult, but it was the most effective naval option open, and if Dibich so wanted, a brigade would be equipped and prepared to storm the European defences of the Bosphorus prior to an attack on Constantinople itself.[21] Fireships that had been prepared earlier for a possible assault on the Turkish fleet in Büyükdere were also kept ready. These preparations were not needed, however; on 19 October Greig received additional orders about returning the Fleet, while leaving enough ships for Dibich's needs in Rumelia.

Ten days later the Black Sea Fleet returned to Sevastopol. During the war it had captured three Turkish brigs, thirty transports and merchantmen, and had managed to destroy a Turkish line ship, a corvette, and thirty-three transports and merchantmen.[22]

Hostilities in eastern Anatolia ceased on 11 October when the Serasker informed Paskevich that he had received private intelligence regarding the Treaty; he requested a ceasefire, to which Paskevich agreed, providing the Serasker as a sign of good faith disband his troops.[23] The agreement ended hostilities between Russia and Turkey.

The Adrianople Treaty had sixteen articles.[24] Given the Russian expenditure of blood and treasure, it was remarkably moderate, although it was not perceived as such in London and Paris. Violations of maritime rights and treaty obligations had figured strongly in Russian grievances prior to the war. Russian merchantmen had been detained in violation of Article XI of the 1774 Küçük Kaynarca Treaty and Articles I and XXX of the 1783 Commercial Treaty.[25] Seizure of Russian cargoes (especially wheat and tallow) had disregarded Articles XXX, XXXIII, and XXXV of the 1783 treaty, as well as Article VII of the 1826 Akkerman Convention.

Article III of the Adrianople Treaty gave Russia control of the Sulina mouth of the Danube, which allowed it to regulate shipping on the river.[26] Article IV recognised Russian possession of the Black Sea coast from the mouth of the Kuban to the fort of Saint Nicholas, as well as the *de facto* Russian presence in Georgia. Article VII protected Russian shipping from the petty vexations of the Turkish customs officials, and specifically forbade them from interfering with the transhipment of grain; it also opened the Bosphorus to the shipping of all nations.[27] It was quite specific on the harsh consequences of future Turkish tampering with Russia's international Straits trade;

> ...and if...any of the stipulations...come to be broken without the Russian minister's claims on the subject receiving a thorough and prompt satisfaction, the Sublime Porte acknowledges in advance the right of the Russian Imperial Court of considering such an infraction as an act of hostility and of taking immediate reprisals towards the Ottoman Empire.[28]

Article VIII provided for Russian financial claims dating from 1806 to be met by a lump sum payment of 1 500 000 Dutch ducats, to be paid within eighteen months. In a magnanimous gesture by Tsar Nicholas (who had consistently maintained throughout the conflict that he was fighting the Ottoman empire to redress specific Russian grievances), Article X forced the Porte to accept the Treaty of 7 July 1827, thus providing for true Greek independence.

Nicholas in reality found the terms Dibich had wrung out of the Turks overly severe, especially his long-term occupation of the Principalities as a surety for Turkish compliance with the treaty. He 'perfectly approved' of Dibich's negotiations, but that rather than occupy the Principalities for ten years, Russia should instead occupy the shore of the Gulf of Burgas up to Constanţa and Satunovo. Dibich was to try and obtain Kars, Akhaltsike and Batum, perhaps in partial compensation instead of money. As many troops as possible were to return to Russia before the bad weather set in.[29] Nicholas later wrote to Dibich approving his plans for evacuation, but the lateness of the season meant that quarantine would be almost impossible to maintain, and that the second and third echelons of troops would have to remain until March or April. Army losses from illness continued to soar, and returning troops brought their maladies back with them. Plague had already broken out at Odessa and Sevastopol, in spite of strict quarantine procedures.[30]

Of the Treaty's various terms, the reparations were what most troubled the Porte. The Russians had considered the possibility of accepting material instead of money, 'amongst . . . equivalents, ships, ship timber, raw silk, and copper of the finest quality from the mines near Trebizond' but the idea was abandoned in favour of cash.[31] The payments so distressed the Turks that they were willing to trade the Principalities in return for their cancellation. When Nicholas told the British ambassador of this offer, he added that he could not see the Ottoman empire lasting much longer.[32] In considering the best way to approach Tsar Nicholas on the subject, the Turks contemplated using the *Nimetullah*-44 [ex-*Rafaiil*-44] to send Halil Pasha to Odessa to begin his journey to St Petersburg, whereupon the ship would be returned to the Russians.[33]

The Sultan also briefly considered a loan to buy off the Russians; in a meeting with Wellington on 11 October, the prominent banker Nathaniel Rothschild asked if Britain would be willing to underwrite such a loan, and received a brief 'no' in reply.[34] Despite the refusal, Rothschild authorised the Vienna branch of the family bank to offer to Mahmut a loan of 4 000 000 Dutch ducats with the copper ore of Tokat to be used as collateral; the bank estimated its resources to be worth 6 000 000 ducats. Due to the Halil's success in St Petersburg, the credit negotiations came to naught.[35] Nicholas proved flexible on the reparations; by mid-April, Lord Heytesbury reported that Nicholas had reduced the amount from 10 to 7 000 000 ducats.[36] Russian demands for reparations were not as unreasonable as they appeared to Russia's contemporaries; war, insurrection and widespread bad harvests during the early years of Nicholas's reign forced Count Egor Frantsevich Kankrin, the Finance Minister, to search abroad for loans. By 1832 the amount negotiated totalled 82 000 000 rubles.[37]

As the Russian army returned to a peacetime footing, the 'common people' were most relieved by the army draft levy being reduced from three men to one man per 500.[38]

The Adrianople Treaty dealt solely with merchantmen passage; nowhere in the Treaty was the right of warships to pass the Straits mentioned, but Foreign Minister Nesselrode remarked that Russia would prefer that the Straits were closed to all warships.[39] Russian views on warship passage through the Straits were clearly shown when Count Mikhail Semenovich Vorontsov, Governor-General of New Russia, was authorised to use the Black Sea Fleet's *Utekha*-10 yacht to send his family to Italy; 'You will make your entry into Constantinople with the gunports masked and 'en flûte' to avoid all complications with the Porte. . .'.[40]

Such a stringent attitude towards warship passage of the Straits was unacceptable to some; one Royal Navy officer now decided to test Russian and Turkish reactions to foreign warships in the Black Sea. Captain Edmund Lyons in the frigate HMS *Blonde*-46 now passed the Straits, and spent several weeks visiting Turkish and Russian ports. The Russians protested to Heytesbury; when he subsequently attempted to discuss the possibility of changes in the Adrianople Treaty he was told,

> it is singular that you should be so scrupulous with respect to the passage of Ships of War 'thro the Bosphorus, having yourselves set the example by the entrance of the Blonde frigate into the Black Sea. . .despite. . .our Treaties with the Turks, by which they engaged never to allow the passage to foreign Ships of War. If they grant this permission to you, what right have you to object to our making a similar demand?[41]

Heytesbury himself mused, 'It seems singular that the Turks should have consented to give an example of ships of war passing the Bosphorus at the present moment.'[42]

Lyons was later reprimanded.

If Nicholas and Nesselrode thought their post-war moderation would gather them plaudits in London and Paris, they soon learned otherwise.[43] Heytesbury believed in the Tsar's sincerity:

> But I confess, I have a higher opinion, than you appear to entertain, of the personal character of the Emperor – I believe in the frankness & sincerity of his professions, & in the moderation of his views, in so far as he is the Master, which an Autocrat, as he is, is not always the case.[44]

In reply, Aberdeen acidly observed that Heytesbury was 'a little bit like Candide in the best of all possible worlds', and hoped that he would soon open his eyes 'to the realities of things'.[45]

Despite the disagreements about the passage of foreign warships through the Straits, maritime trade immediately profited from the peace. In 1827, Russian exports through the Black Sea had totalled

£1 201 119; the war had reduced them to £95 535 in 1828. In the last three months of 1829 revenues revived to £337 327, and increased sixfold the following year to £2 258 277.[46] The war had severely crippled Odessa's shipping; while 666 foreign merchantmen had visited the port in 1827, the following year the number shrank to eighty, of which fifty-eight ships were Austrian. Despite the lateness of the season in 1829 following the Adrianople Treaty, two hundred ships made the passage, while the following year seven hundred merchantmen visited the port.[47]

Russian trade was not the only beneficiary of the peace; British trade with Turkey also increased. In 1827 British exports to Turkey had amounted to £531 704. In 1828 British exports had totalled £1 255 000, which shrank again to £525 000 in 1829; the Dardanelles blockade diverted most European merchantmen from Constantinople to Smyrna. The increased maritime freedom brought about by the Adrianople Treaty nearly tripled the value of the 1830 British trade to £1 476 000, which nearly doubled again in 1831 to £2 885 000.[48]

While the Adrianople Treaty had curbed the arbitrary exactions of Turkish officials for individual merchantmen, the application procedure to trade in the Black Sea was still a tedious process, before the necessary ferman was granted.[49] Russian shipping was largely freed from these vexations by the Adrianople Treaty; Russian outward-bound shipping simply picked up the necessary document in Constantinople, which removed the need to stop at the Outer Castles, Kilit Bahir and Sultani Kalesi.[50] Many Greeks coming up to Constantinople now sailed under the Russian flag for convenience, a practice which greatly annoyed the Russian ambassador, and for which he refused to grant permission. The Russians still allowed the Turks their 'rayet' maritime visitation rights, which led the British ambassador to hope,

> that it is the intention of Russia to cancel so much of the Treaty as is manifestly unjust or derogatory to the dignity and independence of the Turkish government.[51]

Foreign trade under the Adrianople Treaty increased so rapidly that many Russian merchants began to complain that the Russian Mediterranean – Black Sea trade was monopolised by foreigners taking advantage of the relaxed Turkish regulations instead of Russians.[52]

The character of this trade began to change as rapidly as its volume. Russian Black Sea trade increasingly came to be dominated by grain exports: during 1826–40, it eventually averaged 15.3 per cent of total Russian exports.[53] In 1827 grain worth 868 397 rubles had been exported from the Black Sea; while the war had decimated exports, in 1829 the trade had recovered to a value of 1 053 231 rubles; the following year produced a grain trade worth 1 651 603 rubles.[54] In 1830 the price of a chetvert of Russian grain eventually rose to six rubles eighty-five kopecks.[55]

The major Russian Black Sea port remained Odessa. Its duty-free status had been initially responsible for its emergence as southern Russia's leading port.[56] The port possessed a number of natural advantages over its Russian competitors. Despite the rigours of the winters, which not only froze up the bay, but the sea itself up to ten miles from shore,[57] the port was capable of holding three hundred merchantmen simultaneously, while the water was sufficiently deep for the largest ship.[58]

Russia's southern maritime commerce with Europe was not its only area of southern regional commercial growth; trade with Turkey, Persia, and the Central Asian khanates was also increasing. During the period 1827–9, despite two regional wars, Russian trade with its southern neighbours increased by nearly twenty-five per cent from 15 963 000 to 21 156 000 rubles.[59] This revival and expansion of trade would increasingly influence Russian foreign policy considerations towards its southern neighbours.

While the economic life of the Eastern Mediterranean and southern Russia revived and the Allies prepared to run down their naval presence, the Ottoman Empire and Egypt were more concerned with rearmament than trade. Mahmut now wanted the Imperial Fleet to return from Alexandria, where it had spent the previous two years recuperating from Navarino. Mehmet had not been idle while 'blockaded'; in October 1829 the British consul reported the imminent launch of two double-banked frigates, while a third frigate of 44 guns on the slips neared completion. Within the next two years, these would be joined by four more frigates and four three-decked line ships.[60] The Egyptians were receiving help from French navy personnel in reorganising their dockyard; Kergrist, commander of a French warship, worked along with Cérisy for over six months in 1829–30.[61]

Mehmet was aware that Sultan Mahmut wanted the combined Turkish–Egyptian naval forces to winter in Constantinople, but he told the British consul that his ships would accompany the Sultan's squadron only as far as the Dardanelles.[62] Mehmet coyly explained the previous delay had been due to the presence of two Algerian warships that had limped back from Navarino and taken refuge in Alexandria from the French blockade of Algiers; he was worried that the French might try to seize the two vessels.[63] In reply, Mahmut simply expanded his demand to include the two refugee vessels.[64] The ships Mahmut wanted returned were one 74-gun line ship, six frigates, six corvettes and four brigs; during their two-years' idleness in Alexandria, Mehmet had had no maintenance work done on them, as he conserved his supplies for his own vessels.[65]

The combined squadron finally set sail on 18 November; fifteen Turkish ships were accompanied by nine Egyptian warships, four Tunisian ships, and two transports.[66] The Turkish and Tunisian ships entered the Dardanelles on 15 December.[67] The Egyptians remained at sea on manoeuvres, and returned to Alexandria at the end of February 1830.[68]

With Mahmut's long-lost ships returned, the Ottoman navy numbered thirty-four vessels – of the eight line, the largest were the *Mahmudiye*-120 and *Selim*-80; the others were 74-gun ships. There were also ten frigates ranging from 36 to 60 guns, thirteen corvettes, a brig and two steamers, with 'some of the vessels being so old that they are unable to put to sea.'[69]

With the remains of his fleet now returned, Mahmut attempted to improve the Navy's personnel. Carpenters were levied from Khios, and Henry Eckford, an American shipbuilder, was hired to manage a section of the Tersane-i Amire.[70] Eckford worked in a strictly private capacity, a point made clear by the Secretary of State:

> let it be understood by. . .the Porte. . .that this is exclusively and entirely a private and individual enterprise of Mr. Eckford himself, in which this government has no concern whatsoever, and with which it is in no way connected.[71]

In the months following the signing of the Adrianople Treaty, the Allies continued to run down their Levantine squadrons from their August–September strengths. The French contingent was cut to one line ship, three frigates, and ten smaller craft.[72] Malcolm ordered all Royal Navy warships to rendezvous with him at Aiyina.[73]

Russian forces were also withdrawn from the immediate vicinity of the Straits. The Black Sea Fleet and Geiden's squadron had acquitted themselves honourably – apart from the surrender of the *Rafaiil*-44, no ships had been lost in combat; in the Black Sea, adverse weather claimed the transport *Zmeia* and lugger *Strela*-10.[74]

Army losses were of a different calibre. Helmuth von Moltke served with the Russians in the Balkans; his meticulous notes put Russian casualties during the two campaigns there at 25 000 men killed in combat, while illness had claimed 'at least' 60 000.[75]

The Black Sea Fleet now spent the next fifteen months ferrying the ill troops along with military stores from Sizepol, Varna, and other ports back to Russia.[76] In the Mediterranean, Geiden began to prepare his command for its return to the Baltic, dividing his forces in two. One division was to stay in the Aegean under Captain Rikord to cooperate with the French and British in implementing the July 7 Treaty; the other was to return to Russia.[77] In orders dated 6 October, Geiden was directed to leave six vessels in Greek waters. The *Aleksandr Nevskii*-74, *Fershampenuaz*-74, *Elizaveta*-44, *Uliss*-20, *Akhilles*-16, and *Telemak*-20 were to remain under Rikord; the remainder were to be back in Kronstadt no later than 13 May 1830. The squadron was to winter to Poros, 'and only in extreme necessity in Toulon'.

Despite the availability of British facilities in Malta, the two year's Mediterranean service had been hard on the Russian squadron. The *Emmanuil*-64 had so deteriorated from rot that Geiden requested permission to either sell her or break her up for firewood, as she would not survive the return voyage. The ship was to be carefully examined, and if no longer fit for service, to be disposed of in a way 'profitable to the Exchequer.[78] In January 1830 Prince Menshikov reported to the Tsar that the *Emmanuil*-64 was being used as a hospital (lazaretto) hulk; before the squadron's departure she was to be stripped of all useful materials and sold.[79] Nicholas noted with annoyance on the report, 'this only proves with what inexcusable negligence ships were previously constructed...'.[80]

Geiden appointed Lazarev to command the squadron on its return voyage.[81] Geiden himself remained in Greek waters, returning later to Kronstadt on the *Vladimir*-74 in company with the corvette *L'vitsa*-26 under the command of his eldest son, Lieutenant Login Loginovich Geiden.[82]

Lazarev's squadron sailed from Malta on 14 March 1830.[83] In accordance with his orders, Lazarev made no landfalls, and the ships arrived back in Kronstadt on 12 May. Contrary winds slowed the squadron's progress, while from Dagenrot to Gotland, the ships encountered foggy weather and heavy pack ice. The result of Nicholas's eagerness for the return of his fleet was that every ship lost nearly two hundred leaves of copper hull sheathing from forcing its way through the Baltic ice. Lazarev thought it a senseless loss. He attributed the government's incompetence in naval matters to the fact that the navy was headed by Menshikov, who was not a 'Navy' man.[84] Lazarev referred to the damage suffered by the squadron from its forced early return:

> This example will at any rate lie heavily on future commanders of squadrons, especially today, as our concerns are attended to by one who is not Navy, but Army, and of whom one is able to say, is completely ignorant of his business.[85]

In complete contrast to this acerbic professional description of the Chief of Naval Staff, the head of the Third Section, Count Benkendorf, in a report to the Tsar stated that Menshikov's attentions had revitalised the Main Naval Staff, and that while the officer corps was 'earnestly striving' for excellence, all were 'unanimously agreed' that Menshikov was a 'clever man'.[86]

Such irascible bluntness was typical of Lazarev; he was not afraid to speak his mind, even to the Tsar. Lazarev was still relatively unknown to Nicholas when he returned from the Mediterranean, but he was still able to voice his beliefs without compromising himself, as the *Fershampenuaz*-74 inquiry proved.

The *Fershampenuaz*-74 was sent back to Russia in October 1831 by Rikord, along with the *Aleksandr Nevskii*-74 and *Elizaveta*-44, as he found them unsuited to the constricted Aegean waters.[87] Upon entering Kronstadt, the ship burst into flames and quickly burnt to the waterline.[88] Arson was suspected, especially as the ship had been carrying the Mediterranean squadron's accounts for the previous five years. Nicholas appointed Lazarev to head an investigation.

After an exhaustive inquiry, Lazarev concluded that carelessness rather than arson was to blame for the conflagration. When Nicholas next visited Kronstadt, he asked Lazarev about the incident, expecting the arson theory to be confirmed. Lazarev stated only that the ship *had* burned, to which the Tsar replied, 'I'm telling you that the ship was burned.' Lazarev was deeply offended by the slur on his integrity and responded, 'Sire, I reported to you that the ship burned, but I did not say, that the ship *was* burned.'[89]

Despite such incidents, Nicholas had been very pleased with the performance of his navy; in addition to his generosity with honours for his officers, he did not forget the common sailor. Two ukazes eased terms of service for those who had served in the war. Those serving in the Guards were allowed to retire after twenty years' service instead of the previous twenty-two, while those in the line, working, and transport crews were allowed to leave the navy after twenty-two years' service, down from the previous twenty-five.[90] Those wishing to continue after they became eligible for retirement would receive a second bonus in addition to the one due them, while those who stayed for five years after their discharge date would receive the second bonus, plus half again as much in the form of a pension following their retirement; if one had been disabled in the line of duty, then support in the form of a full bonus pension was to continue to death. All of these awards were to be independent of pensions awarded for military excellence, or those with the order of St Anne. All those who participated in the 1828 – 9 campaign were to receive a special medal on a St George ribbon.[91]

After the return of his ships, Nicholas held a second Imperial review. Lazarev wrote that the Tsar had praised everything he saw on the *Azov*-74, but then remarked,

> it is sadly necessary to inform you, that all this improvement is in the light of a fleet such as the English, and is for us in our present position useless, despite the great wish of the Tsar to raise the fleet to the utmost perfection.[92]

Lazarev now served for two years in the Baltic Fleet; his career encompassed many of the profound changes occurring in nineteenth-century navies. As a volunteer, he served in the Royal Navy for five years during the Napoleonic wars.[93] In 1854, three years after his death, a squadron of Black Sea Fleet ships under the command of one of his ablest 'Band of Brothers,' Rear-Admiral Pavel Nakhimov, demonstrated at Sinop the terrible efficiency of shell guns against wooden ships; the guns themselves were an innovation that had been introduced into the Black Sea Fleet by Lazarev.[94] While the Soviets disavow much of their pre-revolutionary history, 'Soviet sailors value highly the service of Admiral Lazarev, as one of the greatest commanders of the Russian Navy.'[95]

Mikhail Petrovich Lazarev was born on 15 November 1788, the son of Petr Gavrilovich Lazarev of Vladimir, a minor noble. He entered the Naval Cadet Corps in 1800, and was joined in the service by his two brothers, Aleksei and Andrei.[96] In May 1803 Lazarev was commissioned gardemarin and sent to England to serve as a volunteer.[97] In 1808 he returned to Russia, and served in the Baltic Fleet. Lazarev then experienced a different form of British hospitality;

on 26 August 1808, his ship, the *Vsevolod*-74, was attacked and captured by HMS *Implacable*-74 and HMS *Centaur*-74. Casualties on the *Vsevolod*-74 were forty-five killed and one hundred wounded; Lazarev spent several months as a prisoner-of-war.[98] After his release, Lazarev sailed for the next five years in the Baltic Fleet, and in August 1812 participated in an amphibious landing at Danzig.

During 1813–16 Lieutenant Lazarev commanded the Russian American Company ship *Suvorov*, ferrying supplies from Kronstadt to Sitka by way of the North Sea, Portsmouth, Rio de Janeiro and Australia, discovering several islands.[99] Lazarev then returned to the Baltic Fleet.

In 1819 Captain Faddei Faddeevich Bellinsgauzen led an expedition of two sloops to explore Antarctic waters; Lazarev commanded the *Mirnyi*-20. The voyage was very successful; the ships sailed to 69 degrees 25′ south, and discovered more than thirty islands, among them the Annenkov and Vallis islets near South Georgia, and the Markiz-De-Travers group.[100] During the voyage Lazarev covered more than 84 475 miles, and logged 751 days at sea.[101] In 1822 Lazarev commanded the *Kreiser*-36 for his third world voyage.[102] Upon his return, Captain Lazarev was appointed to oversee the building of the *Azov*-74 in Archangel, where he introduced a number of innovations during the course of her construction. Lazarev then captained the *Azov*-74 at Navarino. There was now no better-rounded officer in the Imperial service.

Following his return from the Mediterranean, Lazarev served on the 'Committee for Improving the Fleet', which met from November 1830 to February 1831.[103] Others serving on the Committee were Admiral Greig, Lazarev's future commanding officer; Intendant-General Rear-Admiral Aleksandr Pavlovich Avinov;[104] Vice-Admiral Ivan Fedorovich Kruzhenshtern, Director of the Naval Corps; Lieutenant-General Iakov Iakovlevich Brun-Sen-Katerin, Inspector of the Corps of Ships Engineers; and Lieutenant-General Vil'son, head of the Admiralty Izhorskii works.

Lazarev worked hard and made a number of recommendations, nearly all of which were approved and implemented. Among his innovations were: the introduction of iron drying stoves to prevent rot aboard wooden ships, new spar fastenings, a new method of bowsprit construction, a new design for carronade carriages, a new mode of interior bracing for schooner construction, improved cannon-tackle rigging, improved lighting for night cruising, and the instruction of the lower ranks in sabre practice:

in the event of necessity they will have, in contrast to English and French sailors, a firm instruction in this skill, art and adroitness in equal parts, acquiring by these exercises dexterity and familiarity....[105]

Despite his endeavours, Lazarev had a typically tart view of the ultimate value of the Committee's activities; '... the more I observe all this, the more I am convinced that our fleet will never achieve the level of perfection which existed under Chichagov'.[106]

While Lazarev laboured on the Baltic Fleet in the tranquil surroundings of St Petersburg, the southern regions of the empire continued to suffer from the war's after-effects. Both plague and cholera returned to Russia in her soldiers' knapsacks. Plague also entered Russia via Orenburg, where it was transmitted by Kirghiz nomads, and from Persia, from where it spread to Tiflis and Astrakhan.[107] In early September 1829 two shiploads of Turkish prisoners infected with typhus arrived in Constantinople from Odessa.[108] Many of the Turks interned in Russia had already come down with typhus, and they transmitted it to the Russian crews repatriating them.[109]

The plague had first appeared in the Russian army following the capture of Kars in July 1828; strict quarantine measures had blunted its impact, but the army had to suspend its advance for nearly a month as a result.[110] In Thrace Dibich's command was now savaged by cholera; many regiments lost up to two-thirds of their troops, and thirty generals died.[111] Reports reached Constantinople of 13 000 Russian casualties in Varna alone.[112] One Russian military writer put the total number of Russian casualties in 1829–30 as 17 590 from combat, while illness claimed 79 132 soldiers.[113] Russian ships transporting their stricken countrymen homeward themselves became infected.

In a typical instance, a doctor aboard the *Erivan*-60 on 17 November 1829 noted forty-three of the crew were ill; fifteen days later the number had risen to eighty, while by the end of the next month 180 sailors, nearly one-half the entire crew, had fallen ill with contagious diseases, primarily typhus.[114] Treatment was an improved diet, purgatives, tea, and lemon juice in beverages.

The civil authorities made strenuous efforts to halt the contagions. Count Vorontsov immediately issued quarantine orders for the entire area. Sevastopol was sealed off by troops; a quarantine centre was established to the north of the town, while in Sevastopol itself a

'Commission for the Liquidation on the Plague' was set up, headed by the Inspector of the Tauris Board of Health, Dr Lang; the Fleet's medical personnel were placed under his direction.

The restrictions were quite harsh for Sevastopol's residents – one community of shipbuilders on Korabel'naia Bay had 136 guards for its 967 inhabitants.[115] Free movement was halted, and food and fuel were distributed by the authorities. The orders made the winter far more severe than usual, and as the plague abated in the spring, people saw no need for such draconian quarantine regulations to continue. When in early June one group complained to their priest, he told them to be patient and to continue to obey Vice-Admiral Paniuti's orders.[116] The patience of the Sevastopol residents was near the breaking point.

On 12 June 1830 Zinov'ia Shcheglova died in Korabel'noi village; under the quarantine regulations, a doctor was sent to determine the cause of death, who decided that she had died from plague.[117] Dr Lang confirmed the verdict, and wanted to isolate the settlement for a further fourteen days. The villagers refused to release the corpse to the authorities, insisting that she had died from old age. They attacked the soldiers sent to collect the body, killing one and wounding several, and rioting quickly spread.

Soldiers called out by the authorities refused to fire on the rioters, and additional troops were only able to restore order on 19 June. Father Gavrilov's home was attacked by rioters, among whom was a sailor wearing a St George Cross, and several officers. Instead of killing the priest, however, they asked him to sign a paper stating that there was no longer any plague in Sevastopol.[118] They then left.

When troops restored order after quelling the 'popular tumult', ten people had died, including Lieutenant-General Stolypin, military governor of Sevastopol, and the quarantine inspectorate's brigadier, Stulli.[119] Nearly 2000 were arrested, and retribution was swift.

Nicholas received confirmation of the uprising from Menshikov on 29 June; letters from Sevastopol ascribed the revolt to the strict measures taken to combat the plague, 'in whose existence there no one believed'; Vorontsov had already arrested thirty men, among them five officers.[120]

Two weeks later Nicholas sent orders to Vorontsov. All sons of participants in the revolt of any rank were to be despatched to military settlements as cantonists. All lower ranks in Sevastopol who had taken part in the riot were to be sent to Kerch and assigned land for houses; all women living in the riot-turn settlements were to be given identity papers and sent from Sevastopol, and the settlements were to be burnt.

Married sailors who had participated were to be sent to Greig for distant reassignment, while their wives were to be sent from Sevastopol and their settlements burnt. Finally, all Greek Black Sea Fleet officers (with the exception of the two Paniutis) were to be transferred to the Baltic fleet. The total tried by the military courts was 1580; seven received death sentences, while others were exiled to Archangel and other harsh maritime locales.[121] Heytesbury had a difficult time obtaining precise details;

> There is no country in the world where events of an unpleasant nature are so cautiously kept from the public knowledge, as in Russia, particularly during the absence of the higher authorities.[122]

Such incidents undoubtedly further convinced the Tsar that changes were needed in his naval forces. Nicholas instituted a number of surveys, reforms, and improvements in both the Navy and merchant marine. In February 1830 a merchant marine academy was established with the aim of providing Russia with more shipwrights, captains and navigators. The school was under the control of the Finance Ministry. There were thirty-two students, between fifteen and seventeen years old. Each annual class was to contain eight students – two from St Petersburg (of which one every two years was to be from Kronstadt), two from Riga (of which one every two years was to be from Pernau), one from Reval or Libau, one from Taganrog or Kerch, one from Odessa, and one annually from Archangel or other White Sea ports. The four-year course included ship design and construction, astronomy, arithmetic, history, geography, German, French, English and navigation. Practical exercises included cruises, gunnery and swimming. The students were to be chosen by the municipal officials of the various ports, with preference being given to orphans and children of poor families.[123]

Within the Navy itself, earlier educational reforms were starting to produce results. On 4 February 1830 graduated the first seven members of a 'special officers class' (the equivalent of a Naval Technical School) which had been established in the Naval Cadet Corps three years previously. The 'six to eight outstanding members' of the Corps selected annually spent three years studying analytical geometry, differential and integral calculus, astronomy, ship construction theory, history, geography, Russian literature, mechanics, and fortification.[124] Efforts were also made with the matériel of the Fleet, but the Baltic Fleet continued to receive more money and attention

than the Black Sea Fleet; while the Baltic Fleet had seven steamers at
this time, the Black Sea Fleet had only four.[125] The growing strength
of the Black Sea Fleet was underlined by the launch of the *Pamiat'
Evstafii*-84 in September and the *Adrianopol'*-84 in November 1830.[126]

The fleets also underwent administrative reforms; in 1831, the Naval
Staff was reorganised as the Main Naval Staff, under the command of
General-Adjutant Prince Menshikov; the Navy Minister remained
Vice-Admiral Anton Vasil'evich Fon-Moller.[127] Shipbuilding
ekipazhs (which included prisoners) and naval artillery brigades were
also established at this time.[128]

Officers and their professional needs were also provided for; 49 000
rubles were set aside for the purchase in London, Munich, and other
cities of telescopes and other optical equipment. The items were to be
imported without duty, and naval officers were to be allowed to
purchase them very cheaply, paying in instalments if they so wished.[129]
Despite new restrictions on studying abroad, one officer, Aleksandr
Shaunburg, was continuing a four-year course of shipbuilding in
England.[130]

Despite these modest improvements, however, many officers were
still highly critical; a Third Section report contained a number of
trenchant observations on the Navy by its officers. Many criticised 'the
carelessness with which they build ships'. Many of the shipwrights
were lacking in skills, and it was claimed that many were hired only to
enrich the builders, who received bribes from the contractors. The
sailors themselves felt that their line ships were badly constructed.
Many believed that Fon-Moller consistently deceived the Tsar about
the true state of affairs. Sailors gossiped about Greig, whom they felt
was an excellent officer, but that 'his business is not conducted entirely
correctly and the accounting is not in order'.[131] Despite the sombre
tone of the report, Benkendorf reported that many felt that there had
been improvements 'on a massive scale'.

The ships themselves also came under scrutiny; with the example of
the *Emmanuil*-60 still fresh in his mind, Nicholas issued orders for a
survey of all ships of both Fleets. In both Fleets the Chief Commander
was to establish a 'Committee for the Examination of Warships'
Defects and Their Resolution'. The survey was in four parts – the
first concerned the ships' construction. The second section evaluated
the ships' sailing qualities. The third part of the report was concerned
with the actual state and defects of the ships' hulls, masts, and spars.
The fourth section was concerned with repairs that might be made to
eliminate defects that appeared in the previous three sections.[132] In

order that the survey was carried out swiftly and effectively, specialists were to examine their own area of expertise; hulls and masts were to be surveyed by the Ship Engineer, the Tacklemaster was to do the rigging, and so on. The recent conflict had highlighted a number of short-comings in the navy that Nicholas was determined to overcome.

Another maritime legacy of the recent war, one that could not be inspected away, was the rising level of conflict in the Caucasus. The Black Sea Fleet was not to begin to play a very different role from its wartime service, as the growing Russian presence in the Caucasus was resisted by the indigenous tribes without the previous support of their Turkish co-religionists. The Adrianople Treaty in ceding Anapa and Poti to Russia had in reality only rectified border anomalies that had long represented a source of irritation and smuggling to the Russian authorities in Georgia. Anapa had the dolorous reputation of being the main port for Turkish slavers transporting Circassians to Constantinople, while Poti had long been used by the mountaineers as a transhipment point for Russians captured during raids.[133] The scale of the problem was substantial; one raid on Ekaterinfel'd shortly before the outbreak of the war had captured 140 Russians, mostly women, who were shipped out from Poti.[134] The struggle was to continue for more than thirty years.[135]

For Russia the Black Sea eastern coast was a porous frontier that had to be closed. The 1828 Turkmanchay Treaty gave Russia the sole right to maintain warships on the Caspian, while Russia had also a monopoly in trade with Persia by that route. This had closed Georgia's eastern maritime frontier, but no such possibility existed for its western shore. The Adrianople Treaty had opened Black Sea trade to the shipping of all nations; Russia now wanted to direct that commerce into only a few ports strictly supervised by the Russian government, in order to eliminate all contraband trade. Over the next decade the Russian coastal presence on Georgia's western shore would evolve into a chain of thirteen forts backed by trading stations and extensive naval cruising.

The indigenous resistance to Russian penetration of the Caucasus acquired a religious basis when Imam Gazi Mulla now issued a call to gazivat among the Daghestanis.[136] As resistance hardened, Russian attempts to assert direct control became more overt. The Caucasus was one of the most ethnically diverse areas in the world, which made Russian efforts to bring the area under their control both simpler and difficult.[137] Bad relations between the mountaineers and Russians had been simmering for some time; the recent war and peace treaty had only made things worse. A government official earlier had summed up the causes of the dissatisfaction:

> The causes of the animosity of the Circassians against Russia are: (1) the bad conduct of the Zaparozhan Cossacks and other government employees towards them, (2) the succession of internal wars, (3) a prediction that exists among them that they will be destroyed by Russia, (4) the instigations of the Turks, (5) the hope of taking prisoners.[138]

The author ominously predicted, 'Great sacrifices of men and silver will be required to destroy these people.'

In general, the Muslim mountaineers were much more hostile to the Russians than the Christian population. Russia followed policies ranging from allowing relative autonomy to cooperative local rulers to outright annexation and military conquest, attempting with their limited resources to assert their military presence where it was most needed. The only princes in Daghestan allowed to retain power were those that accepted Russian 'advisers'.[139] In Abhazia, Prince Michael was allowed to maintain nominal control; however, his Muslim uncles were largely in control of the areas outside of the Bzyb district, and their hostility meant the Russians had to attempt to maintain their control there by military means.[140] Russia also sent promising young Caucasians to study in Russia.[141] None of these policies was more than marginally successful.

As the conflict intensified and spread, so did the need to interrupt the arms shipments, many of which came by sea from Turkey. The Black Sea Fleet in the context of both stopping smuggling and undertaking amphibious operations was considered an essential adjunct to any army operations that might be undertaken.

General Paskevich regarded a military presence on the eastern coast of the Black Sea as essential to Russian security there, a view reinforced by his recent campaigning there. He now began to plan military operations for the area. In January 1830 Paskevich submitted a plan to the War Minister for operations in Abhazia that would provide for 'the extension and opening up of land communications by way of the coast from Anapa to Poti'.[142]

Other officers were also considering the problems of pacifying the coast. The basic premise of General Vel'iaminov's report was that only force could pacify the region, which meant if necessary the destruction of 'all means of existence' including crops.[143] All supplies coming in from abroad had to be stopped, and Vel'iaminov recommended the construction of small fortresses at all points where the mountains opened on to the plains, as well as at the mouths of all rivers flowing into the Black Sea. Five separate units each consisting of 7000 troops should be formed for 'incessant' action along the mountains' lower slopes, while another 7000-man detachment should operate along the coast. Vel'iaminov believed that such a course of action would result in the area's pacification within five years. The Fleet would provide communications and provisioning for the forts, as they would be isolated from one another by land routes.

The scale of the problem grew increasingly serious; in February 1830 Gazi Mulla and 6000 mürşid followers besieged and captured Kunzakh and attacked Derbent.[144] Smuggling also worried the Russian government – in the spring of 1830, twenty Russian ships were sent to the Caucasus coast during the Gagra operations,[145] while by the end of the year the number of Turkish smugglers visiting the Georgian shore had reached two hundred vessels.[146] Warships of the Black Sea Fleet had been cruising the Caucasus coast since 1804, when Prince Tsitsianov opened a port town at Redut-Kale, but there had been no regular routine established.[147] The government now moved to institute a periodic schedule of cruising.

In April 1830 the Foreign Ministry received information that a Turkish ship had landed munitions in Abhazia for Pasha Said Ahmet, a Turk who was staying in the mountains attempting to incite anti-Russian feeling. Nesselrode considered that in view of this and other incidents, 'how useful it would be for us to break all communication by sea between the Turks and Abhazians, perhaps by quickly establishing cruisers along the Black Sea coast from Taman to Poti.'[148]

Nesselrode asked Greig to send all the relevant information in his possession so that the Emperor could make a well-informed and prompt decision.

Eight days later Nesselrode wrote to Menshikov about another incident where a Turkish ship out from Trabzon had landed gunpowder and lead at Sudzhuk-Kale in exchange for local products. Menshikov noted on the margin of the report that 'The Imperial decision is to despatch cruisers to the Abhazian shore...'.[149] Menshikov ordered Greig to have the Black Sea Fleet take up cruising along the Black Sea eastern coast, using Redut-Kale as a rendezvous and troop transhipment point for other operations.[150] Two squadrons of cruisers were established; one was based at Sukhum-Kale, and the second operated from Gelendzhik.[151] All foreign ships putting into shore between Anapa and Redut-Kale were to be searched 'without exception'; all ships carrying contraband were to be seized, as was any vessel that refused to be searched. Those that were found to be legitimate traders were to be allowed to proceed 'under the strictest and most attentive supervision'.[152] Redut-Kale served as a landing port for trade goods destined for Tiflis, and from there, Baku.[153]

The coastline was extremely difficult to patrol. The coast from Taman to Batum, nearly 300 miles, had only four large bays – Sudzhuk-Kale (now Novorossiisk), Gelendzhik, Sukhum, and Batum. The remainder of the coast offered no safe anchorage for large ships running from storms. Sudzhuk-Kale and Gelendzhik were both dangerous in the autumn and winter from the north-eastern 'bori' winds, as their roadsteads offered no protection from gusts from that direction.[154] Sukhum roadstead was closed to northern, eastern and southeastern winds, with the most dangerous breezes coming from the northeast.[155] The depth of the harbour was sufficient for the largest ships, and the bottom was earthern, providing for good anchoring.

Turks were not the only illicit traders intercepted by the new Black Sea Fleet patrols; on 25 May 1830 the brig *Orfei*-20 was cruising from Anapa to Sukhum-Kale, and stopped the British merchantman *Adolfo*; a search uncovered six casks of gunpowder.[156]

In addition to the inauguration of the naval patrols, Paskevich's plans for coastal security were now carried out; from 13 July to 13 August, troops under Major-General Gesse built a fort at Gagra.[157] The fort was to obstruct communications between the Abhazians and Circassians. The site chosen was near the mouth of the Zhukvara river, commanding a narrow defile.[158]

The 'Black Sea Coastal Line' as the chain of fortifications was to be known, was semi-independent of the general commanding the Caucasus Corps; orders and communications went directly through the War Ministry.[159]

Despite such forceful measures, the scale of resistance to the Russians continued to grow as their presence increased – in September, Gordon sent materials regarding an uprising in Karbada the previous month. The insurgents' strength had been estimated at 30 000; General Bekovich was marching to the scene of the conflict with an army corps, while ships of the Fleet blockaded Sukhum-Kale and landed a second corps there.[160]

One area where the Russian government felt it might achieve success without bloodshed was in its diplomatic relations. European complicity in the clandestine Caucasus trade spurred the Russian government to clarify its Georgian maritime trade policy for legitimate merchants.

The last ukaz to deal with the region had been issued ten years earlier; the new frontiers and expanded trade brought about by the Adrianople Treaty meant that many of its provisions were outdated. As a result, a long ukaz was issued on 15 June 1831. The Black Sea coast was put under the 'European' regime of customs duties, rather than the 'Asiatic'. Section 19 elaborated on Russian restrictions on unauthorised trade and the reasons behind it:

> On the shores of Abhazia . . . it is constantly necessary to have cruising warships, for the defence of maritime trade from plunderers ('khishchnikov'), and for ensuring that no ship land anywhere but at Customs, and especially to stop the slave trade. Moreover, on the shore . . . itself . . . it is necessary to have armed customs vessels with hired oarsmen supplemented by the necessary armed force from the army and fleet under the local main command.[161]

All Fleet cruisers were obliged to render all possible assistance to the Customs vessels.

The new regulations were badly needed, as European merchants had continued to flout Russian attempts at regulation. The previous year, Fleet cruisers stopped three foreign ships along the Caucasus coast. One was the *Adolfo*; another was flying an Austrian ensign, and refused to follow Russian cruisers into port.[162] The authorities estimated that they only intercepted a small percentage of the contraband trade; clarification of the Russian position might persuade the smugglers' port consuls to restrain them. The new regulations were communicated to both the Porte and the foreign ministers in Constantinople. All ships found trading in unauthorised locales after 13 April 1832 were to be confiscated, except those having anchored in unauthorised areas in order to ride out a storm.[163] The British would become increasingly irritated with the restrictions, until the issue broke into a major diplomatic incident five years later.

With Russian attempts to expand legitimate maritime trade with the Caucasus came an increased need for accurate navigation aids. While Captain Bellinsgauzen had surveyed part of the Caucasus shore in 1816, surveying had only been resumed in 1827 when the Black Sea Fleet Hydrographic Department issued a chart based on observations of Sukhum Bay done by Lieutenant Romanov.[164] In 1830 Lieutenant Polianskii surveyed Sudzhuk-Kale Bay and Lieutenant Arkas measured Gelendzhik. Additional measurements were taken along the coast from Anapa to Cape Adler, as well as the coastline from the

Bzyb River to Cape Iskuriia.[165] Surveying the Caucasus coast occupied the Black Sea Fleet for the next twenty years.

The growing estrangement between Russia and the European governments over Black Sea smuggling was mirrored by increasingly strained Allied relations in the Mediterranean. The Adrianople Treaty had removed the major reason for further Allied cooperation in the Levant. As Greece was now independent, it lost its immediacy as an issue. Wellington later observed, 'the Greek affair since the year 1830 is scarcely deserving notice in our foreign transactions. The great affairs are Holland and Portugal...'.[166]

The continued Russian presence in the Eastern Mediterranean was now openly questioned by the other Allied governments. Parliament debated the Greek policy of Wellington's government. Wellington stated that there had been no blockade of the Dardanelles by the Navy following Navarino because 'our principle was to confine hostilities to the circumstances which rendered them necessary'. When questioned about the outcome of the war, Wellington remarked that he had felt that it would end in a Russian victory, but that he had expected the conflict to end after the first campaign. In response to criticism of a lack of British hostilities to force the Turks after Navarino to abide by the July 7 Treaty, the Prime Minister stated that his government had been following Canning's intentions, who had 'insisted . . . it was the principle that the Treaty should be carried into effect without any act of hostility'. Wellington then added that his government had considered other measures, 'and the battle of Navarino was one of the results'.[167]

The major questions for the Allies now devolved from military to diplomatic ones about the territorial extent of Greece and its system of government. The uneasy unity produced by Allied intervention began to unravel when faced with the more complex diplomatic vagaries of the new kingdom. Divergences of European opinion about the amount of direct Allied support to be given the adolescent state became especially pronounced during the 1831 Idhriot revolt.

The Greeks had initially provided sufficient resistance to their Turkish overlords to provoke Egyptian (and ultimately, Allied) intervention. The terrain of the nascent Greek state was uniquely suited to the influence of seapower, and the Greeks had quickly assembled naval forces for their struggle. By the time of the outbreak of the Russo-Turkish war the Greek Navy included the frigate *Hellas*-64, schooner *Athena*, the corvette *Idhra*-28, steamers *Karteria*-8 and *Epicheiresis*, along with three gunboats, twelve brigs, twenty-five feluccas and other smaller craft.[168] Under Cochrane's command the motley fleet practised innovative naval tactics such as using steamers and hot shot.[169]

Despite such inspired leadership, anarchy asserted itself to the extent of rendering nearly impossible the creation of a tightly disciplined national navy consistently capable of adhering to government policy, with the result that the Greek navy played a minor role after the arrival of the Allies. One noted military writer has observed, 'The conduct of the Greek fleets was signalled rather by brilliancy of isolated enterprise than by a sound continuity of naval policy adapted to the circumstances of the case.'[170]

The civilian counterpart of 'isolated enterprise' was piracy, which continued as a problem in the eastern Mediterranean long after Navarino. The Allies now found themselves spending most of their time chasing the swift, small Greek vessels which pursued their 'enterprises'. One of the more noxious piratical bases was in Crete, an area about to pass again under Egyptian control.

In August 1830 Mehmet received a reward for supporting the Sultan in the form of a ferman formally granting him the governorship of Crete.[171] He quickly assembled 3200 troops to occupy his new territory; the expedition of twenty-one warships sailed on 17 September.[172] Mehmet planned to disband the irregular troops there under Mustafa Pasha, as well as the Turkish troops under Süleyman Pasha, as they were under the Sultan's control instead of his own.

Crete was a valuable springboard for Mehmet's maritime ambitions. The British consul in Alexandria wrote,

> His Highness the Vice Roy is highly pleased with the extension of his govt. to a country, to maintain a communication with which will afford him opportunities for the employment of a naval force, for which he has a decided predilection.[173]

In altering his new fief, Mehmet planned to build a new breakwater at Khania and improve Paros harbour, rebuild its derelict Venetian arsenal, and plant trees in the mountains to provide wood for his Fleet. Of the Egyptian government's total expenditure in 1830 of £2 093 679 the Navy consumed £285 690, nearly fourteen per cent of the budget, which represented a level of expenditure more than double that of the Russian government's percentage of its revenue apportioned to the Navy.[174]

In Crete the Egyptians also inherited a Greek garrison at Grabousa, which was not above the occasional act of piracy.[175] The garrison was to be evacuated, and the fort held by Allied forces for ten days prior to the Egyptian takeover. On 21 October, a small contingent of Cretans seized the fortress, and had to be driven off by forces from HMS *Alligator*-28 and the Russian brig *Akhilles*-16.[176] A month later, Malcolm wanted to evacuate all the Allies' forces, but Rikord insisted on remaining until he had received further orders from Ribeaupierre.[177] British forces were withdrawn on 9 December, while the French and Russian garrisons remained until the end of the year, in an attempt to prevent the place being reoccupied before the Egyptian takeover.[178]

Rikord's squadron, based at Nvplion, now consisted of four ships; the frigate *Kniagina Lovich*-44, *Telemak*-20, *Uliss*-20, and *Akhilles*-18.[179] In addition to chasing pirates, Rikord carried on Geiden's earlier mapping and surveying of Greek waters. To the earlier efforts which produced soundings and surveys of the Gulf of Poros, Thasos, Panagis Bay, Napoli di Romani Bay, Astro fortress, and the Kroliko Islands, Rikord's ships produced further surveys of Saros Bay, Salamina port, Vatte Bay, Grabousa, Patrai, Epidàvros Bay, the Petaloi Islands, part of the southwestern Negropont shore, Piraeus and Salamis, all of which were used by the Hydrographer-General in the preparation of new Mediterranean charts.[180]

Rikord also continued Geiden's policy of close cooperation with the Greek government; after Capodistrias purchased several small warships, the Russians assisted in their fitting out and arming.[181] Rikord also loaned the frigate *Elizaveta*-44 to Capodistrias for use in his capacity as the President of Greece, and closely identified with the former Russian minister's policies. Rikord interpreted his orders to support the Greek government very strictly, and when Idhra broke into revolt, he had no doubt where his duty lay. During the revolt at Poros in July 1831 Admiral Maioulis seized the port and its ships, which included the *Hellas*-64 and *Karteria*-8. Rikord was the only Allied naval commander to support the Greek government, and rather than surrender, Maioulis blew the two ships up.[182] Such unquestioning support of the Greek government led alarmist elements in Parliament to warn that Russia was determined to establish a protectorate over the new state, an event that would fundamentally alter the balance of power in the eastern Mediterranean.

While the relative influence of the Allies on the Mediterranean littoral was shifting, it was France, not Russia, that was increasing its authority. The French conquest of Algiers even more graphically illustrated the fragile postwar unity of the Allies. As Russia drew closer to Greece, so France found itself interested in advancing her interests in Algiers in conjunction with Mehmet Ali.

Algiers had long been a thorn in the side of the maritime powers; Lord Exmouth's bombardment of the town in 1816 had been merely the latest in a long series of European and American attempts to coerce the Dey to harass Christian shipping in a more civilised manner. France had been blockading the port since June 1827, when a squadron consisting of a line ship, three frigates and three brigs took up their station.[183] The French outlined five main conditions for peace – all transgressions against French shipping were to be severely punished, quarantine procedures were to be followed, the French consul was to receive full reparations for French losses due to Algerian attacks, 'due respect' was to be shown to the French flag, and friendly relations were to be re-established. The note ended with an ominous warning, but the Dey Hussein was not included to take it seriously.[184] Similar impudence had been shown by the harbour forts firing on the *Provence*-74 under Captain La Bretonnière as she left the port under a flag of truce on 30 July 1829. Following the incident, Drovetti, the French consul-general in Egypt, submitted a proposal to the government for the conquest of Algiers.

Drovetti's plan foresaw a number of difficulties in a direct French invasion, the least of which would be the adequate provisioning of the invasion force. Drovetti suggested that a simpler solution would be for France to encourage Mehmet Ali to invade. Such a scheme would be less upsetting to the Sultan, as Mehmet was ostensibly his vassal, while the Egyptian troops would be acclimatised to the fierce Magribi weather. The French blockade would isolate the Dey from any possible aid, while France would be free of aroused European suspicions of colonialist ambitions. The results of such an expedition would be applauded, 'from Stockholm to Naples'.[185]

Drovetti's memorandum aroused considerable interest in Polignac's government, which, however, saw a number of uncertainties. Among them were the naval forces under Mehmet's control, the possibility of joint French–Egyptian naval activity, and the method of notifying the Russian ambassador.

The consul-general replied that left to his own devices, the Viceroy would prefer to 'liberate' Syria. Mehmet could field four frigates and a large number of corvettes, more than enough ships to blockade the port while attacking it. The French squadron would carry on its activities apart from the Egyptians, in order to avoid British jealousy. As for notifying the Russian ambassador, he would receive written notification of the expedition well before it took place.[186]

Subsequent French offers of aid to Mehmet to secure his participation were very seductive. His dragoman, Boghos Efendi, confidentially informed the British consul that a 10 000 000 franc subsidy had been offered by the French, or, 'what they knew would be a more potent allurement', a gift of four ships of the line.[187] The offer was later modified to an outright gift of money in lieu of the warships.

Mehmet was disinclined to pull the French *marrons* out of the fire; he declined the offer, a gesture which was appreciated at Constantinople almost as much as the $500 000 he sent as a present.[188] The Viceroy was to benefit directly from the upcoming French campaign, as it provided him with a plausible excuse to strength further his shoreline defences at Abu Qur, Rosetta and along the coast as far as Damietta.[189] Given Mehmet's lack of cooperation, the French government decided on the expedition on 31 January 1830.[190]

Dey Hussein was no longer in as strong a position to resist attack as before. Immediately before Navarino, he had felt confident enough to engage the French blockading forces under Commander Collet with twelve ships carrying 252 cannons and 3000 crew, retiring only after they were 'malmenées.'[191] After Navarino, despite the loss of two ships that sailed with the remainder of the squadron to Alexandria, Hussein still had two frigates, two corvettes, about ten brigs and thirty cannoniers.[192]

Algerian seapower had been built with European assistance; marine stores and timber were obtained from northern Europe, while the Dey's right to every eighth person captured led him to take, 'the most valuable in rank, person, or abilities, particularly the carpenters.'[193] Captured ships in suitable condition were added to the fleet, while captured sailors could be pressed into service. Naval personnel numbered about 3000, although 6000 could be raised in an emergency.

The French blockade continued in earnest. In September 1829, Hussein sent four feluccas out to cruise against French shipping. On 1 October the French blockaders pursued three of the cruisers while they were attempting to enter the harbour and ran them aground, cannonading them and the fortifications for four hours. The Algerians had managed to capture two French merchantmen.[194]

By mid-March 1830 French intentions were obvious in Algiers itself, and news of the impending attack dismayed all except Hussein, who would not allow the European consuls to evacuate their families, an act he felt would further harm public morale.[195] The British resident believed that the French would probably attempt a minor incursion, after which they would force the Dey to pay an indemnity 'à la Russe.'[196] For his part, Hussein insisted that he would exact an indemnity from the French.[197]

In Constantinople, French evasiveness about their real intentions produced considerable uneasiness; Guilleminot told Gordon in early March that he had no knowledge of a pact between France and Egypt for attacking Algiers. Gordon felt that the French ambassador was being dishonest, especially when Guilleminot remarked that any such expedition would fill the depleted Turkish treasury, and help alleviate the Russian war debt.[198]

Mehmet adroitly handled the Algerian question, maintaining his distance from both French inducements and British fears of Egyptian participation. On the evening of 7 March he explained his views at length to Barker. As Mahmut was satisfied with the behaviour of the Barbary States, the Sultan could not sanction the raid by the French.[199] When the British consul asked if the Viceroy would act in such a situation without the Porte's permission, Mehmet replied that he considered such approval a 'slight formality'. Barker than asked if he had promised to aid the French, to which Mehmet emphatically replied that he had not.

Mehmet had a precedent for action against Barbary. Egyptian forces had been previously sent to Tripoli to capture some Arabs in the Viceroy's employ that had sought sanctuary there. Mehmet's troops had been provisioned by sea, and he told the Dey that if he would not surrender the men, then he would seize the country. Drovetti had been present when the deserters were returned, and he had then broached his project of subduing the Barbary States with the aid of 40 000 French troops and a French subsidy. As the story was now related to Barker, Mehmet's observation that prior British approval would be necessary had considerably dampened Drovetti's enthusiasm.

In April French warships turned back from Algiers two British merchantmen carrying munitions, which caused a brief ripple of anti-French feeling in Britain, and led to the temporary cessation of the loading of French merchantmen in British ports.[200] The effects of the three-year French blockade were now obvious in the Dey's navy – immediately before the invasion it numbered two decrepit frigates, seven brigs and xebecs, and a flotilla of thirty-two shalloupes. It was intended to draw up the motley armada in a line before the harbour forts, where they would help repel a naval assault.[201] The two Algerian ships that had taken refuge in Alexandria were still there, under the nominal command of the Algerian admiral Mustafa. The corvette had deteriorated to the point of decrepitude but the frigate of Portuguese construction was still of value as a transport.[202]

Hussein's agents made frantic last-minute efforts to find allies –
unsuccessful attempts were made to enlist Tunisian support.[203] At the
time, the Tunisian navy consisted of three frigates, three corvettes, a
xebec, a schooner, and a brig.[204] The Bey of Tunis was more
concerned with placating the French and avoiding a threat to his
own kingdom than helping a brother Muslim ruler, however, and sent
Selim Ağa as Envoy Extraordinary to the commander of the French
forces to assure him of his goodwill.[205]

Russia was similarly well-disposed towards the French expedition.
Terming the Algerians 'pirates', Nicholas told the first secretary of the
French embassy that he had originally wanted to offer Russian troops
to the French to use, but that 'France did not need this'; instead the
Minister of War was to collect from the archives 'all that has bearing
on the mode of making war with eastern peoples'; maps were also to
be provided.[206] Colonel Aleksei Filosofov, aide-de-camp to Grand
Duke Mikhail, was appointed to accompany the French forces as a
'military commissioner'.[207]

Off the Algerian coast the conflict took a nasty turn. On 15 May
two French brigs ran aground near the port; the crews initially
managed to save themselves by claiming to be British. Ninety-three
heads were later brought back to the town; a week later, eighty-seven
'half-starved' prisoners along with more heads were brought in.[208] The
eventual death toll reached 109, with the Dey paying $100 for each
severed head.

The French squadron that set sail from Toulon on May 25 was the
largest ever assembled in the Mediterranean – 675 ships (of which 103
were warships) carried 30 000 troops, 4000 horses, eighty-two siege
ordnance, fourteen cannon batteries and nine mortars.[209] They landed
at Sidi Ferruch on 14 June, and encountered only slight resistance as
they moved to surround Algiers. The French position on negotiations
was now simple; Vice-Admiral Duperré wrote to Hussein that as long
as his flag flew over Algiers, a state of war continued.[210] Bowing to the
inevitable, Hussein surrendered two days later. Twelve warships were
captured in the harbour.[211]

The expedition achieved little of immediate value for France; it
raised no enthusiasm for the government, which fell the next month.
The British attempted to put a brave face on the *fait accompli*; as *The
Times* noted, the strategic importance of Algiers for France was slight;

had the conquest, indeed, been made by a Power that possessed no
other ports in the Mediterranean, the case would have been widely

different; but of what great use are the ports of Algiers to the fleets of France, who has already a line of coast abounding with havens of every description on the same sea, extending from the third to nearly the eight degree of east longitude, from the eastern Pyrenees to the maritime Alps of Savoy. The accession of the ports of Algiers would best serve to divide and sever the naval armaments of France....[212]

The new French government was undecided about what to do with its prize; in September the Council of Ministers debated the question. Molé wanted to retain Algiers, as did Louis-Phillipe; the Council finally backed this resolution.[213]

Although Algiers did not prove of any immediate worth to France, its loss weakened the Porte by depriving it of its one substantial remaining source of reserve naval support, and even more importantly, skilled sailors. It was the second such loss suffered by Mahmut in three years, while Mehmet Ali had emerged unscathed from both the recent Russian war and the Algerian conquest. At the time the French expedition set sail, the Arsenal at Alexandria employed 4000 workers, with sufficient stockpiled materials to complete eight more three-decked line ships, which would bolster within two years the total number of ships of the line available to the Viceroy to ten.[214]

The stockpiled stores were quickly utilised; on 3 January 1831 the *al-Muhallat al-Kubra*-100 was launched, the first 100-gun ship to be built in Africa.[215] The hull was coppered, as were those of four other line ships that had been laid down, the largest to be of 136 guns.[216] Later in the month a corvette of 26 guns was launched; it was to be a 'present' for the Sultan. Four months later, the *al-Mansurah*-100 was launched; its armament consisted of thirty-two long 32-pdrs, thirty-two short 32-pdrs, and thirty-four 30-pdr carronades.[217] The capital ships would be necessary for Mehmet's projected Syrian campaign.

While Mehmet was unable to buy line ships abroad, he still hoped to be able to purchase British assistance in the form of suitably qualified officers seconded from the Royal Navy. In August 1831 he sent Colonel Light to London, to hire if possible, two Port-Captains, two Commanders, several lieutenants, and fifty to sixty petty officers and naval seamen.[218] As Barker noted,

It is now apparent that the Viceroy has given a preference to British sailors and means henceforth to employ not only officers of the British Navy, but also first-rate seamen such as Master's Mate, Boatswains, Gunners, etc.[219]

Such concern for the calibre of his navy was not misplaced; Mehmet's naval forces were to play a crucial role in the upcoming Syrian campaign, allowing him to capture Acre, a prize that had eluded Napoleon. Given the Turkish re-arming that had been going on since November 1829, Mehmet felt that he should strike against his sovereign before his forces became too powerful. The major question for Mehmet would be the reaction of the European powers. France was increasingly favouring him; the attitude of the British was unknown, and the opinion of the Russians largely discounted.

3 The Empire Strikes Back: the First Egyptian Revolt, and Muslim Revolt in Caucasus

'Barbarous as it is, Turkey forms in the system of Europe a necessary evil.'[1]

'One is able to think that in general the sole important point of the Straits question appears to be the passage of Russian warships in peacetime.'[2]

As Colonel Light left Alexandria, Barker reported that the Acre expedition was again under consideration, and that it would depart on 20 August.[3] Cholera now broke out, however, and the severity of the epidemic suspended the projected expedition. As Mehmet waited for the contagion to abate, he continued to look for outside support: 'there are every day fresh indications that the Viceroy is in correspondence and alliance with the rebels in Albania and Bosnia...'.[4]

Mehmet's troops eventually left Cairo on 15 October 1831; his army totalled 26 400, and was under Ibrahim's command.[5] Ibrahim himself sailed for Jaffa on the frigate *Kafr-al-Shaikh*-60 with three brigs on 4 November and reached Jaffa four days later.[6]

Naval considerations had helped to persuade Mehmet to invade Syria; while the Viceroy insisted his conflict with the Pasha of Acre, Abdullah, was primarily over the repatriation of fellahin draft-dodgers, Mehmet had also insisted on his right to import ship timber.[7] The Sultan had also antagonised Mehmet by appointing Tahir Pasha as governor of Adana. Tahir had commanded the Turkish ships at Navarino, and was a bitter opponent of Mehmet's. Adana was a province rich in ship timber and Tahir now forbade its export, which deprived the rapidly-growing Egyptian marine of one of its best supply sources.[8]

Mehmet's navy was in much better condition than the Ottoman fleet. His naval forces numbered twenty-six ships; two line ships of 100 guns, three 60 gun frigates, four smaller frigates, five corvettes, ten brigs, and several smaller vessels.[9] On the slipways in Alexandria a third line ship neared completion. After the *Iskandr*-100 was launched, the *Abu Our*-84 would be completed within two months, with a three-decker following her three months later; work would then immediately begin on four more line ships.[10]

Mehmet's navy was extremely heterogeneous, including ships built in France, Italy, Algeria, the United States, Britain, and Russia.[11] Ibrahim's flagship, the *Kafr-al-Shaikh*-60 had been built in 1828 in Archangel by a merchant named Amosov.[12] The ship was built largely of fir, and had started life as a transport;[13] sold to Egypt via Britain, she was now under the command of a British officer, Captain Prissick, who had brought her out from London.[14]

The personnel of the Egyptian fleet were similarly cosmopolitan. In addition to the foreign officers who laboured in the Arsenal and commanded Egyptian warships, nearly one hundred and fifteen Egyptian students had been registered with the Paris Mission since its inception; of these, six had been sent in 1828 to Toulon to study naval construction.[15] Hassan Bey, who now commanded a line ship, had spent five years in the French navy, entering in 1826 with two other Egyptians, Mahmut and Muhammed-Chenan. After two years studying French, design and mathematics, the three entered the naval school at Brest and served aboard ship. The intrepid Hassan found himself sailing via Rio de Janeiro around Cape Horn, twice crossing the Equator. The return voyage caused him to write, 'Les temps affreux que nous avons éprouvés au cap Horn tout ce que l'imagination peut concevoir...';[16] his reward for his sufferings was the flag rank of Rear-Admiral, which he achieved in 1834. The commander of the Fleet, Osman Nureddin Pasha, had studied in Paris in 1820, and was the first student that Mehmet had sent to study abroad.[17]

In contrast to the care lavished on the officer corps, the recruiting of lower ranks was carried out in a brutally direct manner. A circular was sent to the village shaikhs and magistrates, stipulating the number of men required; any shortages were made up from either the officials' families, or by the officials themselves.[18] Mehmet's international recruiting drives meant that his fleet also included sixty Greeks manning seven fireships; commanded by Captain Agonistes of

Ipsara, the Greeks were former colleagues of Admiral Kanaris and had, while serving under Cochrane in June, 1827, burned a Turkish warship in Alexandria itself.[19] The Turks vainly attempted to pressure the Allies into forcing the· Greek government into recalling their nautical mercenaries from Egypt.[20]

The Ottoman Navy contrasted sharply with the Egyptian in the quality of both men and ships. In addition to the loss of his Greek and Algerian reserves, Mahmut was further stripped of potential naval reserves by the destruction of the Tunisian Navy, which remained under nominal Ottoman control. In August 1831 three days of gales had destroyed Hassan Bey's force of three frigates, three corvettes, a brig, schooner, and xebec near Hamman el-Euf, with a loss of 2000 lives.[21]

In response to the Egyptian invasion, the Turks began a desultory programme of cruising, but their campaigning season ended well before the onset of winter and three line, four frigates, four corvettes and two cutters under the command of the Kapudan Pasha returned from Rhodes to the Dardanelles on 5 October.[22] After their return, Mahmut replaced the lack-lustre Halil as Kapudan Pasha with Tahir; the 6000 Fleet personnel were issued with winter clothing to enable them to fight a winter campaign, though there was little other indication that any such campaigning was contemplated.[23]

The Egyptian naval bombardment of Acre began on 8 November. The fort was the most powerful position on the Syrian coast, and had to be captured to secure the Egyptian coastal flank if an advance into Anatolia was to be secure. Two corvettes and a frigate were to attack from the west, while five frigates fired on the position from the south. The action began at 8:45 a.m. and lasted nearly nine hours. The Egyptian ships fired 60 000 rounds, and in return suffered twenty-five dead and one hundred and thirty wounded.[24] The commanding Egyptian admiral had stated that there was insufficient water for large vessels to work in close to attack the fort, but Captain Prissick disagreed; after sailing in, he retreated with two hundred and twenty shot in his hull, having lost most of his masts and rigging; 'the whole fleet hauled off in nearly the same mutilated condition, without having displaced a stone of Acre...'.[25] Intermittent naval attacks continued throughout November.

On 8 December Ibrahim's army bombarded Acre. The next day, the Egyptian navy again appeared off the fort. Five frigates moored before the fortress with shallops, four corvettes and two brigs anchoring off to the northwest. At 9 a.m. a joint bombardment began.

The assault continued for seven hours, with the fort replying in kind. The Egyptians lost one shallop, and many frigates were severely damaged. When the Egyptians retired to Jaffa, they had thirty dead and one hundred and thirty-five wounded.[26] Naval bombardments continued throughout December, and Egyptian casualties eventually reached nearly one hundred and fifty dead; among the injured were two British officers, who were badly burned along with twenty crew, while handling Congreve rockets.[27] The navy's lack of success reaffirmed the widely-held view that ships were unable successfully to attack strong shore defences; as one military writer observed at the time,

In the present state of artillery, no fleet, however numerous, can effect anything against well constructed forts and land batteries; and for this simple reason, that every shot which strikes a ship must, to say nothing of red-hot shot, do some mischief; whereas, hundreds of shots may be fired by the floating and unsteady artillery of a fleet, without hitting the object aimed at, and hundreds of shots may even strike a fort or battery without, in the slightest degree, injuring its defences.[28]

Despite the lack of immediate naval success, preparations continued feverishly in Alexandria. Cérisy now readied four line, seven frigates, five corvettes, three brigs, five goelettes, five fireships and twenty-one transports, an impressive total of fifty ships.[29] Five three-decked line ships were building on the stocks, while five ships captured from the Turks during the previous campaign (including a corvette of forty guns) were prepared.

Events were also shaking the Ottoman navy out of its customary lethargy. Within the Tersane-i Amire, work continued to fit out the Turkish Fleet of four three-decked line ships, five two-deckers, eight frigates, twelve or thirteen corvettes and brigs, and two steamers; an observer doubted that the Fleet would be able to put to sea before the end of March.[30]

Among the many problems facing the provisioning of the Ottoman Fleet was the heterogeneity of the ships' weaponry. The Fleet's flagship, the *Mahmudiye*-120, carried guns ranging from three-pounders to gigantic cannon mounted on the main deck, capable of firing stone shot weighing 500 lbs.[31] The flagship had considerable dry rot, despite being only a few years old.[32] While many of the Ottoman line ships were old and decrepit, some of the smaller vessels were of more recent, sturdier construction. Among the Sultan's newest ships was the former *United States*-26 corvette, bought from Eckford for $150 000.[33]

Despite the intensity of the Egyptian campaign in Syria, the British response was initially slight; Vice-Admiral Hotham on 13 April 1832 sent only the frigate HMS *Madagascar*-46 to the Syrian and Egyptian coasts to protect British interests, and to make provisions for protecting the Christians in Tarsus and Salakia.[34] In London, Mehmet's insurrection was regarded as sufficiently minor that the Sultan could cope alone.

As the Empire's first maritime line of defence, the Dardanelles forts were hurriedly strengthened. Throughout March, April and May, new batteries and flat-bottomed gunboats were built.[35] Regulations on the passage of the Outer Castles by merchantmen after sunset were also rigorously enforced; previously, many ships had ignored them in order to take advantage of favourable winds after sunset, anchoring off Nara Burnu for the night.[36] Turkish nervousness about the nocturnal passage of shipping was undoubtedly increased by their awareness of Egyptian fireships. As in the Russo-Turkish war four years earlier, the Ottoman navy initially assumed a passive defence, rather than seeking out the Egyptian navy for a decisive engagement. For their part, the Egyptians did not actively seek combat, as Mehmet was still unsure of the eventual attitude of the European powers.

Farther north, the Russians were having a similar lack of success in quelling their rebellious subjects. The military stalemate in the Caucasus gave Russian seapower an increasingly valuable role to play if a vigorous commander could be found. The Tsar considered Lazarev to be such a man, and on 29 February 1832 appointed him Chief of Staff of the Black Sea Fleet.[37]

Lazarev immediately began to work; the day after the formal announcement of his appointment, he wrote to Greig in Nikolaev, stating that unfinished business in St Petersburg delayed his immediate departure, but if Greig wanted to send him work to do in the interim, he would be pleased to begin.[38] This energetic disposition produced results; shortly after his arrival in Nikolaev, Lazarev had constructed along advanced lines two sloops and several smaller vessels, and so impressed his fellow officers that they wrote to Menshikov,

> the appointment of this admiral as Chief of Staff. . . is extraordinarily pleasing to the entire corps of ranks here, especially to the commanders of ships, and they feel as if they have received some

sort of courage to be able to hope for the improvement of the Fleet....[39]

Such a energetic commander would be invaluable with the increased responsibility that the Black Sea Fleet was now assuming.

The Black Sea Fleet now maintained a continuous presence off the Georgian coast with its smaller ships, a hazardous peacetime duty off a dangerous shore. The dangers of cruising in winter were illustrated by the loss of the brigantine *Nartsis*-10; while at anchor in Anapa roadstead, she was caught by a strong southwesterly wind, driven onshore and wrecked.[40]

Despite the increased patrolling, the Gelendzhik commandant complained to the Black Sea Coastal Line commander Major-General Berkhman that the number of ships assigned to the task was inadequate. The Gelendzhik detachment at this time consisted of the brigantine *Nartsis*-18 and cutters *Sokol*-12, *Zhavoronok*-12, and *Lastochka*-12, which had recently been joined by the transport *Revnitel'*.

Borovskii protested that such a force was insufficient, and gave an example. The *Zhavoronok*-12 had been sent to cruise the shore between Cape Issupa to the Manai River; during a sweep of Sudzhuk Bay, she found two Turkish ships that had been trading. On leaving the bay, she met a third Turkish ship, which they were unable to pursue, as their two captives were under full sail. The *Sokol*-12 which usually stood guard in Sudzhuk was off participating in an expedition against the Abhazian coast. *Revnitel'* was despatched to arrest the two ships and confiscate their sails and rigging in order to immobilise them. The *Zhavoronok*-12 went back to Sudzhuk Bay to search for the third ship, but the ship escaped. After a twenty-five mile chase, the ship was captured. On it were six Caucasian Muslim pilgrims and twenty-five Turkish families who had fled into the hills after the Russians captured Anapa.

Borovskii recommended that the squadron be reinforced to two transports and a 'constant' presence of five warships, which should include two brigs or brigantines. One warship should be constantly on station in Sudzhuk Bay as a guardship, where no ship had yet been posted. The second could be stationed in Gelendzhik with the remaining vessels constantly cruising. A steamer would also be useful.[41]

Gelendzhik as a base suffered from a number of drawbacks, however. Quite aside from the threat of attack by the mountaineers, anchorage was not good, and the roadstead was open to westerly winds and off-shore squalls.[42] None of these problems would be solved in the near future.

Lazarev arrived in Nikolaev on 21 July 1832 and spent the next ten days with Greig aboard the yacht *Rezvaia*-10 and lugger *Glubokii*-10 cruising the Abhazian coast, surveying the ports and harbours.[43] They visited Poti, Redut-Kale, Sukhum-Kale, Bombori, Pitsunda, Gagra, Gelendzhik, and Sudzhuk-Kale. Lazarev was shocked by what he saw: 'Our garrisons in these places . . . especially in Poti and Gagra . . . are rotting, surrounded by swamps and lacking hospitals.[44]

During the cruise Greig met with Major-General Vakul'skii, commander of the troops in Mingrelia, aboard the *Rezvaia*-10 at Redut-Kale and discussed the problems of pacifying the coast. As previous arrangements had proved inadequate, they agreed to maintain two detachments of warships for patrolling. One would be based at Anapa, and cruise between Anapa and Gagra; the other would be based at Redut-Kale, and patrol between there and Gagra.[45] Eight small warships and two transports were assigned to the two ports.

The problem was not only foreign smugglers – the Abkhazians themselves built ships capable of carrying one to three hundred men.[46] A shipbuilding wharf had been located on the Sogumi river, not far from the Sukhum fort.[47]

Russian attempts to subdue the coastal insurgents followed the time-honoured tradition of a scorched-earth policy; at the time of Vakul'skii's and Greig's meeting, Russian troops burned the fifteen buildings in the Sudzhuk bazaar in an attempt to interrupt the mountaineers' trade.[48] At the end of the cruise Lazarev and Greig went to Sevastopol, from where Greig sailed to Nikolaev. Lazarev remained in Sevastopol for ten days. It was his first visit, and he ecstatically wrote,

> 'What a port. . . .! Marvellous! It appears that bounteous Nature has poured out all her generosity and provided everything necessary . . . for the best port in the world. . . .'.[49]

In contrast to Nature's generosity, he found the Admiralty 'impoverished'; the site had a small number of magazines, while most of the dwellings were wattle cottages. Only two barracks were habitable, having floors and ceilings; financial stringencies meant 'as they won't give us a kopeck, we don't know what to do'. The ships were also unimpressive; their exteriors were satisfactory, but their interiors were 'bad', as were their masts, spars and sails. The ordnance was in an even more pitiful condition, and the ships' boats were largely useless; 'in a word, it is better, and much worse [than expected.]'

While Lazarev headed the Black Sea Fleet Staff, Greig remained Commander of the Black Sea Fleet, a position he had held for over fifteen years. His initial dealings with Greig were chilly. Lazarev felt that he had lost his drive and enthusiasm; 'everything bored Greig, and he was indifferent to everything. His quarrel with Prince Menshikov is highly injurious to the Black Sea Fleet'; as a result, Greig's reports were largely ignored. Greig's torpor also infected the Fleet; Lazarev incredulously observed, 'already for the third year running the Fleet has not gone to sea, and God knows, for what reason!'[50] Lazarev felt that while Greig had been a formerly capable naval officer, he was long past his prime, and 'everything got on his nerves'.[51]

Lazarev's work was cut out for him; in addition to a jaded superior, the condition of the Fleet's matériel also left much to be desired. The Black Sea Fleet personnel completed the grim picture; in 1832 6000 new 'recruits' had been added to the Fleet ranks, a number that included 2000 Poles; despite the influx of labour, the Fleet still found itself 2400 men short for its needs. Lazarev would spend the next two decades, but with limited success, attempting to raise the Black Sea Fleet from the torpor he had found it in when he assumed command.

While the Russians wrestled with the problems of subduing their rebellious subjects, the Sultan's rebellious subjects continued with their military preparations for a spring offensive. Acre had proved to be a more difficult operation than the Egyptians had originally intended. Mehmet began to use his 'command of the sea' to strip troops from rear positions for the upcoming campaign. On 25 April the Egyptian Fleet returned from Crete carrying two regiments bound for Acre, 'along with the new 101 gun ships commanded by a French officer'.[52] Construction work on the Fleet continued at a feverish pace; two days previously, a 24-gun corvette had been launched, while a 136-gun line ship was building on a slipway.

In Constantinople three line ships (including one of 120 guns), six frigates, and six corvettes were finally ready to sail. The Fleet was to sail to Rhodes and stay there a month, and would then be stationed on the Asia Minor coast in the Gulf of Simi, from where they could intercept any attack on the Dardanelles.

As before, Gordon's informants felt the Turks were not actively seeking a decisive battle; 'It is more to assume an attitude and prevent the Egyptian squadron from advancing than with any intention to fight unless forced into action.'[53] On 10 May the entire Turkish Fleet of eighteen sail moved from Constantinople down to Gallipoli.[54] Turkish reluctance about committing the Fleet to relieving Acre stalled it in the Dardanelles; as a result, on 27 May Acre finally surrendered.[55] Egyptian losses during the siege were 512 killed and 1429 wounded.[56]

Despite the campaign lasting six months rather than six weeks, the Egyptians had scored a great victory. The position was sufficiently stout to have resisted an assault by Napoleon in 1799. As a result of the loss of Acre, the Turks lost their one commanding coastal position south of the Taurus mountains capable of halting Ibrahim's advance; the way into Asia Minor was now open.

Consul Barker was not impressed with the Viceroy's new acquisition;

> Acre is a heap of *Rubbish* and it will require a treasure like that which Mehmed Ali *expected* to find to rebuild it; yet he has issued orders for the fortifications being immediately restored, and has even already written to England for heavy artillery for the batteries....[57]

Sultan Mahmut was sufficiently infuriated by the loss inflicted by his loyal subject to declare Mehmet to be in rebellion; when the news reached Alexandria, it produced a 'sensation, even though expected'. For his part, Mehmet was more concerned about how the ambassadors in Constantinople would react to the Sultan's order. The outlawing had removed the convenient fiction that Mehmet was merely chastising a neighbouring vassal in the Sultan's name. While the British and French reactions were ambivalent about the capture of Acre and Mehmet's outlawing, the Russian and Prussian chargés informed the Viceroy that all commerce between their countries must cease.[58]

After the capture of Acre Ibrahim's troops swept swiftly forward – Damascus was captured on 15 June. Ibrahim moved to capture as much territory as quickly as possible, as the relentless Egyptian war effort was beginning to strain severely the Egyptian population. While Mehmet could field twenty to twenty-five thousand regular troops, four to five thousand irregulars and an equal number of Bedouins, he was now making concerted efforts to recruit for his army and navy in the towns, as the peasantry were exhausted.[59] Recently 15 000 men 'of all types' had been press-ganged in Cairo alone.

The loss of Acre was recognised as a major set-back in Constantinople, and the Turkish Fleet now adopted a more combative stance.
Six line ships, six frigates, twenty-two corvettes and brigs, and a
number of smaller vessels sailed from the Dardanelles on 24 June in
search of the Egyptian Navy.[60] Mehmet's three line ships cruised off
Alexandria, while a corvette was sent to watch the Dardanelles for any
Turkish activity.[61]

Ibrahim continued to advance, and in early July, his troops clashed
with the Ottoman army at both Homs and Belen. Belen was a disaster
for the Turks, who lost 2500 killed or wounded, thirty-nine cannon,
munitions and their supply train, for a cost to the Egyptians of around
twenty casualties.[62] To complete the *débâcle*, the Egyptians captured
1400 prisoners the next day. Belen finally made the Turks aware of
their inability to halt the Egyptians, and they began to cast about for
aid; it would be provided by their traditional enemy to the north.
Mehmet now suspended Ibrahim's advance, hoping that diplomacy
could give him all of Syria without further struggle. On 6 August
Mahmut requested Canning to influence the British government to
provide direct military assistance.[63]

There were a number of reasons that Mahmut turned to Britain in
his search for aid. An immediate influence was that the British
ambassador in Constantinople, Stratford Canning, was the most
puissant foreign representative. A Turkophile, he strongly supported
Ottoman interests to the British government.

A second, equally powerful reason for requesting such assistance
was nautical. British naval aid in the setting of Constantinople and the
Straits would be uniquely useful in resolving the conflict, as Colonel
Francis Rawlinson Chesney pointed out in a long memorandum.
Chesney was one of the most widely-travelled British officers in the
Middle East, and was well-qualified to comment on the Turkish–
Egyptian conflict. Turkey possessed a number of advantages by virtue
of Constantinople's geography:

> Defended as Constantinople is, by a chain of hills and lakes,
> connecting the Black Sea with that of Marmora at 25 miles
> distance . . . and possessed of one of the very finest harbours in
> the world – the Golden Horn, – with its unequalled capacious and
> commodious Arsenal in which 14 Line of Battle ships may be armed
> and equipped at once–each literally touching the Gun-Wharf
> (within a few feet of a line of store-houses, containing the rigging
> of each vessel separately below, and sails on the loft above) yet

remaining afloat until all is completed, and she goes into the Bosphorus...[64]

Unlike many of his contemporaries, Chesney felt that Turkish naval power could be used effectively against Mehmet.[65] While for Egypt 'the wood of the Lebanon Mountains (and that of Caramania for the same reason) make...Syria an important object', the geography of Syria made it extremely vulnerable to seapower. The Sultan, 'having a superior fleet, and the means of a descent on Egypt itself, in its present weakened state, or, any part of Syria...ought, and must as I presume, in the sequel, succeed in reducing the Pacha to subjection...'.

Chesney saw further that a strong Egyptian navy might ultimately prove a threat to British interests:

> The growing maritime importance of Egypt would seem to offer another decided motive for lending our assistance to the Sultan; Mahomet Ali proposes to have a fleet of 14 sail of the line, with numerous frigates, and an extensive transport service for commercial purposes or those of war equally.

Chesney predicted that if Mehmet allied himself with a European power, such a concentration of naval force could threaten British interests in the Mediterranean. The most effective long-term support that Britain could offer the Ottoman Empire to help it resolve the Egyptian crisis was its naval officers;

> the simple addition of some few Officers to direct the Sultan's fleet, and give advice in the field, would alone (most likely) cause the fall of the Pacha...for it can scarcely be doubted that other nations would readily give the Sultan the necessary assistance in the hope of securing him as an Ally in the event of a General War, by which means we should be excluded from the passage of the Dardanelles into the Black Sea, so evidently the most vulnerable part of Russia on the side of Europe as well as Asia...

Any aid would need to be swiftly sent; Mehmet was already drawing up contingency plans for an attack on the Turkish fleet in the event of negotiations proving unsuccessful. The Turks were to be attacked at their base at Marmoris on the southwestern coast of Anatolia, 'one of the best stations that could possibly have been selected for a fleet wishing to act on the defensive.'[66] Batteries placed on surrounding heights would bombard the ships at anchor, while Egyptian frigates attacked the vessels moored at the entrance to the bay.[67]

The gravity of the situation was completely misunderstood in London. Palmerston still regarded Mehmet's invasion as a typically minor Ottoman provincial uprising, not worthy of British interference; genteel stalling would resolve the issue.

> ...probably the Sultan will ask us for military assistance to crush Mehemet, while Mehemet requests our interference to persuade the Sultan to give him Syria. Under all the circumstances perhaps I had better plead the dispersed state of the cabinet as a reason for further delay...[68]

While the Egyptians resumed their advance on land, the hostile navies continued to maintain their distance. Despite the increasing severity of the Egyptian threat, the Ottoman Fleet was now ordered back to Constantinople for the winter. On 11 October 1832 it quit Marmoris for the Dardanelles; shadowed by the Egyptians, the Turks reached Tenedos six days later, but waited there nearly a month for favourable winds before entering the Straits.[69] The Egyptian fleet broke off its pursuit and sailed southwest, reaching Soudhas on 24 October. Orders to return to Alexandria were received there, and the fleet sailed for home on 6 November.[70]

The contrary winter winds and currents at the Dardanelles which delayed the Turks would now also hinder any Egyptian attempts to force the passage; as a contemporary sailing manual observed,

> The whole dread of this [the Black] sea resolves itself into the difficulty, and often danger, experienced in making the entrance of the Dardanelles.... There is always a very rapid stream to be encountered in these passages; and this difficulty is increased by the prevailing winds, which blow in the same direction with the current for at least ten months out of the twelve....[71]

The Turks were fortunate that Nature was on their side; many Royal Navy officers doubted the ability of the Ottoman Navy to even defend itself, much less undertake offensive operations. Captain Maunsell of HMS *Alfred*-50 had been cruising the Egyptian and Syrian coasts since June, observing both fleets. The only action the Turkish Fleet had undertaken was to escort some transports from the Gulf of İskenderun to Lanarca and the Gulf of Antalya. While the Turks had six line ships, eight frigates, ten corvettes, eighteen brigs, a steamer and cutter, they were 'very indifferently handled, numerously, but very badly manned, and I understand, have never exercised their guns with powder, certainly not once during the time we have been with them'.[72] Captain Maunsell was much more impressed by Mehmet's ships. The Egyptians had four line, seven double-banked frigates, three corvettes and two brigs; the ships were

> better handled and manned, and the crews well-trained to their guns, and altho' inferior in numbers, would I am confident, beat the Turkish fleet . . . the extraordinary activity in the Dock Yard at Alexandria is such that it is necessary to witness it in order to give credit to it.[73]

Two line ships had joined the Egyptian fleet since June, while another would shortly be ready for sea; a fourth line ship of 120 guns had been laid down, and would be ready for sea in less than six months. Preparations were advanced for laying down a further three line ships that would be ready within a year. Within a little over a year, Mehmet had brought his fleet from nothing up to fifty per cent of parity with the Ottoman navy in line ships; in a further twelve months, the Egyptian navy would reach equality.

Mehmet's hurriedly-assembled navy was not a balanced force. While Egyptian superiority in matériel was evident, Mehmet's reliance on foreigners was a weakness as well as a strength. Recruiting drives in Britain had managed to find four quartermasters, four gunners, six to eight able seamen for captains of the tops, a boatswain, sail-maker, and several others at the rate of £4 per annum, but they proved drunken and disorderly, and had demanded their discharges when the fleet returned to Soudhas.[74]

With the onset of winter weather and the naval campaigning season over, both the Egyptians and the Turks laid up their ships until the spring. In Constantinople, after Eckford died from cholera, his foreman took over control of the shipyard, with the fifteen other Americans there supervising six hundred workers.[75] Unlike the remainder of the Tersane-i Amire, which employed four to five thousand men, the American section was entirely under American control and American regulations.

While the weather slowed the military efforts of both sides, Turkish attempts to enlist British support increased. In October Mavroyenis, the Turkish chargé d'affaires in Vienna, arrived in London to attempt to secure a Turkish–British alliance. Despite Palmerston's coolness, British aid was still regarded by the Porte as the only possible means of blocking Mehmet Ali.

Such aid was regarded as due the Ottoman empire for past British actions:

. . . all the hope of the Empire and of our ministers rests, from a practical and political point, on the defensive alliance with England. Your Excellency consequently will act in such a way as to try and obtain from the English Cabinet all that which the Empire hopes and expects from that quarter, in making clear that that which the Sublime Porte is suffering is the result of the destruction of her fleet at Navarin. This is why she hopes, as it is completely just, that an indemnity will come to her by which she can make good her losses.[76]

The value attached to an alliance was such that Namık Pasha was sent to London in an attempt to 'accelerate and confirm' Mavroyenis's negotiations. Namık brought an Imperial letter which again stressed the value the Porte placed in the projected alliance, which would compensate for the damage British seapower previously had done to the Turkish navy:

Concerning the maritime assistance demanded as a result of the Navarin disaster where an English admiral commanded the naval forces, I think that the Porte is justified in expecting compensation for the side of England.[77]

European aid would prove essential to defending Constantinople, as the Ottoman fleet and army were certainly not capable by themselves of the task. Captain Maunsell estimated that 'one-half' of the Turkish fleet was fit to go to sea, 'and if they attempt to keep the sea in the winter, many of them will be lost'.[78]

Despite the increasingly urgent entreaties of the Turks, the British government's attention was still focused largely on the crises in Belgium and Portugal, both of which required the assistance of the Royal Navy.

The Belgian imbroglio immediately distracted the Royal Navy from events in the Levant. Following the outbreak of the Belgian revolt in August 1830, France and Britain had tried to get Holland to accede to the October 14 Treaty, providing for the cessation of hostilities. Belgium had accepted the Treaty on 2 November 1832, and agreed to evacuate her troops from the contested area; Holland had refused, despite a warning that a refusal would be countered by an Anglo-French blockade of Dutch ports, with Dutch ships in the Allies' ports being embargoed.[79]

The British blockaders were based in Deal, and consisted of the line ships HMS *Donegal*-74 (Vice-Admiral Malcolm's flagship), HMS *Talavera*-74, HMS *Revenge*-76, HMS *Spartiate*-74, frigates HMS

Vernon-50, HMS *Southampton*-52, HMS *Stag*-44, and HMS *Castor*-36, along with the smaller ships HMS *Volage*-26, HMS *Conway*-26, HMS *Larne*-18, HMS *Scout*-18, HMS *Rover*-18, HMS *Satellite*-18, and HMS *Snake*-18.[80] In Plymouth, HMS *Malabar*-74 was preparing to sail to join Malcolm, which would bring the total number of ships under his command to seventeen.[81] On 8 November Admiral Villeneuve arrived with eight ships, including the line ship *Suffren*-90.[82] The combined squadrons set sail two days later.

The blockade quickly took effect; within a week five Dutch merchantmen had been sent into British ports, while the French government detained nine Dutch vessels in Bordeaux.[83] On 16 November a Dutch decree barred British and French shipping from entering Dutch ports.[84] The blockade was to continue into the spring. Disruptive effects were felt far beyond the Dutch coast – when news of the blockade reached Batavia in the East Indies, the 'richly-laden' ships there set sail for the more secure anchorage of Surabaya, where the coast was defended by heavy artillery and the local militia.[85]

While the blockade of the Dutch coast was proceeding smoothly, there was the possibility that the Dutch Navy would try and break it. It was not an inconsiderable force, with seventy-two warships (including seven line ships and twenty-five frigates) and a number of gunboats and smaller vessels; fifteen vessels were also under construction.[86] The ships had been drawn up the Scheldt to Flushing, but were still available for offensive operations if necessary. Governmental prudence dictated that such a maritime situation in the English Channel took precedence over more distant operations.

Portugal was similarly in need of British naval support. In the dynastic struggle for the Portuguese throne, Britain was firmly on the side of Dom Pedro against Dom Miguel. At sea, Miguel's forces were stronger, with two line ships, a fifty-gun frigate, three corvettes and four or five brigs.[87] In contrast, Pedro had three frigates, a brig, and two corvettes.[88] A British admiral was in charge of the Pedroite forces, but they were not in a fit state to attempt offensive operations; of Sartorius's frigates cruising off the Douro, one writer noted, 'they were in such a crippled state that it was thought necessary to send them to England or Vigo to undergo repairs'.[89] In order to 'protect British interests', a nine-ship British squadron was moored in the Tagus at Lisbon, which included the line ships HMS *Britannia*-120, HMS *Caledonia*-120, HMS *St. Vincent*-120 and HMS *Asia*-84; in addition to the Lisbon squadron, four smaller British warships cruised off Oporto.[90] On 2 November Palmerston wrote to the British ambassador in Lisbon that he had been right to call in the Royal Navy to anchor in the Tagus and prevent a clash between the two warring factions for the Portuguese throne, though he was to refrain from using it except in a case of extreme necessity. While Mavroyenis and Namık pleaded the Turkish cause, Palmerston indicated the relative value he attached to the Portuguese and Turkish crises by telling Hoppner that another line ship was to be detached from the Mediterranean squadron, and would arrive in a fortnight.[91] The two crises soaked up British naval resources that might otherwise have been sent to the eastern Mediterranean.

In complete contrast to Britain's preoccupied indifference, Russia had followed closely the Turkish–Egyptian conflict from the outset. By late November it was obvious to St Petersburg that Mehmet's revolt had the potential to overthrow the Ottoman government, something that could completely alter Russia's security in the Black Sea. Mehmet's insurrection threatened both the post-Adrianople military balance of power that had been established and Russia's new-found southern maritime commercial prosperity.

Russia's aid to the Ottoman empire was not altruistic; her Black Sea commerce was the fastest-growing area of her international trade. This was still concentrated primarily in Odessa and Taganrog, and not the Georgian coast. In 1832 six hundred and twenty eight ships of various countries had entered Odessa; in contrast, only twelve Russian ships and eight Turkish merchantmen had dropped anchor in Redut-Kale.[92] During the same period, Fleet cruisers along the Georgian coast had captured sixteen contraband trading ships.[93] A militant Egyptian-led government in Constantinople might attempt to support directly the Caucasian insurgents, gravely weakening the Russian position there.

Despite the relative paucity of legitimate Caucasian maritime trade, the level of smuggling was such that General Vakul'skii complained that the squadron agreed upon by him and Greig proved to be too small. The mountaineers had many galleys with which they pillaged honest merchantmen, and even attacked patrolling warships. Nicholas was opposed to increasing the number of Fleet warships permanently on station on the Georgian coast, however: 'if the Circassians build galleys and sail in them, then is it not possible our gunboats are not able to serve these shores?'[94]

Despite the Tsar's reluctance to commit more forces, the difficulties to the Caucasus coast continued to increase. Major-General Vishlavtsev, commander of Anapa, complained that no cruisers had arrived from Gelendzhik. Informants among the mountaineers had told him that Turks were landing at the Dzhubge stream 'to trade with the Abkhazians'; they were waiting for the earliest moment after the Spring thaw to sail, taking with them 'Russian captives'. Several small ships in the area of Sudzhuk and Pshade had also brought Turkish 'provocateurs', who would sail in the Spring, taking a number of mountaineers with them. Due to the lack of cruisers, Vishlavtsev was unable to communicate with the authorities in Gelendzhik and Sukhum-Kale.[95]

As part of the Russian government's plan to increase legitimate trade in the Black Sea, the possibility of steam service between Russian ports and Turkey was considered. Vorontsov suggested the value of a regular steamship service between Constantinople and Odessa.

Nesselrode's subsequent reply was lukewarm in the vein of cautious Russian conservatism. No one wanted such a service established more than he, as it would allow for swift communications with the 'Orient'. Balanced against this were a number of shortcomings, primarily financial; preliminary surveys indicated that the projected profits would not cover expenses. Nesselrode promised to act favourably if the circumstances changed.[96] The unsettled state of the Ottoman empire doubtless contributed to Nesselrode's hesitation.

Given the continued British and French reluctance to intervene in the Ottoman empire, Nicholas increasingly weighed the possibility of aiding his traditional enemy. Menshikov now wrote to Greig that the Tsar wanted the Black Sea Fleet readied for sea 'if circumstances demanded it', and asked for a report on the measures necessary to prepare the Fleet.[97] A week later Greig ordered Lazarev to ready the Fleet for sea.[98]

In mobilising the Fleet, Lazarev faced climatic hardships as well as man-made ones. The same day that Lazarev received his orders, the Russian merchantman *Charikleh* had sailed from Odessa. Four hours out of port, the brig was overcome by a storm that raged for four days and foundered, with only two of her crew being saved.[99] The storm sank twenty-five other ships.

Despite the increasingly desperate pleas of the Turkish envoys and alarming reports from the Admiralty and Constantinople, Palmerston continued to ignore the seriousness of Mehmet's rebellion, believing that the real threat to Turkey remained Russia; 'Russia expresses a decided interest in favour of the Sultan, but in a manner and tone that bespeak anything but sincerity and zeal...'. He suspected that Russian interests were 'to advance a little towards the Black Sea, perhaps taking a northeastern Turkish province in the process.'[100] Meanwhile, Ibrahim continued to advance 'a little' from the southeast into Anatolia.

Ignoring the Tsar's magnanimous offers of immediate aid, the Turks continued to attempt to procure British assistance. His Majesty's Government received more 'confidential overtures' for British naval assistance from Mavroyenis during a discussion ostensibly concerning unresolved Greek territorial issues. The Turkish government was even willing to pay the expenses arising from such aid, and as an added incentive, 'to grant to British subjects within his [the Sultan's] domains fresh privileges and facilities for carrying on their commerce...'.[101]

Palmerston, however, resisted these blandishments, as he still expected the inherent strength of the Ottoman empire eventually to bring Mehmet Ali to heel. On the subject of British naval assistance he wrote,

> [it] is one of greater difficulty than at first sight it may appear to the Porte to be, but whether His Majesty's Government should or should not find it possible to comply with the wishes of the Porte on this subject, at all accounts they consider the application as a striking and gratifying proof of the conviction which the Sultan feels of the sincerity of that friendship and regard which His Majesty entertains towards His Highness....[102]

Palmerston would only commit himself to writing to Mehmet to tell him that it was still possible to reconcile himself to the Sultan by direct communication.

Nicholas displayed no such hesitation. On 6 December Menshikov ordered Greig to arm five line ships, four frigates, and a number of smaller vessels. The squadron was to be ready to proceed 'without delay' to Constantinople under the command of Lazarev the moment the Tsar received a formal request for assistance. Lazarev was to block any Egyptian assault on Constantinople and interrupt attempts by Ibrahim to cross into Europe, while simultaneously giving the Turkish government any aid that would prove beneficial.

The Russian defence was not to be limited to Constantinople and the Bosphorus; any further aid needed in either the Black Sea or Sea of Marmora also was to be provided. Any Turkish requests for assistance in the Aegean were to be declined, but if the Egyptian fleet penetrated the Dardanelles as far as Cape Baba and the Turks prepared for battle, then the Russian ships were to 'attempt... the final destruction of the enemy'.[103] Greig was to maintain constant contact with

Butenev, the Russian ambassador in Constantinople, in anticipation of a probable request for support. After the departure of Lazarev's squadron, work was to continue 'unceasingly' to prepare the remainder of the Fleet to support Lazarev if necessary. Butenev received authorisation to send naval forces if the Turkish government should formally request assistance.[104]

Such aid was vital; Ibrahim defeated the Ottoman army at Konya on 21 December. Reşit Pasha had advanced through heavy snow towards the Egyptians; his left flank was vulnerable to the massed Egyptian artillery, while his own had been parcelled out at intervals along the Turkish line. A cavalry change outflanked the right of the Turkish position, and Ottoman resistance evaporated with enormous losses; one regiment losing 3000 men.[105] Mehmet's navy enjoyed some success as well, capturing six Turkish vessels.[106] Supplies for the Egyptian forces were now being provided by sea through Beirut and Latakia.[107] The Egyptian success at Konya cleared the way for an Egyptian advance clear through Asia Minor to the Dardanelles.

Once the decision was made to intervene, the Russians moved quickly. On 25 December General Nikolai Nikolaevich Murav'ev arrived in Constantinople to work in conjunction with the Ottoman government. The same day Nesselrode informed Count Vorontsov that Nicholas had resolved that aid would not be limited to verbal assurances. While the situation could change dramatically, 'if the same dangers recur in the spring, the Emperor has decided to send the fleet to aid the Sultan.'[108]

On 1 January 1833 news arrived in Constantinople from Mavroyenis that the British government would definitely not send aid.[109] In a final attempt to avoid accepting the proffered Russian assistance, the Sultan now sent Halil Rifat Pasha to Alexandria, in an attempt to negotiate directly with Mehmet.

With the prospect of imminent departure, Lazarev quickly went to work. He issued Order No.1, consisting of forty sections. It was extremely comprehensive, covering everything from daily exercising of the gun crews and crewmen manning the sails under the direct supervision of the flagship (Art.5), to attempting to lessen the risk of fire by forbidding all officers to take their samovars ('not excluding myself'). (Art.27) Every opportunity was to be taken to exercise the crews, with 'cruising in the Black Sea to be taken as usual exercise'. (Art.40)[110] Twelve days later Greig ordered Lazarev into Sevastopol roadstead to await further orders; when they were received, the squadron was to cross the Black Sea, but rather than directly enter the Bosphorus, they were to remain outside the passage until ordered to enter.

Lazarev felt that this was idiotic and strongly protested to Menshikov:

> cruising at the present time of the year before the˜Bosphorus, which is subject to cruel northern winds, in such a cold season with the shoreline constantly enshrouded in mist, would be attended by an inevitable loss of life; to cross directly from Sevastopol to the Bosphorus would be less difficult, even if the frost remained as strong as at present...[111]

Lazarev concluded by stating that whatever his orders, he would attempt to fulfil them to the best of his ability.

The next day, eight ships moved into Sevastopol roadstead. Lazarev hoisted his flag aboard the *Pamiat' Evstafii*-84; the remainder of the squadron consisted of the line ships *Chesme*-84, *Anapa*-84, and *Imperatritsa Ekaterina II*-84; the frigates *Erivan*-60, *Arkhipelag*-60, *Varna*-60, and the brig *Pegas*-18. The *Sizepol*-24 had been sent on 7 January to Constantinople with despatches, but had not yet returned. The weather remained severe, with constant snowstorms, frost, and extreme cold.[112] Despite such hardships, Lazarev's endeavours ensured that the ships were ready to sail when orders were received.

Even as Lazarev's ships weighed anchor, Palmerston still dismissed the question of naval aid for the Ottoman Empire:

> We are not prepared to accede at once to the Sultan's application for immediate naval assistance, but at the same time we are anxious to preserve his empire from dissolution or dismemberment, considering it to be an essential element in the balance of power...[113]

On 2 February, obviously fearing 'dissolution or dismemberment', Mahmut formally requested Russian aid. Two days later, Palmerston wrote to Campbell in Alexandria that while he had been aware of the Russian offers of aid, he still felt disinclined to proffer British assistance. Palmerston was aware of the disadvantage Turkey suffered *vis-à-vis* Egyptian seapower:

> The fleet of the Sultan suffered at Navarin losses, which have mainly contributed to deprive the Porte of that maritime superiority, which in a contest with the Pasha of Egypt, it might otherwise have expected to command...

Campbell was to 'treat freely' with the French and Austrian representatives and to be friendly with the Russian chargé, but not to take him into his 'confidence'.[114]

Russia continued its mobilisation; Butenev on 7 February received a letter from Greig stating that in order to save time, he should communicate directly with Lazarev. Six days later the *Shirokii*-10 sailed into Sevastopol with despatches from Constantinople addressed to Greig, as well as a letter from Butenev. Lazarev found Butenev's request for the immediate sailing of the first squadron; if the entire squadron was not ready for sea, then the Sultan requested the immediate sailing of as much of it as was ready, especially the amphibious marine detachments.[115] The same day Lazarev informed Greig that he would sail the following morning if the winds were favourable.[116] Regarding the troops, Lazarev decided that to collect them would waste too much time; as more Fleet ships were being fitted out, they could later transport them if they should still prove necessary. The squadron sailed the next day.

A formal request for assistance was again made to Butenev on 17 February. He replied he had written to Admiral Greig 'by land and sea' ten to twelve days previously to send the Fleet; if the *Shirokii*-10 had reached Sevastopol, then the squadron would sail shortly afterwards; if it had already sailed, 'then it is possible to await at any minute its appearance at the entrance to the Bosphorous'. Butenev requested the Porte to furnish him with instructions in the event of the imminent arrival of the Fleet, noting,

> It is an important observation, that at the present time of the year the Russian squadron is not able to cruise in the open sea, without being exposed to significant dangers.[117]

Butenev ended by reminding the Reis Efendi that he no longer had a ship at his disposition for communicating with the Black Sea Fleet.

Nicholas was not overly pleased with his commitment to uphold the Ottoman Empire; in a conversation with Count Fiquelmont, the Austrian ambassador, the Tsar commented;

> I have taken the engagement and shall keep my word. I do not conceal from you that it is a sacrifice that I make. It is too opposed to all our old relations with Turkey for Russia to behold it with pleasure; besides religious principle is opposed to it. However, I shall keep my word. But that is all I can do. I have no power to give life to the dead.... [118]

Lazarev's squadron arrived off the Bosphorus on 20 February and became becalmed. The pasha commanding the entrance forts came out to the *Pamiat' Evstafii*-84, and using Lieutenant Stavraki as interpreter, asked Lazarev why he had come so close to the Bosphorus. Lazarev remarked that the Sultan had requested Russian assistance, to which the pasha replied that he had received no information; he subsequently requested Lazarev to remain outside the Straits until he had received definite instructions. Lazarev tartly pointed out that the freshening wind which had arisen might expose the pasha to risk if he did not hurry back to his fort. The pasha hesitated, whereupon Lazarev gave the order for the squadron to set sails, and form line of battle; the Russian ships then sailed into the Bosphorus.[119] At the same time, a Russian officer was sent to inform the pashas of Erzurum and Trabzon that, should Ibrahim march towards their districts, Russian forces would be sent to protect them.[120]

Russian seapower would now be involved should the Egyptians attempt an attack on Constantinople; its help would be essential. On paper, the Ottoman Fleet looked impressive; it now had six line ships, eight frigates, eight corvettes, twenty brigs, two cutters and two steamboats; they were all, however, 'sadly neglected'.[121] In the absence of any aid from Western Europe, Nicholas had little choice but to send his forces. The significance of Ibrahim's advance across Anatolia for the Russian deployments in the Caucasus was not lost on General Rozen, commander of the Russian forces there. Rozen thought Mehmet's aim was to 'restore the glory of the Muslim, an take their revenge for the shameful peace concluded by the Sultan with Russia'. The unrest an Egyptian victory would cause in the Caucasus was obvious:

> Therefore, if he [Mehmet Ali] does not turn his main [military] strength against us, then it will devolve into hostile relations with us, the consequences of which will be invasions of our frontiers by militant border peoples; Kurds, Adzharians, Lazes, and others; while, together with this, there will be arising disorder in the mountains, in Abhazia and Daghestan, whose populations are largely Sunni, the faith predominating in Asia Minor.
>
> For us to be able to repel him, it is necessary to strengthen [our] border tribes with military detachments, and therefore not only will it henceforth be impossible to move troops away to the Caucasus Line, but it is possible that the need will arise to bring them for the border into Georgia from the Line....[122]

With the alternatives so obvious, Russian commitment to Turkey remained firm. Menshikov sent orders to Greig concerning Fleet dispositions. If Lazarev, 'contrary to expectations', was still within Russian waters, he was to sail to Odessa and embark the 3rd Brigade of the 26th Infantry Division before heading for Constantinople. Otherwise, a detachment of three line ships and a frigate under Rear-Admiral Mikhail Nikolaevich Kumani was to sail to Odessa and embark as many of the 26th Infantry Division's troops as possible. Kumani was to charter merchantmen to carry supplies and the additional troops of the 26th Infantry Division, and then convoy the ships to Constantinople. Greig was to cooperate with Governor-General Count Vorontsov and Lieutenant-General Otroshchenskii, commander of the 26th Infantry Division, over all aspects of the convoy's organisation. Major-General Zalesskii was to be sent to Constantinople, along with a number of 'efficient' naval artillery officers, to aid the Turks in preparing any possible land defences.[123] Later that day, couriers brought news from Constantinople about the arrival of Lazarev's squadron.[124]

On 2 March Lazarev reported that the Ottoman government remained extremely discomfited by the Russian presence. During the previous eight days, the wind had blown steadily from the north,

> which had not allowed the fulfilment of the desire of the Porte, already thrice expressed, that is, the squadron leave the Bosphorus and henceforth relocate to Sizepol to be on call.[125]

Although previously the wind had been favourable, Lazarev had remained in Constantinople because during a conference in the Russian ambassador's home, Ahmet Pasha had indicated the Porte's indecision about either accepting Russian aid, or relying instead on the French ambassador who had promised to try and influence Mehmet Ali. The offer had been accompanied by veiled threats that if the Turks did not decline Russian assistance, then a French squadron might be forced to enter the Dardanelles and assist Ibrahim. In light of such pressure, Lazarev felt that to remain, while unsettling the Turks, was ultimately more beneficial to both Turkish and Russian interests.

The following week Tahir paid a courtesy call on Lazarev. 'Looking over the ship and praising everything he saw', the Kapudan Pasha invited Lazarev to visit the Tersane-i Amire. Several days later, when Lazarev and a retinue of officers visited the Mint, the Sultan announced that commemorative gold and silver medals would be struck for distribution to the officers.[126]

The French continued to pursue an ambivalent policy; on 18 March Aberdeen informed Wellington that intelligence indicated that Admiral Roussin appeared to negotiate directly for Mehmet in Constantinople, accepting the terms laid down by Halil Pasha.[127] Aberdeen added that both the Austrian and Russian ministers seemed unaware of the discussions.

Despite Lazarev's presence in the Bosphorus and the equivocation of the French, the crisis continued to be lightly regarded in London in comparison to events in Portugal and Holland;

> in truth our Governments are so much occupied by internal affairs and by their revolutionary negotiations in the Peninsula and in Holland that they have not leisure to attend to nor means to interfere effectually in affairs at a greater distance and of minor importance . . . they now prefer the establishment of French influence to that of the Russians in the Levant, and I dare say, that there is no man in the Cabinet who has taken the trouble of ascertaining facts and considering how the interests of this nation might be affected by this arrangement. . . .[128]

Even if Wellington had begun to reconsider the government's position, intelligence from Holland indicated a possible heating-up of the Dutch crisis; on the same day that Wellington wrote to Aberdeen, the Dutch fleet moved downriver to the mouth of the Scheldt from its previous position at Flushing.[129]

In contrast to continued British indifference to events in the Mediterranean, the French were now beginning to respond to the growing Eastern crisis. Not only was the French ambassador in Constantinople attempting to influence Mehmet, but the government began to consider strengthening its Mediterranean forces. The Minister of Marine applied in the Chambre of Deputies for a supplemental sum of 780 500 francs, to be used to build two new line ships to be stationed in the Mediterranean.[130]

Such preparations could not have an immediate effect, however; Russia was still the only European power directly involved. Russian army preparations to aid Turkey with ground forces continued. General Kiselev, President of the Principalities, published in Iaşi a proclamation about the passage of a Russian auxiliary corps. Kiselev was to be in overall command of the troops. An advance guard of 4000 troops with eight field guns under General Varpakovskii left Iaşi on 28 March. The Prut was crossed on 13 April.[131]

With the onset of warmer weather Lazarev was increasingly concerned about the health of his men, and issued an order that all commanders 'without fail' were to supply their men with fresh meat twice a week, on Sundays and Thursdays, as he was aware of the 'harmful consequences' of keeping the men on a constant diet of salt-cured meat. In addition, fresh vegetables were to be purchased for the lower ranks with no scrimping for economy's sake, while for the sick, fresh meat and supplies were to be purchased 'when necessity demands it, even if this means every day....'.[132]

The second Russian naval echelon was now ready; Rear-Admiral Kumani set sail from Odessa on the morning of 30 March, having been delayed for several days by unfavourable winds.[133] Six days later Kumani's squadron, including the line ships *Imperatritsa Mariia*-84, *Adrianopol*-84, and *Parmen*-74, the frigates *Tenedos*-60, *Arkipelag*-60, a steamer, four military and seven merchant transports carrying 5000 troops arrived in the Bosphorus.[134]

Even as Kumani weighed anchor, the Turkish government continued to seek British naval aid. If Nicholas found sending aid to the Turks a 'sacrifice', the Turks found it even more of one to accept it. In a letter dated March 30, the Ottoman government spelled out their requests:

It is therefore presently of the most urgent necessity to remove from his [Mehmet's] hands...ships, in order to render these areas [the Mediterranean coasts] orderly and secure, by land and sea...the Ottoman squadron finds itself consisting of some ships, but few in number...His Highness the Sultan constantly recalls the sincere and continual friendship which happily exists between him and England, ...and...appeal[s]...by an autograph letter to His Majesty the very High, powerful and magnificent King and Padishah of Great Britain...the British government would well want to reinforce the Imperial squadron of His Majesty with the number of fifteen warships which England would be able to send from some port where she has her maritime forces...nothing would be more effective than superiority of the British fleet....[135]

Russia continued to monitor closely the unsettled situation in Constantinople. Ibrahim's troops had occupied Kütahya in February, and Mehmet had threatened to march on Constantinople if the Sultan did not now cede Cilicia as well. One of Count Benkendorf's intelligence sources wrote to him,

...in general, one is aware of the disintegration of Turkey, seeing the impossibility in which the Pasha of Egypt will find himself in overthrowing the throne, of conserving all the states which compose this vast empire. It is believed most probable that there will be a separation of Turkish Africa from European Turkey, and a division between them of the asiatic provinces. . . In effect. . . there will be a sanctioning of the separation of the empire into two independent parts. . . But that which knowledgeable men fear the most is war.[136]

Mehmet Ali meanwhile continued to pretend to be the Sultan's most loyal subject; Campbell reported that

[Mr. Boghos] assured [me]. . . that the Viceroy was anxious to follow the counsels of Great Britain, and had no desire to shake off his allegiance to the Sultan, or to diminish his Power or greatness. . . The Pasha said that the Serasker had deceived him in calling in the Russians whilst Halil Pasha was treating for peace. He asserted that it was the interest both of France and England to support him, as in so doing, they would give the best support to the Ottoman Empire. He declared that he had no desire to throw off his allegiance to the Sultan, or to render himself independent, and that his only object was to assist in liberating the Sultan and his Empire from the yoke of Russia.[137]

Though the Egyptians went through the motions of proclaiming loyalty to the Sultan while threatening him, the Russian presence had completely changed the situation. In reality, Mehmet Ali could gain now by negotiation and prevarication, and he knew it. Russian mistrust of Mehmet's motives meant that they continued to strengthen the defences of Constantinople, and even extend the effort to the Dardanelles. On 1 April Lazarev wrote to Menshikov about possible future Russian reinforcement of the Dardanelles forts. Contrary winds and navigational hazards meant that steamers would be necessary for any attempt to place three hundred men in each of the Dardanelles forts, should such an action become essential.[138]

Palmerston now belatedly began to act, two months after Lazarev's arrival in Constantinople. On 3 April orders were sent to Vice-Admiral Hotham to collect his forces and cruise off Alexandria; from there he was to communicate with Campbell. If negotiations proved successful in restraining Mehmet Ali, he was to sail for Tenedos; if not, then he was to remain to assist Campbell. Palmerston still seemed to believe that the mere appearance of the Royal Navy would deter Mehmet:

> It is to be hoped that the moral influence of Great Britain, united with that of her allies, and a knowledge that the Great Powers of Europe are determined to prevent the dismembrance of the Turkish Empire will be sufficient to bring Mehmet Ali to submit to reasonable terms of accommodation with his sovereign....[139]

If Mehmet continued his belligerence, Hotham was to break all communications between Ibrahim and Egypt. Should a French squadron appear off Alexandria, Hotham was to act in conjunction with it; should a Russian squadron appear, he was to treat it as a 'friendly power'.

As Palmerston finally acknowledged the seriousness of Mehmet's rebellion, the Russians continued to send their forces to Constantinople. On 11 April in Odessa a detachment of the third and final contingent of Russian naval aid to be sent to the Bosphorus, the line ships *Parizh*-110, *Pimen*-84, *Ioann Zlatoust*-74 and bombship *Uspekh* under the command of Rear-Admiral Iosif Ivanovich Stozhevskii arrived in quarantine.[140]

Nicholas wanted Russian troops to occupy two forts on the Bosphorus, one on each side of the channel, in order to secure the passage. If necessary, additional artillery could be sent from Sevastopol.[141] Lazarev recommended that Anadolu and Rumeli Kavaks as the best positions if such a step was undertaken: he himself felt that it was not essential.

> The taking now by our troops of two forts does not appear necessary, as it was earlier; for Ibrahim Pasha in the present circumstances knows that he would meet 10 000 of our troops, and does not dare to begin offensive operations....[142]

Lazarev further reported that Ibrahim had cut an 'enormous amount' of ship-timber in Adana province.

The Dardanelles were not neglected, either. Lieutenant Vladimir Kornilov was sent on the *Erivan*-60 to the Dardanelles to survey the defences there, and make recommendations for their improvement. On 13 April the frigate set sail from Büyükdere – among the officers on board were Kornilov, Lieutenant Putiatin, Colonel Diugamel of Nicholas's staff, and an infantry colonel and staff-captain. Basing themselves at Gallipoli, they spent the next three weeks sailing around the Dardanelles fortifications, taking measurements and soundings.

Contrary winds delayed the *Erivan*-60 in the lower channel, so on 8 May Kornilov and Putiatin returned overland to Büyükdere.[143]

Lazarev approved of his subordinate's work, which had produced highly detailed and extremely accurate maps. The two officers had with 'tireless energy' over more than two months in both the Bosphorus and Dardanelles, measured not only the height and size of the forts' walls, but the calibre of their ordnance as well.[144] They also surveyed the two lighthouses at the Bosphorus entrance. The information was incorporated with previous materials, and the following year the Military Topographic Depot in St Petersburg was able to offer for sale a thirteen-sheet 'Atlas de plans et déscriptions des détroits de Constantinople, des Dardanelles et des principaux lieux de l'empire ottoman, situés sur les bords de la Mer-Noire' for fifty rubles, and a two-sheet 'Plan de Constantinople avec les détroits' for twenty rubles.[145]

The British carefully followed Kornilov's intelligence activities. Consul Lander reported that the Russians 'had been occupied incessantly in taking places of all the Batteries erected within the Dardanelles'; six hundred men were employed in throwing up earthworks around Gallipoli, and several of the Russians' suggestions for improvements were being incorporated.[146] The Bosphorus and Dardanelles forts were not the only Turkish military resources examined by the Russians. In addition to constructing two quays on the Asian Bosphorus shore for the offloading of troops and artillery, Lieutenant Ivan Dmitriev drew plans of the *Mahmudiye*-120, as well as a frigate under construction by the Americans in the Tersane-i Amire.[147]

Mehmet meanwhile continued his hard bargaining; Campbell reported that while the Sultan was going to give Syria to Mehmet, 'the Pacha will endeavour to have Adana added, on account of the excellent timber which it affords, but that this will not in any degree stand in the way of peace...'.[148]

While the negotiations continued, the Turks were careful not to give offence to their traditional enemies, now turned protectors. The Sultan's solicitude for his 'guests' extended to sending the Russian soldiers 25 000 eggs for their Easter celebrations.[149] The common people were for the most part friendly. Several battalions and squadrons of the Sultan's guards with their artillery joined the Russian camp. The naval officers received sweets and wines, while the sailors were sent rum, oxen meat, and six piastres (about one and one-half rubles) per man; the infantry were able to drown their boredom in a mug of vodka provided by the Sultan.[150]

Rear-Admiral Stozhevskii entered the Bosphorus on 23 April with the third and final Russian squadron. Stozhevskii had three line ships, two bombships, one military and eleven civilian transports carrying 5000 troops, which were offloaded at Hünkâr İskelessi.[151] The troops were under the command of Lieutenant-General Otroshchenskii and consisted of the 2nd Brigade of the 26th Infantry Division and one light infantry artillery company.[152] Almost all of the Black Sea Fleet's operational strength was now stationed in the Straits.

A notable aspect of the Russian presence was the relatively low level of illness and mortality among the troops; prior to Stozhevskii's arrival, only two men had died. The warmer weather increased the spread of disease, so the Turks constructed a hospital in Büyükdere and stocked it with provisions, where all casualties were subsequently treated.[153]

While Russian warships guarded Constantinople, other Fleet ships continued skirmishing with Turkish smugglers on the Caucasus coast. On 17 April the *Zhavoronok*-12 captured two Turkish merchantmen in Sudzhuk-Kale; eight days later, she captured a third Turkish ship in the same area.[154] Nine days later, naval forces from Gelendzhik discovered three contraband traders off Vulani at the mouth of the Chabin river.[155] The same day, the *Lastochka*-12 captured three Turkish smuggling ships at Sudzhuk-Kale.[156]

In Constantinople the Russian forces continued to straggle in; the line ship *Panteleimon*-84 arrived from Sevastopol carrying provisions along with several smaller ships and the *Meteor*-2 steamer, while the brig *Paris*-20 joined the squadron from Alexandria.[157]

As the crisis began to wind down, the new British ambassador, Lord Ponsonby, finally arrived on 1 May, sailing up the Dardanelles past the Gallipoli batteries that were to be 'materially strengthened'. When Lander asked the pasha in charge of the position if the Russians would be supervising, the Turk was silent, 'but his look indicated yes....'.[158]

With nearly the entire Black Sea Fleet moored in the Bosphorus, 11 000 Russian troops camped at Hünkâr İskelessi, and Russian engineers fortifying the Dardanelles, Palmerston finally decided to commit the Royal Navy to Turkey's defence and to send 'two 3-deckers, two large -74s and two fifty-gun frigates . . . and a large armed steam-vessel mounting four heavy 32-pounders....'.[159] His belated decision was a question of tardy overreaction, but the number of capital ships committed represented less than a third of the number that the Turks had requested on March 30.

Parliament now also awakened to the Russian presence at Constantinople, and began to ask awkward questions about Government policy in the Levant. The Foreign Secretary was queried on a number of issues. Why had there been no British ambassador in Constantinople at the time of the Russian incursion? Why had there been no Royal Navy ships in the Dardanelles 'to give efficacy to the remonstrances he might have had occasion to make?' Why had the French ambassador been left to try and contest the Russian presence alone? The fierce grilling seemed justified; Russian naval strength at Constantinople stood at ten line ships, five frigates, two corvettes, a brig, two bombships and two steamers.[160]

Palmerston's answers had little substance. There had been an ambassador posted to Constantinople following Canning's departure, but Ponsonby's frigate had been held up for over a month in Naples by contrary winds. On the subject of the Fleet's non-appearance in the Dardanelles, Palmerston went on the offensive and asked, 'where would it have been if the hon. Member's motion for cutting off 7000 men from the number of men voted in the Navy Estimates had been carried?'[161]

Palmerston's incipient Russophobia blinded him to the true state of affairs in the East; he still felt the Russian threat to the Ottoman Empire to be nearly equal to the Egyptian one;

> The matter of the greatest interest and importance after the restoration of peace in the Levant, will be the complete evacuation of the Ottoman territory by the Russian land and sea forces, and to the early accomplishment of this object....[162]

The new orders sent out by the Admiralty took full notice of the changed political climate. When peace was re-established, the new Mediterranean commander, Vice-Admiral Sir Pulteney Malcolm, was to anchor off the Dardanelles and await Ponsonby's instructions. If any Russians remained after the peace, Ponsonby was to act in conjunction with the Austrian and French ambassadors in telling the Sultan it was time for them to leave. Ponsonby could dismiss Malcolm's squadron if he felt its presence was no longer needed. If the Russians did not depart after peace was concluded, Malcolm was to remain in contact with London, but not to begin hostilities nor attempt to enter the Dardanelles without express orders from the Admiralty.[163] In a belated gesture of support, HMS *Malabar*-74 sailed for Constantinople with a gift for the Sultan from the British government; twenty 18-pdr cannons modified to fire 32-lb shot, mounted on newly-invented carriages, a design which had been rejected by the Royal Navy.[164]

The maritime trade which the Black Sea Fleet intervened to protect was ironically in temporary decline; a snowless winter followed by a drought had resulted in an almost total crop failure in southern Russia, severely reducing wheat exports; in Odessa the price of a chetvert of wheat rose to twenty rubles.[165] In 1832 Russian wheat exports had been worth £1 153 366; in 1833 they fell to £553 383, while the following year saw revenue shrink even further to £114 760, nearly £50 000 less than 1828, when Russia had been blockaded.[166]

With the Black Sea Fleet at Constantinople and an Anglo-French squadron off the Dardanelles, Mehmet Ali and the Sultan hammered out an agreement that satisfied neither. Mehmet Ali came out ahead, as he wound up with both Syria/Lebanon and Adana. The Turco-Egyptian stalemate was formally ended by the Kütahya peace treaty, signed on 6 May 1833. Palmerston was opposed to Mahmut granting the Adana pashalik to Mehmet.[167] Three weeks later the Foreign Secretary bowed to the inevitable, and instructed Campbell not to oppose the Porte's decision.[168] Adana was essential to Mehmet Ali's plans for maritime expansion, as nearly all his ship-timber came from there; while Egyptian troops occupied the province, Egyptian timber-ships went there 'to help themselves'.[169]

Tension remained high at Constantinople, with the Turks anxious not to offend their Russian guests. On 25 May the *Mèsange*-14 attempted to pass the Dardanelles, and was turned back by cannon-fire from the Outer Castles.[170] The French schooner had no ferman for passing the Straits; after a formal complaint by the French ambassador, he was told that the officers responsible would be punished.[171]

Russia's policy was already affecting Western European polity. The Russian presence in Constantinople had an immediate effect on French naval estimates – in a report on the proposed 1834 naval budget submitted to the May 30 meeting of the Chambre of Deputies, the authors wrote,

> Dans la Baltique, la Russie n'a rien diminué de sa marine, qu'elle a doublée dans la mer Noire. Au moment ou nous parlons, elle présente dix vaisseaux de ligne à l'ancre dans le Bosphore; elle y conquiert le droit ou la faculté de déboucher avec ses escardes dans la Mediterranée....[172]

Suspicion of Russia and her motives was to become a constant factor in French and British policy during the next eight years. Distractions to Anglo-French naval power that might be used in the Levant meanwhile continued to lessen. In the North Sea, the combined squadron was now released from its tedious blockade duties; four days before the attack on the *Mèsange*-14, William had signed the Treaty of XXIV Articles, and the blockade that had diverted so many resources was lifted.[173]

Despite the peace, post-intervention Russian–Turkish relations had yet to be clarified. In the interim, the Russians continued to enjoy Constantinople. Russian soldiers were even allowed to visit the armoury collection in the old Byzantine church of Haghia Eirene, located within the first courtyard of the Serail itself beyond the Bab-ı Hümayun, an area that had previously been strictly off-limits to Europeans.[174] Black Sea Fleet officers also inspected the Turkish Fleet, moored in the Golden Horn. As one Russian was being rowed around the channel, he was surprised by the smart appearance of the vessels, to which his Turkish oarsman replied, 'Yes, our ships are good, but the men who man them are rotten...'.[175]

In a move that seemed to portend increased Russian privileges as regarded the Straits and warship passage rights, St Petersburg now decided to send Rikord's ships to the Black Sea Fleet rather than return them to the Baltic. On 29 May a Tartar arrived at the Dardanelles Outer Castles with fermans for the four small ships to pass the Straits. When Lander questioned the Pasha about the fermans he was told, 'the Russians, you know very well, do as they like just now, and if they want more vessels in the Bosphorus, they will no doubt order them from where they are to be found...'.[176] Only one Russian officer now remained in the Dardanelles forts supervising construction.

The *Sizepol*-24 and *Redut-Kale* transport were sent to Odessa with news of the peace agreement; all troops preparing to embark in Odessa were to be stopped, and if the ships were met on the way, they were to be turned back, even if they were at the 'very mouth' of the Bosphorus.[177] Aided by favourable winds, the *Sizepol*-24 made the passage in forty-four hours, and found that none of the ships had left, but were still loading. The *Sizepol*-24 rejoined the Fleet at Büyükdere on 11 June.[178] The brig *Uliss*-20 from Rikord's squadron now also passed the Dardanelles to join the Black Sea Fleet ships.[179]

The aggravation produced by French and British protests about the continued Russian presence in Constantinople nettled the Russian diplomats: Orlov wrote to Nicholas, 'Nous n'avons qu'un seul regret ici, c'est de partir sans nous mésurer avec la flotte française...'.[180]

The Royal Navy now asserted its presence within the Straits by sending HMS *Beacon*-8 and HMS *Mastiff*-6 into the Dardanelles to carry out surveys similar to those of the Russians.[181] Vice-Admiral Malcolm informed Ponsonby that in light of the circumstances he had decided to sail directly for the Dardanelles instead of Alexandria. Malcolm had HMS *Britannia*-120, HMS *St Vincent*-120, HMS *Malabar*-74, HMS *Alfred*-50, and HMS *Rover*-18; HMS *Barham*-50 and HMS *Rainbow*-28 were to rendezvous several days later with the other ships at Besika Bay.[182]

On 23 June Malcolm arrived off Tenedos with seven line ships, a frigate and a cutter.[183] The next day Malcolm's squadron was joined by the tender HMS *Hind* and HMS *Meteor*-2 steam ship.[184]

The situation regarding ship passage of the Straits was now in a state of flux; the pasha commanding the Outer Forts received orders on 27 June that no warships of whatever nation were to be allowed to pass the Straits without a previously-issued ferman. When Malcolm attempted to send HMS *Hind* up to Constantinople with despatches, permission to pass the Straits was forbidden; however, the Pasha said that if no ferman was received in the next few days, then HMS *Hind* could pass on Sunday night.[185]

Just at the moment of its greatest postwar triumph, the Black Sea Fleet now lost its most illustrious officer from the last war; on 28 June the brave Kazarskii, hero of the *Merkurii*-20, met a horrific and untimely end from poisoning.[186] Evidence pointed strongly to the chief of police in Nikolaev, Avtomonov. An investigation by Admiral Greig had uncovered nothing, nor had a second investigation. When Nicholas received the Third Section's report on the affair, he sent Benkendorf to Nikolaev to attempt to uncover the truth, 'laying it personally on your conscience. It is all too horrible.'[187]

In Constantinople, the negotiations continued between the Ottoman and Russian governments. In a further gesture of gratitude, Sultan Mahmut attended a review of the Russian troops at Hünkâr İskelessi. Count Orlov, General Murav'ev accompanied by a splendid suite, and General Butenev with the members of the mission received the Sultan on his exit from his ship.[188]

The Russo-Turkish negotiations on July 8 produced the infamous Hünkâr İskelessi Treaty, one of the most misunderstood documents in Middle Eastern history. Ostensibly a purely defensive agreement, its vaguely-worded secret clauses would give rise to European suspicions that Russia had established a unilateral protectorate over the ailing Ottoman Empire. The outcry was immediate; shortly after the signing of the Hünkâr İskelessi Treaty Palmerston was being grilled in Parliament as to why His Majesty's Government had not been sufficiently vigilant to prevent such a treaty being concluded. One member of the Opposition remarked that the Treaty was a visible manifestation of the fact that,

> Russia . . . is slowly but steadily advancing on Constantinople, and determined at no distant day to take possession of the Dardanelles, when all her energy, enterprise and ambition will be directed to the extension of her maritime power. . . .[189]

Attempts to have the relevant papers produced for parliamentary scrutiny had Palmerston reply that the timing of such disclosures would be inauspicious, and that he personally believed in Russia's claims of disinterest.

The Russians now began to prepare for departure. The Turks were impressed with the efficiency of the Russian forces, which the Serasker noted in a letter he sent to Nicholas:

> The landing on shore after the arrival of the troops, and similarly, their departure back to the ships, done in one day during several hours, represented an example of discipline, precision and firm serviceability in which all parts coordinated in a striking fulfilment of the objective.[190]

Western Europe was now not only interested in a Russian departure, but an abrogation of the Hünkâr agreement. Suspicion of Russian motives would become the cornerstone of Anglo-French foreign policy for the next eight years, and linger until it eventually burst forth in the Crimean War.

4 The Hünkâr İskelessi Peace, Russophobia, and a Middle Eastern Arms Race

'Russia has . . . three sources of weakness, inherent and irremediable – Poland, the Caucasus, and the Fleet. All these deprive her of immense sums of money and large masses of men.'

Lord Durham[1]

'I have always thought that military operations alone would not allow us to achieve our end; that it will be necessary to combine force with a system of moderation and commerce, but I have encountered so many obstacles and opposition that I am discouraged.'

Count Nesselrode[2]

'. . . it would be unforgivable for us not to manage to do a landing in the Bosphorus before the appearance of an enemy squadron.'

Admiral Lazarev[3]

'Our fleet could blow the Russian navy from the seas.'

Lord Palmerston[4]

The Russians embarked their troops the day after the Hünkâr Treaty was signed; on 10 July the squadron weighed anchor from Büyük-dere.[5] Russian efficiency impressed Mate William Mends, later admiral commanding Royal Navy transport during the Crimean War. As he observed the loading from HMS *Acteon*-26, Mends took copious notes:

100

...most excellent and expeditious they seemed to be, the whole force of 22 000 men with all their stores and belongings being on board before 6 p.m., the embarkation having been commenced at 6 a.m. The Russian naval commander was Admiral Lazareff, who had been trained in the British service, and was in some of the ships of Nelson's fleet at the battle of Trafalgar. He was a strict disciplinarian, and his ships were in a high state of efficiency.[6]

During the northward passage the wind shifted and left Lazarev's squadron in the Black Sea while Stozhevskii and Kumani remained stranded in the Bosphorus. Lazarev took the *Pamiat' Evstafii*-84, *Imperatritsa Ekaterina II*-84, *Adrianopol*-84, *Ioann Zlatoust*-74, *Shtandart*-44, *Varna*-60, *Erivan*-60 and *Sizepol*-24 and sailed for Feodosiia, arriving there on 14 July. By the end of the day Lazarev was joined by the *Imperatritsa Mariia*-84, *Arkhipelag*-60, *Anapa*-84, *Tenedos*-60, and *Uliss*-20; Rear-Admiral Kumani and the merchantmen remained stranded in the Bosphorus by contrary winds until the following day, and arrived on 17 July.[7] The troops went into quarantine after landing. When the ships returned to Sevastopol, they anchored for several days and then went out on manoeuvres; following their return, the ships underwent quarantine.[8]

Farther south, the bulk of Rikord's squadron in Greek waters had sailed on 2 July for the Dardanelles; only the *Aiaks*-18 and *Paris*-20 remained for the use of the Russian representative in Greece to communicate with Constantinople.[9] The Russian army presence in the Principalities was also run down; one of the three divisions was to be withdrawn immediately, while the other two would take part in autumnal manoeuvres near Bucharest, and winter there.[10]

For his success in handling the Turkish expedition, Lazarev now advanced quickly through the hierarchy of the Black Sea Fleet. The day before he arrived in Feodosiia he was appointed Adjutant-General.[11] A month later Greig was appointed to the State Council, which left the way free for Lazarev to assume control of the Black Sea Fleet.[12] As Lazarev dropped anchor in the Crimea, combined British and French squadrons totalling fourteen sail were cruising off the southern coast of Tenedos.[13] Little was accomplished by their aimless cruising, however, and by mid-August 'a great portion' of the ships had been withdrawn to Urla and the Aegean.[14]

Farther afield the Russian departure was causing uneasiness; Mavroyenis reported from London that the British government believed that a defensive treaty between Russia and Turkey was imminent, or had already been signed. Despite his initial reluctance to aid Turkey, which had forced the Sultan finally to accept Russian assistance, Palmerston had very negative views about such a treaty;

> I am cannot conceive of the advantage that you can have from this, I see there instead to the contrary an increase in the protection that Russia would want to exercise over you, because she would pledge to contribute to your defense against attack in an external war, and to intervene at every opportunity in your domestic affairs; and this now will happen when you submit to a dependence on Russian protection who will, at any event, be able to march her troops into the territories of the Ottoman Empire.[15]

In Constantinople the rumours continued; it was believed that a multi-national force of five British, five French, and five Russian line ships would be stationed in the Bosphorus to protect the Turkish government.[16] While the increased British naval operations in the eastern Mediterranean indicated a more belligerent British stance, newspaper reports that Malcolm was to force the Straits were declared false. The admiral had decided that a journey to Constantinople might be beneficial, and had wanted to raise his pennant on a corvette and sail to Constantinople. Given the new mood in the capital, Ponsonby stated that such a voyage might be provocative and Malcolm subsequently dropped the idea.

Despite the growing clamour over the Hünkâr Treaty and its vaguely worded Secret Article[17] Nicholas felt that it was both defensive and honourable; regarding the British and French protests he remarked, 'Russia will not threaten any one, but will always defend, as far as possible, her rights.'[18] Nesselrode saw the Treaty's Secret Article as not binding Turkey to any conditions not previously observed by her in her international relations;

> ...the treaty... does not impose on the Porte any onerous condition, and it does not provide any new obligation. It serves solely to restate the fact of the closure of the Dardanelles to the flag of war of foreign Powers; a system which the Porte has maintained at all times, and from which she is not able to deviate without prejudicing her most immediate interests.[19]

This benign interpretation was not shared by Britain. On 24 August the House of Commons again discussed recent events in Turkey. Palmerston again argued that the Royal Navy had been too involved in the Portuguese and Belgian crises actively to assist the Sultan, an explanation 'almost too simple to be believed'.[20] Palmerston was asked if the Russians had been sent with British and French approval; if not, had a protest been made? Questions were asked about rumours that the Russians had been fortifying the Dardanelles, as well as whether a treaty had been concluded.[21] In reply to a further question about a Turkish request for naval assistance, Palmerston noted that an approach had been made to the British Government by the Turks *before* they accepted the Russian aid, 'but his Majesty's Government did not, at that moment, comply with that request.'[22]

On 29 October the British ambassador in St Petersburg delivered a formal protest, followed several days later by his French colleague. Nesselrode continued to maintain that the Treaty had an exclusively defensive nature.[23] Palmerston wrote about Mehmet's forces and their effect on subsequent Russian mobilisation to defend Turkey:

> It is evident that the state of preparation in which the Pacha's army and navy have been kept ever since the arrangement of the differences between him and the Sultan, has been the pretext, if not the cause, for the state of readiness in which the Russian Troops and Squadron in the Black Sea have also been maintained...

Despite the Egyptian threat, Britain 'under no pretext whatever' wanted Russia to reoccupy Constantinople.[24] This 'pretext' formed the foundation of Palmerston's foreign policy for the next eight years.

Western European perceptions continued to focus on Russia and its Hünkâr 'coup' rather than the continuing unsettled state of Turkish–Egyptian relations. Despite Nesselrode's disinclination to acknowledge formally the French and British protests, he understood clearly their fury and its future implications for Russian foreign policy:

> ...our treaty of alliance has given rise for us to a serious quarrel...Palmerston wants to avenge himself on us for the sad role he played in the affairs of the Orient...I hope that all will be limited to an exchange of notes and despatches; and yet all is possible with men so enraged and deprived of common sense as those who govern England today; because they are guided by passions and revolutionary sympathies, and not the interests and calculations of sound reason. I will not be sorry now to learn that one is occupied at all events to place Sevastopol in a state of defence...[25]

Continued Anglo-French nervousness about Russian intentions caused both countries to maintain a larger naval presence in the

Levant than they had had there prior to the Treaty. By November 1833 there were four squadrons anchored at Smyrna – Austrian, American, French and British. The Austrians had four warships, while the Americans were represented by the *United States*-44 and *Constellation*-38 frigates, with the line ship *Delaware*-100 expected shortly. The French had the *Ville de Marseilles*-76 line ship, *Iphigénie*-60 and *Galathée*-56 frigates and some corvettes, while the line ship *Duquesne*-78 was at Naples. The Royal Navy maintained HMS *Britannia*-120, HMS *Alfred*-50, HMS *Malabar*-74, and HMS *Champion*-18, for a total of fourteen major warships.[26] On 3 December the line ships HMS *St Vincent*-120 and HMS *Caledonia*-120 also arrived, which resulted in 'the greatest number of three deckers assembled there for some years.'[27] The following month the British squadron at Urla had increased to eight warships, with the line ships HMS *Talavera*-74 and HMS *Meteor*-2 steamer having arrived. The French had been reinforced by the line ship *Superbe*-74, while several others were expected from Toulon.[28]

The European Mediterranean powers were not the only forces maintaining battle stations in the Levant. Despite the Kütahya agreement, the Egyptian forces were not demobilised. Mehmet used a projected expedition to the Yemen as his excuse for maintaining his forces on full combat footing.[29]

British opposition to the Hünkâr Treaty swiftly moved beyond mere diplomatic opposition; at the end of January 1834 Admiralty sent to the Mediterranean commander a secret order authorising him to comply with any request of the Turkish government for aid 'against any threatened attack of the Russians' if the request came through Ponsonby, even if it meant sending the Royal Navy through the Dardanelles, an action which would violate the new agreement.[30] On the diplomatic front, Britain continued to complain about the Treaty, which Nesselrode found excessive and obnoxious: 'Puisque l'Angleterre devient aimable, nous le serons aussi...'.[31] In order to allay British fears of Russian naval forces, Prince Lieven was to state 'avec certitude' that the Black Sea Fleet was not being augmented, while the number of ships in the Baltic Fleet was the same as it had been under Catherine II and Alexander I.

Lieven also gave to Palmerston a copy of the Treaty.[32] Palmerston was not completely convinced; the same day he sent to the British ambassador in Constantinople a copy of the Admiralty's instructions to the new Mediterranean commander, Vice-Admiral Sir Josias Rowley. If Ponsonby should 'at any time' inform Rowley that his squadron off the Dardanelles or any other part of the Levant 'would be attended with important advantage with reference to political transactions', then Rowley was to proceed to whatever locale was agreed; no forcible passage of the Dardanelles was to be attempted without specific instructions from the Admiralty.[33] The despatch ended with a British commitment very differently to any previously given to Turkey;

> ...it is the desire of His Majesty's Government to cultivate the best understanding with Mehemet Ali, while at the same time, it is their firm determination to oppose even by force if necessary, any attempt on his part to make a renewed attack upon the Sultan....

Britain continued to maintain an expanded Mediterranean presence, and use it in an aggressive manner. In May six line, two frigates and a transport with 1500 marines under Vice-Admiral Rowley sailed to Urla and carried out exercises in the area for the next three months.[34] Such menacing manoeuvres made the Ottoman government uncertain as to possible British reaction to its own naval activities; Rowley replied to an enquiry about whether the Royal Navy would interfere with a cruise along the Syrian coast by the Ottoman Fleet by noting that Great Britain and the Ottoman Empire were at peace, and that fact precluded any possible British interference.[35]

In the Black Sea, Lazarev took note of these new 'forward' deployments and responded in kind. The Black Sea Fleet now began a programme of annual summer cruises, sending four or five divisions of the Fleet out to cruise for three months in order to practise their seamanship.[36]

Western European worries about increased Russian influence in the Black Sea and Eastern Mediterranean were confined to the military sphere; if the Black Sea Fleet disturbed other European maritime powers, then the moderate growth of Russian Black Sea commercial shipping did not. The Russian merchant marine suffered from a number of shortcomings that allowed its more efficient foreign competitors to continue to dominate Black Sea trade, despite the Russian government's increasing efforts to stimulate the growth of commercial shipping.

Among the many factors inhibiting its expansion were personnel shortages; 'One of the main reasons why Russian shipping does not participate in international trade is its lack of suitably-trained skippers.'[37] In an attempt to alleviate this shortage, on 19 February 1834 a merchant marine school was founded in Kherson; twenty-four students studied at government expense, and the rest (ten to fourteen annually) privately during the four-year course.[38] During the four years 'not less' than two were spent at sea.[39]

Attempts were also made to stimulate shipbuilding and commerce among the littoral population. The main centres of Russian Black Sea commercial shipbuilding were Bereslavl', Aleshëk, Kherson, Nikolaev, Odessa and Izmail. Bereslavl' was a major shipbuilding centre for coastal 'kabotazh' vessels.[40] As a result of increased opportunities, the several thousand inhabitants of Aleshëk and Nikopol now formed a corporation of free mariners. In order to enroll, sailors had to first serve five years in the Navy, during which time they did not acquire a formal rank.[41] Following their service they could join the corporation and received a patent which allowed them to work on Russian merchantmen free from taxes, conscripted military service, and other governmental obligations.[42]

Kherson had been the original site of the Fleet's shipyards, where the Dnepr broadened to four and a half miles and was fifty feet deep. The shipyard had been situated on an island close to supply and store sites, but it had the major drawback of shallow water at the Dnepr's entrance, a problem which had eventually forced the transfer of the Fleet's Admiralty and shipyards to Nikolaev.[43] Ships entering from the Black Sea usually used the Kizim channel, which had a depth of only seven feet; ships leaving Kherson would sail half-loaded, and receive the remainder of their supplies when they had crossed the river's entrance.[44]

Warship construction had begun at Kherson in 1779. Over one hundred gunboats, brigs and transports had been built there, in addition to seventeen frigates and twenty-five line ships (which included six 100-gun vessels).[45] A commercial shipbuilding wharf had been established in Kherson in 1797.[46] With the establishment of shipyards at Nikolaev in 1788, Kherson's importance as a Fleet shipyard gradually declined. Before the recent war little major shipbuilding had been done; the luggers *Shirokii*-10 and *Glubokii*-10 had been built in 1827, but they were relatively small ships, sixty-five feet in length and twenty-one feet wide, which drew only nine feet of water.[47] Six iuls were built the following year; these iuls along with the *Dromodor* were the last warships built there.

In contrast to the facilities in Kherson, the Nikolaev yards were fully equipped to handle the largest warships; the Black Sea Fleet's first 120-gun line ship was built there. The *Varshava*-120 was two hundred and six feet long on its main gundeck, fifty-two feet wide, and drew twenty-six feet of water when fully loaded.[48] The government did not completely abandon Kherson as a commercial shipyard; 50 108 rubles were now allocated to building a new harbour and dredging.[49] Foreigners occasionally built merchantmen in Kherson, but such an event was 'rare.'[50]

While governmental efforts were made with the merchant marine, its intended cargo remained in short supply. The southern Russian grain failure continued; in Constantinople 'small vessels, which used formerly to traffic in corn from the Black Sea, are now begging freights in this port; several Greek vessels of this description have turned pirates even in the Sea of Marmora...'.[51] By May 1834 the price of corn had risen twenty per cent in Odessa and twenty-five per cent in the Crimea, due to early fears of a second year of bad harvest; despite such uncertainties, more than one hundred and twenty merchantmen had arrived in Constantinople during the last two weeks of May, hopeful of a cargo of grain.[52] The shortage of suitable cargoes was reflected in shipping figures; while in 1832 3237 ships had visited Constantinople, two years later only 1817 ships had arrived.[53] It was reported from Smyrna that piracy had 'recommended in this neighbourhood;' four misticos had been attacking shipping in the Gulf of Contessa and at Kavalla and Thasos, with the brigands feeling powerful enough to attack an armed Turkish galliot from Salonika, massacring thirty of the crew.[54]

The Turkish Fleet at this point did not produce a very favourable impression on foreigners; 'The Sultan's fleet of 15 sail, although maintained at a great expense in the Bosphorus, is described as in a most shocking plight, filthy to such a degree as to endanger the lives of the men on board...'.[55] The Ottoman Navy had now recovered somewhat from Navarino, and consisted of seven line, eight frigates, three sloops and a brig; in addition, four line ships, two 'large' frigates and sixteen smaller vessels were laid up in the Tersane-i Armire.[56] A British officer noted at Gemlik in the Gulf of Mudanya a 'very fine ship' pierced for 86 guns on the stocks, ready for launching.[57]

Mehmet's armed forces continued to present a very different spectacle from the Turkish military; European diplomats now took a close interest. Lieutenant-Colonel Prokesh sent information to the Tsar about the capabilities of the Egyptian Navy. While Egyptian warships deteriorated sharply after six years, they were built with amazing speed, in contrast to Russian warships, which took forever to build, and decayed quickly. Nicholas found the abilities of Mehmet's shipwrights incredible:

For example, one Egyptian frigate was built in forty-two days. I'm totally unable to comprehend this. I thought that the ship was built very (let's even say too) quickly; true, the circumstances led me to this conclusion, but despite this, I have never succeeded in building a frigate in less than six or seven months. To build a frigate in forty-two days is simply incredible; it also seems to me, that Prokesh is exaggerating somewhat. . . .[58]

Mehmet's seapower continued to expand at a dazzling pace; the Egyptian navy now possessed twenty-seven warships mounting 1302 guns and manned by 13 155 crew. In less than three years, the Egyptian navy had built six line ships; these were the *al Qahirah*-100 (also known as the *Misr*), the '*Akka*'-100, the *al-Muhallat al-Kubra*-100, *al-Mansurah*-100, *al-Iskandriyah*-96, and *Abu Qur*-84. The Alexandria Arsenal had built extensive numbers of smaller vessels, including most of the fleet's seven frigates: *al-Jafariyah*-60, *al-Buhairah*-64, *Kafr-al-Shaikh*-60, *Rashid*-64, *Shir[-i] Jihad*-60, *Dimyat*-56, and *Miftah-el-Jiha*d-62. The fleet also included the corvettes *Tanta*-24, *Palang[-i] Jihad*-22, *Jamah Bahri*-22, *Fuwah*-22, and *Jihad Paikar*-22; brigs *Samand[-i] Jihad*-18, *Shahbaz[-i] Jihad*-18, *Timsah*-16, *Washintun*-22, [*Washinton*], *Bad-i Jihad*-10, *Shanin[-i] Darya*-22, *Sa'igah*-20, and *Feshna*-20. The Fleet also had the cutter *al-Nuzhah*-4, six fireships and thirty transports.[59] In the six years following Navarino, Mehmet had purchased and built a fleet nearly as large, and in many ways, superior to his sovereign's.

The Sultan was sufficiently alarmed by this growing menace to attempt to restrict the flow of naval stores to Egypt. Timber exports from Moldavia through Galaţi had been worth 500 000 francs in 1832; after the wood was floated in large rafts down the Danube, it was shipped to Constantinople.[60] In an attempt to deprive the Egyptian navy of further shipbuilding supplies, Sultan Mahmut now forbade its export to Egypt.

Given Mehmet's recent treaty acquisitions, this restriction was less of a blow than it might have been. With the Kütahya peace, Mehmet acquired Cilicia; 'The plains of Cilicia, 25 leagues long and 12 to 15 wide. . . dominated by mountains covered with good building timber, could easily by itself supply a significant amount of trade'.[61]

In the tense post-Hünkâr situation, the Turks began to deploy their naval units more forcefully. Pirates were not the only problem facing the Ottoman navy; a revolt on Samos required quelling. On 27 April 1834 a squadron under the command of Vice-Admiral Hasan weighed anchor from Constantinople to go and blockade Samos.[62] Hasan had twenty ships; the rest of the Fleet was readied, and messengers were sent to Tunis and Tripoli with orders to send xebecs and tartans. In addition, 'a considerable levy of seamen has been made'.[63] Four warships sailed for Tripoli from Constantinople on 7 September 1834 to support Ali Pasha, who was engaged in a civil war.[64]

News of the Ottoman cruising on the North African coast was badly received in Egypt; Mehmet told the Russian consul,

> I will command my fleet in person, and if the Ottoman squadron comes to pass Rhodes, I will consider this as a hostile act, and I will not hesitate to engage in battle. . . Yes, I swear, if we come to blows, not one of the vessels of the Grand Seigneur will return to Constantinople.[65]

No skirmishing occurred, however, and on 13 October the Ottoman Fleet returned to its anchorage off Beşiktaş in the Bosphorus.[66] Despite the lateness of the season, a substantial portion of the Ottoman Fleet was kept ready for sea. Two three-decked line ships, three two-decked line ships and two frigates remained ready to sail at the Tersane-i Amire, while two corvettes and a brig were anchored off Tenedos.[67]

Like Mehmet, Mahmut was also attempting to upgrade his fleet as quickly as possible; nineteen ships were nearing completion in Ottoman shipyards, among them two three-decked line ships of 120 guns, two two-deckers with 90 guns, two two-deckers with 70 guns, seven large frigates, three corvettes, three steamers and a smaller ship.[68] Mahmut was following Mehmet's lead in another area as well; seven new warships were being built abroad, including a 74-gun line ship. Among the available resources was 'timber of the finest quality' in Trabzon; other naval stores were also exported from the region.[69] Timber was also exported from Ereğli on the Black Sea coast, and warships were occasionally built there.[70] Although the majority of the Ottoman Fleet vessels were built in the Tersane-i Amire shipyards in Constantinople, other Empire shipyards built warships; a 60-gun frigate on a slipway in Mitilini was 'nearly ready' for launching.[71]

The overall effort of the Ottomans was still very uneven, however; the Ottoman naval yard at Rhodes had launched its last frigate in 1832. As it had remained on the stocks for more than twelve years, many of its timbers had rotted and had to be replaced.[72] The use of unseasoned wood only compounded the shipyards' inefficiency. The Turks possessed sufficient supplies of timber; the Black Sea coast, the

Bay of Nicomedia, Karamania and the Principalities were all rich in wood, especially ship timber.[73] The Turkish dilemma was efficiently to utilise its resources, a problem exacerbated by a shortage of suitable personnel. Twelve officers were sent abroad to study, with eight going to Vienna, and two each to Paris and London.[74] In addition, a colonel and two captains were doing 'un voyage scientifique' through Europe The Turkish ambassador in London had fourteen officers attached t his suite, of whom four were in naval school; a number of Turkis officers also studied in Paris. Turkish officers were not alone in Portsmouth; the Egyptian Yusuf Efendi studied gunnery there aboard HMS *Excellent*-76.[75]

Besides increasing the efficiency of its naval forces, another problem that the Ottoman Empire shared with its northern neighbour was improving its merchant marine, the 'nursery of seamen' labour pool that might prove decisive in a future conflict. The relative lack of a Turkish commercial fleet meant that most of her trade, like Russia's, was carried by foreigners. The Trabzon–Constantinople trade was largely monopolised by Genoans and Ragusans, while much of the rest of the traffic had percolated into the hands of the Greeks, who had recaptured 'a good portion of the trade of the Black Sea.'[76] A survey of the Greek merchant marine found of the kingdom's 2683 vessels, 1107 ships were involved in trading with Turkey.[77] For both Russia and the Ottoman Empire, the post Hünkâr period was one of steady economic growth.

Despite the fractiousness which the Hünkâr treaty introduced into Russia's relations with Western Europe, it did have one immediate and positive result for Russia; with its barring of foreign warship passage through the Straits, Russia was now formally freed from overt Western aid and interference in the Caucasus insurgency. The Caucasian rebels presented Russia with severe strategic and tactical military problems, which increased the value of any non-military solution. The most important component of a bureaucratic approach to the Caucasus 'question' was trade. Many in the government hoped that this would prove more successful and less costly than armed conflict, as 'nothing draws peoples together as much as trade; nothing is able more quickly and assuredly to weaken the hostile tendencies of peoples as much as trade links with a civilised people...'.[78] It was hoped that the eastern Black Sea ports acquired under the Adrianople Treaty, especially Anapa, would become important enterpôts for Russian trade.

This commerce was initially modest; in 1833 the total value of Russian trade through Anapa with the indigenous tribes was a mere

10 112 rubles in goods and 3485 rubles in cash. Native 'exports' were valued at 13 809 rubles in goods and 119 currency rubles. The most valuable single import was 2418 rubles worth of white linen, while the mountaineers 'exported' 396 head of cattle to the Russians, worth 7222 rubles.[79]

Trade with the Georgian capital Tiflis presented further difficulties, the usual routes for goods were down the Volga through Astrakhan and across the Caspian to Baku, then overland to Tiflis, or across the steppe through Ekaterinograd, Karbarda and along the Georgian Military Highway. Enterprising merchants experimented with finding more profitable routes. A Georgian trading house now investigated with two different itineraries. Iron goods produced in Moscow were sent in April down the Volga to Astrakhan; shipped across the Caspian to the Terek, they were then floated upriver to Kizliar and then sent by land to Tiflis via Ekaterinograd, Karbarda and the Georgian Military Highway. The second load was sent from Moscow in May down the Volga as far as Dubovka, where it was portered to the Don at Kachalinskaia Stanitsa; the goods were then floated downriver via Azov to the Black Sea, landed at Redut-Kale and sent to Tiflis by road.[80] The goods shipped by the Volga-Terek route arrived in Tiflis in mid-November 1834, while those sent through Redut-Kale had arrived in mid-July; freight charges on the merchandise sent through Redut-Kale were less than two kopecks per pound higher than those levied on the first shipment.

Despite these attempts to increase foreign commercial interest in Georgia, governmental restrictions hindered the growth of the region's international trade; foreign trade was still to be confined to Anapa and Sukhum-Kale.[81] Sukhum at this time was hardly a major emporium:

> Sukhum made a most unfavourable impression on me. The bazaar, located in front of the fort, consisted of not more than a dozen mud shop-taverns, in which were indiscriminately displayed for sale wine, vodka, tobacco, saddles, weapons, beef, salted fish, vegetables and the rudest Turkish cloth. The shopkeepers were Greeks or Armenians. . . .[82]

Russian short-sightedness in restricting trade on the Black Sea coast to one or two sites was largely responsible for its small volume; Vorontsov estimated that between Anapa and Redut-Kale there were up to twenty-five coastal locales suitable for establishing emporiums; he particularly valued Pshade.[83] In the conflict between security and commerce, the need for security won.

In contrast to legitimate commerce, smuggling flourished; the Circassians still carried on 'un commerce actif' with the Turks, especially those based in Trabzon. The Turks brought gunpowder, lead, arms, salt, household utensils, cotton cloth and textiles which they traded for hides, beeswax, honey, nuts, fruit, and cereals and slaves. Russian attacks on beached craft would be met by hundreds of warriors, while the ship was hauled to safety. One observer noted a large number of light vessels hidden in the forests and bushes between Gelendzhik and Gagra; another traveller found contraband vessels hidden only seven miles from Gelendzhik.[84] As well as attacking the smugglers, Russia attempted to halt the traffic by appointing port agents in Turkey who put pressure on local officials and merchants.

Lazarev's defensive concerns were divided between an immediate requirement for light, numerous boats for maintaining the Caucasus blockade, and the long-range need to sustain heavier forces of a more strategic nature. He now wrote to Menshikov about the need to augment Sevastopol's defences:

> They are as necessary as they are essential, and I somehow believe, that if Your Highness does not participate in the fortification of Sevastopol (knowing you as an engineering enthusiast), then this port will remain in its remoteness, perhaps for a long time, as it was fifty years ago....[85]

If Lazarev's remarks on Sevastopol's defences caused irritation and disquiet in St Petersburg, then his subsequent secret report on the Black Sea Fleet ships themselves must have produced an uproar. Of the Fleet's twelve line ships, the *Parizh*-110 and *Parmen*-74 were 'completely worthless'; to correct their defects, 'it would be necessary to alter all their above-water sections, which would be extraordinarily expensive...'; Lazarev estimated the total cost of the *Parizh*'s work at 687 586 rubles, and the *Parmen*'s at 407 917 rubles. Associated problems would render all such corrections temporary, and the subsequent sums involved after only a year or so would be so substantial that it 'would not cost more to build new ones in their place'.[86] In contrast, the complete cost of building and commissioning a 100-gun line ship was 800 000 rubles.[87]

Worse news followed. The *Pimen*-84, *Panteleimon*-84, and *Ioann Zlatoust*-74 had 'extremely extensive rot' which demanded 'almost complete replacement'. The *Imperatritsa Mariia*-84, *Chesme*-84, and *Shtandart*-44 had all had basic refits the previous spring, when so much rot had been discovered that was untreatable without drydocking the ships, that they would 'not last three more years'. The same life-span applied to the *Tenedos*-60, *Erivan*-60, and *Arkhipelag*-60. Lazarev concluded, 'from such a survey of the Black Sea Fleet, in the course of a short period of time it will necessarily be deprived of seven line ships and four frigates, or more than half of its complete strength'. In addition, the yacht *Utekha*-10 was being rebuilt due to extensive rot, as was the frigate *Flora*-44. The *Merkurii*-20, *Orfei*-20, *Solovei*-12 and *Lastochka*-12 all needed re-timbering above water, while at the end of the current campaigning season the *Akhiollo* and other transports would have to be hauled onshore for work, along with the steamer *Meteor*-2 and brig *Georgii*.

Lazarev referred back to Greig's report of the previous year, which proposed a construction rate for the Black Sea Fleet of two line ships, a frigate, and several smaller ships every two years; current shortages in trained shipbuilding personnel alone would render this a difficult, if not impossible, rate of production. Lazarev concluded by requesting permission to hire civilian carpenters when necessary, a practice followed in St Petersburg and Kronstadt 'in extremely large numbers,' along with a sufficient sum of supplemental money to be made available for such hirings. Of the line ships needing extensive rebuilding, the oldest were the *Pimen*-84 and *Parmen*-74, both built in 1823; the youngest was the *Parizh*-110, commissioned in 1826. Of the frigates, the *Shtandart*-44 had been launched ten years previously, while the *Erivan*-60 and *Arkhipelag*-60 had been launched only in 1829.[88]

The real condition of the Black Sea Fleet was not known to the British or the French, however, who continued to see it as extremely menacing. Sir James Graham outlined a sufficient British response to the Board of the Admiralty;

> ...the paramount importance [is] of keeping at all times ready to receive men, 12 sail of the line, and 6 large frigates, in addition to the ships which may be, in commission. France, Russia, all the naval powers keep constantly a large proportion of their fleet in this advanced state of preparation...[89]

The Royal Navy now sent an officer to southern Russia to inspect these worrisome developments. In December 1835 Lazarev wrote to Menshikov about Captain 'Drinkworth's' (sic) visit; he had asked for plans of the *Tri Sviatitelia*-120 under construction; in return, Captain Drinkwater promised to send from England plans of the *Medea* steamer. Lazarev added that initial surveys of the Black Sea would be completed during the next year and a general chart was to be drawn up, on which work had already begun. As the Pulkovo observatory was to be built, perhaps the Tsar might want to base all new charts' longitude meridian measure on the new observatory, 'in place of Greenwich or Paris', in which case the necessary coordinates were to be forwarded for inclusion in the new charts.[90]

The Russian army was also busy; on 22 July 1836 General Vel'iaminov began a long campaign overland from Ol'gin to Gelendzhik, which lasted until 14 November. The pace was slow due to the terrain and the mountaineers' attacks; the Russian columns often covered only three or four miles per day.[91] The campaign resulted in the construction of the Abin fortification; the 6000 men and twenty-eight cannon were continually harassed by the mountaineers, whose equipment included eight light cannon that had been given them by the Pasha of Anapa before his surrender in 1828.[92] The Russians suffered sixty-two dead, four hundred and eight wounded, and three men captured.[93] A high casualty rate would become chronic among troops operating in the coastal zone.

The coastal forts that were established in the course of the campaigns were of little real value, or so it seemed to troops in them. One soldier wrote of his time in Ilori,

> The Ilori 'redoubt,' barely able to qualify for the title, is an irregular pile of mud at the aforementioned spot, where breastworks were later to be erected; placed within its boundary walls was a company of a Georgian grenadier regiment. The soldiers lived in shacks built from stakes and reeds, and literally wallowed in mud. ...It was difficult to understand for what purpose a redoubt was erected in Ilori, where it defended nothing besides its own soldiers.[94]

For the ships manning the blockades things were little better, as a tour of duty lasted six months.[95]

Despite the burgeoning Russian coastal presence, the guerillas continued to inflict increasingly substantial losses on the Army of the Caucasus. Following a successful attack from seaward by the mountaineers on Bombori, General Rozen and Admiral Lazarev were ordered to agree on the number of ships necessary to secure the coast. Rozen wanted a squadron in Gelendzhik of one frigate, eight smaller ships, six iuls, and eighteen Turkish kochermas. Rozen felt that the Turkish vessels would be more suitable for the shallow inshore work than the larger ships of the Fleet. The kochermas were to be armed with falconets and under the control of the customs establishment.[96]

Rozen wrote to the Russian consul in Trabzon about the possibility of acquiring the vessels there; they would cost 655–89 rubles each, but as their sale was limited to Turkish subjects, an approach through the Foreign Ministry would be best.

Lazarev was outraged; it would be impossible to allow the Russian naval standard to fly from such 'disgraceful' vessels. Their main advantage was that they could work close inshore and be hauled ashore where the Fleet's larger ships couldn't operate; for preventing smugglers from reaching the open sea, Lazarev felt that a force of twelve schooners and cutters would be best.[97] The fact that the larger ships of the Black Sea Fleet were often unable to capture the smaller, more nimble Turkish vessels had been an object of concern for some time; many army officers felt that the solution lay not on the sea, but in an expanded military presence on the coast. General Vel'iaminov observed,

> Experience has shown that our warships cruising the eastern shores of the Black Sea were not in a condition to track and capture the Turkish vessels supplying the mountaineers with supplies and military goods.... Turkish boats are very small and skillfully concealed in the mouths of rivers . . . where they are unable to be pursued by larger craft. A better means of halting Turkish trade with the Circassians is the construction of small forts in all places where the Turkish ships put in. To break the mountaineers' relations with the Turks is important because if from the Kuban we will be able to make raids on Circassian lands, to trample down their fields and drive them always farther into the mountains where they have little pasturage, then not having a supply of grain from the sea, they will be exhausted and in several years will submit to us....[98]

The danger that blockaders faced increased as the weather turned cold. One fierce autumn storm in 1834 sank more than thirty commercial ships, mostly Turkish; Greek, Ionian, Austrian and Russian craft were also lost.[99] Despite the hazards of navigation so late in the season, by late October southern winds blowing for several days had brought a 'great many' merchantmen to Odessa, while more than one hundred were reported in the Black Sea as sailing towards the port.[100]

In contrast to the growing Russian naval presence on the Caucasian coast, Russian maritime policy towards Turkey was marked by the greatest moderation, in spite of Hünkâr 'advantages'. When Lazarev in late 1834 recalled the *Aiaks*-20 and *Paris*-20 from the Aegean, and

ordered the *Themistokl*-18 to Greece,[101] continued British and French
sensitivity to the passage of warships through the Straits led Butenev
to recommend that 'preferably only small ships' be sent for the use of
the Russian mission, a suggestion that Nicholas approved.[102]

Nicholas's restraint towards Turkey was in increasing contrast to
British policy; in Constantinople, the Russophobe British ambassador
was not hesitant about using his ability to call in the Royal Navy.
When Ponsonby learned of a plot against Sultan Mahmut during the
last week of January 1835, he feared that the Turks would send for
Russian aid. Frantic appeals to Vice-Admiral Rowley arrived at Malta
on 3 February; ships were prepared in three days of intense labour,
and the ships reached Urla on 14 February.[103] In addition to Rowley's
ten ships (including five line ships), HMS *Edinburgh*-72, HMS *Vernon*-
50, and HMS *Endymion*-50 were sent to Smyrna, where they joined the
sole French line ship in the Levant, *Ville de Marseilles*-76.[104] Rowley's
squadron remained idle at Urla for over a month, where 'Its presence
produces no more sensation among the Turks than King Log's among
the frogs...'.[105] Despite such idleness due to the lack of a definite
'threat', the British Mediterranean squadron continued to be maintained at a much higher level than before the Hünkâr İskelessi Treaty;
it now numbered fifteen warships (of which six were line) mounting
772 guns, and manned by 5595 men.[106]

Aware of Ponsonby's inclination to use the Royal Navy at the
slightest opportunity, on 16 March 1835 the British government
cancelled his authorisation to summon unilaterally the Mediterranean
squadron to Constantinople.[107] Despite Wellington's personal scepti-
cism of the Russian 'threat', the spectre of the Russian navy increasing
its influence in the eastern Mediterranean at the expense of the Royal
Navy continued to haunt British governmental policy. Three days
before Wellington reined in Ponsonby, the House of Commons
discussed the upcoming Navy Estimates. When one MP suggested
that the number of Navy personnel ought to be cut to 20 000, Sir
James Graham rose up to defend the Royal Navy:

> [Graham]...could not conceal from himself the fact, that many
> large and effective fleets were maintained by foreign powers
> ...Russia had a fleet of 27 ships in the Baltic, and 12 ships in
> the Black Sea. And he would remind the house that the present vote
> would furnish men sufficient to man any ten ships of the line.[108]

In reality, Russian naval power was not quite so menacing. Nicholas
now settled on a total of sixty-nine warships for the Black Sea Fleet,

which, when implemented, would give the Black Sea Fleet the actual number of ships which Graham stated that they already had. The Black Sea Fleet estimates included three 120-gun line ships, twelve 84-gun line ships, four 60-gun and three 44-gun frigates, and two naval steamers. If there was a new threat to the Royal Navy's influence, it was that the Black Sea Fleet was now under the capable command of a Royal Navy-trained officer who might completely overturn the inertia of the Greig years.

Lazarev was beginning to achieve results; in 1835 the Black Sea Fleet received four million rubles over its regular budget allotment to finance new warship construction. The money was to be used to build three 84-gun line ships in succession, and to buy oak ship-timber 'necessary for the incessant construction of ships, located on the slipways'.[109]

Lazarev was not the only officer in southern Russia looking for additional funds; as the war in the Caucasus expanded, pressure continued to grow among local officials for an expanded military–naval presence on the Black Sea coast. The governor of Kerch-Yenikale recommended fortifications at all coastal points between Anapa and Mingrelia frequented by smugglers, with military operations to be mounted from the sites already occupied.[110] Smuggling continued to be a major problem; the British consul in Odessa put the number of vessels in 1835 either captured or destroyed by Russian cruisers along the Caucasian coast between forty and fifty.[111]

The human cost of manning the coastal forts remained high; service in Gagra was sufficiently grim for a Decembrist assigned there to request that his case be raised with the Emperor for a possible transfer:

> But I'm convinced that His Imperial Majesty in promoting me to . . . Gagra did not intend [this], as fatal as this coast of the Black Sea is, buried between scorching sun and cliff, devoid the year round of fresh food and water, and even air. . . . For me, already half-dead, Gagra will be an inescapable grave. . . .[112]

To the men in the Coastal Line, the short-sightedness of governmental policy was all too evident;

> In St Petersburg they did not suspect that we were having to cope with a half-million people in the mountains who were never unaware of their power; brave, martial in their mountainous thickets of impenetrable forest, which presented a strong natural fortress at every step. There they still thought that the Circassians were not

more than rebellious Russian subjects, transferred to Russia by their legitimate sovereign the Sultan in the Adrianople Treaty![113]

While the Caucasus increasingly distracted Lazarev's attention and resources, the continuing unsettled state of Egyptian–Turkish relations, combined with Western European hostility, began to force the formulation of a commensurate Russian response. Contingency plans were now drawn up for Black Sea deployments in wartime. In January 1836 Lazarev received a secret despatch in which Menshikov asked for Lazarev's opinions on three possible scenarios: 1) the arrival of an enemy fleet in the Bosphorus before Russian troops could manage to stage a landing there, and its subsequent entry into the Black Sea; 2) if a hostile fleet entered the Black Sea while the Black Sea Fleet had already weighed anchor for the Bosphorus; 3) if a superior enemy fleet appeared before Sevastopol which forced the Fleet into the harbour, what possible defensive deployments might possibly be made.[114]

Lazarev felt that the appearance of an enemy fleet in the Black Sea would be linked to Turkish agreement to allow its passage. Should the Hünkâr prohibitions remain in force,

> ...in such an event it would be unforgivable [for us] not to carry out successfully a Bosphorus landing before the appearance there of the enemy squadron, providing only that the troops appointed for this would be gathered in complete readiness...

Lazarev had definite views about the second scenario;

> ...it would be necessary to return quickly to Sevastopol and disembark the troops, for in meeting the foe, all disadvantages would be on the side of the ships carrying troops, who would be encumbered with a quantity of equipment which due to a lack of space is usually stored between the guns.

If the Fleet then went to sea without amphibious forces, the question of attacking or retreating would depend on the strength of the enemy.

In answer to Menshikov's final query, Lazarev had a number of suggestions. The ambassador in Constantinople should have a steamer at his service at all times, in order to be able to relay intelligence about enemy movements. Should they appear before Sevastopol in overwhelming strength, successful defence would depend on the fortifications which Lazarev had been trying to convince the government to build:

The main defence of Sevastopol consists of the good condition of its fortifications (of which there are none presently), skillful gunners and a sufficient number of infantry in the event of a landing, without which a decisive blow is not possible...

Lazarev filled the remainder of the report with grim news about shortages, rot, and a lack of personnel.[115] Menshikov replied to Lazarev's request for the Pulkovo coordinates by informing him that they had not yet been accurately determined, and it was consequently 'not necessary to wait for them to publish a map of the Black Sea'.[116] The Navy Minister then added:

The [British] papers tear us to pieces... our Treaty with Turkey still completely blinds British perceptions, though I don't presume any activity, for they would lead Europe into a general war. None the less caution is necessary, and these reasons were the basis for the demand for us for information about the arming of the fleet.

This prudence was echoed in the government's trade policy. Russian attempts to expand trade in the Black Sea still involved the two-pronged approach of encouraging foreign merchantmen on the one hand and stimulating indigenous trade on the other, an approach that would involve little direct governmental spending. Nesselrode still believed that steam communication between Greece, Constantinople, and Odessa would prove unprofitable:

To establish steamships solely for transport only a bit more prompt and slightly more regular than our current political correspondence, the game is not worth the candle. The sad reports from Greece arrive for me too quickly. In any case, this project is premature.

Nesselrode did favour the establishment of regular steam service between Odessa and Redut-Kale.[117] Steam communication between Odessa and Constantinople had been established in August 1831 when the *Neva* began making a regular passage.[118] Two years later the Black Sea Steamship Company was established, chartered for ten years.[119] The government had helped the Company to acquire three steamers, and regular steaming began in 1834.

While deferring to Nesselrode's doubts about an extensive Black Sea–Mediterranean service, the Council of Ministers decided to establish regular steamer service between Odessa, the Crimea and Azov ports.[120] Three steamers were required; the *Petr Velikii*-2 was built in England, while two other older Russian-built ships were

acquired, the *Naslednik* and *Odessa*. Russian steamers were not alone
in the Black Sea; a British steamer now began to ply regularly
Constantinople–Samsun–Trabzon route, while the next year an Ottoman steamship began covering the same route.[121]

The increasing importance of the southern trade to Russia was
reflected in the trade statistics. Russia overall ran a slight trade deficit
– in 1835 total exports were valued at 227 174 351 rubles, while imports
totalled 250 994 338 rubles. This compared unfavourably with 1834
exports of 230 419 880 rubles against imports of 218 093 352 rubles.[122]
The Baltic still accounted for nearly three-fourths of Russia's foreign
trade. In contrast to the Baltic, however, the Black Sea–Azov region
had a favourable trade balance, with 1835 exports totalling 35 875 213
rubles and imports valued at 19 953 957 rubles. Major Russian exports
were agricultural; the most valuable items were wheat (11 576 738
rubles), sheepwool (6 384 800 rubles), and hemp (6 327 860 rubles).[123]
The most important imports were fruit (3 315 405 rubles), wine
(2 689 802 rubles), and lamp-oil (low-grade olive 168 oil, 1 972 446
rubles). Agricultural products were shipped largely through Odessa,
while industrial goods came largely from Taganrog via the Don.

Despite Taganrog being the second largest port in southern Russia,
it had a number of drawbacks. Its shallowness meant that ships
drawing more than twelve feet of water had to stand twenty miles
out to sea, and receive their cargoes from lighters.[124] The harbour's
silting up was aggravated by ships dumping their ballast there, and the
harbour froze up earlier than Odessa.[125] In order to stimulate trade
through the port the payment of duty on foreign trade was postponed.[126]

Odessa became increasingly preeminent in Russia's Black Sea trade,
despite the government's modest efforts to diversify; of the two-
hundred and sixty-two Russian ships which arrived back in Russian
ports from abroad during the first six months of 1835, fifty-five
returned to Odessa out of a total of sixty-five ships for the entire
Azov–Black Sea region.[127] This prosperity could be jeopardised by a
revitalised government in Constantinople. Mehmet Ali represented a
mode of westernisation that could transform the moribund Ottoman
Empire into a much more difficult neighbour.

Mehmet had now a navy numbering forty vessels – eight line, six
frigates, four corvettes, seven brigs, fourteen transports and a cutter;
three additional 100-gun line ships were on the slipways, along with a
60-gun frigate and a transport.[128] Completion of the line ships would
give him an operational strength that was one line ship more than

Admiral Lazarev's. Egyptian naval innovations consistently surpassed Turkish efforts. French officers had armed the Egyptian ships with standardised artillery and ammunition, which simplified supply problems and made the ships' gunnery more efficient.[129] The Ottoman Empire was mobilising as quickly as possible to cope with the Egyptian threat, while Mehmet continued to press the westernisation of his navy as quickly as possible on a large scale. His interest in seapower rivalled that of Lazarev. In his 'Report on the political and moral state of Syria and the Egyptian Government', Wood noted that the needs of the Egyptian fleet meant that 60 000 trees were to be felled, 'the greatest part of these cut down and sent'; in order to process the lumber, the population of the entire district from Alexandretta to Adana had been mobilised.[130] Mehmet attempted to guarantee his supply of ship-timber by establishing a government monopoly over all timber cut in the Lebanon.[131] Given its proximity, this force could be a greater threat to Sevastopol than the Royal Navy.

While Lazarev wrestled with the knotty problem of building a balanced fleet that could both operate effectively off the Caucasus as well as conduct a 'preemptive' Russian strike on the Straits, some thoughtful Royal Navy officers were wrestling with the knotty problem of Lazarev and the Black Sea Fleet. A Royal Navy officer in September 1836 put the Russian force at thirty-four operational warships, including ten line ships, eight frigates, eleven brigs, and four corvettes.[132]

This estimate bore little relation to the condition of the forces actually under Lazarev's command. Despite his strenuous efforts, Lazarev again sent to Menshikov a dispiriting report about the Fleet. The *Kniagina Lovich*-44, *Arkhipelag*-60, *Tenedos*-60, *Panteleimon*-84, and *Paris*-20 brig were all 'extremely bad', and 'after a thorough examination by a commission, are fit only for one more campaigning season'. The *Shtandart*-44 and *Ioann Zlatoust*-74 both required complete underwater retimbering. The *Merkurii*-20 had just been repaired and relaunched; the ship was 'entirely new' except for her keel and two futtocks. Rot was also appearing in the frigate *Flora*-44.[133]

Lazarev then returned to possible Anglo-French action in the Black Sea:

I reread several times with particular attention Your Highness's note...and...I venture to make some observations on...an attack by the enemy...with landings on our coast and the defence of Sevastopol, with the intention of inflicting the most damage... while conserving our Fleet as much as possible, in order that our Fleet can attempt to complete the dispersion of our foe. In the first place success in battle... ships... are completely manned to the limit of the... regulations... presently these levels are not met, and in the lower ranks the shortages are extremely pronounced. Secondly, I agree completely that it would be impossible to wait for a large-scale landing on our shores, if only because before the landing occurred, it would be necessary for the enemy to force vigorously through the Dardanelles and Bosphorus; but if his passage into the Black Sea in such circumstances was with Turkish agreement and if the main aim of Britain and France (united as allies) was truly the inflicting of a decisive blow at Sevastopol and the destruction of its Fleet, as all of its establishments are in this port, then the strengthening of our Fleet would put them in the position of landing an extremely sizeable force in the Crimea. But for all this it is impossible to state that by the time of the appearance in the Black Sea of a fleet we will have done a strong landing; a great number of merchantmen are required for gaining mastery of the Dardanelles and Bosphorus, while the northeast winds can produce great difficulty and a substantial loss of time. Consequently... would it not be preferable to preserve our Fleet from all harm....

The Fleet presence at Sudzhuk at this time was the *Shtandart*-44 (flagship), a corvette, two brigs and two smaller vessels.[134] In addition to the Fleet ships, each of the three commanders of the Coastal Line had access to steamers belonging to the Caucasus administration; each fort also possessed two barkases rowed by 20–30 men and armed with several small cannon.[135] The barkases were so useful for inshore work that 'the mountaineers feared them more than the cruiser squadrons'.

In the event of future conflict, any Royal Navy attempt to deliver a 'decisive blow' against the Black Sea Fleet via the Straits would prove increasingly difficult, due to the continuous improvements the Turks were making to the Dardanelles forts under the direction of Moltke and Copke.[136] While sites could be improved, the calibre of the men manning them was another matter; in attempting to clear the anchorage off Numasie, enthusiastic Turkish gunners sank an Ionian vessel anchored in the channel. The Kapudan Pasha explained to Lander that the incident had been a mistake, and offered compensation totalling £2000; 'fortunately', no one was hurt in the incident.[137]

The Pasha commanding the Outer Castles was ordered to find 4000 recruits aged 16–65, who would be trained by the forts' 500 gunners to form a militia which would serve for six months each year.[138] In view of the difficulty in locating the recruits, the required number was soon halved.[139] Further work included attempting to standardise the calibre and ammunition of each site as far as possible, with the exception of the large cannons.[140] Copke and Moltke continued to work throughout October 1836.[141]

The Straits were not the immediate site of confrontation between Russia and Britain, however; a British merchantman off the Circassian coast now brought the entire issue of the Russian blockade into sharp focus, and further soured relations between London and St Petersburg. On 24 November the *Aiaks*-20 under Lieutenant Vul'f stopped the *Vixen* off Gelendzhik, stated that the ship was trading in an unauthorised zone and had broken an established blockade, and that he would therefore have to take the ship to the Crimea to appear before an Admiralty court. The ship's owner told Vul'f that Britain had never recognised the blockade and that he would not allow the ship to be boarded. Vul'f replied that resistance would be met by the ship being sunk and sent the crew to battle stations, whereupon Bell surrendered. Taking Bell aboard the *Aiaks*-20, Vul'f sent a boarding party aboard the *Vixen*; the two ships then sailed for the Crimea.[142]

Lazarev was in no doubt as to the guilt of the British merchants; an Admiralty court declared the *Vixen* a prize, a verdict supported by Bell's admission that the ship had arrived in Sudzhuk-Kale with the specific intention of trading.[143] One of Sudzhuk-Kale's advantages for smugglers was that its depth was only eighteen feet, which barred the entry of large warships, and made the navigation of even light frigates extremely hazardous.[144] Lazarev reported that the merchantman was an 'extremely good ship', which had outsailed the *Aiaks*-20 on the passage to Sevastopol.

The first news of the *Vixen*'s capture was received in St Petersburg on 2 January 1837. Nesselrode was waiting for Lazarev's report before discussing the matter with the British ambassador, Lord Durham, and Nesselrode felt Russian rights were so strong that protests would be slight:

> After all the precedents, which we have taken so perfectly in the right order, the *Vixen* is declared to be a lawful prize, and her captain and above all Bell sentenced as smugglers.[145]

In Tiflis news of the *Vixen*'s capture aroused little comment.[146]

Nicholas's decision on the seizure of the *Vixen* was 'according to the contraband laws of all countries, the individuals who took part in this infamous expedition ought to be shot without mercy'; Nicholas, however, had pardoned Bell and the crew, and was to send them all at his own expense to Constantinople.[147]

In Constantinople reports of the seizure of a British ship off the Caucasus were originally doubted; the Russian position on trading there had been clearly established by the 1831 ukaz, as well as his note to the Turkish government and foreign ambassadors in September of that year.[148] At the time, Butenev's circular notes 'did not solicit the slightest remark...'; nor, in 1831–2 when Russian cruisers intercepted large numbers of Turkish ships off the coast and sent them as prizes to Sevastopol, did the Turkish government dispute the decisions.[149]

Nesselrode felt that a second investigation might prove useful, as the *Morning Chronicle* alleged that the *Vixen* had been delivering gunpowder. A search of the ship had found a wide cavity in its ballast, where it appeared that the gunpowder had been stored. Nicholas was making every effort to be fair in the case:

> before he decided to release the intriguer Bell, the Emperor wanted to know if he had had gunpowder on board the *Vixen*. As the visit to the ship had not found any, the Emperor had consented that he would be repatriated with the rest of the crew.[150]

Nesselrode felt that David Urquhart, the rabidly Russophobe first secretary of the British embassy in Constantinople, was behind the affair.[151]

Despite clear evidence of the blatant provocation that had produced the incident, Palmerston believed that the Russians' case for confiscation differed in two respects from accepted legal definition:

> This *Vixen* affair is very provoking.
>
> The fact is that Russia has never declared a blockade, but has established customs regulations confining commerce to one or two points where customs-houses are established, and pretends that ships trading to other ports on the coast are seizable as smugglers.
>
> Now to entitle her to make such regulations, she ought to possess the coast *de jure* and *de facto*. Her right *de jure* depends upon the Treaty of Adrianople, which conveys to her, not Circassia, but the sea-coast from the Cuban to St. Nicholas. But then arises the question, did the Turks possess that which they thus ceded, or, on the contrary, was not their occupation confined, like that of the

Russians at present, to Anapa, Poti, and one or two other points on the coast? . . . even at Anapa and Poti her garrisons dare not stir far from the glacis.[152]

On 24 February 1837 Count Vorontsov informed Nesselrode that Bell and the *Vixen*'s captain had arrived in Odessa prior to their repatriation to Turkey, and that he had met them both. Passage had been arranged on a British ship, which would sail when the ice in the harbour broke. His opinion of Bell was that he was a 'very intelligent' man who was 'very careful' in what he said. Bell persisted in his defence that he was a 'simple trader' looking for new outlets.[153]

In spite of Palmerston's spirited defence of his countrymen, the evidence against the *Vixen* seemed daunting; bolstering the Russian case was the deposition of a Circassian deserter at Anapa detailing the cannons, muskets, swords and gunpowder which had been offloaded in Sudzhuk bay the previous November.[154] The *Vixen* subsequently was taken into the Black Sea Fleet as a transport under the name *Sudzhuk-Kale*.[155]

The issue continued to inflame British politics, and on 17 March the *Vixen* affair was discussed in the Commons. After criticism of the government's handling of the situation, Palmerston rose to reply. He based his defence on the fact that the issue was not whether the blockade was valid and recognised by the British government, but whether the *Vixen* had breached Russian quarantine and customs regulations:

[Palmerston] wished to draw the attention of the house to the distinction that exists between a blockade, and the establishment of certain municipal regulations . . . I declined to give to Mr. Bell any communication as to what the bearings of the municipal regulations, established by Russia on the eastern coast of the Black Sea, might be upon the particular voyage he was about to undertake; but I referred him to the Gazette, where he would find that no blockade had been declared or communicated to this country by the Russian government, consequently none was acknowledged. This closed the correspondence.[156]

Palmerston's rhetoric soothed the more ruffled members of the Commons, and the motion to produce all relevant papers was dropped.

For the Russians the *Vixen*'s smuggling represented a continuing problem; the same day as the House of Commons debate, Butenev sent to Lazarev a despatch that seemed to confirm the possibility of further incidents with British merchantmen. Butenev's sources indicated that the *Wizard*, which was salvaging guns from the wrecks in Navarino harbour, would afterwards sail to Constantinople and then the Georgian coast with 'secret communications and supplies'.[157] The ship would be armed with several guns, and Urquhart's backing was again suspected. In addition, several British merchantmen in Smyrna were also loading with contraband for voyages to Abhazia. The intelligence was not conclusive, but Butenev wanted Lazarev to know so that he could augment coastal patrols should he feel it was necessary to do so.

If Bell had put the British government in the awkward position of clarifying its policy on an issue it would rather have ignored, it still remained to salve national pride. While Palmerston privately admitted his doubts about the legality of Bell's actions, he was not inclined to settle the matter quietly. Nearly six months after the incident Palmerston lectured Pozzo di Borgo, the Russian ambassador, on the subject of Circassian independence: 'l'Angleterre doit remplir son rôle *comme protectrice de l'independence* des nations...'.[158]

When di Borgo attempted to remonstrate, Palmerston grew more abusive; in commenting on the recent Turkish work in the Dardanelles, Palmerston stated that the Prussian engineers had been sent to the Sultan by Nicholas in order to avoid the public outcry that would have resulted from Russian officers. When di Borgo observed that the Turks as a sovereign nation had the right to fortify any part of their domains, particularly the maritime approaches to their capital, Palmerston interrupted him; 'Non, monsieur, il fortifie les Dardanelles *contre nous*, car il n'y a pas d'autre Puissance qui pourrait tenter de les forcer'. Tempers eventually abated and the *Vixen* ceased to be an issue the following month.[159]

If the resolution of the *Vixen* crisis temporarily shelved the issue of Circassian independence and blockade, Anglo-Russian interests still clashed in the Black Sea. About the same time as the *Vixen* incident the firm of Bell and Anderson based in Wallachia complained that their chartered British merchantman *Hero* had been fired upon by a Russian cruiser patrolling the Danube's entrance; later the firm protested that another vessel, the *Star*, had been wrecked at the Sulina Danube passage as a result of interference from a Russian cruiser.[160] The British consul in Iaşi believed the reports to be without foundation. As George Bell was the brother of James Bell of the *Vixen*, his suspicions were well-grounded.

The Principalities were sharing in the increasing Black Sea grain trade, due to enlightened trade policies introduced by the local government under Russian tutelage. Brăila had been declared a free port in 1836 and Galaţi the following year.[161] With the increasing prosperity of the lower Danube came pressure from Austria on the Turkish government to help open up the river entrances. The Austrians suggested that dredging and widening work be done on the St George Danube channel to allow the free passage of merchantmen. Its greatest advantage was that the channel lay solely under Ottoman control; other benefits would include a shorter quarantine, faster passage, and Turkish retention of all customs duties.[162] The disadvantages of the Sulina channel was not only that it was under exclusive Russian control; the shifting Sulina sandbanks had resulted in 1836 in the loss of two merchantmen.[163]

Grain was not the Principalities' only commodity. Wood exports were also increasing. Interest in timber was not limited to Turkey and Mediterranean countries, as Russia also considered importing timber from the area. Russian Crimean stocks of ship-timber were insufficient for all the Black Sea Fleet's needs. Short-sighted forestry policies followed by the great landowners there meant that the local timber resources were badly managed:

> It is really inconceivable with what rapidity the finest forests of the Crimea are disappearing; year by year whole hills are totally stripped, and the government. . .takes no means to check this fatal devastation.... Several great landowners. . .cut timber as fast as possible. Foremost. . .is Admiral Mordvinof....[164]

A supplementary source of wood for the Fleet was timber rafted down the Dnepr, but in addition to problems caused by the wood's long immersion, shallow water in the Dnepr cataracts could hold up its passage; low water in 1835 and 1836 so diminished supplies that Lazarev was forced to halt work on the *Tri Sviatitelia*-120.[165] Timber in Georgia was either in insurgent-controlled areas or decimated by the constant conflict:

> At the present time. . .are preserved only those woods over forty years old, which old settlers of the region assure us were once extensive. Russian settlements were surrounded by mountaineer brigands, who hid in the local woods, which allowed them the chance to raid the settlements. The settlers were thus forced to destroy deliberately the forests. As a consequence of insufficient

visibility the process of destruction was carried through to completion, and now the region is extremely poor in wood. . . .[166]

Exploitable wood was in sufficiently short supply in Guria for the
government to bar its export 'for the time being'; the ostensible reason
was that the Crown forest had not yet been properly delineated.[167]

Given the increasingly valuable resources in the area, the Russian
government began to expedite the development of the communication
and transport infrastructure of the Black Sea littoral. Beginning in
1837, the following five years saw a burst of activity in the Black Sea
Fleet's mapping and surveying of the eastern coast. Lieutenant
Rodionov surveyed the Cape Adler roadstead in 1837, while the
following year midshipman Akimov charted Sudzhuk-Kale bay.[168]
In 1839 Akimov took detailed astronomical observations from ten
fortified sites along the coast. Additional astronomical sitings were
made in 1840 from positions along the Black Sea northern and eastern
coasts, and followed up with supplemental data from other surveys. In
1841 Captain-Lieutenant Egor Pavlovich Manganarii took trigono-
metric and topographic measurements of Sudzhuk-Kale bay and
measurements between Sevastopol and the western Turkish Black
Sea coast, while Lieutenant Rodionov surveyed Sukhum.[169]

The value of these surveys was profound. By the measurements in
the 1842 atlas of the Black Sea published by the Black Sea Fleet
Hydrographic Department, a 1772 French chart[170] had placed the
eastern Black Sea coastline from Batum to Cape Adler thirty-five miles
to the northeast of its actual location, while the Kerch Straits were
forty miles out of place.[171] Later maps and charts had considerably
reduced these discrepancies, but so recent a work as Gote's 1822 chart
had still placed Poti four miles northeast of its true position. The Fleet
had to wait until 1851 for a government guide to the entire Black
Sea.[172]

Accurate navigational aids were also essential to the safe passage of
Russian troops and supplies on the eastern coast, as movement by
land between the various forts continued to be hazardous and risky. In
1837 the Black Sea Coastal Line was strengthened by the construction
of fortifications at the Pshade and Vulani rivers, while a naval
expedition was mounted to capture Cape Adler (Konstantinovskii),
where Sviatoi Dukha was built. On 22 May 1837 Lieutenant-General
Vel'iaminov led troops out of Ol'gin towards Abin; from there, the
soldiers marched to the mouth of the Pshade to begin building
Novotroitskoe, remaining on the Pshade from 1 June to 22 July.[173]

Sniping and skirmishing took their toll of the Russian troops, who lost fifty-five dead since they quitted Abin.[174]

Despite the continuous Russian possession of the Caucasus shore for eight years, the scope and savageness of the conflict continued to grow. Constant skirmishing forced the Russians to defoliate the forests around their positions; around Abin the trees had been felled for three to four miles in all directions in an attempt to lessen the risk of ambush. The guerillas had the occasional help of committed British Russophobes playing the 'Great Game'; while the Russians were skirmishing on the Pshade, the Englishman Longworth was 'advising' their war council,

> to storm one of the other fortresses, Gelendzhik or Aboon, while the enemy was occupied with the new erection on the Pchat, but they did not relish the suggestion. . . .[175]

For the Russian soldiers, such caution from their opponents would have provided a welcome respite. The calibre of the infantrymans'' weapons and marksmanship was not all it could be, a fact ruefully acknowledged by one of the expedition's officers;

> our infantry were very badly armed and shot poorly; in respect to this, the enemy enjoyed a great superiority over us. I can't say that the mountaineers were excellent shots, but their muskets and rifles . . . were far more accurate than our weapons, and for defensive purposes they were able to conceal themselves and await our approach. They utilised the terrain very skillfully, and with instinct the mountaineers combined a remarkable bravery and ease of movement in the mountains.[176]

When the palisades at Novotroitskoe were completed, the Russians marched down the coast to the Vulani. Construction was begun on the Mikhailov position, which occupied the Russians until mid-September.[177] Cape Adler was taken by amphibious assault on 18 July 1837. Russian casualties were nineteen killed and forty-four wounded. Construction of the fortress took until mid-November, with a further loss of thirty-one dead and one hundred and fourteen wounded.[178]

While the Army of the Caucasus suffered badly from the mountaineers, in operations near the coast they had a valuable ally in the Black Sea Fleet. The Black Sea Fleet had a increasing capability for amphibious operations: each line ship carried two barkases armed with two cannon and two falconets, each of which could carry seventy men. Every line ship also carried two polubarkases; armed with two cannon, they could each carry thirty men.[179] Every line ship also possessed two light twelve-oared cutters. A 100-gun line ship had the potential to carry and land 460 men (equivalent to more than half its complement of crew) for amphibious operations.

The potential of Russian armed forces to pacify the region overrode the immediate difficulties in the Caucasus to convince some optimistic officials who felt that the region had a great future; one stated that in terms of natural wealth, Imeretia, Mingrelia and Guria were the equal of France and Italy.[180] While he conceded that 'the ports of these provinces are very deleterious to health', Tribodino felt these problems could be avoided by building flat-bottomed steamers which could navigate up the Rion river, opening up the inland areas to trade. In addition to the valuable timber resources, the lush semi-tropical climate could be used to grow lemons and oranges, while sugar-beet cultivation and refining could produce a revenue of more than 2 500 000 rubles per year.

The military reality of the area continued to be rather different; as General Vel'iaminov noted, 'As long as we are unable to maintain communications by land between the forts, it is necessary to move by sea on warships...'.[181] While Russia's long-term needs stipulated a strong 'blue water' fleet on the Black Sea, Lazarev had also to develop an extensive local force for the tedious blockade and amphibious operations along the Georgian coast. The unsettled international situation in the eastern Mediterranean continued to fuel the naval arms race, especially in the Ottoman Empire, where Mahmut's desire for revenge was an added incentive.

Like Lazarev, Sultan Mahmut was stymied in his search for naval superiority. Like the Black Sea Fleet, the Ottoman Navy was still plagued by a shortage of suitable sailors. One of the best sources for skilled mariners were the Greek Aegean islands still under Ottoman rule. Fermans were now sent to Tenedos, Limnos, Imroz, Samothraki and Mitilini to enlist a certain number of Greeks for the Ottoman Fleet.[182] The officer corps was also in dire need of improvement. According to one British officer, only eight officers in the Fleet could determine their latitude by observation and calculations; for longitude they relied on 'dead reckoning'.[183] There were no regularly published Turkish nautical tables, while insufficient fluency in foreign languages prevented the use of foreign compilations.

While these second-rank naval powers struggled to overcome these obstacles, Western European perceptions of the threat posed by these efforts continued to grow. Despite consistent Russian forbearance in utilising its advantages (according to Western European judgements) granted by the Hünkâr İskelessi Treaty, misinterpretation and hostility were now a constant feature of Russian diplomatic relations with France and Britain. The Russian government now briefly considered an action which would have confirmed Britain's deepest suspicions. Tsar Nicholas considered sending two line ships and one or two sloops from the Baltic to the Mediterranean; after stopping and replenishing in Sardinia, they were to pass the Straits and join the Black Sea Fleet.[184]

Unlike Nicholas and Menshikov, Nesselrode was under no illusions that the projected cruise would benefit Russia in any sense whatsoever. His views on the closure of the Straits to all foreign warships in peacetime were identical to those upon which Palmerston based his diplomacy;

> In the midst of the difficult . . . circumstances in which the affairs of the Orient are found, Your Majesty has invariably adopted as a principle to put in order the security of the southern province of Russia rigourously to watch that the entry to the Dardanelles remain closed to foreign flags of war.
>
> This principle, in accord with interests well understood and the ancient political traditions of the Porte, has come formally to be enshrined in the treaty concluded between Turkey and England in 1809.
>
> It is this gap that our treaty of alliance of 26 June-8 July 1833 has served to fill.[185]

It was only a 'special exception' that fermans were granted to light warships to pass the Straits for the use of the Russian representative in Greece; such rights did not extend to all Russian warships.

> The Adrianople Treaty, confirmed by that of Constantinople, stipulates explicitly in our favour the free passage of *merchant* ships; but no provision allows us to demand, in the Bosphorus, the admission of our *warships*.

Nesselrode felt that if a request was made and refused, Russia's prestige would suffer, while if the Russian request were granted, Britain and France would immediately attempt to pass a squadron of their own into the Black Sea. Nesselrode was strongly against the projected voyage, and it was subsequently shelved.

The Baltic units that Nicholas considered transferring to the Black Sea would have been of little real use in the Black Sea Fleet's Caucasian campaign. Russian control of the eastern Black Sea coast continued to be contested by their obstreperous subjects, which in turn hardened governmental resolve to bring its recalcitrant citizens to heel. 1838 saw further construction on the coastal fortification system with the most vigorous campaigning so far, which included most ships of the Black Sea Fleet. On 25 April a landing at Sochi was successful, at an eventual cost of thirty-one Russian dead and one hundred and seventy-seven wounded. After the landing construction immediately began of Fort Aleksandrovsk, which was completed eleven days later. Five days later six infantry battalions and twenty-two cannon under Major-General Simborksii were landed at the mouth of the Sochi river in Ubykh territory to build Fort Navagin.[186]

On 24 May there was a second amphibious landing at Tuapse. Major-General Nikolai Nikolaevich Raevskii commanded eight infantry battalions, two companies of sappers and four Black Sea Cossack infantry regiments, armed with twenty-eight cannon.[187] The troops spent the next month building Fort Vel'iaminov; to reduce the chance of sniping, all vegetation was felled for nearly a mile around each site.[188]

Added to the Russian battle-losses were now some inflicted by nature; one of the Black Sea's worst summer squalls raged over two days in June, causing great havoc among merchant and naval shipping on the Caucasus coast. Lazarev assessed the damage to the Fleet:

> As far as the ships go, then the tender *Skoryi* and transport *Lanzheron* do not constitute a great loss for the Fleet. But it is impossible not to regret the loss of so many officers and men, or the beautiful steamer *Iazon*, the *Themistokl* brig and *Luch* tender, all brand-new ships of excellent quality....[189]

Lazarev was determined to replace the *Iazon*-7 as soon as possible; the Fleet needed another steamer, 'if not so large, then at least one hundred horsepower...'; Lazarev hoped to acquire two other steamships, if possible by May 1839.[190] Lazarev requested that the Tsar allow the ships to be bought in London, as he believed that the ships could be purchased more cheaply in Britain than in Russia. Besides Fleet losses, the great storm of 11–12 June wrecked fifteen merchantmen.[191]

It had been a difficult summer for the Russians; besides the naval and mercantile losses, the three expeditions to fortify the coast had cost over six hundred dead and wounded. The forts all shared a number of characteristics – their locations were unhealthy and isolated, and provisioning had to be done largely by sea. Complete control of the surrounding countryside by the mountaineers made the garrisons prisoners rather than pacifiers. Among the additional hazards of serving in the Abin and Nikolaev positions were 'two or three old Turkish cannon' which the mountaineers sporadically used to fire on the forts; such attacks occurred 'without doing especial harm, but keeping the garrison in a constant state of anxiety'.[192]

The coastal fort troops' sense of isolation was increased by still being visited by warships only once or twice a year. Rostov was the major supply point of the forts for both provisions and military supplies.[193] The fortification project continued; in the following year the last two forts in the Line were completed. Fort Golovin was built at Subashi, which was taken by amphibious assault on 15 May at a cost of twenty dead and one hundred and seventeen wounded. Fort Lazarev was later built at Psezuape in six weeks between early August and mid-September. The hasty erection of these forts meant that like the earlier constructions, they did not have the design that gave them the strongest and sturdiest topographical profile, and in consequence, they were undermanned.[194]

While Lazarev did not have to worry about Georgians attacking Sevastopol, he continued to be concerned about the increased possibility of an attack by foreign navies. Lazarev's efforts to increase Crimean security at Sevastopol were aided by the development of a bombardment gun for shore defence, which had a range of over a mile and a projectile weight of 108 lb.[195] Artillery for both the fortifications and the Fleet was supplied by the Lugansk Factory in Ekaterinoslav province.[196]

Menshikov shared Lazarev's concern about security, and reported to Nicholas about possible Fleet mobilisation in wartime. In accordance with the discussed 'forward projection' scenarios, the Black Sea Fleet would transport two divisions without horses or supply trains in two trips to the Bosphorus; for this it would be necessary to assign to the Fleet administration up to one and a half-million rubles in order to purchase and store the necessary naval supplies. Nicholas wrote extensive comments on the report:

It is all very good; order the provisions to be prepared; about the money, I have given orders to the Finance Minister, and you are now able to demand it from him.

Our actions will have to be swift and decisive, in order to take the Bosphorus, and perhaps the Dardanelles; for this it is only necessary to transfer more troops.

It is to be understood that if we were late, it would be not to the business of the landing, but to the defence of our shores. It is to be understood that we are not able to remain at home, and if the enemy visits us, we will array against him an equal strength, sufficiently strong to remain at sea and await the weather. When the weather is appropriate, I will send infantry directly to Tsargrad [Constantinople].[197]

Menshikov wanted more specific information about the Fleet's mobilisation capabilities.[198] The Chief of the Main Naval Staff was interested in four areas: 1) what money would be needed to acquire naval stores and arm the entire Fleet for a six-month campaign involving the transport of a 9000-men landing force; 2) if it was presently possible to sail with such a force, how long could it remain at sea before it required resupply; 3) if it was currently impossible to go to sea without fresh supplies, what time would be needed to procure and load them, and 4) did the Fleet possess the capacity to take either two divisions or 18 000 men to two points in Abhazia.[199]

The Black Sea was not the only area of naval interest to St Petersburg; as in 1831, Egypt was also attracting attention.

Mehmet-Ali is forcing us to cautious measures. I believe that all will end amicably and that the despatch of our troops to the Bosphorus will not be necessary, but the Emperor would like to be prepared for action where necessary and against whomever necessary. The main question to be resolved now is what measures to take in order to arrive in Constantinople before the British and French if under some pretext they conceive the idea of appearing before the walls of the Seraglio in order to destroy our influence at the Porte. There is no other remedy other than being ready to act at the first receipt of news. But if the Turks in the Dardanelles do not detain the foreign fleets, then we will hardly be able to arrive in time.

What measures are you thinking of taking for the winter? It is impossible for the fleet to remain armed due to the expense, and because this would obviously reveal our intentions or expectations. . . .[200]

Despite such interest in prophylactic measures, Russian interpretation of its Straits passage rights continued to be strictly defensive; on

3 September 1838 Nesselrode told the British ambassador in Vienna that the Hünkâr Treaty 'did not secure to Russia a right to pass her fleet through the Dardanelles'.[201]

While Russian naval forces continued to operate under governmental restraint, Nicholas's Black Sea Fleet caused increasing disquiet among certain visionary Royal Navy officers, among them Captain Charles Napier, future conqueror of Acre. Napier numbered the Black Sea Fleet at twelve first-class line ships, ten 60-gun frigates, four 24-gun corvettes, and ten 20-gun brigs, contrasting it with the current British Mediterranean squadron of seven line ships, and the combined Turkish–Egyptian strength of nearly twenty line. Napier was in little doubt as to whom Nicholas intended to threaten with his fleets;

> It was never before known in the history of England, during a profound peace, that a foreign power kept a fleet of nearly thirty sail-of-the-line within a few days sail of our own shores, without our having a fleet to protect us....[202]

If Napier had been aware of the rate of construction of Russian merchant shipping, its extent would doubtless have infuriated him still further. In 1838 6681 vessels were built for internal trade, at a total cost of 6 128 883 rubles.[203] This was not as impressive as it might have been; the previous year 8197 craft had been built, at an average cost per vessel of 1527 rubles.[204] Despite Russia's modest but energetic interest in the carrying-trade of the Black Sea, the quality and relative cheapness of her naval stores made them a popular item of export, despite their military potential to possible enemies. Prior to the Hünkâr Treaty there had been a certain amount of trade between Russia and Turkey in naval materials; the Turks had imported various naval stores from Odessa, among them iron, sail-cloth, cordage and anchors.[205] Russian supplies to Greece of naval stores were also significant; 'Turkish and Greek wharves are equipped exclusively with Russian rope...'.[206] As always, Russian participation in the Aegean carrying trade was slight; of the 4811 ships arriving at Siros in 1837, only sixty-two were Russian.[207]

This modest but steady improvement was reflected in the government's trade statistics. The total value of Russian exports in 1838 was 313 525 687 rubles, which represented an increase of nearly 50 000 000 rubles on the previous year's trade. The largest single item of export was now grain, with the value of 1838 exports being 53 048 374 rubles, a figure nearly double two years previously when grain exports had had a total value of 25 497 952 rubles. Shipping in Russian ports was increasing as well; in 1838 6001 ships entered Russian ports, 741 more than the previous year.[208]

This growth in the southern regions continued, but in a lop-sided manner despite governmental efforts to diversify. Odessa's preeminence in Russia's Black Sea trade was now firmly established; in 1838 exports through Odessa were worth 38 380 000 rubles.[209] Seven marine insurance companies now operated out of the port. The importance of the port was underlined by a grant of 502 700 rubles to build a mole to protect the harbour and provide for a small commercial shipbuilding yard.[210] Exports from the Black Sea ports (excepting Odessa) in 1838 were worth 26 134 827 rubles; Odessa accounted for 59.4 per cent of the region's total trade.[211]

Such prosperity carried a naval commitment; for the growth of southern Russia's trade to continue, it was necessary that the Ottoman Empire remain peaceful and the Straits stay open. This tenuous stability was now directly threatened by increasing Egyptian unrest. The Sultan had never been fully able to accept the terms of the Kütahya peace. Mahmut now resolved to attempt to throw Mehmet Ali out of Syria, and began to prepare the war. The Turks shipped 50 000 rifles off to be used by Syrian insurgents and the Ottoman government bought up all powder depots in the empire, which had been banned from sale from the previous three years.[212] In view of the imminent conflict, particular attention was paid to preparing the Ottoman Fleet; the 'armament of the whole fleet is being actively carried on....'.[213] In early March 1838 the *Phocien* steamer purchased from France arrived in Constantinople, while a steamer designed and built in the Tersane-i Amire underwent its sea trials and fitting-out.[214] Fleet personnel also received foreign stiffening; a Captain Tylden, formerly of the US and Brazilian navies, arrived in Constantinople in mid-March, where he was promptly given command of a brig.[215]

Despite such ominous war preparations in the East, the British government continued to be largely mesmerised by the Russian 'threat'. During a discussion in the Commons in March about the Navy estimates, Wood of the Admiralty was asked if the British Channel Fleet would be able to repel the twenty-six line ships of the Russian Baltic Fleet, or if the Royal Navy Mediterranean contingent was a match for the sixteen line ships of the Black Sea Fleet. Wood stated that the Channel Fleet could cope with any threat from the Baltic, while the Black Sea Fleet contained nine line ships, *not* sixteen; the British fleet 'on that station are in a condition to meet the Russian whenever occasion offers.'[216]

Mahmut's reforms had worked substantial improvements in the navy. An indication of the increased efficiency of the Ottoman Navy was the despatch of a twenty-three-ship squadron (which included six line ships and six frigates) to the Macedonian coast in July to deal with an outbreak of piracy.[217] The cruising again aroused suspicions in Alexandria that a Turkish attack was being readied. Mehmet had his fleet put into readiness:

> ...and the Pasha declares that the appearance of a single warship of the Sultan in Syrian or Egyptian waters, that is to say, on this side of the islands of Rhodes or Crete, in the present circumstances, will be regarded by him as a provocation and in consequence as an act of aggression, and he will not hesitate, in that case, to fight.[218]

As a result of the Turkish deployments the Egyptian fleet spent August and most of September incessantly cruising the Egyptian and Syrian coast.

Mehmet's restlessness was again followed closely in St Petersburg, and intervention was again considered if events made it necessary. Menshikov once more inquired about the Fleet's preparedness and ability to carry two divisions of the 5th Corps to either the Bosphorus or the 'Circassian shore'. Lazarev replied that the Fleet would be held in complete readiness at all times 'if not for a six month campaign, then at the very least for a four month one'.[219]

On the question of beating the French and the British to a landing in the Bosphorus, the Fleet would have to be kept in 'constant readiness to sail at the first order', and northern or northeasterly winds would be necessary. Lazarev suggested a number of preparations that the Fleet could make despite its usual winterisation procedures; with such preparations, the necessary ships could be ready to sail two days after receiving orders. The main shortcoming to such a projected expedition would be the lack of a suitable troop collection point; no such locale existed in Sevastopol, and if the Fleet had to sail to Odessa to embark troops, not only would time be lost, but ice in the harbour there might make embarkation impossible. Britain was attempting to stiffen the Ottoman Navy against attack by either Egypt or Russia by allowing Royal Navy officers to enter Turkish service.

While the Russians discussed sending ships to aid the Turks, the British continued with the idea of sending personnel. On 29 October 1838 the Admiralty informed Commander Massie that an appoint-

ment on a Turkish ship was available; he could go out to Constantinople with Commander Legard, who was to be offered command of a
frigate, while Lieutenant Foote of HMS *Sapphire*-28 would be offered
command of a corvette.[220] Massie was to have the rank of Commander in the Turkish navy, at an annual pay of £400; should the
circumstances require it, he might occasionally have to command a
vessel smaller than a frigate. Massie's half-pay as a Royal Navy
Commander was to continue during his Turkish employment. The
Lords of the Admiralty were explicit about his service in the event of
conflict;

> You have their Lordships' permission to remain in the service of the
> Ottoman Porte, in the event of a War between Turkey and any other
> country except England, but you are of course at liberty to retire
> from Turkish service when you may think proper to do so....[221]

Prejudice against foreigners still ran deep, however, and Ponsonby
eventually wrote that, following a conversation with the Ottoman
Foreign Minister, he saw 'no hope' that the Porte will give the
'command' of an Ottoman warship to any foreigner.[222]

Given the relative lack of success of his threats, Palmerston now
attempted to bargain directly with Nicholas about the mobilisation of
his naval forces. On 29 December 1838 the Foreign Minister wrote to
Ambassador Clanricarde outlining the British Government's views.
Clanricarde was to state that Her Majesty's Government would
'probably feel it their duty' to propose to Parliament early in the
following year an increase in the British 'Naval Force'. Palmerston
was blunt about the reasons for the increase:

> The main ground upon which a larger Naval force is considered
> requisite for Great Britain is the great extent of naval armament
> maintained by Russia....[223]

The size of the increase would be proportional to the number of
Russian ships mobilised for spring operations;

> For in the midst of profound Peace, when... Great Britain, France,
> the United States and all the other Maritime Powers of Christ-
> endom, with the single exception of Russia, have long ago placed
> their Fleets upon a Peace Establishment, Russia alone keeps up Her
> Naval Armaments upon a War Footing.

Palmerston numbered the Russian fleet as 27–28 line ships in the
Baltic, and 12–14 line in the Black Sea.[224]

These views were not 'official', and Her Majesty's Government 'by no means partake in these opinions and apprehensions....'. If the Tsar would agree to mobilise a percentage of his warships, then the British government could allude to the fact in Parliamentary debates, and the Royal Navy increases might be avoided. Palmerston suggested that the Baltic Fleet mobilise one division of ships and one-third of the Black Sea Fleet for the upcoming year.[225] If the Russians objected to the British naval presence in the Mediterranean, Clanricarde was to point out that it consisted of 8–9 line ships, which were not a match for the Black Sea Fleet, but perhaps a match for Mehmet's navy. While the Black Sea Fleet didn't immediately threaten England, it was 'kept up with a view to intimidate, if not to attack Turkey'.

Clanricarde did not feel that the Russian naval forces represented a direct challenge to British seapower;

> The Emperor is certainly very anxious to have a powerful and efficient Navy, but I do not believe that this desire is combined with any particular, or ambitious project.
>
> His Imperial Majesty seems to have conceived notions of the identification of a Navy with the memory of Peter the Great, and with Russian greatness, which he vainly endeavors to impress upon his people, and which he will not readily lay aside.
>
> The Emperor's Nautical passion is not shared, or admired by his subjects, who place little confidence, or affection in their Navy....[226]

Turkish preparations continued for the imminent conflict; besides arming the Fleet and army, in all of the Dardanelles forts sites large mortars were being prepared; all the work was *highly* secret.[227] A second clash was inevitable; when war broke out less than two months later, it differed from the 1831 conflict in that the Sultan was now the aggressor.

5 The Second Egyptian Revolt and an Uneasy Peace

'Perhaps all of the naval policy of Egypt from 1830 to 1840 can be explained by this single consideration by which Mehmet Ali, without ever having articulated, but rather obeying his instinct, an awareness that the Navy is the element which, in times of peace, determines the ranking of nations.'[1]

'In an audience. . . the Emperor entreated that. . . the maintenance of tranquillity depended on the strength of the British Navy, adding that he could put soldiers on board his ships, but that his own Navy was a forced Plant, and without a Commercial Navy he could never get sailors.'[2]

'No invasion of Syria, it is well known, is to be feared from the side of Egypt, from any army which cannot command the co-operation of a powerful fleet.'[3]

Turkish mobilisation produced an inevitable reaction in Egypt; on 11 March Mehmet gave orders to prepare the navy for sea.[4]

Russian inclinations were not to act unilaterally under the Hünkâr Treaty in order to support the Turkish aggression; Nesselrode was 'confident' that Mahmut would maintain the peace, but felt it was essential that the Russian and British ambassadors 'hold to the Divan the same language on that subject'.[5] Clanricarde reported from St Petersburg that the other ambassadors were convinced that Nicholas sincerely desired that conflict was avoided, and he agreed with their observations. The Russian disinclination to aid Turkey was made clear to the other European powers; Granville stated that he had received information that Butenev had informed the Turks that military assistance would not be provided if they initiated hostilities.[6] Despite this Russian inclination to neutrality, the Sultan still declined to hire any of the Royal Navy officers sent out from London, remarking,

It appears from enquiries made that there are fifteen or sixteen English Naval Officers employed as instructors in the Ottoman Marine, and that there is no need of more.[7]

Such modesty did not influence Mahmut's determination to crush Mehmet, however; on 21 April 1839 a Turkish army of 20 000 men under the command of Hafiz Pasha crossed the Euphrates near Bir.[8] Syria was in open rebellion; harsh Egyptian taxes and conscription policies had done much to incite revolt. An observer saw little chance of the uprising succeeding, 'because. . . he (Mehmet) brought all of his army and navy against them'.[9] The chance to strike back at Mehmet when he was distracted by the revolt was an opportunity that the Sultan could not resist.

Unlike the torpor he displayed in 1831, Palmerston moved quickly. His intentions were from the beginning to bind tightly Turkish policy to British designs, not allowing Russia a chance to intervene unilaterally. Reşit's discussions with Palmerston began the last week of April and continued for nearly a fortnight, during which time a draft treaty of alliance was quickly hammered out. The treaty would allow British warships to detain not only Egyptian warships and merchantmen, but declared that the Ottoman fleet would stop and search neutrals, and if they were found to be carrying 'warlike stores and provisions' for the Egyptians, their cargoes would then be seized. The Turkish and British fleets were 'to act in concert on the coasts of Egypt and Syria'.[10]

In his calculations Palmerston considered many scenarios, including the possibility of an Anglo-Turkish war against Russia. Palmerston persisted in viewing Russian policy as specifically directed towards weakening the Ottoman empire by encouraging diversity in its military forces:

[the Turks] send pupils for instruction in small numbers to 3 or 4 different countries & to encourage them to take officers of all lands: Italians, Prussians, Frenchmen, Austrians, etc. etc., each of these instructing his battalions according to the school of his own country and thus producing a chaos of tactics in which Turks and Christians must lose all fixed object and aim.[11]

The author of another memorandum written for Palmerston's consideration saw a possibility of a Franco–Prussian–Russian alliance against Turkey. In the event of a Russian attack on Turkey, a joint 'coup de main' against Constantinople was,

> only possible if the Russians remain masters of the Black Sea, but as the result of an Anglo-Turkish League, would be the immediate destruction or blockade of the Emperor's naval forces in the Euxine, it cannot be reasonably admitted that a similar surprise deserves to be considered as feasible after the union of the Allied Squadron.

In pursuing a land war against Russia on her Black Sea coastal areas, '20 000 English troops on either front, using the Black Sea for transport would probably decide the campaign'. If Russian forces should manage to occupy Constantinople

> *before* the British fleet reaches the Marmora & can join the Turkish fleet, the *expulsion* of the Russians (if possible), from these points – (once firmly occupied) – will be a matter of no usual exertions and sacrifices.

Basing the Royal Navy at Malta was useless in such an event; the fleet would have to be based 'within a *few hours* sail of the Dardanelles...'.

Such aggression by the Russians against the Ottoman Empire was pure fantasy; Russian naval forces were at the time involved in 'coups de main' against their own disaffected subjects on the Georgian coast. Amphibious landings on the Georgian coast had increased in both frequency and size since the first one in 1837. On 14 May 1839 a unit under Lazarev's command anchored at Subashi.[12] In one of the largest operations to date, the squadron contained the *Silistriia*-84, *Imperatritsa Ekaterina II*-84, *Pamiat' Evstafii*-84, *Sultan Makhmud*-86, *Adrianopol'*-84, the frigates *Brailov*-44, *Agatopol'*-60, and *Shtandart*-44, and five smaller ships; this was nearly half of the Black Sea Fleet's capital ship strength.[13] Some troops were disembarked that evening, while the rest were to be put ashore the following morning. The mountains suddenly blazed with several thousand fires which burned all night, 'presumably to warn us that they were prepared for us...'.

The next morning after a heavy fog lifted, over 3000 mountaineers were observed drawn up into columns. After a fifteen-minute bombardment to soften up the landing site, Lazarev embarked 2700 soldiers into boats for the landing. Shallows prevented the larger ships from getting closer than three miles, while many of the mountaineers were able to take refuge from the bombardment in ravines and gullies. After returning 'extraordinarily strong fire' the insurgents threw themselves on the Russians with 'the greatest frenzy'. The skirmishing was vicious enough for the Russian troops to make repeated use of their bayonets. Despite the insurgents' custom of retrieving their dead, they left forty-eight corpses on the battlefield. The Russians lost one hundred twenty-eight men.[14]

Farther south things continued to grow more unsettled. In Constantinople the Ottoman Fleet was readied for sea; on 22 May Ponsonby was informed that the Fleet would operate from Jaffa, and part of it would sail in two days; the Kapudan Pasha would shortly follow with additional ships.[15]

The two Muslim navies were by now roughly equivalent. Mahmut had thirteen line ships – the *Mahmudiye*-120, *Selimiye*-126, *Fethiye*-96, *Makademi-Lair*-76, *Burj(i) Zafer*-74, *Bekberi-kufret*-74, *Mesudiye*-118, *Fivrie*-74, *Teṣrifiye*-96, *Ainduie*-74, *Tifihie*-74, *Nizamiye*-72 and *Nuzretiye*-72. The Turkish Navy had nine frigates; the *Ṣerefresan*-64, *Hifzirraman*-52, *Mazkheri-Tersik*-48, *Mezimi Zafer*-52, *Annibakh*-50, *Parlibakh*-44, *Iaveri-Tersik*-50, *Qa'id Zafer*-52, and *Zafer*-48. In addition, there were two other frigates, a half-armed seventy-four gun line ship and a fifty-gun frigate, built by the Americans in the Tersane-i Amire. The Imperial Fleet had six corvettes – the *Mesır(-ı) Ferah*-26, *Seri-Zafer*-26, *Mediafter*-26, *Rezemrazi*-26, *Medzhirai-Zafer*-26 (used as a prison hulk), *Hilâli-Zafer*-26, and an American-built corvette-26. The Fleet's two brigs were the *Manzur'e*-16 and *Teozi-Sifind*-16. In addition, the Fleet possessed eight cutters, one goelette, six cannon boats and two steamers. A frigate and line ship were building, and a line ship was in the Tersane-i Amire being altered. The total number of ships actually ready for sea was less impressive; of the forty-six available warships, only twenty-six were seaworthy.[16]

In contrast, the oldest of Mehmet's eleven line ships was eight years old. Since 1831, the *Hims*-100, *Beylan*-86, and *Alep*-100 had been added to the Fleet.[17] His forces included the steamer *Nile*-2 which mounted two shell guns, making it one of the most progressive ships in any navy.[18] All the line ships had been built in Alexandria; in contrast, only two frigates, a corvette and a brig had been built there, as Mehmet preferred to purchase smaller ships abroad and husband his limited resources to construct those ships he was unable to buy.[19] In contrast to the Ottoman Fleet, nearly all the Egyptian vessels were ready for sea.

Despite Mehmet's qualitative edge, his forces were still in need of improvement. One of Mehmet's most trusted and knowledgeable foreign advisers now prepared a confidential report; Jomard's 'Notes' covered forty-seven folio pages, and contained a number of trenchant observations on the Mehmet's armed forces.[20] Jomard felt that the Syrian economy should be fully integrated with the Egyptian, in order to procure sufficient wood for the Fleet; in addition, a forestry school should be set up. The Naval Academy needed improvement, and ought to be merged with a remodelled Polytechnique, to create a sufficient number of sailors to allow Mehmet to dispense with using Greeks.[21] With Mahmut's attack, however, such improvements would have to wait.

The Ottoman Fleet weighed anchor on 8 June for the Dardanelles, where it was to remain for six to eight days before proceeding to Syria; 11 000 troops were on board.[22] Eight days later Mehmet's fleet began leaving Alexandria. When Campbell told Mehmet that its departure was 'a bad and useless measure', the Viceroy replied that it was not sailing with the intention of seeking out and destroying the Turkish fleet, but rather to protect the people and foreign interests in the Syrian coastal towns, which had been stripped of nearly all their troops as a consequence of the Sultan's hostile deployments.[23]

Despite Palmerston's intense interest in events in the eastern Mediterranean, British tardiness in agreeing upon joint instructions for their Levantine squadron distressed the French. Seven French line ships were already off Smyrna, another had sailed from Toulon for Turkey the previous day, while two more were soon to follow, producing a French presence of ten line ships, 'besides frigates and sloops'.[24] The French had no doubt about the effect the combined Allied squadron would have. With the British contingent numbering ten line and other smaller ships, Roussin's command deploying ten line and four or five frigates, with 'at least' four steamers and other lighter vessels, the Allies could force the Turks and Egyptians to negotiate. The Duke of Dalmatia saw an additional benefit in joint naval action in that it would lessen the chance of unilateral Russian assistance:

> leur développement, en rendait la guerre presque impossible, ôtera à la Russie tout prétexte de mettre en mouvement sa flotte de Sébastopol, ou même son armée de terre.[25]

He suggested an Austrian presence in the squadron of one or two frigates and light vessels, an idea that Metternich also favoured.

Like the British, the French were paying close attention to the unrest in the eastern Mediterranean. The need for augmenting French naval forces in the Mediterranean led the Minister of Marine to introduce a bill in the Chambre of Deputies on 25 May for a supplemental grant of 10 000 000 francs to cover mobilisation and additional building costs.[26] It seemed that Britain and France might work in close conjunction in resolving the crisis. Palmerston sent Granville a copy of the proposed orders for Admiral Stopford; despite his understanding with the French, he remained greatly concerned about the possibility of the Sultan calling in the Russians:

> The part of these instructions which relates to the possibility of the English and French squadrons going up to Constantinople in the event of a Russian force entering Turkish territory may require some consideration. It seems clear that such a measure would, in such a case, be highly desirable, and that it would be the best, if not the only way, of effectually counteracting the bad consequences which might result from the entrance of the Russians into Turkey; that if the movement were to be effected against a vigorous resistance on the part of the Turkish forts in the Dardanelles, it would be difficult to accomplish it, unless the fleet were accompanied by some force which could be landed to carry the forts by taking them in the rear. This operation would not be difficult, and would not require any large amount of force; for though the batteries are formidable against ships, on account of the narrowness of the channel, the strength of the current which sets downward toward the Mediterranean, and because at this time of year the wind sets chiefly the same way as the current, yet these forts are weak on the land side, and might be taken one after the other, by any moderate force which attacked them in the rear.
>
> It is probable, however, that if the Turkish troops were defeated and if the Russians had entered Turkey, the Sultan would cheerfully permit, if he did not actually invite, the British and French squadrons to go up to Constantinople, and as those squadrons would come as friends to protect the Sultan, and not enemies to attack him, it is difficult for the Russians to suggest to him a plausible reason for refusing to achieve a peaceful solution.[27]

As if to underscore the need for prompt Allied action, Mehmet now began to exercise his fleet off Alexandria. Stopford reported a squadron of ten line ships and two double-banked frigates cruising off Alexandria.[28]

The situation in Turkey was also shifting rapidly; on 24 June the Turks and Egyptians clashed at Nezib. As the Turks had more than 80 000 troops in Anatolia as opposed to 'not more' than 45 000 Egyptian troops in all of Syria, Hafız decided to go on the offensive. Ibrahim drew his 35 000 troops into four columns to attack the Turks, who had 30 000 regular troops, 111 cannon and 3000 Kurds.[29] The result was a rout in which 1000 Turks were killed and 17 000 captured, along with the Turks' entire artillery park; the Sultan could now muster only 15 000 men at Konya and 10 000 at Malatya with two hundred artillery to oppose a second Egyptian advance into central Anatolia.[30]

As if this were not a sufficient calamity for the Ottoman Empire, Sultan Mahmut died on 30 June. This was followed by the sudden defection of the Turkish fleet to Alexandria, which completely altered the maritime balance of power. On the morning of 4 July the Kapudan Pasha received official notification of Sultan Mahmut's death, and the accession of Abdulmecit I. That afternoon the Kapudan Pasha took a squadron of eight line ships, twelve frigates, a corvette, four brigs, three fireships and a steamer out of the Dardanelles on a course assumed to be for Syria.[31] According to the Kapudan Pasha, he was taking the squadron to unite it with the Anglo-French naval forces.[32] Off Tenedos the following morning the Turks met with Admiral Lalande, who was cruising with two line ships and a brig, and informed him that their destination was Rhodes. The squadron passed Rhodes on the night of 7 July.[33] Orders were received while the Fleet was near Castel Rosso to return at once to Constantinople.[34]

The news of the Kapudan Pasha's treachery had not yet reached Europe when Palmerston wrote to Ponsonby to direct him to state to the Porte that if the Turkish government asked for or accepted military or naval aid from any European power, 'Her Majesty's Government trust that the Porte will at the same time address itself to Britain to the same effect'.[35] Ponsonby was to state that Stopford possessed orders to go to Constantinople the moment a request was made for the British fleet, and that Roussin had received similar orders.

There was still a considerable variance of opinion between the European powers on how best to restrain Mehmet. Metternich was willing to allocate a role to the Russians that Palmerston could not abide; he suggested that if Mahmut's forces were defeated, a Russian army could occupy Constantinople, while a combined British, French, and Austrian naval squadron could pass the Dardanelles.[36] Events in Constantinople meanwhile continued to overtake diplomacy. Ponsonby received information that the Kapudan Pasha, Ahmet, had accused Halil and Husrev of murdering the Sultan, as they were Russian agents and determined to betray the Empire. Ahmet had decided to take the Ottoman fleet to Crete and offer it to Mehmet Ali.[37]

News of Sultan Mahmut's death reached Alexandria on 8 July; the next day a Turkish corvette arrived carrying Naip Bey, the Kâğıtcı of the Kapudan Pasha. Naip stated that the Fleet was at Stankio on its way to Rhodes, where it would be placed under the Viceroy's control if he would accept it.[38] The next day Akif Efendi arrived at Alexandria, sent by Abdulmecit to announce Mahmut's death. Akif brought despatches for Mehmet; before opening them, Mehmet told Campbell that if Ahmet offered him the Turkish fleet, he would not accept it; he would, however, attempt to mediate between Ahmet and Husrev.[39] Ahmet could stay in Egypt if he wished, and the Fleet sail without him.

Akif's despatches gave Mehmet nearly everything he wanted; a pardon, the right to hereditary succession in Egypt and for his family, and news that Turkish troops would be withdrawn from Syria. Mehmet now sent couriers to Ibrahim and ordered him to withdraw across the Euphrates.[40]

On 12 July the Turkish squadron met Mehmet's steamer *Nile-2* and sailed southwards. Two days later they joined eleven Egyptian line ships, three frigates and two brigs, cruising ten miles off Alexandria.[41] The Kapudan Pasha's intention to defect was not known to more than four officers, with the result that most of the Turkish warships cleared for action upon sighting the Egyptian fleet.[42] Two days later the combined fleets entered Alexandria.[43] Rear-Admiral Walker, one of the few Royal Navy officers that Mahmut had accepted, stated he was unable to serve under Mehmet Ali, and left for Constantinople.

Mehmet now possessed a formidable naval force – Egyptian naval personnel totalled 15 000 men, in addition to the 4000 Arsenal workers; combined with the 14 000 sailors of the Ottoman fleet, the Viceroy could field a force of nineteen line ships and fourteen frigates, manned by 33 000 men.[44] The Turkish contingent under Egyptian control totalled twenty-three ships – eight line ships, twelve frigates, three brigs and corvettes.[45] Five of the Turkish line ships remained outside Alexandria harbour, due to the restlessness of their crews; as a precaution, all their ammunition was unloaded, as well as the Fleet's war chest, which contained 5 000 000 francs (£120 000).[46] Unrest among the Turkish crews caused the Egyptians to land many of them.[47] In an attempt to placate the Turkish sailors the authorities sent fresh food supplies to the ships, while they exhorted the local populace to be friendly to their unexpected 'guests'.[48]

While the presence of the Turkish fleet gave Mehmet Ali a naval force far superior to the few ships remaining in Constantinople and a most valuable bargaining chip, he continued to pretend that both fleets were under the ultimate control of the Sultan. In an interview on 13 July Mehmet restated his loyalty:

> The fleet does not belong to me, it is the Sultan's, the same as my own, my army and all the countries under my command. Thus, whether the Ottoman Fleet is at Alexandria or Constantinople, it is always in the Sultan's dominions, and is able to be deployed according to his wish. If he wants it to return to Constantinople, he need only speak and I will go myself if he so wishes.[49]

Despite this massive concentration of seapower now under Egyptian control, Palmerston was determined to avoid any Black Sea Fleet ships passing the Straits and operating with European Levantine squadrons;

> ...there is a marked distinction between the co-operation of the four flags in the Sea of Marmora, or in the Bosphorus for the defence of Constantinople, and the junction of these flags in the Mediterranean'.[50]

Palmerston also authorised Ponsonby to offer the British squadron's aid to the Turkish government should Mahmut die; similar instructions were to be sent to the French admiral.[51]

Turkish Straits defences were still in a neglected state; Palmerston received a report on the Bosphorus and Dardanelles which analysed the possible Russian 'threat' from the north. The author (later to command Turkish forces in Syria) stated that a hostile Russian force attempting to occupy the Dardanelles via a landing north of Sestos could capture all important positions 'with a trifling loss if resistance were made, or possible'.[52] The Dardanelles fortifications would only protect Constantinople against an attack *'by sea'* from the *'Mediterranean'*; the Kapudan Pasha wanted to construct fortifications in the Bosphorus which would secure the channel from an attack from the north. The crucial difference between an attack from the north and an attack via the Dardanelles was that the Russians would always have the advantage of surprise, while a Mediterranean-based attack would be obvious well in advance; if the Dardanelles remained open to the Royal Navy Mediterranean squadron, then it would nullify any possible Russian advantage.

For their part, unlike Palmerston, the Turks seemed to view their southern 'threat' as the more menacing. Bereft of their fleet, the Turks continued to alter and improve their Dardanelles defences rather than waste resources on the Bosphorus channel. Large bronze ordnance were moved closer to shore and mounted in carriages in an attempt to increase their manoeuvrability, and earthern outerworks were constructed around the batteries. The Dardanelles forts now mounted 320 cannon, which threw a total broadside of 14 400 lb.[53]

Neither Mahmut's death nor the Ottoman Fleet's defection were yet known in London, so Palmerston continued to focus on the dangers of Russian intervention under the Hünkâr Treaty terms. On 18 July Palmerston further extended Ponsonby's prerogatives; should the Black Sea Fleet 'for any reason whatever' enter the Bosphorus, then Ponsonby was immediately to apply for British permission to do the same.[54]

Palmerston's reactions were not based on information from Russia. Reports from St Petersburg continued to indicate a sincere desire for cooperation:

> Upon every occasion Count Nesselrode has expressed to me the desire of the Russian Government to obviate the possibility of a *causus foederis* arising under the Treaty of Unkiar Skelessi. His Excellency has held the same language to all my colleagues, and I believe this desire to be sincerely and anxiously entertained.
> I have every reason to believe that the Sultan deceived M. de Bouteneff, and that his commencement of hostilities was as disagreeable to, as it was unexpected by His Imperial Majesty....[55]

Beauvale noted from Vienna that a likely precondition to full Turkish recognition of Mehmet's claims would be a limiting of his fleet, which would annoy France as they saw Mehmet's forces as a counterweight to the Mediterranean-based Royal Navy.[56]

The Allied Powers were in agreement that Syria, Crete, and Arabia ought to be returned to the Sultan's control. The Allies' seapower gave them the ability to enforce their will:

> ...if Mehemet Ali should resist, a little reflection will suffice to show what ample means of coercion the Five Powers possess. The fleet of Mehemet Ali, his communication with Syria, his capital, are all at the mercy of the combined squadron; his fleet might be taken and given over to the Sultan; all communication by sea with Egypt and Syria might be cut off; and though it is no doubt physically possible for him with time and expense, to send supplies to Syria by land across the Desert, yet there would be no great difficulty on the part of the Allies in cutting off that communication also, by occupying some position on the line of march.[57]

For whatever aid the Russians might or might not send, Palmerston and Ponsonby remained extremely concerned about the issue of warship passage through the Straits in light of the perceived Russian privileges under the Hünkâr Treaty. Ponsonby subsequently raised the issue with the Grand Vizier. The Grand Vizier stated that the Straits were 'very rigorously shut' against all foreign warships, and that the commanders of the Bosphorus and Dardanelles had orders to fire on any warships that attempted to force the passage.[58]

The Russian government was comfortable with the idea of the British and French handling the Egyptian crisis without direct Russian naval or military aid. Nesselrode considered an Anglo-French Mediterranean squadron as sufficient to compel Mehmet to surrender the Turkish fleet, and stated that he had 'no wish whatever' to have the petite Russian Mediterranean squadron act in conjunction with the Anglo-French squadron.[59]

In accordance with his orders, Admiral Robert Stopford now sailed to Besika Bay near the Dardanelles, where he was joined on 5 August by HMS *Powerful*-84, HMS *Ganges*-84 and HMS *Implacable*-74. Stopford's forces included HMS *Vanguard*-84, HMS *Pembroke*-74, HMS *Bellerophon*-84, HMS *Rodney*-92, HMS *Asia*-84, and HMS *Minden*-74 line ships, the frigate HMS *Castor*-36 and corvettes HMS *Tyne*-26, HMS *Daphne*-18, HMS *Hazard*-18, and the steamer HMS *Rhadamanthus*-1, for a total of fifteen vessels.[60] The French squadron there was of equal strength, with the nine line ships *Montebello*-120, *Hercule*-100, *Iéna*-90, *Jupiter*-86, *Santi-Petri*-86, *Diadème*-86, *Triton*-74, *Généreux*-80, and *Trident*-80, along with thirteen smaller craft.[61]

While Admiral Stopford was a moderate man, content to follow Admiralty orders, his second-in-command was of sterner stuff. Like Palmerston, Commodore Napier was not in any doubt as to the best use for the flotilla, feeling Russia to be a greater threat to the Ottoman empire than Egypt:

> If we are quite satisfied that Russia sincerely wishes to preserve the integrity of the Turkish empire, a fleet of nineteen sail-of-the-line in Busseejah Bay is quite unnecessary; and if we are not satisfied, a fleet there is quite useless....[62]

Napier felt that the Allied squadron should have sailed directly to Constantinople on the receipt of news of Mahmut's death.

The Anglo-French concentration of power off the Dardanelles brought back unpleasant memories for the Russian government. While the British were behaving responsibly, the French were less hostile to Mehmet, and the Russians were concerned that the French might force the Straits under the pretext of protecting Constantinople. In such an instance, the Russian ambassador would deliver a formal protest and then quit the Turkish capital:

> En 1833, nous avons protégé la Porte sans braver les Puissances de l'Occident. En 1839, les escadres étrangères, sans protéger la Porte, viendaient insulter la Russie...'.[63]

If such an event occurred, the Russians might not be able to deal with 'unwanted guests' as quickly as they might; the Black Sea Fleet was not the strong force that it continued to appear to the British and French. Lazarev again sent to Menshikov yet another disquieting despatch about the Fleet's actual state. The *Imperatritsa Ekaterina II-*84, *Pamiat' Evstafii*-84, *Chesme*-84 and *Imperatritsa Mariia*-74 all suffered from extensive rot.[64] Nor was this report an attempt by Lazarev to wheedle more money out of a parsimonious Exchequer; a British officer who viewed the Fleet at the time noted, 'half the fleet would not be able to stand the weather in the Black Sea in the winter'.[65] Lazarev requested additional funds to include a fourth line ship in his building program, as the 4 000 000 ruble supplemental grant that the Fleet had earlier received to build additional line ships would in fact stretch only to building three. The 1 000 000 additional rubles he requested would only be sufficient to build and fit out one line ship hull; any additional money needed he would have to attempt to squeeze from the Fleet's 1840 and 1841 budgets. Other immediate and necessary projects were sapping the Black Sea Fleet's financial reserves, especially the construction of Sevastopol's drydocks. These had been started in 1831 at the head of Korabel'naia Bay. The drydocks were to contain five slips, three for line ships and two for frigates. Fourteen thousand troops were involved in the excavations, in addition to the construction work on Sevastopol's Admiralty and fortifications.[66]

An Allied venture into the Black Sea could threaten or destroy all these undertakings, and Russia's extreme nervousness about possible Allied intentions under the guise of stopping Mehmet Ali was evident. Nesselrode regretted the movement of the Anglo-French squadron from its cruising off Alexandria to Tenedos off the Dardanelles. Clanricarde relayed assurances 'that the Russian Government are most desirous of avoiding any military demonstration, or any necessity for carrying into execution the main clause of the Treaty of Unkiar Skelessi...'.[67]

This nervousness extended to the Navy; Menshikov wrote to Lazarev about the crisis,

> The Turkish business grows more complex, dear Mikhail Petrovich, and the united Anglo-French fleet has not sailed from Tenedos, as it is awaiting our movements. Our policy is motivated by a general concern with the defence of the Sultan, with whom we are in alliance and inspiring the other powers to restrain the Egyptian pasha, along with the necessity of staying away from the defence of Constantinople. But it is impossible to predict the future....[68]

A certain symmetry still existed between the Allies' projected deployments; Granville informed Palmerston that a French fleet would be sent into the Sea of Marmora only if the Russian Black Sea Fleet passed the Bosphorus.[69]

Given the delay in communications, Palmerston attempted to improve Stopford's ability to react swiftly to changing events; on 23 August he directed the Admiralty to order Stopford to obey Beauvale's directions from Vienna, where the Powers were attempting to formulate a united response.[70] In the event of the French not issuing suitable instructions to their Levantine commander, Stopford was given the power to act independently if necessary.[71] In Constantinople work continued to try to outfit and strength the remaining Turkish ships; French officers from the squadron at Tenedos were working in the dockyard alongside the Turks.[72]

For Palmerston, the surrender of the Turkish ships by the Egyptians remained the most important immediate goal, 'an indispensable preliminary to any other arrangement whatever'.[73] His suggestions for concerted action should such a request be refused contained five main parts. 1) An Allied Anglo-French squadron should be off Alexandria, with some ships off the Dardanelles, to stop Ibrahim if necessary. Egyptian warships should be blockaded in Alexandria. 2) If the Turkish squadron remained outside Alexandria, attempts were to be made to get it to return to Turkey. 3) If the Turkish Fleet was in harbour, then a collective note from the Allied naval commanders was to be sent, stipulating its surrender within a specified time period. 4) If the squadron was surrendered, then it should cruise 'for some time' in the company of the Allies in order to ensure that no Turkish officers sympathetic to the Egyptians would attempt an attack on Constantinople once they had repassed the Straits. 5) If the demands for the Fleet's surrender were refused, then the five Consul-Generals ought to indicate their displeasure by quitting Alexandria; should this prove insufficient, the 'various other methods of coercion might be employed, without any positive attack on Egyptian ships'.

Among 'other methods' were the severing of all communications between Egypt and Syria, the capture of Egyptian merchantmen, or the seizure of Crete.

Such action would not be opposed by Russia; the British ambassador in St Petersburg continued to believe in the sincerity of Russian efforts to act in conjunction with British interests.[74] Despite this apparent bonding of Russian and British perceptions, French mistrust of Russian intentions became increasingly evident, with the French contemplating direct unilateral action to neutralise Russian influence in Constantinople. Soult informed Bulwer that in the event of Russian warships entering the Bosphorus, French warships would pass the Dardanelles and enter the Sea of Marmora.[75]

Despite being averse to direct intervention, Russian preparations for possible action in Turkey were underway in the Crimea for receiving a division of infantry to join the two already at Sevastopol, 'although 'tis well known that there are no means in the Peninsula of quartering more than a Single Division of Infantry during Winter....'.[76] On 1 September 1839 five line ships and a frigate had been sent from Sevastopol to the Georgian coast to pick up Raevskii's troops from Psezuape in order to transport them to Novorossiisk for future operations on the coast; they were now to complete this operation as soon as possible and return to Sevastopol.

A fortnight later Lazarev informed Menshikov that the Fleet was ready for possible intervention in Turkey except for a shortage of personnel; supplies had been loaded aboard for a four-month campaign and the ships were fully rigged and armed. If the dispute was quickly resolved, Lazarev wanted to put the Fleet back on its normal winter footing, as 'all possible economies are presently called for...; 'if supplies were left on the ships for long they were liable to deteriorate, while the ships' running tackle would become weather-beaten.[77] Lazarev reported that the two recently-launched line ships *Tri Sviatitelia*-120 and *Trekh Ierarkhov*-84 were being fitted out with ordnance; he planned shortly to go to Sevastopol to take the two ships out on their sea trials. The despatch ended with a postscript that between Tenedos and the Dardanelles France and Britain had concentrated thirty-two warships, of which nineteen were line (eleven British and eight French).[78] The nineteen line represented parity with the ships under Mehmet's control since the defection of the Ottoman fleet. They also represented nearly twice the operational strength in capital ships of the Black Sea Fleet, a display which could most certainly be interpreted by the Russians in more than one way. Butenev had reported that Constantinople and the Dardanelles were quiet, and rumour had it that the Anglo-French fleet would sail for Alexandria.

The tense stalemate in the eastern Mediterranean began to wear on the Egyptian ruler; Mehmet now stated his intention to order Ibrahim to advance if the Allies blockaded Alexandria. In order to counter such a move, the Foreign Office requested the Admiralty to order Stopford to leave a small squadron at the entrance of the Dardanelles, to be ready to sail up to Constantinople if the Turkish government called for such assistance.[79]

Palmerston felt that the first priority for the Allies remained the immediate return of the Sultan's fleet. The indifference he had earlier displayed in 1831–33 had disappeared. Combined with his new awareness was a keen appreciation of how vulnerable the Egyptians would be to a blockade:

> The army of Ibrahim in Syria has hitherto received its supplies from Egypt by sea, a short and easy, and cheap line of communication; but if the sea line were cut off, all the supplies would have to be sent by land, first across the Desert, and then through a long tract of country infested by marauders and insurgent tribes, through which it would require immense means of transport to convey military stores; and where the convoys would be liable to be plundered at every stop, unless escorted by large bodies of troops.
>
>   It must be obvious how such a difficulty would cripple the operations of Ibrahim's army; and instead of a naval blockade leading to his advance to Constantinople, it would much more probably compel him, after a time, to fall back.

Such a blockade would have a twofold advantage; not only would it pen in Egyptian warships, it would also damage Egyptian commercial interests.[80]

Given the lateness of the season, climatic conditions now began to influence events. Stopford had to contemplate the safest anchorage for his ships with the imminent onset of stormy autumnal weather. Besika Bay would soon become unsafe; if the Navy's presence was still required off the Dardanelles, he would run his ships up the channel as far as the 'White Cliffs' anchorage.[81] If the Royal Navy squadron's presence was no longer essential, Stopford suggested a withdrawal to Urla before the second week of October.

The continuing close proximity of the Allied squadrons to the Straits worried the Turks nearly as much as an Egyptian attack. With the onset of bad weather, the Porte discreetly suggested to the Allies that they station themselves elsewhere besides in the immediate neighbourhood of the Dardanelles, perhaps off Alexandria.[82] Among the alternative anchorages suggested were Smyrna, Urla, or Çesme. The Turks had reason to feel threatened; thirty-seven French, British and Austrian warships were now cruising off the Dardanelles.[83] Ponsonby continued to come under pressure from the Turks to withdraw the British squadron from off the Dardanelles to another anchorage, especially as the Egyptian fleet had 'no appearance' of putting to sea.[84] Preparations for a possible Allied–Turkish attack continued in Alexandria; the *Mahmudiye*'s cannon were offloaded for use in the fortifications springing up around the city.[85] No such attack occurred, however; towards the end of October, the French fleet retired to Smyrna, and the British ships made for Urla.[86]

Despite Turkish nervousness about European aid, there were no Ottoman resources sufficient to stop Mehmet Ali. As in the earlier crisis, the only additional naval force that the Sultan might call upon was that of Tunisia, but its value against Mehmet's armaments remained slight. Of Tunisia's thirty-four ships, the largest was a 44-gun frigate, which was disarmed; of the smaller vessels, five were disarmed, while a ten-gun brig and a twenty-two-gun corvette had already sailed for the Turkish capital.[87]

There still seemed a chance that Allied pressure might yet cause Mehmet to yield up the Turkish Fleet; Stopford received intelligence from Alexandria that the Turkish Fleet was to 'speedily depart'. If it proved necessary for the Allies to apply more direct pressure, it now arrived in the form of Admiral Lalande with nine line ships.[88]

Palmerston remained obsessed with possible unilateral Russian aid to Turkey; during a conversation with Brunnov on 3 October, Palmerston stated that the Cabinet wanted a Royal Navy presence in the Dardanelles if Russian forces entered the Bosphorus, in order that each country could guard a respective part of the Straits. The Royal Navy's current deployments were then not particularly suited to the best strategic resolution to the Egyptian insurrection. Brunnov pointed first to Tenedos and then to Alexandria on a map while tartly observing to Palmerston, 'Voila où votre escardre se trouve au-jourd'hui, et voila où elle devrait être pour sauver l'Empire Ottoman'.[89]

Despite his severe tone with Brunnov, Palmerston was increasingly aware of Russian flexibility on the diplomatic issue of warship passage of the Straits. Brunnov understood the British position that the Straits should remain closed to all warships in peacetime,

> and he could assure me, that the Emperor would be perfectly ready to agree to such an arrangement, and to consider the Bosphorus as being as much closed against Russian ships of war, as the Dardanelles against the ships of war of other Powers; and the Emperor would willingly agree, that an Article to this effect should be inserted in the proposed convention....[90]

Brunnov for his part was authorised to say that if such a Convention were signed, then Nicholas would not renew the Hünkâr İskelessi treaty, a cardinal preoccupation of British policy since 1833. Palmerston felt that the unilateral Ottoman closure of the Straits rested upon a 'general and fundamental principle of the Law of Nations', that of a country's sovereign control of its territorial waters to a three-mile limit from low tide, a definition which produced many 'closures' of the waterway.[91] Nicholas's moderate bargaining position represented a goal towards which Palmerston had been consistently bending his energy since 1833; given the increasingly ambivalent French stand towards Mehmet Ali, it would allow him to take a firm position with both the French and Egyptians.

Future French assistance in resolving the crisis might prove conditional, as their policy continued to diverge increasingly from the British and Russian positions. The French government strongly doubted the usefulness of a blockade of Syria and Egypt.[92] In contrast to French vacillation and bellicosity, Russian policy towards cooperation with Britain continued in a moderate, conciliatory vein. The Tsar was now even amenable to an Allied squadron operating in the Sea of Marmora should a division of the Black Sea Fleet anchor in the Bosphorus; his major concern was that the cruising area in the Sea of Marmora be determined in advance in order to preclude any possible misunderstandings between the Russian and Allied forces.[93]

The Tsar's eagerness to cooperate with the British was a relief to all, especially the Royal Navy's Mediterranean commander. Admiral Stopford was well aware of the difficulties of forcing the Dardanelles, especially if Russians manned the batteries. Citing the recent case of the *Belle Poule*-60 being towed up the Straits, Stopford noted that the passage to Constantinople had taken four days; furthermore,

> When their Lordships consider that a Line of Battle ship in tow of the best steamer must have been for two hours under the fire of *200*

pieces of cannon, they will concede in opinion with me that a progress up the Dardanelles under such circumstances is an impracticability.[94]

Added to the military difficulties of such a transit were the ever-present climatic considerations. In the previous eleven weeks' cruising off the Dardanelles, there had been not one day of southerly favourable winds for making the passage.

As French policy continued to diverge from London's, Palmerston became concerned about the French build-up in the Mediterranean. While the French Levantine contingent had nine line ships, six other line ships were fitting-out in Toulon, with the exception of being joined by another two from Brest.[95] France would then have seventeen line ships in the Mediterranean, a number Palmerston regarded as well in excess of any immediate need. The Royal Navy's Mediterranean forces would soon be augmented by three line ships that were being recommissioned, but these were being sent to replace three line ships returning to Britain. If the French could offer no satisfactory explanations for their build-up, then perhaps the three line ships would not be recalled, and additional reinforcements would be sent.

Mehmet's intentions remained uncertain; Turkish sailors and officers were being ordered to wear Egyptian uniforms, while the crews were amalgamated to a fifty–fifty admixture of Turkish and Egyptian personnel.[96] Dissatisfaction and desertion continued among the Turkish sailors, which led to the placing of Egyptian officers aboard the Turkish ships as military police and instructors.[97] Mehmet now stated that he would only return the Fleet when the outstanding differences between him and the Sultan were settled; in the meantime, if Egypt were attacked, he would use the Turkish Fleet in its defence.[98]

Despite Egyptian bellicosity, Napier continued to regard the Russians as the greater threat, observing that while Russia had 'seventeen' line at Sevastopol, the combined Anglo-French force could only muster eighteen.[99] The autumnal weather finally forced the Allies in the Mediterranean to retire their squadrons. The French withdrew two more line ships, while on 14 January 1840 half of the British force sailed for Malta, which left a combined Anglo–French force in the eastern Mediterranean of twelve line ships.[100]

Brunnov in London continued to urge a joint Anglo–French–Russian approach. The Russian position on intervention was based on a strong desire for common action. If Russia was asked by the Sultan to send the Black Sea Fleet and troops to Constantinople to protect the city, the Allies should take appropriate action on the Egyptian and Syrian coasts. In addition, an Austrian–British–French squadron of two or three warships each should be sent up the Dardanelles to cruise in the Sea of Marmora between Gallipoli and the Gulf of Mudanya. Any Allied action should cease as soon as stability was restored. Russian governmental attitudes on the question of foreign warship passage of the Bosphorus and Dardanelles and the Sultan's sovereign rights were summed up in Section 12 of Brunnov's memorandum;

> It will be expressly understood at the outset that the admission of foreign flags into the Bosphorus at the same time as into the Sea of Marmora will be considered as an exceptional measure adopted at the demand solely of the Porte itself and solely towards the end of its defense; this measure does not impair in the least the existing principle, in view of which the Sublime Porte has always considered the straits of the Dardanelles and that of the Bosphorus as before to remain closed in times of peace as in times of war to all foreign Powers. This principle has invariably served as the law of the Ottoman Empire, at all times as an inherent right of the Sultan's sovereignty, as master and guardian of the two straits; the Allied Courts, to manifest the respect that they unanimously have for the independence and repose of the Ottoman Empire, accordingly recognise formally today the closure of the straits of the Dardanelles and the Bosphorus, and agree to consider for ever this principle as being part of European state law.[101]

Far from considering unilateral aid to Turkey, Russia was serving notice that it would abandon its rights in return for an international agreement closing the Straits in peacetime to everyone's warships except Turkey.

Such moderation on Russia's part continued in marked contrast to French attitudes. The French drifted further from the possibility of joint action; Granville now reported that it was unlikely that the French would accede to Russian proposals for joint naval intervention in the Dardanelles.[102]

Despite Russian reasonableness, suspicion of Russian intentions persisted among many influential British officials and naval officers. Napier again wrote to Palmerston with his suggestions for resolving the 'Eastern Question'. As the Commodore felt that the Turks were unwilling pawns of the Russians, the solution was to send the combined fleet to Constantinople, where it could protect the Turkish capital from both the Egyptians and the Russians. Napier suggested that a 2000 man British force capture the Dardanelles, and then the French be informed of a request that the combined fleet sail up to Constantinople. Once there, the Royal Navy could confront the Turks' real enemy:

> The next thing to be done is to settle Russia. She has sixteen sail-of-the-line at Sevastopol; the English fleet, without the assistance of the French, would put them in check – so there would be no fear from that quarter.... Give Russia a choice of war or disarming....[103]

Napier felt that Russia was 'very probably' backing Mehmet, and noted as proof that 'this is the first winter she has kept her Black Sea Fleet ready for sea...'.

The news from Syria was increasingly grave. The Egyptians were taking energetic measures to fortify Acre; 500 cannon had been sent out from Egypt, while 250 were already mounted.[104]

Farther to the north, Russia's position in the Caucasus continued to deteriorate. Russia had more immediate pressing tasks for its Fleet than fulfilling the sombre predictions of a Royal Navy Russophobe. The severe autumn and winter of 1839–40 had caused illness in the garrisons of the Black Sea Coastal Line to the point where they were not only unable to finish work on the sites, but were left with insufficient troops adequately to man the positions.[105]

The harsh weather made things equally bad for the insurgents outside the palisades. Hunger was now an added fillip to religious antagonism driving the warriors. A bad harvest of several years' duration culminated in a nearly complete crop-failure in late 1839 which left the mountaineers desperate; bread supplies were nearly exhausted, and cattle plague had broken out.[106] Ten years of skirmishing had left many of the most productive areas in the Caucasus laid waste; heavy snowfalls and severe frosts in the western regions completed the grim picture. Attacks on the hated Russians responsible for such deprivation were not long in coming. On 19 February 1840 Fort Lazarev, posting of the newly-created battalion, fell to an assault of the mountaineers.[107]

As Russian soldiers fought and died at their posts, ministers in St Petersburg ironically were aware of the shortcomings of governmental policy in the region. Count Aleksandr Ivanovich Chernyshev, Minister of War, now outlined his low opinion of previous Russian military efforts in the western Caucasus;

Many years' military action against the unruly Circassian tribes at
different locales but without a consistent policy, for all its partial
successes, has not had the slightest influence on the general
pacification of the region. Trade links with Turkey, military and
all other aid which the mountaineers have received, and the hostile
support reaching them through unhindered communications via the
open eastern coast of the Black Sea, ceaselessly stimulated them to
new unrest and insurrection. Towards the interruption of such
communications the cruising of our warships continues unabated,
but this appears insufficient, and there remains no other means of
limiting them, then capturing the shore itself, and the construction
of fortifications in the main anchorages. The government never
counted these measures as sufficient for decisively pacifying the
mountaineers, but by taking them and relentlessly pursuing their
implementation a two-fold aim is achieved...first, depriving the
mountaineers of all foreign assistance, and second, to force them to
return all their trade via our borders....[108]

Driven by desperation and hunger, the mountaineers pursued their
own 'partial successes'. On 12 March the mountaineers attacked and
captured Fort Vel'iaminov.[109] The situation on the Black Sea Coastal
Line now became critical. It looked unlikely to most of the remaining
garrisons that naval support would be sent in time, so they hurriedly
prepared their positions and waited for the worst.

Even as the soldiers sharpened their bayonets their officers in Tiflis
considered other ways of pacifying the mountaineers. Major-General
Raevskii wrote to General Golovin with his views on alternatives to
warfare:

One peaceful means of dealing with the Circassians able to lead to
their lasting submission and different from the other, founded on
destruction and bloodshed, harmful and contrary to the magnanimous intentions of the Emperor, is trade; drawing the mountaineers
closer to us, furnishing a great profit to the garrisons, decreasing
smuggling, and not producing harmful consequences.... Raids and
expeditions only postpone the time of Circassia's pacification....[110]

For the soldiers in the Black Sea Coastal Line, raids and expeditions
mounted by the mountaineers were about to intensify. A Circassian
spy on 28 March 1840 brought news to the five hundred-man
Mikhailov garrison that 11 000 insurgents were preparing to attack.
While the position was prepared for battle, private Arkhip Osipov

stated that at the moment the attack seemed successful, he would blow up the powder magazines.[111] The troops had the small consolation of being safe from a night attack, as the Circassians never raided then. Skirmishing began on the morning of 3 April.

The initial attacks were driven off by bayonet charges; the swarm of mountaineers was so dense that the troops fired at random, being sure of a target. The outer ditch began to fill up with corpses. As the attacks continued throughout the morning, ammunition began to run low. The walls were breached in several places, and hand-to-hand fighting began. When the insurgents rushed for the magazines, Osipov fulfilled his vow and fired the powder. The mountaineers with heavy losses now captured the position, along with a handful of dazed survivors.[112]

While the Russians grappled with their insurgency the Ottoman Empire took a further pummelling from theirs. One hundred and thirty-five Turkish cannon captured at Nezib were being taken to improve the defences of Acre; in addition, 15 000 trees were cut to provide material for a palisade around the fort.[113] Mehmet now appointed Ahmet as commander of the combined fleets.[114]

In light of French prevarication, a joint Anglo-Russian response to possible Egyptian naval action was now coalescing; Palmerston felt sufficiently trusting of Russian sincerity to order the Admiralty to have Stopford pass up the Dardanelles to the Bosphorus with a 'sufficient' naval force if the Porte made a request for assistance to the British ambassador.[115] It was fortuitous that British commitments to the defence of Constantinople freed Russian seapower for purely Russian concerns; the major units of Black Sea Fleet would be essential in re-establishing Russian control on the Caucasus coast.

News of the Caucasian attacks began to reach Sevastopol in the first week of April 1840. According to fragmentary reports, the mountaineers had attacked Forts Vel'iaminov and Navagin with more than 7000 men, and lost more than 700 dead.[116] The ferocity of the attacks was such that only fifteen Russian soldiers had been reported captured. Lazarev immediately despatched the *Brailov*-44 to Sudzhuk-Kale and the *Penderaklii*-24 to Gelendzhik to support the garrisons. The mountaineers continued their relentless onslaught, and on 14 April attacked and overwhelmed Nikolaev.[117]

The following day Lazarev sent to Menshikov more information. According to two Cossacks who had been captured after the storming of Mikhailov and then escaped, the 480-man garrison had been attacked by more than 7000 mountaineers. Osipov's explosion had killed more than 2000 of the attackers. Major-General Raevskii was taking steps to stiffen the remaining forts; arriving in Sevastopol aboard the steamer *Moguchii*-7, he hurriedly assembled a company from the Black Sea Line battalion troops and artillery, and along with the schooner *Smelyi*-16 sailed for Gelendzhik.[118] In such circumstances, Russian aid to Turkey would only squander valuable resources desperately needed at home. By the time troops and ships would return, perhaps all the coastal positions would have been lost. Lazarev gave in to a rare moment of despair: 'How long will this continue? Our fleet had been ready for a long time, and impatiently awaits only troops. . .'.

Menshikov informed Lazarev that reports had been received about the loss of Vel'iaminov; unofficial reports indicated that Novotroitskoe had also been captured.

> These positions in general, in the reports of eyewitnesses, are in the most defenceless state, and I am not in the least astonished by the mountaineers' successes; having seen the troops of the 5th Corps, I am afraid for any great success in subsequent mountain raids....

Menshikov then turned his attention to the Egyptian crisis:

> The Egyptian question is not resolved by the conduct of France in favour of Mehmet-Ali, but the feeble British ministry does not dare to act decisively. Whom do I fear? – the vile French fleet!. . .If Ibrahim took it into his head to go towards the Bosphorus in the early spring, no one would be able to stop him from possessing the throne of the Sultan....[119]

Despite Menshikov's continuing distrust of the Egyptians, Russia's most pressing need was to regain control of the coast. Plans were made for immediate counter-attacks. Raevskii was ordered to send a punitive expedition into the Ubykhs' territory; the troops were 'to burn and destroy their crops, harvesting, and stores':[120]

The first Russian counter-attack was on 22 May at Tuapse. Raevskii's troops quickly recaptured the desolate Vel'aminov position.[121] The insurgents' successes at Tuapse would make future operations more difficult; while they had left the large cannon in place, they had captured and carried away more than thirty smaller ones.[122] The mountaineers felt confident enough on 7 June to attack Abin with 12000 men; the seven hundred-man garrison repelled the attack, killing nearly seven hundred insurgents while suffering twenty-seven casualties.[123]

Quite aside from concerns of national pride, economic interests were also increasingly influencing the Russians to bolster their Caucasian presence. General Evgeni Aleksandrovich Golovin considered using local wood in the construction of shoreline fortifications, but the difficulties of operating in hostile country combined with the swampiness of the coastal areas seemed to rule it out. Despite these obstacles, the perceived value of the region's timber resources was such that Nicholas now issued orders to survey the wood of Guria, Mingrelia, Samurzakani and Abhazia; large quantities of timber suitable for shipbuilding and artillery were subsequently found.[124] This new source of timber was so highly regarded that despite the fierceness of the insurgency an order was issued by the Artillery Board that all wood needed for the Kiev and southern military districts was to be cut there.[125]

Farther south the situation continued to unravel. Mehmet began to bestir himself; aware that the Allies were considering intervention, his troops now began to press forward, attempting to capture as much territory as possible to trade in any future negotiations. An Egyptian line ship, fourteen Egyptian and Turkish frigates and six Egyptian and Turkish corvettes and brigs with 'mixed crews' on 22–3 June landed 15 000 troops in Beirut.[126] Discipline was rigidly enforced; four Turkish commanders who attempted to withdraw their ships from Egyptian service were strangled and thrown overboard.

Work feverishly continued on the Egyptian defences at Acre.[127] The 10 700 man garrison worked under Lieutenant-Colonel Schultz, a Polish officer in the Egyptian service. The fort's magazines were completely filled, with a further 800 barrels of gunpowder being stored in the hospital's storage area. In Alexandria two divisions totalling nineteen vessels were readied, including nine Turkish frigates, ensuring an Allied attack would destroy many of the Sultan's vessels.[128] The cost of these preparations combined with presence of the Ottoman Fleet severely strained Mehmet's finances; the Egyptian government began to sell its cotton harvest cheaply in order to raise some quick cash.[129]

Despite increasingly bellicose Egyptian operations in Syria, Mehmet's room for manoeuvre shrank as Allied attitudes hardened. Diplomatic discussions in London resulted in a Convention signed on 15 July 1840 by Austrian, Russian, Prussian, British and Turkish representatives. Palmerston now decided to call France's bluff, and act unilaterally if need be. The five-power Convention ensured France's isolation, and Palmerston doubted that France would actually go to war over Mehmet's independence, if for no other reason than the fact that British seapower was superior:

> France has, it is true, a fleet of fifteen sail of the line in the Mediterranean, and she might soon add three more to that number, but that is nearly the whole amount of her available fleet; and she could not send to sea a much greater force if she were to go to war with the Four Powers. Great Britain, on the other hand, could, in case of war, send to sea a fleet which would sweep the Ocean.[130]

On 25 July Commodore Napier informed Stopford that the entire Turco-Egyptian squadron remained moored in Alexandria.[131] Napier was certain that the Royal Navy could subdue Mehmet without outside aid; he reported that a 'very small force' with guns and ammunition could pacify the Lebanon. The Egyptians' most vulnerable point north of Acre was Beirut.[132]

On 4 August Menshikov informed Lazarev of the recently concluded Convention. If Mehmet persisted in his aggression, then the Royal Navy was to break all maritime communications between Egypt and Syria; 'Russia will be called upon to defend Constantinople in the event of an attack.'[133] It was necessary to keep the Black Sea Fleet in 'complete readiness' in order to send it immediately if needed. The 14th Division was ready, and three companies of the 13th Division were available. Menshikov ended by noting that the Fleet had 'yet another obligation' in Abhazia, possibly at the same time as the projected Bosphorus expedition.

Admiral Stopford now wrote to Commodore Napier that he was sending him HMS *Ganges*-84 and HMS *Thunderer*-84 from Malta, while retaining HMS *Asia*-84 and HMS *Bellerophon*-84; two additional ships were expected from Naples, while HMS *Revenge*-76 and HMS *Cambridge*-74 were being sent out from Britain.[134] Three line frigates and steamers were ordered by Ponsonby to be kept off the Dardanelles 'to protect the capital, in conjunction with the Russians, from any attack on the part of Ibrahim Pasha'. The British Mediterranean squadron now had twelve line ships and thirteen smaller vessels, including six steamers.[135]

For the Russians, the French continued to replace the Egyptians as the greater threat. Prince Menshikov believed that the Egyptians would probably not move directly on the Bosphorus, but would instead penetrate Asia Minor, seizing Urfa and Diyarbakır. Russian action therefore 'might be against the French if they enter into the Dardanelles...'; if the British did not support the Russians, then they would not be 'sufficiently strong' to repel such an attack.[136] A second 'secret' despatch from Menshikov informed Lazarev that Count Orlov would have supreme command of the Russian land and naval forces, should they be sent. Orlov would be exercising the same rights and privileges that he had had during the 1833 expedition.[137]

The Royal Navy began to deploy to protect the remaining Turkish ships in the eastern Mediterranean. Stopford sent HMS *Asia*-84 and HMS *Wasp*-18 to accompany a Turkish expeditionary force sailing to Famagusta, Cyprus.[138] Farther to the east, Napier also began to arrange his forces off the Syrian coast. On 16 August Napier issued secret orders to Captain Collier of HMS *Castor*-36 to proceed to Beirut and search all Egyptian vessels he encountered; Collier was also to detain any Egyptian warships he met.[139] Napier also wrote to the head of the Egyptian army that he was detaining all warships or merchantmen carrying troops, military stores, or provisions between Egyptian or Syrian ports.[140] Süleyman Pasha replied that such a course of action was unacceptable.[141] Napier's aggressive blockading soon captured an Egyptian frigate loaded with supplies, bound for İskendurun.[142] During the first five days of the blockade Napier's forces also captured a cutter, two merchantmen loaded with ammunition, and several vessels stocked with provisions.[143]

Two British line ships, a frigate and two steamers along with two Austrian frigates and a corvette under Admiral Bandiera remained off Alexandria, forcing Mehmet to deploy his naval forces.[144] A number of smaller vessels were dismasted and drydocked and all nineteen line ships were drawn up in battle order.[145] It was obvious that a blockade of Alexandria was imminent.

On 26 August a squadron of two Egyptian line ships and five frigates, eleven Turkish frigates, two Egyptian and a Turkish corvette, three brigs and seven transports had weighed anchor for Syria, with three more Egyptian line ships being readied.[146] Unrest continued among the Turkish officers; Mehmet uncovered a treasonous plot to burn both fleets at anchor. Mehmet rebuked seven 'superior' officers and sent them under arrest to Abu Qur fortress; thirty-eight others were arrested.[147]

Russian commitments in the Black Sea continued to rule out the despatch of substantial aid to Turkey. Lazarev noted that the *Chesme*-84 was 'completely unreliable and extremely dangerous for transporting troops...'; in addition, the Fleet had shortages due to other demands. Lazarev stated that if he did not receive orders to the contrary, then he would send a squadron of three line ships and three frigates under Rear-Admiral Ivan Iakovlevich Zakharin on 4 September for the use of Major-General Raevskii to transfer troops to the Georgian coast.[148] Eight line ships and three frigates would be left for use in any Bosphorus action, though any such operation would stretch Fleet capacities to their utmost.

In addition to possible ship shortages, Lazarev reported a possible lack of troops for the projected Turkish expedition. If the expedition occurred before the return of the Vil'no regiment, then the total number of troops available in Sevastopol totalled 7000 men, which Lazarev regarded as 'extremely insufficient'. While provisions were adequate except for supplies of biscuit and fresh meat, a number of ships were less than completely reliable. Besides the line ship *Chesme*-84, the *Gavriil*-84, *Tenedos*-60, and *Imperatritsa Mariia*-84 were all unavailable due to rot and decay. Lazarev hoped that with the British pressure on Mehmet the Egyptian revolt could be brought quickly to a conclusion.[149] As for immediate Fleet concerns, the Fleet's shipbuilding programme was progressing, with Lazarev hoping to launch the line ship *Uriil*-84 and frigate *Messemvriia*-60 by mid-November. The launch of the line ship *Dvenadsat' Apostolov*-120 had to be postponed until the spring, due to a lack of sufficient copper hull sheathing.[150]

The possibility of Russian intervention was now communicated to Mehmet.[151] In the interests of appearing unified, everything done by the British was to be done in the Sultan's name; as a result, Captain Walker was serving as a commissioned Turkish officer and not as one from the Royal Navy.

The agreed-upon British Mediterranean contingent was to consist of 'at least' sixteen line and three large steamers, while the French, if they participated, would send thirteen line ships. On 9 September Beirut harbour held an impressive total of thirty-three warships; twenty-three British, three Austrian, and five Turkish craft were observed by an American and a French ship.[152] Nearby were anchored nearly forty captured Egyptian and Syrian merchantmen.[153] The Allied blockade of the Egyptian and Syrian coasts had begun the previous week.[154]

Russia also began to mobilise in earnest for possible intervention. Russian naval assistance was not to be limited to the Black Sea; in Kronstadt a division of the Baltic Fleet of nine line ships and six frigates which had been laid up for the winter were readied for sea.[155] If needed, the ships would sail to Sveaborg before the Gulf of Finland froze, in order to make for the Mediterranean as soon as possible in the spring.

Despite Napier's ingrained Russophobia, the magnitude of the British commitment on the Syrian coast caused him to temper his attitude; he wrote to Ponsonby and complained that he was short of troops, asking him to call in the Russians to land in İskendurun.[156] Stopford informed him that the British would be acting alone on the Syrian coast, as no Austrian or Prussian aid would be forthcoming; 'as for the Russians, we had rather not.'[157]

On 26 September Napier attacked and captured Sidon; the action lasted five hours, with the 1400 Allied and Turkish troops defeating an Egyptian force numbered at 2700 men.[158]

Stopford's squadron included several small steamers, marking the first time that steam vessels had participated to any extent in large-scale naval operations. Their usefulness was such that he was moved to write to the Admiralty:

> The steam vessels have been eminently useful in constantly moving along a great extent of coast with troops and arms, and taking part in the attacks upon the different forts, which service has been executed entirely to my satisfaction.[159]

French collusion with Egyptian interests was further illustrated by the arrival in Alexandria of Colonel Galisse of the French army Engineer Corps.[160] Galisse inspected all the positions in Alexandria and along the coast, and began to draw up defensive plans for Abu Qur and Alexandria.

Despite such French gestures of support, Palmerston felt that Britain's naval policy was producing moderation in France; after congratulating Napier on his 'brilliant achievements,' the Foreign Minister stated, 'Your successes have produced a decisive Effect at Paris, and have reconciled the French to seeing the whole of Syria rescued from the tyranny of Mehmomed Ali'.[161] In an effort to temper any excess of zeal in his subordinate's 'brilliant achievements,' Ponsonby informed Stopford that the blockade was not to be enforced on neutrals, as the belligerent right of blockade by one state against another was only applicable in a declared state of war.[162] Information from Alexandria indicated that Mehmet did not intend to challenge the Allied blockade.[163] Ponsonby was to tell the Turks that the militant language of the French ambassador was only bluster; Palmerston believed that seapower would cause the French to back down, noting, 'By sea, France is inferior to England alone; but much more so to England and Russia united. . .'.[164]

As in 1798 and 1831–2, Acre remained the key to coastal operations in Syria. Stopford and Napier accordingly made plans to attack and capture the citadel. The steamers HMS *Gorgon*-6, HMS *Phoenix*-4,

HMS *Vesuvius*-4 and HMS *Stromboli*-4 arrived off Acre on 1 November, and began bombarding the fort. The steamers' attack continued into the next day; inaccurate Egyptian fire largely missed the ships.[165] The fort's defences were by now formidable; besides cannon the fort contained a number of eight-inch shell guns mounted 'en barbette'.[166]

Admiral Stopford arrived off Acre during the evening, with HMS *Powerful*-84, HMS *Princess Charlotte*-104, HMS *Thunderer*-84, HMS *Revenge*-76, HMS *Bellerophon*-80, HMS *Edinburgh*-72, HMS *Carysfort*-36, HMS *Talbot*-28, HMS *Hazard*-18, HMS *Wasp*-16 and HMS *Pique*-36.[167] The British were joined by three Austrian ships and a Turkish contingent under Walker (Yaver Pasha), who hoisted his flag on the *Mukhuddinay-i Hive*-74.

The *Mukhuddinay-i Hive*-74 was not an impressive vessel; an Englishman who boarded her at Beirut noted she was 'patched-up, old, lumbering and leaky; none, in fact, but a most daring sailor would have risked himself to sea in her for any time....'.[168] After the Fleet's defection, Walker had found his flagship lying decrepit and dismasted in the docks of Yeniköy, 'where, being considered unseaworthy, she had suffered to remain...for many years'. Her crew was similarly improvised; of her complement of six to seven hundred men, 'not more than twenty' had previously served aboard ship, which caused Walker's visitor to note, 'How can I describe things below decks!' The night of 2 November was spent laying buoys and taking soundings of the water near the fortress. Plans for lashing the steamers to the warships to manoeuvre them into range were abandoned on account of heavy swells.[169]

Stopford divided his force in two; HMS *Revenge*-76, HMS *Powerful*-84, HMS *Princess Charlotte*-104, HMS *Thunderer*-84, HMS *Bellerophon*-80 and HMS *Pique*-36 were to attack Acre from the northern side, while the others along with the Austrians and Turks were to approach the fort from the south; the steamers were to continue their bombardment from wherever they found their contribution to be most effectual.[170] The Austrians had a modest presence in the frigates *Guerriera*-44 and *Medea*-44 and the corvette *Lipsia*-24.[171] Attempts to work in close to the fort at 10 a.m. were stymied by light winds; the vessels were becalmed until 1 p.m.

The bombardment continued for the next three hours, with the fort replying in kind. At 4.20 p.m. a magazine in the fort blew up,[172] killing between one and two thousand men.[173] Following the explosion, the fort's fire rapidly slackened. When the ships worked in close to the fort to continue their assault the next morning, they found that the Egyptians had evacuated the position during the night.[174] Allied losses were eighteen killed and forty-one wounded.[175] Damage to the British warships was relatively slight.[176]

Even before the attack, Ibrahim realised that the superiority of the Allies could damage his position in Syria: 'Si la mer ne sera bientôt libre, la Syrie ne sera pas tenable...'.[177] The Allies controlled the sea passage from Egypt to Syria; their capture of Acre now threatened to close the coastal road, marooning the Egyptians in Syria.

Stopford reported that a 'great quantity' of arms and ammunition was found in the ruined fort, and that the 'fortifications were rapidly getting into a state of preparation against attack'.[178] The same day Mehmet learned of the French fleet's departure for Toulon; there was now no possibility of any hope for French support for further resistance.[179]

The capture of Acre produced a strong reaction in Constantinople: 'The *do nothings* here see how easily it (Acre) was taken and ought to be *ashamed*...'.[180]

Naval pressure was now brought to bear directly on Egypt. Napier was given command of the squadron cruising off Alexandria, which was to be increased to six line.[181] Napier sailed from Beirut on 15 November; before joining his command, he reconnoitred Alexandria's seaward defences.[182] Napier estimated that Alexandria contained 'about' twenty line ships and as many frigates.[183] The Egyptians now began a rapid withdrawal from Syria; three weeks after the capture of Acre there remained only 26 000 Egyptian troops in Syria, as opposed to 60 000 two months before.[184]

For Mehmet the game was up; his forces could no longer operate beyond Syria, as the Royal Navy could interdict his supply lines by both land and sea. To continue his struggle might lead first to the loss of his fleet, and then to his overthrow as ruler of Egypt. Ever the pragmatist, Mehmet now began to negotiate with Napier about withdrawing from Syria and returning the Turkish Fleet to the Sultan's control in return for the hereditary control of Egypt. Napier communicated a despatch from Palmerston which stated that Mehmet could have hereditary control of Egypt in return for his fulfilling conditions 'at once'.[185] A convention between Napier and Mehmet for the implementation of the terms was agreed upon and initialled,[186] despite Turkish protests, which caused Ponsonby to write to Napier, 'you have no Power or Authority whatever to justify what you have done, and... the Convention is null and void...'.[187]

Palmerston informed the Admiralty that Her Majesty's Government approved the Convention, although it was unable to give Mehmet a four-power guarantee of the Sultan's offer.[188]

The Egyptian withdrawal from Syria was proceeding sufficiently well for Reşit to tell Ponsonby on 2 December that the Syrian blockade was to be lifted.[189] The Egyptian defeat was seen as a golden opportunity to aid Turkey and restrain Russia; Londonderry outlined both his own views and those of the Turks:

> [we shall] impose upon her naval and military instructors and aid her in her attempts at civilized institutions.... It is alleged here that Russia, having twelve or fourteen sail of the line (which she can always command now at Odessa) can arrive by the Black Sea in a few days at Constantinople supporting her fleet by a large army through Servia by land and then, holding the entrance of the Bosphorus and Dardanelles, the Empire of the East falls into her hands. But these are *phantoms* and *shadows*.... If the great gates from the Sea of Marmora and the Black Sea are to be made impregnable, let England assist Turkey with such powerful preparations, and no Russian force would advance from Wallachia or Moldavia or Servia....[190]

Mehmet was still not inclined to return immediately the fleet, as it was his last major bargaining counter. Mehmet stated that the Turkish Fleet was not being prepared, but he would give it up if reinstated as governor of Egypt. Napier suggested that Mehmet send some of the Fleet as soon as possible to Marmoris as a gesture of good faith, but Mehmet wanted the entire fleet to sail together; it could be ready within five days of the arrival of an officer from Constantinople to command it.[191]

The weather was on Mehmet's side; Napier's squadron sustained damage in gales off Alexandria. He doubted the usefulness of a winter blockade of the port, especially as the Egyptians appeared to have no intention of putting to sea.[192] Admiral Stopford off Beirut was also having trouble; on 2 December HMS *Bellerophon*-80 was caught off the coast by a gale which wrecked eight merchantmen.[193]

With the evacuation of Syria proceeding smoothly, Palmerston noted that His Majesty's Government appreciated the 'sound judgement' displayed by Tsar Nicholas:

> there cannot be a doubt that the powerful naval and military force, which the Emperor has kept in reserve to be ready to act in case of

need, has essentially contributed to the successful result which has been obtained; while the circumstance that these forces have been kept in reserve, and have not prematurely been brought into action, has prevented some political difficulties which might otherwise by possibility have arisen.[194]

While Palmerston was paying tribute to Russian moderation, Walker was hoisting the flag over the Turkish fleet in Alexandria.[195] Mehmet promptly released the Alexandrian dockyard resources for repairing and provisioning the Sultan's ships.[196] The following day the entire Turkish Fleet except for two ships was on its way to Marmoris.[197] Farther north in the Black Sea the winter weather was not so benign; twelve ships were wrecked on the Caucasus coast during a severe storm.[198]

The major remaining issue was the form of the hereditary government that Mehmet Ali was to be allowed to establish in Egypt. A ferman of 12 February 1841 set out the major conditions. One-fourth of all revenue collected in Egypt by the government was to be sent to Constantinople; the Egyptian army was to be limited to 18 000 troops, a number that could only be increased by the Sultan; all military uniforms and banners were to be identical to those used in Turkey; no Egyptian governors were to build warships without express permission from Constantinople.[199] This last condition was reaffirmed in a second ferman of 1 June:

> The Pashas of Egypt will not build henceforth any warships without having first obtained the permission of the Sublime Porte and without having been provided with a distinct and positive authorisation in advance.[200]

Mehmet accepted the limitations, but he asked for the revenue demands to be lowered.[201]

On 16 March the Ottoman Fleet dropped anchor off the Golden Horn after cruising in the Sea of Marmora for the previous two days. The nine line ships, eleven frigates, two corvettes and two brigs fired a twenty-one gun salute.[202] Four days later the young Sultan inspected his long-absent ships, and as a sign of his pleasure he had twenty piastres distributed to each soldier and sailor.[203] The ships did not long remain idle; a detachment of ten ships were quickly prepared and sent to Crete.

Mehmet attempted one last assertion of independent authority by ordering the construction of two more line ships. Palmerston felt that this was done with French connivance, and stated that since Mehmet had accepted the investiture ferman of 12 February, this was impermissible.[204] Ponsonby reported that the Egyptian government had decided to build three line ships (three three-deckers and two two-deckers) and five frigates; the problem facing the Egyptians was where to find sufficient timber, now that supplies from Karamania were no longer available.[205]

While the Mediterranean conflict was being resolved through negotiation, the Russian crisis in the Caucasus were no closer to resolution. On 6 May Menshikov approved another expedition against the Caucasus tribes, and authorised the use of three or four Taman battalions in addition to the troops already designated.[206] The Black Sea Fleet was to increase its amphibious operations in an attempt to pacify the region by force.

As a progressive officer, Lazarev had long realised the value of the steamship; the recent action off Acre had given startling proof of their usefulness in wartime. Lazarev consistently attempted to prod the sluggish Naval Ministry into providing an adequate number for the Black Sea Fleet. He now sent on the favourable comments of the Russian consul-general in London about the procurement of two steamers for the Black Sea Fleet in Britain, and he asked Menshikov to approve the purchase of two steamers of one hundred and eighty horsepower each.[207] 'If necessary' the Fleet would settle for one new steamship of one hundred and eighty horse power. Not only were the steamers needed for the Fleet, but Russia's prestige was involved: 'The *Silach*-4 currently stationed in Constantinople plays an extremely pitiful role among the multitude of beautiful steamers of the foreign powers.'[208]

The Caucasus steamers were useless for major Fleet needs; in addition, three of the Fleet's steamers – *Kolkhida*-7, *Boets*-7, and *Moguchii*-7 were either recently repaired or in need of repairs. It must have been particularly galling to Lazarev to have to beg for relatively modest resources; in contrast, Britain would have the following year eighty-four war steamers in commission with a further twenty under construction.[209] The steam revolution was apparent within the Bosphorus itself; small government steamers were towing merchantmen up to the Black Sea for a half-dollar charge per ship ton, 'which must be infinitely preferable to loitering about in the Bosphorus for weeks waiting for a fair wind'.[210]

The question of Turkish sovereignty over the Bosphorus and Dardanelles and the loitering there of foreign warships was finally resolved by the Convention signed between Great Britain, Russia, Turkey, France, Austria, and Prussia on 13 July 1841 in London. Article I clearly delineated Turkey's 'ancient right' regarding Straits passage:

> His Highness the Sultan, for his part, declares that he has the firm intention to maintain in the future the invariable principle established as an ancient law of his Empire, and in view of which it had at all times denied that to foreign warships entrance into the Straits of the Dardanelles and Bosphorus.[211]

Article II reserved the right to the Sultan to issue fermans for 'light vessels under the naval ensign' used by the legations in Constantinople.

The Treaty satisfied all signatories to a certain extent and remained in force until the post-First World War collapse of the Ottoman Empire. For Western Europe the malignant influence of Russia as embodied in the Hünkâr Iskelessi Treaty was finally nullified, while Russia avoided maritime assault by the Western European powers in the event of a war not involving Turkey. Russian–Ottoman maritime parity in the Black Sea was restored.

Russia was spared the possibility of direct European involvement in the worsening Caucasian insurgency; as if to underline the difficulties of suppressing the conflict, an ukaz was now issued banning all gunpowder imports into the Caucasus by land from either Turkey or Persia or by sea via the Caspian.[212]

The recent crisis had brought home the potential of Britain and France to flood the eastern Mediterranean with warships; at the time of the Treaty's signature, Britain's Mediterranean force alone was equal to the Russian Black Sea Fleet in capital ships. HMS *Britannia*-120, HMS *Howe*-120, HMS *Rodney*-92, HMS *Powerful*-84, HMS *Caledonia*-84, HMS *Ganges*-84, HMS *Vanguard*-84, HMS *Thunderer*-84, HMS *Revenge*-76, HMS *Benbow*-72, HMS *Cambridge*-72, HMS *Hastings*-72, and HMS *Implacable*-74 were supplemented by four frigates, several sloops and thirteen steamers.[213] As the second Egyptian crisis was now over, France and Britain began reducing their Mediterranean forces. By October France had laid up six of her line ships at Brest, and the British considered withdrawing an equal number from the eastern Mediterranean.[214] This tranquillity was reflected in Constantinople's shipping; by the end of the year 3318 ships visited the port.[215]

In building their Black Sea fleets, both Russia and Turkey saw one another as their prime enemy. The recently-concluded Convention would ensure that they met as equals. The two traditional maritime protagonists now received an expert and dispassionate comparative analysis. Both were viewed by Sir William Symonds, Surveyor of the Royal Navy and one of the most distinguished naval architects of the nineteenth century. During his visit to the Tersane-i Amire Symonds found the Turkish ships 'in all respects. . .the clumsiest pieces of mechanism I ever beheld'.[216] Symonds's views of Lazarev's ships were also harsh: 'Russian ships show strong symptoms of weakness. . .they complain that a ship is never worth more than eight years. . .'.[217] Symonds felt that the drydocks under construction in Sevastopol would be both extremely expensive and of 'doubtful' utility. Some of the Crimean and Caucasian timber used in shipbuilding was very good, though the amount available was very small. The Surveyor summed up the Black Sea Fleet in one pithy sentence:

I think, upon the whole, the Russian ships and naval establishments in the Black Sea have been overrated.[218]

In contrast to this harsh assessment, when Lazarev wrote to Menshikov about Symonds's visit to Nikolaev and Sevastopol, he believed that Symonds had been very favourably impressed.[219] Thirteen years later an Anglo-French attack would force Lazarev's successors to scuttle their 'weak' ships in their 'overrated' port, while after the port's capture, Royal Engineers would destroy the 'extremely expensive' drydocks of 'doubtful utility'.

Conclusions

'Whosoever commands the sea, commands the trade; whosoever commands the trade of the world, commands the riches of the world itself.'

Sir Walter Raleigh

'War is a business of positions.'

Napoleon

'Among all masters of military art – including therein naval art – it is a thoroughly accepted principle that mere defensive war means military ruin, and therefore national disaster. It is vain to maintain a military or naval force whose power is not equal to assuming the offensive soon or late; which cannot, first or last, go out, assail the enemy, and hurt him in his vital interests...a navy for defence only, in the *military* sense, means a navy that can only await attack. . .leaving the enemy. . .at liberty to choose his own time and manner of fighting.'

Alfred Thayer Mahan, *Lessons of the War with Spain*

In seeking to develop a conceptual framework in which to understand Russian naval performance and actions in the years 1827–41, two very useful authors remain Alfred Thayer Mahan and Sergei Georgivich Gorshkov, former commander of the Soviet Navy and the man most responsible for its current form. While Mahan's works were written fifty years after the events related here, his importance for naval strategic thought was recognised early in Russia, and a number of his observations remain applicable today.[1] Gorshkov's attempts to provide a Soviet analysis of Russian naval history that justifies policy that includes pertinent, albeit brief, perspectives on the Nicholaeven period, as well as broader views of Russian needs and capabilities throughout the nineteenth century.[2] On the question debated by the Russian government in the early twentieth century 'whether a navy is necessary for Russia,' Gorshkov notes that in the 32 wars that Tsarist Russia waged prior to World War I, the Navy served in all but two.[3]

Seapower's primary objective is the furtherance of national interests and policy in both peace and war. Seapower as an element of national military power is uniquely flexible. While 'showing the flag' is a peacetime tradition that continues today, naval warfare is the true test of Seapower. A strong maritime state at war enjoys a number of advantages. To quote Gorshkov, 'The foundation of naval forces is their high manoeuvrability, their ability to concentrate secretly and unexpectedly to appear in powerful groups'.[4] Within a limited context and under special conditions, the Black Sea Fleet was able to achieve this in the period under consideration. What were Russia's intended and actual uses of its Black Sea Fleet in the years 1827–41, and to what extent did Russia succeed in implementing these objectives?

In a Mahanian strategic analysis, the four fundamental concerns of the Black Sea Fleet would be strategic position, 'command of the sea', concentration of force, and communications.

Influencing these concerns would be the six factors of geographical position, physical conformation, extent of territory, population, the character of the population, and the character of the government itself.[5] Did Nicholaeven Russia fit these definitions of a thalassocracy?

While these concerns have remained constant throughout the two centuries of Russia's Black Sea naval presence, the relative importance of these factors has varied considerably. Implicit in these concerns is Gorshkov's observation that,

> Significant difficulties for Russian Seapower arose from her geographical position, which demanded that each of the various theatres maintained an independent fleet capable of securing a decision of the problems faced there.[6]

The Black Sea theatre operated largely in isolation from Russia's other major naval region, the Baltic. Despite this isolation, however, the cooperation of forces despatched from there, as well as from friendly Mediterranean maritime forces, was essential to the Black Sea Fleet's success in 1828–9.

The problems of the Black Sea Fleet during 1827–41 in dealing with the Turks had precedents dating back to Peter the Great, the 'Father' of the Russian Navy. While Peter's Azov campaigns proved ultimately unsuccessful, his Azov flotilla served notice that Russia would eventually challenge the Ottoman Empire's naval monopoly on the Black Sea.

Throughout Nicholas's reign the Black Sea Fleet was in an over-whelmingly advantageous strategic position only as regarded either destroying the Turks' Black Sea forces or attacking the capital of the Ottoman Empire. 'Command of the Sea' could only be achieved as long as the Ottoman Fleet, if it acted alone, stood at parity or less with the Russians. If Turkey entered into a European alliance as she did in the Crimean War, then this advantage would be lost. For Russia to secure her communications within the Black Sea, she had to achieve a concentration of force either near or within the Straits, to prevent passage of hostile ships into the Black Sea. This regional 'command of the sea' meant that the first casualty of any Russo-Turkish conflict would be Russia's unprotected Mediterranean-bound merchant shipping through the Straits.

Of the Mahanian variables necessary for a country to achieve 'command of the sea', the only one which Petrine Russia possessed was a government which desired seapower, whether the populace were inclined towards it or not. In the century that passed between Peter's death and Nicholas's accession, the only other factor that changed in Russia's favour was 'physical conformation' – the annexation of the Crimea in 1783 by Catherine the Great had given Russia a toehold on the Black Sea. In June of the same year Sevastopol was founded, future headquarters of the Black Sea Fleet, and the later scene of two remarkable sieges.

Despite these gains the Straits themselves remained in Turkish hands, able to cut Russian commercial access to the Mediterranean at a stroke. Control of the Bosphorus and Dardanelles gave Turkey 'interior lines' in both the Mediterranean and Black Seas. For Russia to be able to counter this strategic advantage, it was necessary in any war with the Ottoman Empire for Russia not only to have a strong fleet on the Black Sea, but also to have a squadron in the Mediterranean. Such a situation occurred for the first and only time in Russia's history in 1827.

The Russian squadron that fought at Navarino was the successor of the first Russian squadron to operate in the Mediterranean, sent by Catherine the Great in 1770. Geiden unfortunately suffered from the same problems as Orlov nearly sixty years earlier. Both forces could fulfill their combat mission against the Turks only with the support of a friendly Mediterranean power – no Russian help from the Black Sea would *be* possible as long as the Straits were under hostile Turkish control.

In both 1770 and 1827 the friendly Mediterranean naval power was Britain, which allowed the Russians to use their bases and stores for operations. This friendship was extended for extremely limited objectives, however, and could be withdrawn at any time, which subsequently left the Russians at the mercy of hostile powers, as happened to Seniavin in 1807. The Soviet *eskadra* in the Mediterranean since 1967 faces the same intractable logistical problems as Orlov, Seniavin or Geiden. For the Russian Navy and its successors, the Straits represent the Black Sea Fleet's 'choke point' for Mediterranean egress.[7] Whether Russia wanted to ignore the Mediterranean or not, it was nevertheless an important theatre which strongly impinged upon Russian security within the Black Sea itself. As Gorshkov remarks,

> ...we see that the Mediterranean Sea, lying near the southwestern Russian borders, beginning with the era of sailing fleets, appears as a region having an important strategic meaning for her defence. Russian squadrons undertook military action there not to conquer foreign territories or to enslave peoples, but for the sake of guaranteeing the security of their country.[8]

It is important to recognise both the importance and insularity of the Black Sea as considered in isolation from the Mediterranean; control of *both* is essential to shifting the strategic regional balance of power within the Black Sea itself in one's favour.[9] According to Gorshkov, 'The location of her [Russia's] ships in these [Mediterranean] waters is founded not only on geographical conditions (the proximity of the Black Sea to the Mediterranean theatre) but on the centuries-old need for the Russian fleet to remain there'.[10]

In a Mahanian context, the supreme strategic point in the Black Sea theatre of operations *was* the Straits; an absolute precondition for Russia obtaining 'command of the sea' in either the Black Sea or the Mediterranean was at the very least the neutralization or, at best, Russian possession of the Straits in order to be able to localise the theatre of operations.

Mahan wrote extensively in his work *Naval Strategy* about the importance of such a narrow channel:

> A strait is a strategic point, the value of which, like that of other points, depends: 1st, upon its situation; 2nd, upon its strength, which may be defined to consist in obstacles it puts in the way of an assailant and the consequent advantages to the holder; in other words, in its difficulties; 3rd, upon its resources or advantages, such as the facility it gives to the possessor for reaching a certain point,

or for passing from one of his ports to another; upon its shortening distances, etc.[11]

On the basis of his criteria, the Bosphorus and Dardanelles, in closing the passage between two great inland seas were of unique importance for both Russia and the Ottoman Empire. The strength of the passages in both man-made and natural obstacles was extremely formidable, but the passage northwards from the Mediterranean was by far the more difficult. As both Admirals Duckworth in 1807 and De Roebeck in 1915 discovered, the Dardanelles properly fortified could exact a fearful toll from those rash enough to attempt a northward passage in the teeth of sustained opposition.

While Geiden's forces had originally been sent to the Mediterranean in 1827 as part of an Anglo-French-Russian initiative to break the cycle of *revolutionary* bloodshed in Greece, during the subsequent Russo-Turkish war they provided the effective 'concentration of force' needed to cut Turkish supply lines from the Mediterranean. The plight of the Greeks had been a strongly emotive issue in Russia; more so than the French and the British, the Russians were tied to Greece by both cultural and religious links. Geiden's forces were suddenly transformed from neutral policemen to auxilliaries of the Black Sea Fleet.

Geiden's forces would prove passive but crucial in the 1828-29 war. By isolating the Sultan from his north African reserves, Geiden's squadron ensured maximum mobility for Russian land and Black Sea naval forces operating in both the Anatolian and Balkan theatres.

Navarino had temporarily crippled the Turkish fleet as an effective force, and this disability combined with the Russian Mediterranean squadron to give the Russians naval superiority in both the Black Sea–Mediterranean theatres. The actions undertaken in 1828–9 represent the most successful Russian naval operations in their many wars against the Turks precisely because of their ability to concentrate their force on the Straits from both the Black and Mediterranean Seas, allowing the Russians 'command of the sea' in both areas while simultaneously denying it to their opponents.

The malleability of seapower became obvious to the Russians as a result of the war, as the advantages conferred by obtaining regional 'command of the sea' were evident throughout the two-year campaign. The initial stages of the war were marked by the Ottomans using their position athwart the Straits to disrupt completely southern Russia's seaborne trade. Despite this economic setback, the Black Sea Fleet was able to use its superiority to shift troops between the Anatolian and Rumelian theatres, allowing Russia an economy of force relative to the Ottomans. The Fleet proved itself essential in the Anapa, Varna, and Poti campaigns, while in 1829 it allowed the Russian army to risk its tight flank at Šumen and cross the Balkans, penetrating Thrace to within a day's march of Constantinople and forcing a terrified Turkish government to negotiate.

Had Russian intentions in August-September 1829 been to either capture or destroy Constantinople there would have been nothing that the Ottoman Empire alone could have done to prevent it. Navarino and the Russian navy had achieved, 'the utter defeat of the enemy and the destruction of his essential strength and material basis (that is, his ships and crews and weapons stocks or shore objectives located within range').[12]

Black Sea Fleet ships equipped to fire 'hot shot' could have burned large areas of the Sultan's wooden capital to the ground in short order.

While Russian successes in the 1828-29 war were greater than in any other conflict that they fought with the Ottoman Empire up to that time, the cost of the war was high in both blood and treasure. Navarino, European apathy and Egyptian reluctance to intervene also had given Russia a priceless set of strategic circumstances which it could not be assumed would be operational in any future conflict.

By 1829, however, Russian attempts to capture the Straits and Constantinople had been abandoned in favour of a policy of allowing the Ottoman Empire to decay. The Adrianople Treaty and the Secret Committee's recommendations to Nicholas represented a fundamental shift in Russian policy as regarded the 'Eastern Question', for the first time since the time of Peter the Great. Nicholas was much more of a realist than his brother had been, and realised that any Russian attempt to capture Constantinople would involve Russia in a general war with Europe, a coalition war that Russia could not hope to win. The Secret Committee's recommendations supported this supposition, and it became the cornerstone of Russian policy towards the Ottoman Empire until the Crimean War.

Nicholas and Nesselrode increasingly made it a cornerstone of their policy to attempt subsequently to achieve a common European consensus for dealing with both the Ottoman Empire and the issue of the Straits. The thrust of their policy was defensive, not offensive. Russia would henceforth do nothing to weaken the Ottoman Empire; once Russian interests (especially trade) were protected, the Ottoman Empire would be allowed to senilize largely free from Russian pressure.

Should such moderation fail, naval considerations would be paramount in any future Russo-European war. In the south, Russian positional advantages would be largely nullified in any such conflict by the numerical superiority that a European naval coalition could bring into the Black Sea. While the geographical benefits of 'interior lines' within the Black Sea itself allowed Russia to concentrate its naval forces against Constantinople and the Straits more readily than the other European powers, this advantage was limited to being able to arrive earlier than possible Western European opponents.[13] Technological advances in the form of telegraph and steam power would shortly nullify this advantage, as Turkish allies would be able to move immediately after learning via telegraph of Russian activity without bothering about the adverse winds and currents.

In any Russian-Ottoman/Western European conflict, the best that the Russians could hope for in the Black Sea would be the relatively modest achievement of 'sea deniability', not allowing the enemy to exploit fully advantages conferred by a numerically superior 'command of the sea' force projected from an unassailable Mediterranean position. The concentration of nearly forty warships off the entrance to the Dardanelles in September 1829 was a harbinger of European reaction to what was perceived as Russian expansionism. The passage of time has not lessened the value of Mediterranean sabre-rattling; in 1946–7 over forty U.S. warships, including two aircraft carriers and seven cruisers, were deployed to the same area during a tense period of American–Soviet relations.[14]

It might be noted that this Russian self-restraint in limiting its conception of the need to exercise 'command of the sea' in distant waters has an echo in modern Soviet naval thought;

> It follows . . . that from the very beginning of its existence, Soviet naval art completely rejected attempts to identify the concept 'command of the sea' with the concept of 'command of the world'. The gaining of 'command of the sea' was always seen not as an end in itself, but rather a path to creating certain conditions of operational situations using the strength and abilities of the fleet to decide successfully particular missions in definite theatres in a specific period of time.[15]

If Russia did decide to take an initially aggressive posture against Turkey, then she would have to seize the Straits and close them before a numerically superior enemy could force his way up the Dardanelles past Constantinople into the Black Sea. A 'pre-emptive strike' against the Straits in the event of an outbreak of hostilities was proposed as an option by Lazarev during the 1830s. Rear Admiral Vladimir Kornilov forcefully argued for such a course of action in March 1853 prior to the outbreak of the Crimean War, but was overruled.[16] Russian government officials were much more timid, however, than their Nelsonic naval officers.

Such governmental caution was underscored by the fact that throughout the nineteenth century the army remained the principal element of Russian military force. While the Black Sea Fleet possessed the capability for a bold attack on Constantinople, holding the city and the Straits against subsequent determined opposition would be another matter. By the late 1830s Turkey had recovered its maritime parity with Russia; a Russian maritime assault could be only the opening act of a play whose decisive action would be determined by the armies of both sides.

As the 1828–9 campaign showed, a large Russian attacking force would face formidable logistical difficulties in invading the Ottoman Empire even with a naval advantage. By the time peace was signed at Adrianople in 1829, Dibich was down to less than 12 000 healthy troops. The subsequent Russian–Egyptian encounter in 1833 might be best described as an expedition facing down a second expedition. Should a Russo–Turkish conflict escalate into war, then the armies would prove decisive, rather than Hünkâr-sized expeditions with 11 000 men.

Nicholas's post-Adrianople *laissez-faire*, restrained attitude towards the Ottoman Empire presupposed two conditions: first, that no other European power would be allowed to influence the Ottoman Empire to an extent greater than Russia; second, any attempts at internal regeneration of the Ottoman Empire were to be carefully monitored, and if they produced hostility to Russia, opposed. Conversely, if the Ottoman Empire collapsed under the weight of its own torpor, Russia was willing to agree in advance as at Munchengratz to act in concert with other European powers regarding the disposition of Ottoman territorial remnants providing certain Russian 'special interests' were taken into account. By far the most important of these was the status of the Straits, both for commercial and naval ship passage.

Implicit in these considerations was the constant recognition by the Russian government of a British maritime superiority in the Mediterranean and beyond; any 'arrangement' over the carcass of the Ottoman Empire would have to take this superiority into account. A hostile Royal Navy in the eastern Mediterranean at the very least would bottle up Russian trade and the Black Sea Fleet in the Straits or the Black Sea itself; at worst, it could enter the Black Sea, attack Russian towns and shipping, sink the Black Sea Fleet, and overturn Russia's Georgian coastal positions. British hostility in the Baltic would similarly both pen up the Baltic Fleet and completely destroy St Petersburg's trade.[17]

As for a possible resolute British response to Russian 'aggression', British 'command of the sea' would allow them to attack at a place of their own choosing, but as the Crimean War proved, in a land campaign on the periphery of Russian territory an amphibious force could achieve only limited objectives. The 1915 Gallipoli campaign similarly proved the difficulties of projecting seapower onto coasts held by a determined enemy holding secure interior lines of supply and communication.

Throughout the period French naval power remained a secondary consideration for Russia, with the Anglo–French alliance during the Crimean War being the exception rather than the rule. Both powers pursued differing policies in the Middle East during the period under consideration, with France backing Mehmet Ali (and, by implication, weakening the Ottoman Empire), while Britain after 1833 was devoted to upholding the Ottoman Empire.

While these considerations of potential outside 'interference' profoundly influenced Russian defence and foreign policy up to the outbreak of the Crimean War, the new Russian 'peace policy' proved immediately beneficial to both former enemies, and their trade flourished. The period 1829–31 saw a phenomenal growth in both Russian and Turkish foreign trade as a result of the Adrianople Treaty's provisions opening passage of the Straits to the merchant shipping of all nations. Odessa now became the fastest-growing city in the Russian empire, its prosperity based on a flourishing grain trade. The former antagonists now acquired a fiscal incentive to preserve the *status quo*.

Russia's relations with the lands bordering on the Mediterranean and Black Sea were also changing. The post-Hünkâr period saw a further steady growth in Russia's export trade with its immediate neighbours to the south. Internal unrest in the Ottoman Empire would now not be only a military threat; with each passing year it would increasingly damage the Russian Exchequer.

The Adrianople Treaty solved the immediate problem of protection of Russian commerce from arbitrary interference in peacetime; the Turks would not interfere with the grain trade unless they desired war.

Even if war should break out, there was a basis for Russian belief that Britain would vociferously object to Turkish interference with neutral shipping through the Straits, as she had in 1828–9 during the Russian blockade. In such an instance, an Ottoman Empire at war would still behave most cautiously towards neutral shipping. With maritime trade secured by a bilateral agreement backed up by a powerful third-party navy, Russia's major unresolved southern maritime problem remained the possible passage of foreign warships through the Straits, a murky topic *that* the British believed was covered by their 1809 agreement with the Ottoman Empire. Russia began to see the disadvantages in *the* series of Ottoman bilateral accords on this important issue rather than a binding international agreement.

While the post-Adrianople trade explosion benefited the Russian Exchequer, it did not bring about a commensurate increase in the Russian merchant marine. The Mahanian factor of population did not lead to the growth of Russian seapower and its merchant marine. Relatively few of Russia's citizens made their living from the sea. Despite governmental encouragement, the number of Russians engaging in maritime commerce grew slowly; as a result, the majority of Odessa's trade remained in foreign hands. Governmental fiscal conservatism made many merchants loath to venture capital in uncertain maritime enterprises, subject to the vagaries of foreign interference.

On the issue of 'governmental character', Mahan noted that Great Britain had consistently aimed at control of the sea.[18] In peacetime, a government was to foster commerce and maritime trade. In contrast, the shortage of Russian commercial shipping led to a lack of any perceived governmental need to defend that commerce in wartime with a substantial fleet; the symbiotic link between the merchant marine and the fleet was lost. Mahan's remarks illuminate Russia's shortcomings in this regard; 'If seapower be really based upon a peaceful and extended commerce, aptitude for commercial pursuits must be a distinguishing feature of the nations that have at one time or another been great upon the sea'.[19] The prosperity of Russia's southern trans-Mediterranean trade depended not on Russian military means, but on peaceful relations with the Mediterranean naval powers.

This relative lack of merchant shipping deprived the Russian navy of a 'nursery' of competent seamen to use in emergencies. Russia's vast size and large population were in this case of little immediate maritime value, despite an increasing governmental interest in her burgeoning southern trade. The increasing foreign trade increased the responsibilities of the Russian Black Sea Fleet without bolstering its personnel reserve. The growth of this trade largely represented a liability. In the event of conflict this trade would be quickly destroyed, if not in the Black Sea then in the Mediterranean, and its fiscal benefit to the government ended.

Since the government did not muster the naval resources to guarantee the security of either their indigenous or foreign-based Mediterranean-Black Sea trade, Russian interest increased in an international agreement regulating Straits passage which could take the place of a Black Sea Fleet sufficiently strong to force and capture the vital waterways in any circumstances. As Russia's Black Sea trade grew increasingly profitable, so did the necessity for such an agreement. Russia could not bring pressure to bear on Ottoman commerce without having her own destroyed in turn.[20]

Added to governmental reluctance to increase naval resources to 'parity' with Mediterranean powers was a growing need for more Russian Black Sea Fleet assets within the Black Sea itself. Russia during this period had a continuing and increasing need for its southern military establishment; rebellion in Poland and accelerating guerilla warfare in the Caucasus increasingly occupied the peacetime Russian armed forces. While the Black Sea Fleet could operate effectively in an amphibious capacity on the Caucasus coast, it remained of value only in a 'regional' sense; it could only safeguard Russian merchant shipping within the confines of the Black Sea itself. The expanding demands by the southern military commands on slender resources meant that the Black Sea Fleet was constantly stretched simply to maintain its forces. The Caucasus insurgency demanded that the Black Sea Fleet build additional ships different from those required for a 'blue water' force.

The increasingly unsettled state of the Ottoman Empire after the Adrianople Treaty was a threat both to Russia's flourishing prosperity and her overcommitted navy. Like Russia, the Ottoman Empire also faced revolt, potentially more threatening to it than the recent Russo-Turkish war. Unlike the peripheral nature of the Caucasian threat to the Russian government, Constantinople was extremely vulnerable to both Egyptian land and sea forces if they were deployed in a sufficiently aggressive manner.

Alone among the Muslim rulers of this time Mehmet Ali thoroughly understood the value of Western military and industrial technology, and he moved quickly to acquire both. His efficiency in eliminating the Mamluks removed the one serious internal obstacle to his consolidation of power, while his Arabian and Grecian campaigns allowed him to hone the quality of his military.

A strong navy was essential to his plans for expansion and eventual independence. His monopoly of Egyptian agricultural produce gave him large cash reserves, and he began by buying whatever ships he could find in Europe and America. Navarino had destroyed relatively few Egyptian warships, but had severely crippled the Ottoman Navy. Mehmet expanded Alexandria's Arsenal and imported French naval engineers to build line ships.

Mehmet's ambition to control Syria was based on maritime and defence considerations in addition to his desire for the country's wealth. Not only would Syria provide the matériel for ship construction, but a strong Egyptian navy would control the invasion route to Egypt from Turkey, which lay along a narrow coastal area dominated by Acre. By the time that Mehmet launched his revolt in 1831 he had a navy equal to that remaining to the Turks after Navarino.

The Russian government was aware from the outset of Mehmet's revolt of its seriousness, and the consequences for Russia of an Egyptian victory. Quite apart from threatening Russia's growing Black Sea trade, the potential military consequences of such a success were immense. A revitalised Muslim government in Constantinople could draw upon the military resources of Turkey, Arabia, North Africa and Egypt; in 1832 the resurgent combined fleets of Turkey and Egypt alone were more than half again as large as the Russian Black Sea Fleet in capital ship numbers.

Furthermore, a militant Egyptian government in Constantinople might well encourage Caucasian Muslims to intensify their fight against Russia. Russia's coastal position in Georgia remained extremely fragile; a single hostile frigate on the eastern Black Sea coast could overwhelm all the Russian positions there.

Nicholas and Nesselrode consistently attempted to arouse the other European powers to the threat posed by Mehmet's revolt, but to no avail. The French and British saw the Viceroy's aggression as yet another typical incident of the minor unrest which periodically annoyed the outlying provinces of the Ottoman Empire; they were much more preoccupied with events closer to home in Belgium and Portugal. Russia found itself in the ironic position of supporting the Ottoman Empire against internal revolution three years after fighting a war with it.

If Russian aid to the Ottoman Empire was not offered solely for altruistic reasons, it was equally true that Russia was not acting to establish an exclusive protectorate over the Ottoman Empire. Russia was attempting unilaterally to preserve the Middle Eastern/Mediterranean-European *status quo* in view of general indifference.

The Russian naval aid sent to Turkey represented the Black Sea Fleet operating at its peak capability; such decisiveness combined with the tardy remonstrations of the other European powers to convince Mehmet Ali that the time was not quite right to achieve independence. To paraphrase the Chinese strategist Sun Tzu, the Black Sea Fleet had achieved the greatest of all victories, winning without fighting.[21]

Russia's reward for preserving the Ottoman Empire from dissolution was the vaguely-worded Hünkâr İskelessi Treaty, which subsequently poisoned Russian relations with the rest of Europe for twenty years. The Russian aid was perceived as establishing a *de facto* protectorate over the prostrate Turks. Both France and Britain remained unable to understand clearly Russia's peculiar security needs in the Ottoman Empire.

The Hünkâr Treaty, by its nebulous wording, encouraged Western European suspicions, although Russia never used the unilateral Treaty 'privileges' that some believed it accorded her to pass her larger warships through the Straits. The one possible exception to this would have been the passage of Rikord's squadron, but this occurred before the Treaty was ratified. Provocative attempts by Russophobe Royal Navy officers such as Captain Edmund Lyons in HMS *Blonde*-46 to test the Hünkâr Treaty and to heighten tension between Britain and Russia immediately began. On the Georgian coast which Russia had declared to be under blockade, British merchantmen also taunted Russia's pretensions.

Rather than being a devious Russian ploy to gain influence over the Ottoman Empire, the Hünkâr Treaty was a bilateral attempt by Russia to come to an agreement with the Ottoman Empire on the subject of Straits warship passage rights, a limited experiment of eight years duration. The absence of any international consensus made a bilateral agreement the best security that Russia could obtain under the circumstances. Her willingness to trade off her renewal rights of the Hünkâr İskelessi agreement in return for an inter-European agreement on the Straits was a primary element of Russian foreign policy in the 'second' Eastern crisis of 1840–1. Given Russia's overall weakness in the continued presence of superior European naval and commercial forces, the 1841 Straits Convention represented a great accomplishment.

We can divide the maritime situation in a conflict into five categories: absolute control ('command of the sea'), working control,

control in dispute, enemy working control, and enemy absolute control.[22] Up to the battle of Navarino, the Allies had 'control in dispute'; after the battle, the Allies had 'absolute control'. This 'absolute control' was exercised by the Russians throughout 1828–9, although if Mehmet Ali had contributed his naval forces to the Sultan's defence, the situation would have changed to 'control in dispute'. In 1832-3, the Turkish–Egyptian conflict was 'control in dispute' until the arrival of Russian naval aid in Constantinople, after which the Sultan had potential 'working control' if Mehmet should attempt an armed attack on the city.

The Hünkâr Treaty by closing the Straits to foreign warships gave the Russians 'working control' of the Black Sea for the next eight years. Russia could not assume that the unique opportunities provided her in 1827-29 would occur again, but an international convention on the Straits could at least ensure that a future war with the Ottoman Empire would not be with a 'coalition' of naval powers. Such an agreement would allow Russia in the Black Sea to consider the better odds of a Russo-Turkish 'control in dispute' situation rather than a possible Allied-Turkish 'absolute control'.

As Russian intentions were largely misunderstood by France and Britain, the period 1833–9 was one of unrelieved suspicion of Russia. British and French perceptions of Russian 'privileges' from the Hünkâr Treaty caused them to see sinister motives behind every Russian action, and they tailored their foreign and military policies accordingly. Anglo-French eastern Mediterranean naval deployments during this period were consistently higher than they had been before 1833.

Despite this unity in the face of Russian 'aggression', a divergence in Western European foreign policy in the Middle East also became apparent during this period. France tended to favour Egypt, while Britain attempted to establish closer links with the Ottoman Empire.

British interest in the eastern Mediterranean was no longer limited to local trade; the region now began to have an impact on the security of the British Empire itself. Experiments during this period had proved to Britain's satisfaction the feasibility of a mail link to India via the Red Sea, which concentrated British attention on any future instability in the area. A further incentive to British concerns for stability in the Ottoman Empire was the advantageous Balta Liman trade treaty signed in 1837. These two events alone ensured that any future unrest in the region would not be met with the complacency displayed by Britain in 1832–3.

While these considerations had all increased the need for a dynamic Russian presence on the Black Sea, circumstances instead produced paralysis in the Russian navy. Of the Fleet's condition at the time Gorshkov has noted,

> The ships almost never put to sea. The sailors were employed in secondary assignments. There was extensive corruption. The famous Russian Admiral V. M. Golovin wrote, '...if rotten, underarmed and poorly-equipped vessels and senile, infirm fleet commanders without awareness of the sea and its soul, inexperienced captains and officers and farmers and drafted mariners forced into ships crew can form a fleet, then Russia has a fleet'.[23]

In light of these considerations it is ironic that the Black Sea Fleet now passed under the leadership of a man of sufficient calibre to unnerve further Western European politicians and officers. The appointment of Mikhail Petrovich Lazarev as commander of the Black Sea Fleet produced a modest renaissance of Russian seapower.

Lazarev was one of the most remarkable naval men officers of his time. Highly experienced, energetic, and intensely patriotic, Lazarev laid the foundations of an increasingly efficient Black Sea Fleet; Sevastopol was fortified and provided with an aqueduct, barracks, building slips and drydocks. Lazarev consistently pushed an increased building programme for warships, and he was interested in dynamic naval developments such as shell guns and steam propulsion. While objective British naval officers downplayed the immediate 'threat' of the Black Sea Fleet, noting its shortcomings and deficiencies in personnel, matériel (especially quality timber), and training, the Black Sea Fleet's increasing ambitions and capabilities provided proof of sinister Russian designs for European politicians and officers looking to increase their country's naval budgets and their own political credibility.

In reality the Russian Black Sea Fleet increasingly had two mutually exclusive and irreconcilable strategic objectives to fulfill that divided its slender resources; securing the Caucasus against smugglers and possible foreign interventions since 1830, and defending southern Russia and its commerce against hostile maritime attack. Defence of Russian interests in the Caucasus meant maintaining two disparate types of naval forces; light, swiftsailing small craft for combating smugglers, and large warships both for maintaining a formal blockade of the coast and allowing Russian amphibious forces to carry out large-scale landings.

Naval innovations during the 1830s might have allowed Russia to increase her naval strength *vis-à-vis* superior naval powers. With the advent of developments in steam propulsion, shell guns and mine warfare, a progressive naval power had the potential largely to neutralise a numerically superior opponent equipped with obsolescent equipment. As the Russian victory at Sinop in 1853 demonstrated, the future belonged to steam-driven shell-firing warships, while the later defence of Kronstadt in 1854 with underwater galvanic mines stymied an attack by the British fleet.

Although only a few visionary naval officers at the time understood its future ramifications, the Industrial Revolution's impact upon naval warfare would soon render the ship of the line as obsolescent as a dug-out canoe. While iron-hulled, shellgun-equipped ships would allow a complete restructuring of the naval 'balance of power', only those states with a highly developed industrial base would be able immediately to take advantage of the opportunities provided. The Russian deterrent built up with so much effort by Lazarev and his cohorts would prove at Sinop that the future of naval warfare belonged to iron and coal, not wood and hemp. While Russia had abundant supplies of both elements for the new 'arms race', she did not possess the integrated industrial base of a Britain or France to be able effectively to utilise them.

Despite the enthusiastic endorsement of these innovations by progressive officers such as Lazarev, these developments were not encouraged by the Russian government, however, and so the naval reformers achieved only limited success. Prince Menshikov was an aristocratic cavalry officer crony of the Tsar, and his limited vision denied Russia the chance to partake of these innovative, albeit *expensive* technologies. Gorshkov laments the effects of this lack of commitment by the government during the Crimean War by observing, 'The technical backwardness of the Russian fleet produced a defensive, not an active military stance, which ran counter to the essence of the most mobile aspect of power, designed for searching out and destroying an enemy at sea'.[24]

True reform in the Russian navy began only in the wake of Russia's disastrous performance in the Crimean War. If we apply Mahan's criteria of the character of a state's government influencing a nation's development of seapower, then Russia during this period was hamstrung by its autocratic form of government. Nicholas did not have a clear understanding of the fundamental elements of sea-power. Nicholas's own interests were directed more towards the army, with the result that the naval budget during the period 1827–41 never exceeded more than 8 per cent of total governmental expenditures, as opposed to the army's share of income never dropping below 33 per cent. Lazarev had the further problem of competing with the Baltic Fleet for an equitable share of the naval budget. The Baltic Fleet's proximity to St Petersburg gave it a visibility to the government and the Tsar with a subsequent 'favouritism' that the Black Sea Fleet could not hope to match.

The logistical support base of the Black Sea Fleet during this period was also uneven. There were many reasons for this – fiscal austerity, corruption, a severe climate, the relatively weak state of the Russian industrial base, a shortage of skilled personnel, the difficulty of consistently maintaining an uninterrupted supply of high-quality naval stores. The end result was to render the continuous mainte-nance of the Black Sea Fleet an extremely expensive, difficult and uncertain task.

The strain on the Black Sea Fleet's resources was heightened by the constant need throughout the period under consideration to consider as the primary task of the Black Sea Fleet an undisputed 'command of the sea' of not only the Black Sea, but if possible the Straits as well. This meant that Russian strategic planning had to consider four possible scenarios: (1) war with Turkey alone, as in 1828–9; (2) war with the Ottoman Empire drawing freely on all its resources, including the formidable naval forces that Mehmet Ali was gathering in Egypt; (3) war with a hostile European power, or powers; (4) war with the Ottoman Empire allied to one or more European powers.

Had Russia pursued a genuinely aggressive policy against the Ottoman Empire during this period, then the naval forces that she was fielding in the Black Sea Fleet were sufficient only to secure her southern maritime frontiers against Turkey alone. By 1839 Turkey had completely recovered from the losses sustained at Navarino and could match the Russian Black Sea Fleet on a one-for-one basis in line ships and frigates, while from 1841 onwards her Fleet in conjunction with Egypt's would give her nearly twice as many line ships and frigates as Russia.

In any conflict which involved the Ottoman Empire allied to either France or Britain, the odds for Russia were even worse. With no international arrangement regarding passage of the Straits by foreign warships, Russia faced possible conflict with an Egyptian-European-Ottoman maritime coalition that would have an immediate maritime superiority of more than 3:1 in line ships and frigates. Furthermore, any such force would have the advantage of the 'interior lines' of both communications and bases in both the Mediterranean and the Straits. Russia could not even maintain the *status quo* in such a situation. 'It is power plus position that constitutes an advantage over power without position; or more instructively, equations of force are composed of power and position in varying degrees, surplus in one tending to compensate for deficiency in the other'.[25] In such a conflict Russia would have neither power nor position.

It was not as though Russia faced a static Ottoman Empire or Egypt during this period; both were re-arming and modernising their armies and navies as fast as their resources would allow. Mehmet Ali had the advantages of a complete control of Egyptian finances due to the system of monopolies that allowed him to purchase the weapons and technology he wanted. By 1839 the navy he had created from nothing was the equal of his sovereign's, and it was better-trained, with newer ships and weapons.

Mehmet Ali's ultimate weakness was that his military–naval resources were in the end artificial creations of his will-power. While Egypt could press-gang its peasants and hire foreign officers to train and lead them, the material needed to build and sustain a navy had to be purchased abroad. Mehmet bought both timber and finished ships from any European power willing to sell them, while his Alexandrian dockyard concentrated on building line ships. The Egyptian merchant marine was extremely insignificant, which meant that the Egyptian Navy lacked a reliable reserve. Given the Ottoman Empire's abundant timber and resources, it was only a matter of time before the Ottoman Empire overshadowed and crushed Mehmet's forces. To paraphrase modern American arms control negotiators, Mehmet Ali had to 'use it or lose it'.

The Ottoman Empire had problems as well. While its population and natural resources were far richer than Egypt's, the Ottoman armed forces suffered from severe shortages of trained personnel. Mahmut was more restricted than Mehmet in dealing with his bureaucrats, and had to take far more notice of conservative sentiments within both his government and his armed forces. The Ottoman merchant marine was as inconsequential as the Egyptian. Despite such handicaps, immediate and moderate successes were achieved in both training and matériel; in addition, British post-Hünkâr policy towards the Ottoman Empire was to strengthen it both by promoting reform and allowing the Ottoman Empire to use British officers and experts. With a superiority of position, population and resources, time was on the side of the Ottoman Empire. Given his options, Mahmut II decided to strike.

The flashpoint for a second conflict in less than a decade between the Ottoman Empire and Egypt was again Syria, where Mehmet Ali's harsh rule had provoked a massive uprising. The difference in 1839 was in the European response to the conflict. During the previous six years British willingness to intervene directly in the conflict between vassal and suzerain altered completely.

Turkish aggression threatened more than Mehmet Ali when an Ottoman army crossed the Euphrates in early 1839. Southern Russian economic growth (itself a product of the post-Adrianople period) had given Russia the strongest interest in upholding the Ottoman Empire's stability. This Russian desire for equilibrium on its southern frontier nevertheless did not extend to providing unilateral military aid to the Ottoman Empire under the terms of the Hünkâr İskelessi Treaty. Russia instead now sought an international effort from the outset. Furthermore, Nicholas made it clear that he would be willing in a post-conflict situation to trade the Hünkâr Treaty for an international treaty.

This moderation in maritime matters was further buttressed by Russian set-backs in Georgia; violence on the Caucasus coast sharply intensified in early 1840 and resulted in the loss of several positions, despite the major landings of the preceding three years. In addition to amphibious landings the Fleet was committed to a standing blockade of hundreds of miles of coastline. The Black Sea Fleet could not take both a commanding lead in defending Constantinople and recovering Russian positions on the Georgian coast; a defence of Constantinople after the defection of the Turkish Fleet meant a possible attack by nineteen Muslim line ships and as many frigates on a Russian force barely half as large. Unilateral Russian intervention in Turkey might subsequently result in an attack by a superior force of British and French ships.

In spite of the fears of various British Russophobes, the Russian Baltic and Black Sea Fleets during the period under consideration never constituted a serious threat to the Royal Navy, simply in numbers of warships if nothing else. A British naval author evaluating the two navies at the end of 1841 listed the Royal Navy as having 627 warships in commission to a Russian total of 126.

Despite the disparity in numbers, the British view of Russian seapower was very different in 1841 from what it had been in 1827. The Russian performance in Turkey in 1833 had traumatised British perceptions of Russian abilities and intentions to an irrational level, summed up by one of Palmerston's despatches in 1838 to the British ambassador in St Petersburg:

It is in vain for the Russian Government to say . . . that the Navy is The Emperor's hobby, and that it is simply for His Imperial Majesty's amusement that this armament is kept up. Nobody can be blinded by such a Pretext; and it is well known that the present Emperor is not a person accustomed to devote his own time and the revenue of his Empire to trifling pursuits, unconnected with serious views, and with important political objects.

Equally unsatisfactory is the excuse, that unless Russia keeps up her Navy to its War-Establishment in Peace, She will be unable to man and equip a Fleet for her defence in war, seeing that She has not a sufficiently large mercantile Navy to form an adequate nursery for seamen. That might be a reason for keeping up in time of peace a Squadron of Eight or Ten Sail of the Line, as the nucleus for a war-establishment; but it is not true that Russia has no mercantile Navy; and though that Navy may be much smaller than the mercantile Navy of some other Countries; still it would furnish ample and immediate means of complementing the equipment of her Fleet, when war should break out.[26]

Palmerston's comments indicate quite clearly what naval forces he considered sufficient for legitimate Russian needs, as well as how far Russian armaments exceeded the level that Britain felt comfortable with.

Russian pragmatism combined with a willingness to trade the Hünkâr treaty for an international agreement allowed Britain to take a commanding lead from the start in resolving the crisis. While France had originally agreed to act in concert with Britain and Russia to halt Mehmet Ali, French views increasingly diverged from those of Russia and Britain. Russia consistently supported an aggressive British policy in the Mediterranean, while preparing its own navy in the Black Sea and Baltic to intervene in conjunction with Austrian and British squadrons if necessary.

The result was a British squadron under Stopford and Napier blockading the Syrian coast and capturing Acre. The capture of Acre broke the Egyptian resistance, and as French support for Mehmet Ali did not extend to going to war with Britain, the crisis was rapidly defused.

With Mehmet Ali's defeat Russia was ready to trade its Hünkâr 'privileges' for an international agreement, and the Straits Convention was signed in July, 1841. It seemed a satisfactory agreement; the Ottoman Empire reasserted its 'ancient right' of sovereignty over the

Straits, Palmerston relieved himself of his nightmares of a Russian 'protectorate' over the Ottoman Empire, and Tsar Nicholas felt that his southern maritime frontier was at last secure.

The 1841 Straits Convention represented the best 'deal' that Russia could wangle out of the other European powers; in closing off the Straits to all warships while the Ottoman Empire was at peace, Russia could hope for naval parity in any future Russian–Turkish conflict. Similarly, any future Russian–European conflict would see southern Russia's maritime frontier secure from attack.

The one situation which the Convention did not truly provide for was the one which seemed the most unlikely to the Tsar and his advisors, a Russian war against an Ottoman Empire allied to superior, technologically advanced European powers. The Crimean War would prove Nicholas's faith in his European 'understandings' to be cruelly misplaced. The Crimean War's first casualty was the Russian hope of a war with the Ottoman Empire on a purely internal issue without the Turks opening the Straits to their European allies; Lazarev's beloved, increasingly obsolescent Black Sea Fleet was the second.

Appendix 1
Shipbuilding Programme of the Black Sea Fleet, 1827–41

Name & Guns	Date laid down/launched	Where	Shipwright
LINE SHIPS			
Imperatritsa Mariia-84	5-X-1826/29-X-1827	Nikolaev	Razumov
Chesme-84	3-I-1827/6-VII-1828	"	Kaverznev
Anapa-84	3-VIII-1828/19-IX-1829	"	Surovtsov
Pamiat' Evstafii-84	23-V-1829/6-IX-1830	"	Osminin
Adrianopol'-84	9-IX-1829/23-XI-1830	"	Kaverznev
Imperatritsa Ekaterina II-84	9-IX-1829/12-VII-1831	"	Surovtsov
Varshava-120	11-IV-1832/18-XI-1833	"	Osminin
Silistriia-84	5-I-1834/12-IX-1835	"	"
Sultan Mahmud-86	13-II-1835/12-XI-1836	"	Apostoli
Tri Sviatitelia-120	10-I-1836/10-IX-1838	"	Vorob'ev
Trekh Ierarkhov-84	2-XII-1836/10-IX-1838	"	Cherniavskii
Gavriil-84	10-IX-1838/1-XII-1839	"	Akimov
Selafail-84	10-IX-1838/22-VII-1840	"	Apostoli
Uriil-84	10-IX-1838/12-IX-1840	"	Akimov
Dvenadtsat' Apostolov-120	16-X-1838/27-VII-1841	"	Cherniavskii
Varna-84	16-X-1838/7-VIII-1842	"	Vorob'ev
Iagudiil-84	3-X-1839/29-IX-1843	"	Dmit'riev
FRIGATES			
Tenedos-60	26-VIII-1827/16-XI-1828	"	Kaverznev
Kniagina Lovich-44*	13-XII-1827/7-IV-1828	St P.	Stoke
Anna-60*	8-X-1828/1-VII-1829	"	"
Agatopol-60	18-IX-1833/23-XI-1834	Nikolaev	Vorob'ev
Brailov-44	26-II-1835/18-X-1836	Sevastopol	Cherniavskii
Flora-44	6-XII-1837/3-X-1839	Nikolaev	Akimov
Messemvriia-60	16-X-1838/12-XI-1840	"	Cherniavskii
Sizepol-54	4-XI-1838/16-III-1841	Sevastopol	Prokof'ev
CORVETTES			
Sizepol-24	11-VII-1829/18-IX-1830	Nikolaev	Osminin
Penderakliia-24	18-III-1830/18-IX-1831	"	"

Name & Guns	Date laid down/launched	Where	Shipwright
Messemvriia-24	15-V-1831/6-V-1832	Sevastopol	Prokof'ev
Ifigeniia-22	18-IX-1833/12-VI-1834	Nikolaev	Apostoli
Orest-18	10-I-1836/12-IX-1836	"	Akimov
Pilad-20	16-X-1838/5-VII-1840	"	Mashkin
Minelai-20	22-V-1839/21-XI-1841	Sevastopol	Prokof'ev
Andromakha-18	1-VII-1840/1-VIII-1841	Nikolaev	Mashkin
Kalisto-18	2-VII-1841/21-IX-1845	"	"

BRIGS

Name & Guns	Date laid down/launched	Where	Shipwright
Telemak-20*	13-XII-1827/25-V-1828	St P.	Stoke
Uliss-20*	13-XII-1827/25-V-1828	"	"
Aiaks-20*	11-XII-1828/30-V-1829	"	"
Paris-20*	11-X-1828/30-V-1829	"	"
Kastor-18	5-III-1828/6-XI-1829	Nikolaev	Kaverznev
Poluks-18	5-III-1828/21-XI-1829	"	"
Themistokl-18	2-XI-1832/18-IX-1833	Sevastopol	Akimov
Argonaut-12	14-II-1837/15-IX-1838	Nikolaev	Prokof'ev
Endimion-12	6-XII-1837/28-VI-1839	Nikolaev	Cherniavskii
Palamid-18	16-X-1837/17-IX-1839	"	Kirilov
Themistokl-16	16-X-1838/29-XI-1839	"	Afanas'ev
Persei-16	28-VI-1839/5-VII-1840	Nikolaev	Afanas'ev
Neark-12	5-VIII-1840/7-VIII-1842	"	Kirilov
Enei-12	5-VIII-1840/7-VIII-1842	"	Afanas'ev

SCHOONERS

Name & Guns	Date laid down/launched	Where	Shipwright
Kur'er-12	24-V-1830/31-V-1831	"	Ivanov
Vestnik-12	13-VI-1830/13-VI-1831	"	"
Strela-10		"	
Gonets-16	24-IX-1833/24-V-1833	"	Karagurin
Vestovoi-14	24-IX-1833/16-VI-1835	"	Nikolaev
Lastochka-12	22-II-1837/24-VI-1838	"	Nikolaev
Smelyi-16	3-XI-1838/22-V-1838	Sevastopol	Prokof'ev
Drotik-16	6-XII-1837/28-VI-1839	Nikolaev	Venberg
Zabiiaka-16	16-X-1838/5-IX-1839	"	Afanas'ev
Vestnik-12	25-XI-1840/9-X-1841	"	Kirilov

BRIGANTINES

Name & Guns	Date laid down/launched	Where	Shipwright
Nartsis-18	7-X-1826/27-XII-1829	Sevastopol	Osminin

YACHTS

Name & Guns	Date laid down/launched	Where	Shipwright
Rezvaia-10	10-X-1828/11-VI-1830	Nikolaev	"
Satunovo (rowing)	18-III-1829/12-VIII-1830	"	"
Strela-10	24-IX-1834/9-IV-1835	"	Dmitriev
Orianda-10	27-VII-1836/10-IV-1837	"	Akimov

CUTTERS

Name & Guns	Date laid down/launched	Where	Shipwright
Bistryi-12	21-IIX-1832/10-VI-1833	Sevastopol	Cherniavskii

Name & Guns	Date laid down/launched	Where	Shipwright
CUTTERS cont'd			
Skoryi-6	21-IIX-1832/10-VI-1833	"	"
STEAMERS			
Liman	?	?	?
Gromonosets-14	5-III-1829/7-IX-1830	Nikolaev	Osminin
Vezuvii	29-VIII-1830/1-XII-1830	"	"
Petr Velikii-2	7-VI-1834/21-VIII-1834	England	Valis (Wallace)
Severnaia Zvezda-10	3-VII-1834/13-VIII-1835	Nikolaev	Dmitriev
Iazon-7		England	(bought 1836)
Kolkhida-7	(bought 1837)	"	Digborn
Uspeshnyi	1-XII-1836/29-VIII-1837	Nikolaev	Dmitriev
Silach-4	5-XI-1837/27-XI-1838	"	"
Inkerman-2	(bought 1838)	England	
Predpriiatie	3-III-1839/12-VI-1839	"	Ferben
Meteor-2	19-VI-1838/8-XI-1839	Nikolaev	Dmitriev
Moguchi-7	? / 1839	England	
Boets-7	? / 1839	England	
Molodets-7	? / 1839	"	
Molniia-4	12-XI-1840/1-VIII-1842	Nikolaev	Dmitriev
TRANSPORTS			
Sukhum-Kale-6	?/29-VI-1827	Nikolaev	Razumov
Pelageia-4		Sold 1829	
Chapman-5	8-VIII-1831/1-XII-1832		
Slon-12	8-VIII-1831/1-XII-1832		
Persei-8	(bought 1832)		
Andromeda-4	(bought 1832)		
Berezan-6	10-I-1836/17-IX-1837	Nikolaev	Karachurin
Ingul-2	31-X-1836/ "	"	Afanas'ev
Kuban-4	1-XII-1836/17-IX-1837	Nikolaev	Afanas'ev
Dnepr-4	18-X-1836/7-VI-1838	"	Ivanov
Kinburn-2	1-XII-1837/22-IX-1838	"	Prokof'ev
Kodos-4	(bought 1838)	England	
Socha-4	16-X-1838/4-XII-1839	Nikolaev	Mashkin
Ialta-8	15-VII-1839/23-XII-1840	Sevastopol	Prokof'ev
Adler-2	(bought 1839)	England	
Subashi-4	" "	"	"
Mamai-4	" "	"	"
Laba-4	" "	"	"
Gagra-10	4-XII-1839/1-IX-1841	Nikolaev	Mashkin
Sukhum-Kale-2	23-XII-1840/29-IX-1843	Sevastopol	Prokof'ev
Rion-4	1-IX-1840/29-IX-1843	Nikolaev	Mashkin
Dunai-6	1841/17-X-1847	Sevastopol	Deliabel

NOTE: All ships marked with an asterisk (*) either passed the Dardanelles and Bosphorus as part of Rear-Admiral Rikord's squadron in July 1833, or were sent from St Petersburg into the Mediterranean for the use of the Russian diplomatic mission in Greece.

Appendix 2
Warship Construction in the Black Sea, 1827–41 (dates launched)

Year	Line	Frigate	Corvette	Brig	Schooner	Steamer	Transport	Other
1827	1						3	65
(+2 luggers, 3 plashkhouts and 60 pontons)								
1828	1	2						17
(+5 gunboats, 10 iuls, 1 plashkhouts, 1 supply lodok)								
1829	1	2	2					9
(+1 brigantine and 8 iuls)								
1830	2	1	1		2	2		2
(+2 yachts)								
1831	1	2	1					1
(+1 lugger)								
1832							2	11
(+1 dredging ship and 10 pontons)								
1833	1			1				10
(+2 tenders and 8 iuls)								
1834		1	2					1
(+1 plashkhouts)								
1835	1				2	1		13
(+4 tenders, 1 yacht, and 8 podvoznyi bots)								
1836		1	1					1
(+1 podvoznyi bot)								
1837						1	3	34
(+1 yacht, 3 podvoznyi bots, and 30 barges)								
1838	2			1	1	1	2	16
(+8 podvoznyi bots, 2 rowed boats, and 6 pontons)								
1839	1		1	3	3	1	1	12
(+1 tender, 6 Azov lighters, 4 port barges, 1 podvoznii bots)								
1840	2	1	1	2	1 (transport)			4
(+2 plashkouts for heavy work and 2 for supply)								
1841	1	1	1	1			1	20
(+5 gunboats, 5 plashkhouts, 1 bot for Sudzhuk bay, and 8 pontons)								

Appendix 3
Russian Warship Losses in the Black Sea, 1827–41

Ship/armament	Date	Commander	Deaths	Details of accident
Revnitel' (transport)	22-III-1827	Lt Z.N. Talaev	–	Thrown ashore during a storm at Anapa
Strela-10 (schooner)	17-X-1828	Lt V.A. Vlas'ev	–	Thrown ashore during storm on Black Sea E. coast & broken up
Zmeia (transport)	7-XI-1828	Capt.-Lt Tugarinov	–	Sunk by a storm at Cape Inadia
Captured Turk prizeship No. 4	18-X-1829	Lt K. Alekseev(3rd)	–	Lost on voyage from Nikolaev
Sv. Nikolai (Captured Turk prizeship)	13-XII-1829	–	6	Destroyed by explosion at Izmail
Captured Turk prizeship No. 6	26-IX-1830	Lt V.A. Mordasov	–	Grounded near Odessa & broken up by waves
Gagara	24-XII-1830	Capt. G.G. Riumen	–	Driven onshore near Kozlova by storm 38; broken apart
Captured Turk prizeship No. 14	1830	Lt Organovich(3rd)	–	Wrecked at Danube mouth
Nartsis-18 (brigantine)	29-III-1829	Capt.-Lt G.I. Romanovich	–	Wrecked onshore at Anapa; refloated 1833
Sukhum-Kale-6 (transport)	25-III-1833	Lt Ia.F. Khotumov(2nd)	1	Wrecked & broken up by storm at Pitsunda
Captured Turk prizeship No. 1	6-IV-1834	Lt A.P. Nabatov	–	Sunk by fire at Izmail

Ship/armament	Date	Commander	Deaths	Details of accident
Ingulets (transport)	26-VII-1835	Capt.-Lt G.I. Romanovich	–	Grounded on reef at Gelendzhik & broken up
Chaika (transport)	12-VII-1836	Lt N.I. Piatunin	1	Sunk by squall near Tarkhankut
Podobnyi (transport)	29-XII-1836	Lt K.I. Bilim Kolosovskii	7	Driven ashore & wrecked by storm at Sukhum
Varna-60 (frigate)	12-VI-1838	Capt.-2 A.A. Tishevskii	17	Driven ashore & wrecked by storm at Sochi
Messemvriia-24 (corvette)	12-VI-1838	Lt N.M. Budakov	13	As *Varna*-60; 9 crew captured by mountaineers
Themistokl-16, (brig)	12-VI-1838	Capt.-Lt N.F. Metlin	2	Driven ashore & wrecked by same storm at Tuapse
Luch-12 (tender)	12-VI-1838	Lt A.I. Panfilov	3	As *Themistokl*-16; later refloated
Skoryi-6 (cutter)	12-VI-1838	Lt P.I. Kislinskiii	–	As *Luch*-12
Lanzheron (transport)	12-VI-1838	Lt D.A. Motsenigo	–	Thrown ashore at Tuapse by same storm & broken up
Iazon-7 (steamer)	28-VII-1838	Capt.-Lt Ia. F. Khomutov	–	Thrown ashore twice at Tuapse by storm & broken up
Sv. Nikolai (transport)	23-X-1839	Lt F.G. Evlashev	–	Grounded on sandbar at Danube Sulina mouth & broken apart
Gelendzhik-12 (lugger)	5-XII-1839	Lt I.T. Alekse'ev	2	Frozen into ice at Sudzhuk Kale & crushed

Appendix 4
Russian Merchant Ship Construction in Black Sea Ports, 1827–41

Year	Corvettes	Brigs	Tribaks	Golettes	Martigs	Coastal shipping	Total
1827							
Azov	–	–	–	–	–	1	1
Kherson	–	–	1	–	–	–	1
1828							
Azov	–	–	2	–	–	–	2
Kherson	–	6	7	–	–	–	13
1829							
Azov	–	4	2	–	1	–	7
Kherson	–	10	18	–	–	–	28
1830							
Azov	–	2	7	1	–	3	13
Kherson	–	4	22	–	–	–	26
1831							
Azov	–	3	4	–	–	3	10
Kherson	–	2	26	–	–	–	28
1832							
Azov	–	4	15	–	2	4	25
Kherson	–	–	8	–	–	–	8
1833							
Azov	–	1	10	–	3	8	22
Kherson	–	1	4	–	–	–	5
Other	–	–	3	–	–	–	3

Year	Corvettes	Brigs	Tribaks	Golettes	Martigs	Coastal shipping	Total
1834							
Azov	–	2	2	–	–	2	6
Kherson	–	1	5(2)	–	–	–	6(3)
Other	1	–	–	–	–	–	1
1835							
Azov	–	2	18	–	10	12	42
Kherson	–	2(1)	10(2)	–	–	–	12(3)
Other	–	(1)	(2)	–	–	–	(3)
1836							
Azov	–	5	18	–	4	17	44
Kherson	–	2(1)	11(4)	–	–	–	13(5)
Other	–	(1)	(4)	–	–	–	(5)
1837							
Azov	–	9	28	–	3	21	61
Kherson	2	4	18(9)	–	–	–	24(9)
Other	–	–	(9)	–	–	–	(9)
1838							
Azov	–	16	20	5	3	13	57
Kherson	1	7(2)	12	–	–	–	20(15)
Other	1	(2)	1	–	–	–	2(2)
1839							
Azov	–	8	3	–	–	–	11
Kherson	3	14	34	–	–	–	51
Other	–	2	12	–	–	–	14
1840							
Azov	n/a	n/a	n/a	n/a	n/a	n/a	n/a
Kherson	–	9	19	–	–	–	28
Other	n/a	n/a	n/a	n/a	n/a	n/a	n/a
1841							
Azov	n/a	n/a	n/a	n/a	n/a	n/a	n/a
Kherson	–	3	13	–	–	–	16
Other	n/a	n/a	n/a	n/a	n/a	n/a	n/a
TOTAL	8	123	353	6	26	84	600
Ships built 1827–41		(118)	(326)				(444)

1. The Sea of Azov construction sites were at Azov, Rostov, Taganrog, and Starocherkask.
2. Other Black Sea merchantmen construction centres were at Akkerman, Aleshëk, Berislavl', Izmail, Kerch, Nikolaev, Novogeorgievsk, Odessa, and Ochakov.

Compiled from: M. Bukhteev, 'Chernomorskoe torgovoe sudostroenie i moreplavanie', in *Kommercheskaia Gazeta*, 15-X-1840, No. 119, pp. 475–6; 17-X-1840, No. 120, pp. 479–80; and M. Bukhteev, 'Torgovoe sudostroenie v Khersone', *Zhurnal Manufaktur i Torgovli*, August 1843, pp. 265–78; 'Statisticheskoe opisanie Azovskago torgovago moreplavaniia', *Zhurnal Manufaktur i Torgovli*, June 1839, pp. 433–55.

NOTES Discrepancies occur in the incomplete figures given in Bukhteev's two articles, particularly in the given totals. The *Kommercheskaia Gazeta* figures are given in brackets (–).

For the years 1827–32, shipbuilding figures for Kherson are included with those of the other Black Sea ports minus the Azov Sea construction sites.

Appendix 5
Russian Expenditure on the Imperial Navy, 1827–41

	I	II	III	IV	V	VI	VII
1827	24 115 991	27 310 000	161 718 000	421 617 000	.384	.057	(.065)
1828	27 476 374	30 589 000	151 500 000	406 927 000	.372	.068	(.075)
1829	31 284 809	32 149 000	161 751 000	427 906 000	.378	.073	(.075)
1830	31 615 663	33 047 000	153 679 000	427 847 000	.359	.074	(.077)
1831	30 949 623	32 954 000	160 446 000	446 589 000	.359	.069	(.074)
1832	28 550 078	30 184 000	177 692 000	496 614 000	.357	.057	(.061)
1833	30 480 265	32 922 000	175 186 000	495 048 000	.355	.062	(.066)
1834	30 222 486	34 835 000	172 716 000	527 548 000	.327	.057	(.066)
1835	37 534 999	42 695 000	201 446 000	587 093 000	.343	.064	(.073)
1836	35 921 020	38 470 000	197 251 000	583 472 000	.338	.062	(.067)
1837	36 419 376	38 040 000	199 383 000	573 335 000	.347	.064	(.066)
1838	35 518 090	39 989 000	199 692 000	596 515 000	.355	.060	(.067)
1839	37 734 322	40 768 000	222 368 000	627 925 000	.354	.060	(.064)
1840	11 573 519	12 691 000	70 227 000	187 980 000	.373	.061	(.067)
*	40 507 316	44 418 000	245 794 000	657 930 000	–	–	–
1841	11 852 892	12 572 000	68 949 000	195 767 000	.351	.061	(.064)
*	41 485 122	44 002 000	240 971 000	685 184 000	–	–	–

All figures are in millions of rubles. I = Navy Ministry expenditure (Ogorodnikov); II = Navy Ministry expenditure (Finance Ministry); III = Army expenditures (Finance Ministry); IV = Total governmental expenditure (Finance Ministry); V = Army per cent of total annual budget (Finance Ministry); VI = Navy per cent of total annual budget (Ogorodnikov); VII = Navy per cent of total annual budget (Finance Ministry).

Compiled from *Ministerstvo Finansov 1802–1902*, Chast'l, Sanktpetrburg 1902 and S. Ogorodnikov, *Istoricheskii Obzor Russkogo Flota*, Sanktpetrburg, 1902.

NOTE Values for the assignat rubles in the years 1840–41 (the lines marked with an asterisk (*) under 1840/1841) are calculated using a multiplication factor of 3.5 assignat rubles for every silver ruble, a figure decided upon in early 1839 as an official conversion rate.

Notes and References

1 The Greek Revolt and Tsar Nicholas's First Turkish War

1. Seniavin had the line ships *Gangut*-84, *Tsar Konstantin*-74, *Kniaz Vladimir*-74, *Iezekiil*-74, *Azov*-74, *Aleksandr Nevskii*-74, *Sysoi Velikii*-74, *Sviatoi Andrei*-74, *Emmanuil*-64, frigates *Konstantin*-44, *Merkurius*-44, *Provornyi*-44, *Kastor*-44, *Vestovoi*-44, *Diana*-44, *Elena*-36, *Kreiser*-36, the corvettes *Gremiashchii*-24 and *Userdie*-20, and the brig *Akhilles*-16. 'Spisok korablei eskadry Vitse-Admirala D. N. Seniavina', 12-VI-1827, in Nikul'chenkov, K. I. (ed.), *M.P. Lazarev; Dokumenty* (hereafter referred to as *Lazarev*) Moskva 1952–61, 3 vols, Vol. 1, p. 294.
2. A. Aptsimovich, 'Admiral Dmitri Nikolaevich Seniavin', *Morskoi Sbornik* (hereafter referred to as *MS*. Note; all *MS* pre-Revolutionary references are from the 'neofitsial'nyi' [unofficial] section of the journal unless noted otherwise), December 1855 p. 261.
3. M. Litvinov, *Chernoe More; Moria v Raznyia Istoricheskiia Epokhia*, Sanktpetrburg, 1881, p. 51.
4. 'Deiatelnost' Admiralteistva v tsarstvovanie Imperatora Nikolaia I', *MS*, November 1859, pp. 1–4; V. K. Istomin, 'Kontr-Admiral Istomin', *Russkii Arkhiv* (hereafter referred to as *RA*), pt. 1, 1877, pp. 124–6.
5. S. I. Kirilov, 'Zarozhdenie sudostroeniia na severe', *Sudostroenie*, March 1966, p. 82.
6. Moller–Seniavin, 24-IV-1827, in *Lazarev*, Vol. 1, op. cit., pp. 293–4.
7. Ministerstvo Inostrannykh Del'–Seniavin, 24-IV-1827, in *Lazarev*, Vol. 1, op. cit., pp. 289–93.
8. M. Rifaat Bey, *The Awakening of Modern Egypt*, Lahore, 1964, pp. 40–41. Two Egyptians were taken as supernumeraries into the Royal Navy. Melville-Adm., 26-XI-1828 ADM. 1-478; Briggs-Adm., 17-XI-1828, 26-XI-1828 ADM. 12-254.
9. Georges Douin, *Les Premieres Frégates du Mohammed Ali*, Cairo, 1924, p. 78.
10. Barker-Canning, 21-VIII-1827, FO 142–2; Malcolm–Adm., 4-X-1830, ADM. 1-453.
11. Roger Charles Anderson, *Naval Wars in the Levant 1559–1853*, Princeton, 1952, p. 507.
12. C.G. Pitcairn-Jones, *Piracy in the Levant*, London, 1934, p. 282. British merchantmen also suffered. In 1826 sixteen British vessels were plundered; the next year the number had risen to thirty-eight. *Nautical and Maritime Magazine*, March 1828, pp. iii–iv.

13. Nesselrode–Lieven, 15-VI-1827, BM. ADD. MSS. 47248.
14. Lieven–Nesselrode, 3-IX-1827, BM. ADD. MSS. 47248.
15. Liubomir G. Beskrovnyi *Russkaia Armiia i Flot v XIX V.*, Moskva, 1973, p. 494.
16. *Obzor Deiatel'nosti Morskogo Upravleniia v Rossii (1855–1880), Chast' l*, Sanktpetrburg, 1880, pp. 397–9.
17. A.M. Zaionchkovskii, *Vostochnaia Voina 1853–1856*, Sanktpetrburg, 1908, 2 vols; Vol. 1. p. 616.
18. Seniavin–Nicholas, 20-VII-1827 in *Lazarev*, op. cit., Vol. 1, pp. 300–301.
19. Fenwick–FO, 24-VII-1827, 25-VII-1827, ADM. 12-244.
20. Pigot–Adm., 7-VIII-1827, 21-VII-1827, ADM. 12-246; Stopford–Adm., 8-VIII-1827 ADM. 1-339.
21. Nicholas–Geiden, 13-VII-1827, in G. Paleolog and M. Sivinis *Istoricheskii Ocherk Narodnoi Voiny za Nezavisimost' v Gretsii*, Sanktpetrburg, 1867, pp. 5–7.
22. Annex F 12-VII-1827 in *Parliamentary Papers* (hereafter referred to as *PP*), Vol. XLVIII (1831–2), pp. 184–5.
23. Nesselrode–Lieven, 15-VI-1827, 10-VII-1827, 13-VII-1827, BM. ADD. MSS. 47248; Stopford–Adm., 10-VIII-1827, ADM. 1-1338.
24. Stopford–Adm., 10-VII-1827, ADM. 12-246.
25. Stopford–Adm., 10-VIII-1827, ADM. 1-1338; Gray–Stopford, 16-VIII-1827, ADM. 12-246; Benkhausen–Crocker, 20-VIII-1827, ADM. 1-3860.
26. Seniavin–Geiden, 17-VIII-1827, in *Lazarev*, op. cit., Vol. 1, pp. 301–2.
27. Ministerstvo Inostrannykh Del–Seniavin, 16-VI-1827, in *Lazarev*, Vol. 1, op. cit., pp. 289–93.
28. Stopford–Adm., 20-VII-1827, ADM. 1-1339. Geiden took *Gangut*-84, *Azov*-84, *Iezekiil*-74, *Aleksandr Nevskii*-74, *Provornyi*-44, *Tsar Konstantin*-74, *Elena*-36, *Kastor*-44, and *Gremiashchii*-24.
29. Beauclerk–Adm., 1-IX-1827, ADM. 12-246.
30. Fenwick–Adm., 15-IX-1827, ADM. 12-246.
31. Codrington–Bethnell, 28-VII-1827, in Lady Bourchier, ed. *Memoirs of the Life of Admiral Sir Edward Codrington*, London, 1873, 2 vols (hereafter referred to as *Codrington*), Vol. 1, pp. 395–6.
32. Ross-Adm., 24-III-1827, ADM. 106-2050.
33. Charles Colville Frankland *Travels to and from Constantinople in the Years 1827 and 1828*, London, 1829, 2 vols; Vol. 1, p. 108. In addition to the detachment being prepared, Frankland noted seven line ships, three to four frigates, and some corvettes and brigs. All appeared 'dreadfully rotten'.
34. Journal of Captain Bompar of the frigate *Egyptian*, enclosed in Codrington–Adm., 12-IV-1828, ADM. 1-450.
35. 'Statement of dispositions of combined Turkish & Egyptian naval forces August 20, 1827', enclosure in Craddock–Dudley, 21-IX-1827, FO 78-182.
36. Barker–Canning, 21-VIII-1827, FO 142-2.
37. Hamilton–Codrington, 27-VIII-1827, enclosure in Codrington-Adm., 4-IX-1827, ADM. 1-448; Codrington–Adm., 26-X-1827, ADM. 1-448; Codrington–Adm., 2-IV-1828, ADM. 1-450.
38. Dudley–Craddock, 14-VII-1827, FO 78-182.

39. Salt–Canning, 21-VIII-1827, FO 78–160.
40. Barker–Canning, 21-VIII-1827, FO 142–2.
41. Codrington–Hamilton, 1-VII-1827, in *Codrington*, op. cit., Vol. 1, p. 401.
42. Bompar journal, enclosure in Codrington–Adm., 12-IV-1828, ADM. 1-450; Craddock–Dudley, 21-IX-1827, FO 78–182; Barker–Wilkenson, 5-VII-1827, FO 142–2.
43. Hamilton–Codrington, 27-VIII-1827, enclosure in Codrington–Adm., 4-IX-1827, ADM. 1-448.
44. Craddock–Canning, 21-VII-1827, FO 78–182.
45. Salt–FO, 19-VIII-1827, FO 78–192.
46. Salt–Dudley, 27-VIII-1827, FO 78–192.
47. Codrington–Bethnell, 21-VII-1827, in *Codrington*, op. cit., Vol. 1, p. 393.
48. Anderson, op. cit., p. 515.
49. Codrington–Canning, 1-VIII-1827, in *Codrington*, op. cit., Vol. 1, p. 398.
50. Adm.–Codrington, 13-VII-1827, with enclosures, ADM. 1-467.
51. 'You may judge how comfortable it will make me to have to rely on French and Russians. In truth, I will place no reliance upon any but ourselves...', Codrington–Hamilton, 7-VII-1827, in *Codrington*, Vol. 1, op. cit., p. 404.
52. Codrington–Adm., 3-IX-1827, ADM. 1-448.
53. Canning–Codrington, 19-VIII-1827, enclosure in Codrington–Adm., 9-XII-1827, ADM. 1-467. In another despatch of 1-IX-1827, Canning again reiterated the use of 'cannon-shot' if necessary.
54. Codrington–Adm., 3-IX-1827, ADM. 1-448.
55. Bompar journal, enclosure in Codrington–Adm., 12-IV-1828, ADM. 1-450.
56. Codrington–Adm., 12-IX-1827, ADM. 1-467.
57. 'I hardly expect to see Count Heiden during the month of September, but I shall be very glad of the reinforcement of the Russian squadron'. Codrington–Canning, 16-IX-1827, in *Codrington*, op. cit., Vol. 1, pp. 461–7.
58. Codrington–Ottoman Admiral in Navarin 19-IX, enclosure in Codrington–Adm., 25-IX-1827, ADM. 1-467.
59. Codrington–Adm., 25-IX-1827, ADM. 1-467.
60. Annex A, 10-IX-1827, *PP* Vol. XLVIII, op. cit., pp. 186–7.
61. 17-IX-1827, Protocol, *PP* Vol. XLVIII, op. cit., p. 188.
62. Annexes A–C, 17-IX-1827, Vol. XLVIII, op. cit., pp. 12–14.
63. Codrington–Geiden, 30-IX-1827, enclosure in Codrington–Adm., 9-XII-1827, ADM. 1-467.
64. V. Mel'nitskii, 'Tri glavy iz ocherka deistvii russkogo flota pri osvobozhdenii Gretsii', *MS*, February 1861, pp. 356–7.
65. Mikhail Aleksandrovich Rykachev, *God Navarinskoi Kampanii*, Sankpetrburg, 1877, p. 43.
66. Codrington–Adm., 2-X-1827, Codrington–Mustafa, 2-X-1827, Patrona Bey–Codrington/De Rigny [n.d.], Codrington–Adm., 4-X-1827, Codrington–Adm., 6-X-1827, ADM. 1-467.
67. Codrington–Mustafa, 2-X-1827, ADM. 1-467.
68. Codrington-Adm., 10-X-1827, ADM. 1-467.

69. 'He appears to be all I could wish; like one of our service, eager to act under my orders as he is instructed to do'. Codrington–Canning, 14-X-1827, Codrington–Lady Codrington, 17-X-1827, in *Codrington*, op. cit., Vol. 2, pp. 50–51, 57–8.

70. Fellowes–Codrington, 17-X-1827, ADM. 1-467.

71. Codrington–Adm., 24-VI-1828, ADM. 1-467.

72. Protocol, Codrington–De Rigny–Geiden, 18-X-1827, enclosure in Codrington–Adm., 21-X-1827, ADM. 1-467.

73. Fellowes–Codrington, 17-X-1827, ADM. 1-467.

74. 'Iz shkanechnogo zhurnala korablia Azov . . .' in *Lazarev*, op. cit., Vol. 1, pp. 304–7.

75. V.P. Andreevskaia (ed.), *O Podvigakh Russkikh Moriakov, Navarinskii Boi*, Sanktpetrburg, 1911, 3rd ed., p. 20.

76. Fellowes–Codrington, 10-XII-1827, enclosure in Codrington–Adm., 10-XII-1827, ADM. 1-467.

77. Nakhimov–Reineko, 16-XI-1827, in *P. S. Nakhimov. Dokumenty i Materialy* (hereafter referred to as *Nakhimov*), Moskva, 1954, p. 72.

78. There are discrepancies about the exact number of Muslim ships. The Kapudan Pasha's secretary listed three line ships (two-84s, one-76), nineteen frigates (four Egyptian -64s, twelve Turkish -48s, three Tunisian -48s), twenty-six corvettes (eight Egyptian, eighteen Turkish), twelve brigs, five fireships, and a large number of transports. Flueral gave forty-seven warships, forty transports, and six fireships. Bompar numbered sixty-four ships, counting the four Tunisians. Geiden counted one hundred warships. Bompar journal, enclosure in Codrington–Adm., 14-X-1828, ADM. 1-450: Flueral–Codrington, 12-IX-1827, enclosure in Codrington–Adm., 12-IX-1827, ADM. 1-467.: George Finlay, *History of the Greek Revolution*, London, 1861, p. 17: O. Troude *Batailles Navales de France*, Paris, 1867, 4 vols; Vol. 4, pp. 239–40 for Kapudan Pasha's statement: Geiden–Nicholas, 24-X-1827, in *Lazarev*, op. cit., Vol. 1, pp. 320–22. *Lazarev* Vol. 1 also contains a list giving the names of several of the Turkish and Egyptian ships, pp. 323–4.

79. V.E. Nadvoskii, 'Slavnaia pobeda', *Sudostroenie*, October 1967, pp. 69–71. Allied gunnery was not as effective as it might have been; HMS *Albion*-74 expended 11 092 pounds of gunpowder and 52 tons of shot, and did not sink or seriously damage a single ship. A. MacDermott 'Guns and gunners of olden times', *Mariners Mirror* (hereafter referred to as *MM*), 1958, No. 2, p. 149.

80. D. Kallistov, 'Grecheskii vopros, . . . Eskadra Rikorda', in A.S. Grishinskii, N.L. Klado, V.A. Nikol'skii, *Istoriia Russkoi Armii i Flota*, Moskva, 1911–15, 12 vols; Vol. 9, pp. 180–200.

81. *Russkii Invalid* (hereafter referred to as *RI*), 27-V-1834, p. 475.

82. Codrington–Adm., 26-X-1827, ADM. 1-448. At Navarin were ten Barbary warships, three Tunisian, and three Tripolitan, which ranged in size up to 50-gun frigates. Five European transports were also present. A further four Algerian warships were based in Alexandria and doing convoy duty at the time of the battle. 'The Turkish Navy', *United Service Journal* (hereafter referred to as *USJ*), December 1834, p. 514; J. de Courcy Ireland, 'The cruisers of North Africa', *MM*, 1976, No. 3, p. 281.

83. Nadvodskii, op. cit., p. 71.
84. De Rigny–Codrington, enclosure in Codrington–Adm., 21-X-1827, ADM. 1-467; Heyden–Codrington, 24-X-1827, enclosure in Codrington–Adm. 26-X-1827, ADM. 1-448.
85. Geiden–Nicholas, 24-X-1827, in *Lazarev*, Vol. 1, op. cit., p. 322.
86. Greek piracy extended as far as Egypt; on 19 September the Russian schooner *Caraclia* was plundered while loading a cargo of rice. Pezzoni–Ribeaupierre, 19-IX-1827, René Cattaui, *Le Règne de Mohammad-Ali d'après les archives russes en Egypte*, Cairo, 1931–5, 3 vols in 2; Vol. 1, p. 107.
87. Codrington/De Rigny/Heyden–Members of the Permanent Legislation Corps, 24-X-1827, enclosure in Codrington–Adm., 8-XI-1827; also Codrington–Greek Legislature, 19-X-1827, ADM. 1-468.
88. Codrington–Adm., 10-XI-1827, ADM. 1-448.
89. Ponsonby–Husskisson, 6-XI-1827, CO 158-56.
90. Codrington–Adm., 21-X-1827, ADM. 1-448.
91. Eugene Bogdanovich, *La Bataille de Navarin*, Moskva, 1877, p. 107.
92. Ross–Adm., 1-IV-1828, ADM. 106-2050.
93. Ross–Adm., 10-XI-1827, 1-III-1828, 1-IV-1828 ADM. 106-2050.
94. Mel'nitskii, 'Tri . . .', op. cit., p. 374.
95. Ross–Adm., 12-IV-1828, ADM. 106-2050.
96. Richards–Codrington, 21-I-1828, FO 78–182.
97. Barker–Codrington, 28-XI-1827, ADM. 1-449.
98. Barker–Codrington, 28-XI-1827, ADM. 1-449; Barker–Richards, 17-XI-1827, FO 142–2.
99. D'Oysonville–Chabrol, 3-III-1827, in Georges Douin, *L'Égypte de 1828 à 1830*, Cairo, 1935, p. 10.
100. Barker–Canning, 27-X-1827, FO 142–3; Barker–Elphinston, 5-XI-1827, FO 142–3.
101. Annex B, 12-XII-1827, *PP*, Vol. XLVIII, op. cit., pp. 183–4.
102. Hardy–Kerr, 6-XI-1827, FO 360–5; Guilleminot–Damas, 11-XI-1828, Canning–Wellesley, 11-XT-1827; Annexes A, C, 12-XII-1827, *PP*, Vol. XLVIII, op. cit., pp. 191–2, 198–9.
103. Hardy–Kerr, 6-XI-1827, FO 360–5.
104. De Rigny–Codrington, 21-XII-1827, in *Codrington*, op. cit., Vol. 2, p. 155.
105. Nesselrode–Lieven, 6-I-1828, Annex A, 12-III-1828, *PP*, Vol. XLVIII, op. cit., p. 196.
106. 'Mémoire . . . 12-IX-1827' in E.A. Bétant (ed.), *Correspondence du Comte Capodistrias 20 Avril 1827 jusqu'à 9 Octobre 1831*, Geneva, 1839, 4 vols; Vol. 1, p. 220.
107. Capodistrias–Lieven, 2-XII-1827, in Bétant, op. cit., Vol. 1, p. 319.
108. C.M. *Woodhouse, Capodistrias*, London, 1976, p. 341.
109. Dudley–Lord High Admiral 17-XI-1827, FO 195–65.
110. Bathurst–Wellington, 16-XI-1827, in *Despatches, Correspondence and Memorandum of H.M. the Duke of Wellington*, London, 1837–9, 13 vols; Vol. 4, p. 159.
111. 12-XII-1827, Protocol, *PP*, Vol. XLVIII, op. cit., pp. 190–91.

112. Codrington–Adm., 20-XII-1827, ADM. 1-449; Borgo–Lieven, 12-XI-1827, BM. ADD. MSS. 47262; Nesselrode–Lieven, 6-I-1828, BM. ADD. MSS. 47249.

113. *The Parliamentary Debates*, Vol. XVIII, London, 1828, pp. 3–5.

114. Nesselrode–Lieven, 5-XII-1827, BM. ADD. MSS. 47248.

115. Nesselrode–Lieven, 21-XI-1827, 23-XI-1827, BM. ADD. MSS. 47248.

116. Geiden–Nicholas, 25-XI-1827, 'Prikaz A.V. Mollera', 22-XII-1827 in *Lazarev*, op. cit., Vol. 1, pp. 329, 334; N.G., 'Vospominaniia o zhizni i sluzhbe admirala grafa Logina Petrovicha Geidena', *MS*, December 1850, p. 528.

117. Nicholas–Codrington, 20-XI-1827, Nesselrode–Geiden, 21-XI-1827, ADM. 1-449.

118. Lieven–Geiden, 16-X-1827, FO 360–5; Stopford–Adm., 18-IX-1827, 22-IX-1827, 24-X-1827, 25-X-1827, ADM. 1-1340; Ross–Adm., 1-I-1828, ADM. 106-2050.

119. A. Ushakov *Istoriia Voennykh Deistvii v Aziatskoi Turtsii v 1828 i 1829 Godakh*, Warsaw, 1843, 2 vols; Vol. 1, pp. 374–82.

120. Ribeaupierre–Nesselrode, 11-XI-1827, BM. ADD. MSS. 47248; Ribeaupierre–Nesselrode, 16-XII-1827, No. 1 Annex A, 12-III-1828, *PP*, Vol. XLVIII, op. cit., p. 203.

121. D.M. Afanas'ev 'K istorii Chernomorskogo flota 1816 po 1853 god', *RA* 1902, No. 7, pp. 377–8.

122. V.I. Melikhov, 'Opisanie deistvii Chernomorskogo flota v prodolzhenii voiny s Turtsiei, v 1828 i 1829 godakh', *MS*, January 1850, pp. 34–48; February 1850, pp. 88–102, 474–82; March 1850, pp. 115–28, 183–207; April 1850, pp. 267–365; May 1850, pp. 357–404, 537–41; June 1850, pp. 475–528; July 1850, pp. 1–28; August 1850, pp. 99–128; September 1850, pp. 211–26; January 1851, pp. 34–48.

123. Avramii Aslanbegov, *Admiral Aleksei Samuilovich Greig*, Sanktpetrburg, 1873, p. 52.

124. Richards–Codrington, 21-I-1828, ADM. 1-449; Pezzoni–Bokty 30-XII-1827, Pezzoni–Nesselrode, 16-I-1828, in Cattaui, *Le Règne...*, op. cit., Vol. 1, pp. 160–61, 166-70; N.A. and N.N. Epanchin, *Tri Admirala, iz Semeinoi Khroniki 1787–1913*, New York, 1946, p. 12.

125. Keith–Codrington, 7-I-1828, enclosure in Codrington–Adm., 21-I-1828, ADM. 1-449.

126. Barker–Canning, 11-II-1828, FO 142–2; Craddock–Dudley, 12-II-1828, FO 78–182; Pezzoni–Nesselrode, 16-I-1828, in Cattaui, *Le Règne...*, op. cit., Vol. 1, pp. 166–70; John Barker, *Syria and Egypt under the Last Five Sultans*, London, 1876, 2 vols; Vol. 1, p. 87.

127. D'Oysonville–Chabrol, 16-I-1828, in Douin, *L'Égypte...*, op. cit., p. 16.

128. Undated note (March–April, 1828) BM. ADD. MSS. 43231.

129. Geiden–Pezzoni, 13-XII-1827, 17-XII-1827, 12-I-1828, Cattaui, *Le Règne...*, op. cit., Vol. 1, pp. 148–9, 165.

130. D'Oysonville–Chabrol, 20-I-1828, in Douin, *L'Égypte...*, op. cit., pp. 19–20.9

131. Pezzoni–Geiden, 6-II-1828, in Cattaui, *Le Règne...*, op. cit,. Vol. 1, p. 178.

132. Nesselrode–Geiden, 19-I-1828, in Bogdanovich, op. cit., p. 139.

133. Nesselrode–Lieven, 7-I-1828, BM. ADD. MSS. 47249.
134. Nesselrode–Lieven, 27-III-1828, BM. ADD. MSS. 47249.
135. Nesselrode–Lieven, 6-I-1828, 7-I-1828, BM. ADD. MSS. 47249.
136. Annex C, 12-III-1828, *PP*, Vol. XLVIII, op. cit., pp. 205–6.
137. Hamilton–Geiden, 12-II-1828, ADM. 1-468.
138. Geiden–Duke of Clarence, 9-III-1828, in *Codrington*, op. cit., Vol. 2, p. 212.
139. Cockburn–Geiden, 15-II-1828, in *Codrington*, op. cit., Vol. 2, p. 216.
140. Geiden–Hamilton, 5-V-1828, in *Codrington*, op. cit., Vol. 2, pp. 258–9.
141. Capodistrias–Geiden, 8-III-1828, FO 360–5; Lieven–Nesselrode, 6-V-1828, BM. ADD. MSS. 32290; Ross-Adm., 1-V-1828, ADM. 106-2050; Geiden–Capodistrias, 12-III-1828, in Paleog, op. cit., p. 80.
142. Ukaz 29-1829-1827 in *Lazarev*, op. cit., Vol. 1, pp. 334–5; N. Monasterev and Serge Tereshchenko, *Histoire de la Marine Russe*, Paris, 1932, p. 161. The *Azov*-74 deteriorated soon after her return to Kronstadt in 1830. In 1832 in her memory the *Pamiat' Azova*-74 was launched in Archangel, and joined the Baltic Fleet. 'Plavanie voennykh sudov iz Arkhangel'ska v Kronshtat s 1801–1842 god' in *Zapiski Gidrograficheskogo Departamenta* (hereafter referred to as *ZGD*), Vol. 2 (1844), pp. 452–3.
143. Nesselrode–Lieven, 29-IV-1828, BM. ADD. MSS. 43231.
144. Pezzoni–Nesselrode, 19-IV-1828, Pezzoni–Nesselrode, 8-1828, in Cattaui, *Le Règne* . . . , op. cit., Vol. 1, pp. 208–10, 263.
145. Pezzoni–Nesselrode, 8-VII-1828, Cattaui, *Le Règne* . . . , op. cit., Vol. 1, pp. 223–4; Edward C. Clark, 'The Ottoman industrial revolution', *Middle Eastern Studies*, No. 5 (1974), p. 69.
146. Pezzoni–Pozzo di Borgo, 2-V-1828, Pezzoni–Nesselrode, 5-V-1828, Pezzoni–Nesselrode, 8-VII-1828, in Cattaui, *Le Règne* . . . , op. cit., Vol. 1, pp. 220–22, 224, 249.
147. The French blockading squadron took up its position before Algiers on 12 June 1827.
148. Barker–Geiden, 8-V-1828, FO 142-2.
149. Pezzoni–Nesselrode, 28-IV-1828, in Cattaui, *Le Règne* . . . , op. cit., Vol. 1, p. 214.
150. Geiden–Moller, 29-V-1828, in *Nakhimov*, op. cit., p. 87. Nicholas wrote, 'the corvette is considered surrendered; renamed *Navarin*, it will be sent to join the Baltic Fleet.'
151. Geiden–Menshikov, 28-VI-1828, in *Nakhimov*, op. cit., p. 88.
152. Ross–Adm., 1-X-1828, 1-XII-1828, 1-I-1829, 1-II-1829, 1-III-1829, ADM. 106-2050.
153. Liubomir G. Beskrovnyi *Russkoe Voenoe Iskusstvo XIX V.*, Moskva 1974 pp. 180–81. Nicholas also received plans from Kankrin, Buturlin, Kiselev, Jomini, and others.
154. Hardy–McDonald, 13-V-1828, FO 257–3.
155. Helmuth von Moltke, *The Russians in Bulgaria and Rumelia in 1828 and 1829*, London, 1854, pp. 15–9; *Le Spectateur Militaire* (hereafter referred to as *LSM*), No. 9, 1828, pp. 96–8.
256. Adolphus Slade, *Records of Travels in Turkey, Greece, &c and of a Cruize in the Black Sea with the Capitan Pacha in the Years 1829, 1830, and 1831*, London, 1833, 2 vols; Vol. 2, p. 236.

157. Afif Büyüktuğrul, *Osmanlı Deniz Harp Tarihi*, Istanbul, 1970, 2 vols; Vol. 2, p. 336; Charles MacFarlane, *Constantinople in 1828; a Residence of Sixteen Months in the Turkish Capital and Provinces*, London, 1829, 2 vols; Vol. 2, pp. 226–8, 239. Of the line ships, three were in decay. During the summer more fireships were added to the Bosphorus fleet. Tahir in the Dardanelles had a frigate, some sloops, and thirteen fireships. A Russian source gives the Turkish fleet remaining after Navarino as eight line ships and twenty-four frigates, corvettes, and brigs. 'Nyneshnee chislitel'noe sostoianie voisk Evropeiskikh derzhav', *Voennyi Zhurnal*, No. 1, 1835, p. 154.

158. Adolphus Slade, *Turkey, Greece and Malta*, London, 1837, p. 158.

159. In Europe the major forts were Bovali Kalesi (Maydos)-50 guns, Seddülbahir-74 guns, Eski Hisarlık-12 guns, Kilit Bahir-64 guns, Camlı Burnu-30 guns. In Asia the major batteries were Nara Burnu-84 guns, Köşe Kalesi-46 guns, Kumkale-84 guns, Hacı Omer (not yet armed), and Sultani Kalesi (Çanakkale)-192 guns. (Ingestre–Neale, 26-I-1827, enclosure in Geiden–Adm., 5-III-1827, ADM. 1-447; Marie Brzozowski, 'Notice sur la ville de Constantinople, et sur ses moyens de défense', *LSM*, December 1827, pp. 233–52; H. Hoegg, *Türkenburgen an Bosphorus und Hellespont*, Dresden, 1932, pp. 23–57; 'Sur les châteaux forts de l'Hellespont', *LSM*, May 1828, pp. 149–72.

160. Every fort was of embrasured drywall brick, which was hazardous due to splintering from enemy shot. All sites except Eski Hissarlık were overshadowed by nearby unfortified heights.

161. Brigadier J. H. Lefroy, 'An account of the Great Cannon of Mohammed II', *Proceedings of the Royal Artillery Institution*, 1868, pp. 203–26. The great bronze cannon were also carried on Ottoman line ships. Charles M'Pherson, 'Extracts from Life aboard a Man-of-War with a description of the battle of Navarino', in Henry Baynham (ed.), *From the Lower Deck*, London, 1972, p. 200.

162. Henry A.V. Post, *A Visit to Greece and Constantinople in 1827–1828*, New York, 1830, pp. 307–10. The Bosphorus gunners were no better; a Russian ship forced into the Bosphorus by storms sailed down to Büyükdere on jury-masts, and although batteries on both sides opened fire, the ship did not receive 'the least injury'. 'A naval sketch', *Nautical and Maritime Magazine*, December 1827, pp. 377–8.

163. The European positions were Rumeli Feneri-30 guns, Papaz Burun-13 guns, Garipçe-60 guns, Büyük Liman-27 guns, Dikili Tabya-24 guns, Rumeli Kavak-37 guns, Telli Tabya-29 guns, Mezar Burun-58 guns, Ağac Alty-6 guns, Kirec Alty-10 guns. The Asian forts were Anadolu Feneri-27 guns, Poyraz Burun (Yuşa)-54 guns, Fil Burun-19 guns, Anadolu Kavak-46 guns, and Macar Burun Kalesi-58 guns. Lander–Canning, 20-V-1832, FO 195-9; Albert Gabriel *Châteaux Turcs de Bosphore*, Paris, 1943; G.F. Herman, 'The defences of the Dardanelles and Bosphorus', *USJ*, May 1843, p. 49; Sidney Toy, *The Castles of the Bosphorus*, Oxford, 1930.

164. Aslanbegov, op. cit., pp. 52–4; Z. Arkas 'Prodolzhenie Deistvii Chernomorskogo Flota s 1806 po 1856 god', *Zapiski Odesskogo Obshchestva*

Istorii i Drevnosti (hereafter referred to as *ZOOID*), Vol. 6 (1867), pp. 428–9.

165. Nikolai Luk'ianovich *Opisanie Turetskoi Voiny 1828 i 1829 Godov*, Sanktpetrburg, 1844–7, 4 vols; Vol. 1, pp. 45–6.
166. Nicholas–Greig, 27-VIII-1828, in Aslanbegov, op. cit., p. 73.
167. Litvinov, op. cit., p. 62.
168. A.I. Lebedev, 'II. Voennye deistviia na Chernom more v voine s Turtsiei v 1828-1829 gg', in Grishinskii, op. cit., Vol. 9, pp. 203–5; 'Neskol'ko ukazanii o desantakh', *MS*, February 1865, pp. 474–5.
169. Prince Aleksandr Sergeevich Menshikov (1787–1869) began his governmental service in 1809 when, after three years in the forces fighting the Turks he served on military staffs. Menshikov was appointed an Adjutant-General in 1817. He transferred in the diplomatic service for 1823–4, and then in 1827 was appointed Navy Chief of Staff and a member of the Council of Ministers. In 1830 he was appointed to the State Council, and the following year was appointed governor-general of Finland. In 1853 he was sent to Constantinople to attempt to negotiate; when war broke out he served as Commander-in-Chief of all forces in the Crimea, resigning in February 1855. He later served as Governor-General of Kronstadt. As for his service to the navy, one source states,' in 27 years as chief of the Naval Staff did nothing for the improvement of 'he Russian fleet', *Lazarev*, op. cit., Vol. 1, p. 424.
170. N.V. Novikov (ed.), *Boevaia Letopis' Russkogo Flota*, Moskva, 1948, pp. 200–201.
171. Beskrovnyi, *Russkoe ... Iskusstvo ...*, op. cit., pp. 193–5.
172. Novikov, op. cit., p. 201.
173. James E. Alexander, *Travels to the Seat of the War in the East, through Russia and the Crimea in 1829 ...*, London, 1831, 2 vols; Vol. 1, p. 237.
174. Heytesbury–Aberdeen, 24-VIII-1828, BM. ADD. MSS. 41557.
175. Luk'ianovich, op. cit., Vol. 1, p. 253.
176. Aslanbegov, op. cit., p. 82.
177. Afanas'ev, 'K istorii ... 1853 god', op. cit., p. 391.
178. Luk'ianovich, op. cit., Vol. 1, pp. 308–9; Melikhov, op. cit., March, pp. 190–93.
179. Heytesbury–Aberdeen, 19-IX-1828, BM. ADD. MSS. 41557; Bot'ianov, 'Prebyvanie Imperatora Nikolaia Pavlovicha na Chernomorskom flote, v 1828 godu', *MS*, August 1869, pp. 1–31.
180. Nesselrode–Comtesse Nesselrode, 4-IX-1828, in A.D. Nesselrode (ed.), *Lettres et Papiers du Chancelier Comte de Nesselrode 1760–1856*, Paris, 1904–12, 11 vols; Vol. 7, pp. 87–91.
181. Aslanbegov, op. cit., pp. 84–6; Melikhov, op. cit., March 1850, pp. 328–86.
182. Codrington–Ibrahim, 2-V-1828, ADM. 1-469.
183. Codrington–officers, 24-V-1828, ADM. 1-469.
184. Barker–Codrington, 16-VI-1828, FO 142–2.
185. Geiden General Order, 9-VII-1829, ADM. 1-469.
186. Codrington–Campbell 'Secret', 16-VII-1829, ADM. 1-469.
187. Codrington–Heyden, 6-VIII-1828, ADM. 1-469.

188. Pezzoni–Nesselrode, 29-VII-1828, in Cattaui, *Le Règne*..., op. cit., Vol. 1, p. 273.
189. Malcolm–Adm., 12-IX-1828, 17-IX-1828 ADM. 1-469.
190. Rikord also had the *Tsar Konstantin*-74, *Emannuil*-64, *Kniaz Vladimir*-74, *Olga*-44, *Aleksandra*-44, and *Mariia*-44. Northesk–Adm., 15-VIII-1828, 4-IX-1828, ADM. 1-855.
191. Ross–Adm. 1-X-1828, 1-XI-1828, ADM. 106-2050.
192. Nesselrode–Lieven, 27-II-1828, 2-IV-1828, BM. ADD. MSS. 47249.
193. Protocol, 15-VI-1828, *PP*, Vol. XLVIII, op. cit., pp. 216–20.
194. Heytesbury–Aberdeen, 11-VIII-1828, BM. ADD. MSS. 41557.
195. Aberdeen–Heytesbury, 13-VI-1828, BM. ADD. MSS. 41557.
196. Heytesbury–Aberdeen, 'Secret', 17-VIII-1828, 11-XI-1828, BM. ADD. MSS. 41557. Ship-timber was among the materials considered in lieu of cash.
197. Nesselrode–Lieven, 28-VIII-1828, BM. ADD. MSS. 47249.
198. Aberdeen–Lieven, 21-IX-1828, BM. ADD. MSS. 41557.
199. Aberdeen–Heytesbury, 21-IX-1828, BM. ADD. MSS. 41557.
200. Aberdeen–Lieven, 30-IX-1828, BM. ADD. MSS. 43232.
201. Aberdeeb–Heytesbury, 2-X-1828, 'Separate and Secret', 2-X-1828, BM. ADD. MSS. 41557.
202. Aberdeen–Malcolm, 15-X-1828, FO 78–182.
203. Heyden–Malcolm, 18-X-1828, enclosure in Malcolm–Aberdeen, ADM. 1-469.
204. Aberdeen–Malcolm, 15-X-1828, FO 78–182.
205. Ross–Adm., 20-IX-1828, FO 78–182.
206. Rikord–Geiden, 5-IV-1829, in *Lazarev*, op. cit., Vol. 1, pp. 354–5; K.I. Nikul'chenkov, *Admiral Lazarev*, Moskva, 1956, pp. 105–7.
207. Kallistov, op. cit., pp. 195–7.
208. Frank S. Russell, *Russian Wars with Turkey*, London, 1877, p. 110.
209. Duval–Duilly, 17-II-1829, in Douin, *L'Égypte*..., op. cit., pp. 107–8; Pezzoni–Geiden, 16-I-1829, in Cattaui *Le Règne*..., op. cit., Vol. 1, p. 330.
210. Barker–Malcolm, 28-XI-1828, ADM. 1-451.
211. Malcolm–Adm., 14-I-1829, ADM. 1-451.
212. Heyden–Malcolm, 27-I-1829, enclosure in Aberdeen–Adm., 29-VI-1829, ADM. 1-469.
213. Kallistov, op. cit., p. 197.
214. Pezzoni–Ribeaupierre, 28-II-1829, in Cattaui, *Le Règne*..., op. cit., Vol. 1, pp. 333–5.
215. Heyden–Mehmet, 26-II-1829, Annex 1 in Douin, *L'Égypte*..., op. cit., pp. 110–112.
216. Heyden–Nesselrode, 25-II-1829, enclosure in Aberdeen–Adm., ADM. 1-469.
217. MacDonald–Secretary of Government of Bengal, 24-II-1829, FO 60–31; V.I. Sheremet, *Turtsiia i Adrianopol'skii Mir 1829 God*, Moskva, 1976, p. 78.
218. Heytesbury–Aberdeen, 21-III-1829, 1-IV-1829, BM. ADD. MSS. 41558.
219. Ibid.
220. Afanas'ev, 'K istorii... 1853 g.', op. cit., p. 384.

221. Blutte–Cowley, 27-III-1829, FO 97–402.
222. Beskrovnyi, *Russkoe...Iskusstvo...*, op. cit., p. 199.
223. William Monteith, *Kars and Erzeroum; with the Campaigns of Prince Paskevich in 1828 and 1929*, London, 1856, p. 178.
224. Gordon–Aberdeen, 26-VI-1829, 17-VII-1829, 'Confidential' 7-VII-1829, FO 195–82; Francis Rawdon Chesney, *The Russo-Turkish Campaigns of 1828 and 1829*, London, 1854, p. 206; Adolphus Slade, *Record of Travels in Turkey 1828–29*, London, 1837, 2 vols; Vol. 1, p. 161.
225. Gordon–Aberdeen, 26-VI-1829, FO 195–82. The *Rafaiil*-44 was renamed *Nimetullah*-44 ('Grace of God'; she also was known as *Parlibakh*-44) and served in the Turkish fleet until 1853, when she was destroyed during the Russian attack on Sinop.
226. Ukaz na imia Admirala Greiga, 16-VI-1829, in *Polnoe Sobranie Zakonov Rossiiskoi Imperii* (hereafter referred to as PSZ), Series II, Sanktpetrburg, Vol. 1829, p. 1377; Robert Welter Daly, 'Russia's maritime past', in *The Soviet Navy*, edited by M. G. Saunders, London, 1959, pp. 37. Stroiknikov never did marry, and died childless. Zaionchkovskii, op. cit., Vol. 1, pp. 71–2.
227. Lebedev, op. cit., Vol. 9, pp. 211–13.
228. Rikord–Van Lencys, 28-III-1829, ADM. 1-469.
229. Pezzoni–Pozzo di Borgo, 12-V-1829, Pezzoni–Heyden, 6-VI-1829 in Cattaui, *Le Règne...*, op. cit., Vol. 1, pp. 339–41, 345.
230. Malcolm–Adm., 4-V-1829, ADM. 1-451.
231. Aberdeen–Heytesbury, 22-V-1829, BM. ADD. MSS. 41558.
232. Nesselrode–Lieven, 1-VI-1829, BM. ADD. MSS. 47249.
233. Lieven–Geiden, 13-VI-1829, ADM. 1-469.
234. Aberdeen–Adm., 16-VI-1829, ADM. 1-469.
235. Heyden–Malcolm, 25-VII-1829, ADM 1-469.
236. Heytesbury–Aberdeen, 11-III-1829, 17-IV-1829, BM. ADD. MSS. 41558.
237. Kallistov, op. cit., Vol. 9, p. 197.
238. Rikord–Geiden, 3-IV-1829, in *Lazarev*, op. cit., Vol. 1, pp. 354–5; Gazzano, captain of the *Providenza*, quoted in Pezzoni–Rikord, 21-I-1829, Pezzoni–Heyden 16-I-1829 in Cattaui, *Le Règne...*, op. cit., Vol. 1, pp. 330, 332.
239. T.B. Armstrong, *Journal of Travels in the Seat of the War during the Two Campaigns of Russia and Turkey*, London, 1831, p. 212.
240. Gordon–Aberdeen, 26-VI-1829, No. 1, FO 195–82.
241. Gordon–Aberdeen, 26-VI-1829, No. 3, FO 195–82.
242. Nikolai Alekseivich Epanchin, *Ocherk Pokhoda 1829 g. v Evropeiskoi Turtsii*, Sanktpetrburg, 1905–7, 3 vols; Vol. 2, p. 13.
243. Heytesbury–Aberdeen, 22-VII-1829, BM. ADD. MSS. 41558.
244. Gordon–Aberdeen, 'Confidential' 7-VIII-1829, FO 195–82.
245. Aslanbegov, op. cit., pp. 120–27.
246. Nicholas–Dibich, 16-VII-1829, in Epanchin, *Ocherk...*, op. cit., Vol. 2, p. 111.
247. Gordon–Aberdeen, 26-VII-1829, 29-VIII-1829, 5-IX-1829, FO 195–82.
248. Gordon–Aberdeen, 26-VIII-1829, FO 195–82.
249. Fonton–Nesselrode, 13-VII-1829; Fonton–Nesselrode, 17-VIII-1829; Nesselrode–Lieven, 17-VIII-1829, BM. ADD. MSS. 47249.

250. Robert J. Kerner, 'Russia's new policy in the Near East after the peace of Adrianople; including the text of the Protocol of 16 September 1829', *Cambridge Historical Journal*, 3 (1937), pp. 280–90.
251. Nesselrode–Lieven (n.d.), BM. ADD. MSS. 47249.
252. Heytesbury–Aberdeen, 30-IX-1829, BM. ADD. MSS 41558.
253. Melikhov, op. cit., July, p. 18.
254. A. Verigin, *Voennoe Obozrenie Pokhoda Rossiiskikh Voisk v Evropeiskoi Turtsii v 1829 Godu*, Sanktpetrburg, 1846, p. 75.
255. Dibich–Geiden, 1-IX-1829, in Bogdanovich, op. cit., pp. 28–9.
256. Nicholas–Dibich, 9-IX-1829, in Epanchin, *Ocherk...*, op. cit., Vol. 2, p. 167.
257. Nicholas–Dibich, 9-IX-1829, in N.K. Shil'der, *Adrianopol'skii Mir 1829 Goda; iz Perepiski Grafa Dibicha*, Sanktpetrburg, 1879, p. 24.
258. Nesselrode–di Borgo, 11-IX-1829, BM. ADD. MSS. 47249.
259. Gordon–Aberdeen, 'Most Confidential' 10-X-1829, FO 195–83.
260. Geiden–Malcolm, 30-IX-1829, enclosure in Malcolm–Adm., 1-X-1829, ADM. 1-451.

2   The Adrianople Peace and the Growth of Russian Black Sea Trade

1. 'Military reforms of Turkey and Egypt', *USJ*, 1832, Pt. 1, p. 312.
2. 'Memoir on Russia and Turkey Pt. IV', BM. ADD. MSS. 30132.
3. 'On the commerce of Russia', *Nautical Magazine* (hereafter referred to as *NM*), December 1832, p. 536.
4. Nesselrode–Vorontsov, 14-VIII-1829, in P.I. Bartenev (ed.), *Arkhiv Kniazia Vorontsova...bumagi Grafa M.L. Vorontsova* (hereafter referred to as *Vorontsov*), Moskva, 1870–95, 40 vols.; Vol. 40, p. 45.
5. Gordon–Aberdeen, 26-VIII-1829, 29-VIII-1829, FO 195–82; Andrei Murav'ev, *Puteshestvie ko Sviatyam Mestam v 1830 Godu*, Sanktpetrburg, 1835, 2 vols; Vol. 1, p. 14.
6. *The Times*, 5-X-1829, p. 3.
7. Duveluz–Gordon, 23-VIII-1829, FO 195–82. Gordon later numbered Dibich's forces as 'at least 50,000 men perfectly equipped'. Gordon–Aberdeen, 5-IX-1829, FO 195–82.
8. Alexander, op. cit., Vol. 2, pp. 125–7: N.K. Shil'der, 'Adrianopol'skii mir. Po rasskazu Mikhailovskago Danilevskogo', in *Khrestomatiia po Istorii SSSR*, Moskva, 1949–53, 3 vols; Vol. 2 (1682–1856), p. 739. Dibich on August 21 numbered his effective forces as 12 200 infantry, 4500 cavalry and 100 artillery pieces. Dibich–Nicholas, 21-VIII-1829, in Shil'der, 'Adrianopolskii...Dibicha', op. cit., p. 534.
9. Verigin, op. cit., p. 77. Epanchin numbered Russians south of the Balkans at 35 000, while estimating losses from disease as 34 times greater than those from wounds. Epanchin, *Ocherk...*, op. cit., Vol. 1, p. 163.
10. *The Times*, 30-IX-1829, p. 2.
11. 'Brouillon d'une lettre...', 21-VIII-1829, BM. Egerton MSS. 3168.
12. N. Grech, 'Obozrenie deistvii eskadry pod nachal'stvom Kontr-Admirala Rikorda v Sredizemnom more', *MS*, November 1855, p. 22.

13. Proketch–De Rigny (n.d.), enclosure in Gordon–Aberdeen, 'Secret' 30-X-1829, FO 195–82.
14. Rothsay–Aberdeen, 5-X-1829, FO 27–396.
15. Malcolm–Adm., 1-X-1829, 28-X-1829, ADM. 1-451; N.G., 'Vospominaniia... Geidena', op. cit., p. 529.
16. In 1827, 20 of the 40 ships in the Caspian flotilla were merchantmen. During 1828–9 all 20 were involved in supplying the army. P.A. Bogoslavskii, *O Kupecheskom Sudostroenii v Rossii, Rechnom i Pribrezhnom*, Sanktpetrburg, 1859, p. 93; Al. Sk., 'Astrakhanskii port 2 1783 po 1827 god', *MS*, January 1851, pp. 15–18.
17. Paskevich–Nicholas, 18-X-1829, in *Akty Sobranie Kavkazskoiu Arkheograficheskogo Kommissieiu*, Tiflis, 1866–1904, 12 vols (hereafter referred to as *ASKAK*); Vol. 7, pp. 826–8.
18. Gordon-Aberdeen, 10-IX-1829, FO 195–83; *The Times*, 14-X-1829, p. 2. In referring to the erratic southern winds of the Dardanelles one captain observed, '[it] is a fair indication of a chance being afforded of making your passage, and you must therefore take advantage of it, to get as far as you can each day while it lasts'. 'Observations on the navigation of the Dardanelles, Bosphorus and Black Sea...by R. D. Middleton...', *NM*, March 1833, p. 121. He cautioned against attempting to enter the Dardanelles after sunset, 'as...the castles have frequently fired upon vessels attempting to pass in the night' (p. 114). Regarding the difficulty of navigating northwards, HMS *Actaeon*-26 had to tack 145 times to pass from the Dardanelles to the Sea of Marmora. See Bowen Stilton Mends, *Life of Admiral William Robert Mends*, London, 1899, p. 31.
19. *The Times*, 22-IX-1829, p. 2.
20. Aslanbegov, op. cit., p. 110–11.
21. Ibid.
22. Novikov, op. cit., p. 209. Arkas cites 38 Turkish vessels destroyed and 28 captured. Arkas, op. cit., pp. 430–31.
23. Paskevich–Nicholas, 20-X-1829, *ASKAK*, op. cit., Vol. 7, p. 829.
24. For the treaty, see Gabriel Effendi Noradounghian, *Recueil d'Actes Internationaux de l'Empire Ottoman*, Paris 1897–1903, 4 vols; Vol. 2, pp. 166–73.
25. Dmitri de Boukharow, *La Russie et la Turquie depuis le Commencement de leurs Rélations Politiques jusqu'à nos Jours*, Amsterdam, 1877, p. 103.
26. The Prut remained the common frontier from the Danube. F. Martens, *Sobranie Traktatov i Konventsii zakliuchennykh Rossieiu s Inostrannymi Derzhavami*, Sanktpetrburg, 1874–1905, 15 vols; Vol. 8, pp. 144–5.
27. Susan Fairlie, 'Shipping in the Anglo-Russian grain trade, to 1870', *Maritime History*, Vol. 1 (1971), p. 161.
28. Martens, *Sobranie...*, op. cit., Vol. 8, p. 148.
29. Nicholas–Dibich, 22-IX-1829, in Shil'der, 'Adrianopolskii...Dibicha', op. cit., pp. 560–61.
30. Nicholas–Dibich, 10-XI-1829, in Shil'der, 'Adrianopolskii...Dibicha', op. cit., pp. 581–3.
31. Gordon–Aberdeen, 5-IX-1829, FO 195–82.
32. Heytesbury–Aberdeen, 8-X-1829, 14-X-1829, BM. ADD. MSS. 41559; Stuart de Rothsay–Aberdeen, 16-X-1829, FO 27–396.

33. Heytesbury–Aberdeen, 4-XI-1829, 8-XII-1829, BM. ADD. MSS. 41559.
34. Lord Ellenborough, *A Political Diary 1828–1829*, London, 1881, 2 vols; Vol. 2, p. 11.
35. Dibich–Nesselrode, 24-IV-1830, in V.I. Sheremet, 'Turtsiia i Rotshilda v 1828-1830 gg'. *Vestnik Leningradskogo Gosudarstvennogo Universiteta (Istorii)*, 1967, No. 2, p. 42.
36. Heytesbury–Aberdeen, 17-IV-1830, BM. ADD. MSS. 41559; Sergei Zhigarev, *Russkaia Politika v Vostochnom Voprose*, Moskva, 1896, p. 379.
37. Shipov, 'Ocherk zhizni i gosudarstvennoi deiatel'nosti gr. Kankrina', *Biblioteka dlia Chteniia*, 1864, p. 10.
38. Heytesbury–Aberdeen, 3-X-1829, 6-III-1830, BM. ADD. MSS. 41559.
39. Heytesbury–Aberdeen, 24-I-1830; Heytesbury–Wellington, 25-I-1830; Heytesbury–Aberdeen, 25-I-1830, BM. ADD. MSS. 41559.
40. A ship 'en flûte' had some guns removed or stored in her hold to increase the space available for troops or stores.
41. Heytesbury–Aberdeen, 28-XII-1829, 31-XII-1829, BM. ADD. MSS. 41559. The authorities in Sevastopol were not pleased with the arrival of HMS *Blonde*-46; 'partly owing to the quarantine, partly to the jealousy of the Russian authorities...and partly...the state of the weather...nothing could be accomplished either in the way of observation or discovery'. Edward Goodenough, 'Memoir on the voyage of His Majesty's ship Blonde in the Black Sea', *Journal of the Royal Geographical Society*, 1 (1831), p. 108.
42. Heytesbury–Aberdeen, 1-XII-1829, BM. ADD. MSS. 41559. Aberdeen stated His Majesty's Government did not approve of HMS *Blonde*'s voyage, and the Russians accepted the apology. Aberdeen–Heytesbury, 9-II-1830; Heytesbury–Aberdeen 31-XII-1829, 3-III-1830, BM. ADD. MSS. 41559. Unlike the Russians, the Turks raised no objections to HMS *Blonde*'s passage. Gordon–Aberdeen, 2-III-1830, FO 195–85. Aberdeen was obsessed with possible Russian intentions; 'I am inclined to hope that they [the Russians] will scarcely carry their pretensions so far as to send Russian Men of War into the Mediterranean from the Black Sea.... This is the most important point...'. Aberdeen–Heytesbury, 13-XII-1829, BM. ADD. MSS. 43089. Lyons's voyage provided valuable intelligence. Enclosure of maps and plans in Malcolm–Adm., 22-I-1830, ADM. 1-452; Malcolm, 14-X-1830 (Russia, 52-14), ADM. 12-270. Dibich was in no doubt as to the true purpose of the voyage: 'The appearance of the..."Blonde" in the Black Sea and its cruise along the western shore...appears...solely a military reconnaissance for the English...'. Dibich–Nicholas, 28-XI-1829, in Shil'der, 'Adrianopolskii...Dibicha', op. cit., p. 481.
43. Nicholas summed up Russian war aims: 'Dans ces jours...constamment étranger à tout désir de conquête, à toute vue d'agrandissement, nous n'avons jamais cessé d'inviter la Porte à concourir au rétablissement de la bonne harmonie entre les deux Empires. Les Chefs de nos Armées, à chaque victoire, se hâtaient, par notre ordre, de lui offrir paix et amitié. Nos efforts, néanmoins, restèrent toujours steriles...notre conduite...n'était pas de renverser son Trône, mais d'obtenir l'accomplis-

sement des Traités...'. 'Manifesto of the Emperor of Russia, on the conclusion of peace with Turkey – 1st October, 1829' in *British and Foreign State Papers* (hereafter referred to as *BFSP*), London, Vol. XVI (1832), pp. 904–5.

44. Heytesbury–Aberdeen, 22-VIII-1830, BM. ADD. MSS. 43089.

45. Aberdeen–Heytesbury, 25-XI-1830, BM. ADD. MSS. 41559.

46. *PP*, [137] XLVIII (1837-8), p. 185.

47. John Ramsay McCullough, *A Dictionary Practical, Theoretical, and Historical of Commerce and Commercial Navigation*, London, 1834–5, 3 vols; Vol. 2, p. 250; *Le Moniteur Universel* (hereafter referred to as *LMU*), 12-VI-1830, p. 639. This commerce was rarely carried by Russian shipping; in 1829, of the 5122 vessels built in the Russian empire, only 144 were seagoing ships. 'Dopolnitel'nyia svedeniia po vnutrennei Rossiiskoi torgovle za 1829 god' in *Zhurnal Manufaktur i Torgovli* (hereafter referred to as *ZMT*), February 1830, pp. 128–31.

48. *PP*, XVII (1829), p. 252; XXVII (1830), p. 213; (1831-2) XXIV (1831-2), p. 205.

49. Harold William Vazeille Temperley, *England and the Near East; the Crimea*, London, 1964, p. 33.

50. Gordon–Aberdeen, 7-II-1830; Cartwright–Gordon, enclosure in Gordon–Aberdeen, 7-II-1830, FO 195–85: *LMU*, 19-XI-1829, p. 1791; 5-III-1830, p. 253; 24-III-1830, p. 329.

51. Gordon–Aberdeen, 6-I-1830; Cartwright–Gordon, enclosure in Gordon–Aberdeen, 7-II-1830, FO 195–85.

52. A. Sergeev (ed.), 'Gr. A. Kh. Benkendorf o Rossii v 1827-1830 gg'. *Krasnyi Arkhiv*, Vol. 37 (1929), p. 157.

53. M. Pokrovskii, 'Sbornik svedeniia po istorii i statistike vneshnoi torgovli Rossii', *Khrestomatiia...SSSR*, op. cit., Vol. 2, p. 606.

54. V. Pel'chinskii, *O Sostoianii Promishlennykh Sil Rossii do 1832 Goda*, Sanktpetrburg, 1833, p. 72.

55. Vladimir Zolotov, *Vneshnaia Torgovlia Iuzhnoi Rossii v Pervoi Polovine XIX Veka*, Rostov, 1963, p. 46. While there were variants in the measurement of the chevert, it usually measured as equal to eight puds, and as a pud = 36 lb., a chevert could be measured as 288 lb.

56. Vernon J. Puryear, 'Odessa: its rise and importance, 1815–1850', in *Pacific Historical Review*, 3 (1934), pp. 196–7.

57. R. D. Middleton, 'Observations on the navigation of the Black Sea', *NM*, April 1833, p. 179.

58. J. S. Hobbs, *Sailing Directions for the Black Sea*; (n.p.); 1857, pp. 21, 36.

59. M. K. Rozhkova, *Ekonomicheskaia Politika Tsarskogo Pravitel'stva na Srednem Vostoke vo Vtoroi Cherte XIX Veka i Russkaia Burzhuaziia*, Moskva, 1949, pp. 66–7.

60. Barker–Bidwell, 23-X-1829, FO 142–3.

61. G. Durand-Viel, *Les Campagnes Navales de Mohammad Aly et d'Ibrahim*, Paris, 1935, 2 vols; Vol. 2, p. 20.

62. Gordon–Aberdeen, 1-X-1829; Barker–Gordon, 12-X-1829, enclosure in Gordon–Aberdeen, 11-XI-1829, FO 195–83.

63. Gordon–Aberdeen, 10-XI-1829, FO 195–83.

64. Rothsay–Aberdeen, 25-XII-1829, FO 27–397; Guilleminot–Polignac, 11-XI-1829, in Douin, *L'Égypte...*, op. cit., p. 155. The wrangling over the two vessels continued after the French conquest of Algiers; the French eventually gave them to Mehmet, as they were in very bad shape. Mimaut–Polignac, 30-III-1831, in Georges Douin, *La Première Guerre de Syrie; la Conquête de Syrie (1831–1832)*, Cairo, 1931, p. 12.

65. Barker–Malcolm, 9-X-1829, enclosing 'A list of Turkish and Egyptian Ships of War...', enclosed in Malcolm–Adm., 22-XI-1829, ADM. 1-452. Barker listed the 74-gun line ship as 'broken-backed', and thought it likely that it would founder. Barker–Malcolm, 11-XI-1829, ADM. 1-452.

66. Barker–Malcolm, 11-XI-1829, enclosure in Malcolm–Adm., 28-XII-1829, ADM. 1-452; the Tunisian contingent was a corvette and 3 brigs.

67. Gordon–Aberdeen, 15-XII-1829, FO 195–83. On 20 December HMS *Hind* passed twenty Turkish warships (including one 2-decked line ship, four frigates, six corvettes and nine brigs) in the Sea of Marmora. Malcolm–Adm., 28-XII-1829, ADM. 1-452.

68. Durand-Viel, op. cit., Vol. 2, p. 29. Barker stated that the Egyptian fleet returned from Carvalla to Alexandria on 9–11 January 1830. Malcolm–Adm., 30-I-1830, ADM. 1-452.

69. 'Flotte Ottomane', *Annales Maritimes et Coloniales* (hereafter referred to as *AMEC*), 1832, partie non officielle, Vol. 1, pp. 267–8.

70. A.I. Tzamitzis, 'Ships, ports, and sailors' in Stelius A. Papadopoulos (ed.), *The Greek Merchant Marine (1453–1850)*, Athens, 1972, p. 60.

71. Van Buren–Porter, 22-IV-1831, in Patricia De Kay Wheelock, 'Henry Eckford (1775–1832), an American shipbuilder' in *American Neptune* 7 (1947), pp. 188–9. Commodore Porter was sent to Constantinople after Adrianople to conclude a trade agreement. The Turks suggested that they would lose by such a treaty, and that the US should give them several warships as compensation. They then attempted to append a secret article to the proposed treaty that would allow them to build 'whatever quantity of war vessels, such as two-deckers, frigates, corvettes and brigs...'; in addition, any constructed under the agreement would return to Turkey laden with sufficient timber to construct a similar vessel. The Senate refused to ratify the Treaty with the Secret Article, however, and the Treaty was eventually ratified without it. James A. Field, *America and the Mediterranean World, 1776–1832*, Princeton, 1969, pp. 165–6: David H. Finnie, *Pioneers; the Early American Experience in the Middle East*, Cambridge, Massachussetts, 1967, p. 57: Jacob Coleman Hurewitz, *The Middle East and North Africa in World Politics*, New Haven, Connecticut, 1975, 2 vols, Vol. 1, pp. 246–7; Hunter Miller (ed.), *Treaties and Other International Acts of the United States of America*, Washington, DC, 1931–48, 8 vols; Vol. 3, pp. 541–86: Charles Oscar Paullin, *Diplomatic Negotiations of American Naval Officers 1778–1883*, Baltimore, 1912, pp. 142–5. The value of American-built warships was also evident to the Russians; see Evstaf'ev-Mordvinov, 29-V-1829, in V. A. Bil'basov (ed.), *Arkhiv Grafov Mordvinov*, Sanktpetrburg, 1901–3, 10 vols.; Vol. 7, p. 296.

72. Malcolm–Adm., 22-XI-1829, ADM. 1-452; Rothsay–Aberdeen, 13-XI-1829, FO 27–396; *LMU*, 10-III-1830, p. 273; 'Mouvements des

bâtiments du Roi', *AMEC*, 1830, partie non officielle, Vol. 1, pp. 98–104, 888–94.

73. Malcolm–Commanders of HM ships, 12-XI-1829, FO 286–6.

74. Kapt.-Leit, Aleksandr Sokolov, *Letopis' Krushenii i Pozharov Sudov Russkogo Flota, ot Nachala ego po 1854 God*, Sanktpetrburg, 1855, pp. 124–9.

75. Helmuth von Moltke, *Der russisch–türkische Feldzug in der europäischen Türkei, 1828 und 1829*, Berlin 1845, pp. 404–24.

76. Afanas'ev, *K istorii... 1853 god*, op. cit., p. 394.

77. *Nakhimov*, op. cit., p. 92.

78. 'A list of the Russian naval force in the Mediterranean', enclosure in Malcolm–Adm., 22-XI-1829, ADM. 1-452; Menshikov–Geiden, 6-X-1829, in *Lazarev*, op. cit., Vol. 1, p. 359.

79. Menshikov–Nicholas, 10-I-1830, in *Lazarev*, op. cit., Vol. 1., pp. 361–2.

80. Raport Vitse–Admirala Grafa Geidena Delo Kants. M. M-ra in S. Ogorodnikov, 'Sobtvennoruchnaia rezoliutsii Imperatora Nikolaia I po morskomu vedomstvu', *MS*, December 1907, pp. 23–4.

81. 'Nekrolog Admirala Mikhaila Petrovicha Lazareva', *MS*, July 1851, p. 57.

82. Malcolm–Adm., 14-VII-1830 (52/14 Russia), ADM. 12-270; N.G., 'Vospominanie... Geidena', op. cit., pp. 529–30.

83. Malcolm–Adm., 26-III-1830, ADM. 1-452; 11-III-1830 (private), C.O. 714–91. Lazarev had originally intended to sail on 4 March, but was delayed by contrary winds; on 10 March the entire squadron sailed, but contrary winds had forced it back. Malcolm–Adm., 7-III-1830, 10-III-1830, ADM. 1-452.

84. Soviet historians are similarly scathing: 'all his knowledge of the navy consisted of his studying... some books for several months while in the country'. *Nakhimov*, op. cit., p. 684.

85. Lazarev–Shestakov, 3-IX-1830, in *Lazarev*, op. cit., Vol. 1, pp. 372–3.

86. 'Obozrenie proisshestvii i obshchestvennogo mneniia v 1831 godu' in A. Sergeev (ed.), 'Gr. A. Kh. Benkendorf o Rossii v 1831–32 gg.', *Krasnyi Arkhiv*, 46 (1931), p. 140.

87. Grech, op. cit., pp. 23, 43.

88. Heytesbury–Palmerston, 25-X-1831, BM. ADD. MSS. 41562; 'Istreblenie pozharom korablia Fershampenuaz', *MS*, April 1855, pp. 293–9; 'Neskol'ko slov o pozhare na korable Fershampenuaz', *MS*, May 1855, pp. 200–202.

89. Aleksandr Khripkov, 'Rasskazy ob Admirale M.P. Lazareve', *RA*, August 1877, p. 474.

90. Afanas'ev, *K istorii... 1853 god*, op. cit., p. 393; Aslanbegov, op. cit., pp. 124–5.

91. *LSM*, 1830, pp. 507–8; *LMU*, 5-XI-1829, p. 1735.

92. Lazarev–Shestakov, 3-IX-1830, in 'Pis'ma Admirala Lazareva', *MS*, January 1918, pp. 64–5.

93. Boris Genrikhovich Ostrovskii, *Lazarev*, Moskva, 1966, pp. 8–10, 172.

94. Lazarev–Menshikov, 27-III-1839; Lazarev–Menshikov, 6-II-1840, in *Lazarev*, op. cit., Vol. 3, pp. 212, 218–20.

95. *Lazarev*, op. cit., Vol. 1, p. XXVII.

96. *Lazarev*, op. cit., Vol. 1, p. 407; *Russkii Biograficheskii Slovar'*, Moskva 1897–1916, 21 vols, (hereafter referred to as *RBS*); Vol. 'Labzina-Liashenko', pp. 34–5.
97. Greig-Barrow, 6-IX-1804, ADM. 1-3853.
98. T.B. Martin–H.V. Martin, 27-VIII-1808, in Richard Vesey Hamilton (ed.), *Letters and Papers of Admiral of the Fleet Sir Thos. Byam Martin, Vol. 1*, London, 1898, pp. 44–9.
99. 'Leit. Lazarev R.A.K. korabl' Suvorov 1813–1816', *ZGD*; Part 9 (1849), pp. 47–52.
100. 'Kap. Bellinsgauzen i Leit. Lazarev shliupy Vostok i Mirnyi 1819–1821 *ZGD*; Part 7 (1849), pp. 92–105.
101. Ostrovskii, op. cit., p. 78.
102. 'Kap. 2-i rang Lazarev-1 i Kapitan-leiutenant Lazarev-2 (fregat Kreiser i shliup Ladoga) 1822-1825', in N. Ivashintsov, 'Russkie krugosvetnye puteshestviia', *ZGD*, Part 7 (1849), pp. 29–38.
103. Aslanbegov, op. cit., p. 132.
104. 'Vospominaniia o zhizni i sluzhbe Admirala Aleksandra Pavlovicha Avinova', *MS*, January 1855, pp. 68–85.
105. 'Predlozheniia M.P. Lazareva...15-XII-1830/18-II-1831', in *Lazarev*, op. cit., Vol. 1, p. 385.
106. Lazarev–Shestakov, 17-V-1831, in *Lazarev*, op. cit., Vol. 1, pp. 400–413.
107. S. Ia. Gessen; *Kholernye Bunty (1830–1832 Gg.)*, Moskva, 1932, p. 4; Roderick Erle McGrew, 'The first cholera epidemic and social history', *Bulletin of the History of Medicine*, 34 (January–February 1960), p. 61; J. R. von Lichtenstadt, *Die asiatische Cholera in Russland in den Jahren 1829–30 (und 1831). Nach russischen amtlichen Quellen bearbeitet*, Berlin, 1831, p. 180.
108. *The Times*, 30-IX-1829, p. 2.
109. Zakrevskii, 'Korabl "Erivan" 1833 god', *MS*, March 1861, p. 76; Zakrevskii; 'Fregat "Shtandart" 1830 god', *MS*, June 1861, p. 301.
110. Nikolai Gerasimovich Ustrialov, *Istoricheskoe Obozrenie Tsarstvovaniia Gosudaria Imperatora Nikolaia I*, Sanktpetrburg, 1847, pp. 58–9.
111. Heytesbury–Aberdeen, 29-XII-1829, BM. ADD. MSS. 41559.
112. Gordon–Aberdeen, 27-XI-1829, 15-XII-1829, FO 195-83.
113. Epanchin, *Ocherk . . .*, op. cit., Vol. 3, p. 331.
114. Zakresvkii, 'Korabl' . . .', op. cit., pp. 88–91.
115. Zakrevskii, 'Na beregu v Sevastopole', *MS*, April 1861, p. 293.
116. 'O chumnom vozmushchenii v Sevastopole 1830 goda', *RA*, 1867, No. 8, pp. 1380–2.
117. F. Khartakhai, 'Zhenskii bunt v Sevastopole', *Soveremennik*, 1865, No. 10, pp. 377–9.
118. 'O chumnom...', op. cit., pp. 1382–3.
119. Heytesbury–Aberdeen, 1-VII-1830, 16-VII-1830, BM. ADD. MSS. 41560.
120. Menshikov–Nicholas, 29-VI-1830, 15-VII-1830, in Ogorodnikov, 'Sobstvenno...', op. cit., pp. 15–16.
121. A. Polkanov, *Sevastopol'skoe Vosstanie v 1830 g.*, Simferopol', 1936, pp. 58–94.
122. Heytesbury–Aberdeen, 22-VII-1830, BM. ADD. MSS. 41560.

123. *Sanktpeterburgskiia Vedomosti*, 18-II-1830, No. 16.
124. N., 'Ofitserskii klass i akademicheskii kurs morskikh nauk', *Iakhty*, January 1877, pp. 3, 17–19. Heytesbury remained sceptical; 'It is much easier... to make ships, than to make sailors, in this country'. Heytesbury–Aberdeen, 11-IX-1830, BM. ADD. MSS. 41560.
125. S. Th. Ogordonikov, *Istoricheskii obzor razvitiia i deiatel'nosti Morskogo Ministerstva 1802–1902*, Sanktpetrburg, 1902, p. 101.
126. F. F. Veselago, *Spisok russkikh voennykh sudov s 1668 po 1860 god*, Sanktpetrburg, 1872, pp. 460–1.
127. 'Administrative system and policy-making process', in *The Military-Naval Encyclopedia of Russia and the Soviet Union*, Gulf Breeze, Fla. 1978– (hereafter referred to as *MNERSU*), Vol. 2, pp. 106–7.
128. 17-II-1830, *PSZ*, Series II, 1830, Vol. 5(1), pp. 130–1, 29-II-1832, Series II, 1832, Vol. 7, p. 91; Ogorodnikov, *Istoricheskii...*, op. cit., p. 100.
129. 'Po gidroficheskomu depo', *ZGD*, Part 2 (1844), p. xxxii.
130. *Obshchii Morskoi Spisok*, Sanktpetrburg, 1885–1907, 9 vols (hereafter referred to as *OMS*); Vol. 12, p. 284; 2-III-1831, *PSZ*, Series II, Vol. 6(1), 1831, pp. 167–8.
131. A. Sergeev, ed. 'Kartina obshchestvennogo mneniia v 1829', in 'Gr. A. Kh.. Benkendorf o Rossii v 1827–1830 gg.', *Krasnyi Arkhiv*, 38 (1930), p. 130.
132. 6-IX-1831, *PSZ*, Series II, 1831, Vol. 6(1), op. cit., pp. 781–3.
133. *The Times*, 27-X-1829, p. 2.
134. G.V. Khachapuridze *K istorii Gruzii Pervoi Polovini XIX Veka*, Tbilisi, 1950, p. 161; Bernard Eugène Antoine Rottiers, *Itinéraire de Tiflis à Constantinople*, Brussels, 1829, pp. 155–6.
135. Slaving was not exclusively a western Caucasian problem; by 1831, Kirghiz and Turkmen abductions of Russian fishermen from the Caspian numbered more than two hundred per year. H. Sutherland Edwards, *Russian Projects Against India*, London, 1885, pp. 50–51, 80–81.
136. K.K. Abaza, *Obshchedostupnaia Voenno-Istoricheskaia Khrestomatiia*, Sanktpetrburg, 1887, 2 vols; Vol. 2, p. 308; N.A. Volkonskii, 'Voina na vostochnom Kavkaze s 1824 po 1834 g. v sviazi s miuridizm (prodolzhenie), *Kavkazskii Sbornik* (hereafter referred to as *KS*), Vol. 11 (1857), pp. 146–7; M.N. Chichagov, *Shamil na Kavkaze i v Rossii*, Sanktpetrburg, 1887, p. 19; A. Fadeev, 'Miuridizm kak orudie agressivnoi politiki Turtsii i Anglii na Severo-Zapadnom Kavkaze v XIX stoletii', *Voprosy Istorii*, September 1951, pp. 76–96; A.V. Fadeev, *Rossiia i Kavkaz Pervoi Treti XIX V.*, Moskva, 1960; R.A. Fadeev; "O miuridizm' *Sobranie Sochinenii R.A. Fadeeva*, Sanktpetrburg, 1889–90, 3 vols; Vol. 1, Part 1, pp. 281–94; 'Miuridizm', Vol. 1, Part 1, p. 25; N. Khanykov, 'O miuridakh i miuridism', *Sbornik Gazety Kavkaz*, 1847, Part 1, pp. 136–56; 'Ocherk kavkazskoi voiny', *Voennyi Sbornik*, 1864, p. 292; Pavel Przhetslavskii, 'Vospominanie o blokade Derbenta v 1831 godu (Kazy-mulloiu, s istorich. vedeniem), *KS*, Vol. 18 (1864), pp. 159–78; N. A. Smirnov, *Miuridizm na Kavkaze*, Moskva, 1963.
137. A. Berzhe, *Kratkii Obzor Gorskikh Plemen na Kavkaze*, Tiflis, 1858; R. Traho, 'Literature on Circassia and the Circassians', *Caucasian Review*, No. 1 (1955), pp. 145–62.

138. 'Mémoire (extrait du) sur les affaires de Circassie, présenté en 1816 par M. de Scassi', *ZOOID* 22 (1900) Part II, pp. 4–5.
139. 'Daghistan', *Encyclopedia of Islam*, Leiden, 1954, new ed. (hereafter referred to as *EI*); Vol. 2, p. 88; David Marshall Lang, *A Modern History of Georgia*, London, 1962, p. 71.
140. T. Abhazian, 'Liberation in Abhazia and the Abkhazian-Abhazaians', *Caucasian Review*, No. 7 (1958), p. 127; 'Abkhaz', *EI*, Leiden, 1913–38, Series I, 5 vols; Vol. 1, pp. 100–101; G. A. Dzidzariia, *Prisoedinenie Abkhazil k Rossii i ego Istoricheskoe Znachenie*, Sukhumi, 1975, p. 6.
141. Platon Zubov, *Kartina Kavkazskogo Kraia*, Sanktpetrburg, 1834–5, 4 pts; pt 2, p. 231; A. Berzhe, *Istoriia Adykheiskogo Naroda*, Tiflis, 1861, pp. 5–12.
142. Paskevich–Chernyshev, 28-I-1830, in G. A. Dzidzariia, *Makhadzhirstvo i Problemy Istorii Abkhazii XIX Stoletiia*, Sukhumi, 1982, p. 59.
143. Vel'iaminov-Kom-u Otd. Kavkaskago Korpusa, 1-VI-1830, in D. I. Romanovskii, *Kavkaz i Kavkazskaia Voina*, Sanktpetrburg, 1860, pp. 228–9.
144. 'Kazi-Mulla (Gazi Magomet) – iz zapisok pokoinogo Kapitana Pruzhanovskogo', in *Sbornik Gazety Kavkaz*, Part 2, 1847, p. 33.
145. Korguev, op. cit., p. 28. Sukhum alone received annually '70 large Turkish ships'. A. Fadeev; *Kratkii ocherk istorii Abhazii; chast' pervaia*, Sukhum, 1934, p. 162. Despite the increasing Russian naval presence, 'Our cruisers very rarely successfully managed to capture them [Turkish smugglers]'. 'Vospominanie Kavkazskogo ofitsera', *Russkii Vestnik*, September 1864, pp. 9–10.
146. Bolgari, op. cit., p. 33.
147. *OMS*, op. cit., Vol. 8, p. 8; Vol. 9, p. 58; Vol. 10, pp. 250, 278.
148. Nesselrode–Greig, 20-IV-1830, in *Lazarev*, op. cit., Vol. 2, pp. 193–4.
149. Nesselrode–Menshikov 28-IV-1830 in *Lazarev*, op. cit., Vol. 2, pp. 194.
150. Menshikov–Greig, 12-V-1830, in *Lazarev*, op. cit., Vol. 2, pp. 194–5.
151. E. D. Felitsin, 'Deistviia russkikh kreiserov u Kavkazskikh beregov Chernogo moria v 1830–40 godakh' in *Kubanskie Vedomosti*, 18-I-1890, No. 1, p. 1.
152. 'Utverzhdenie nashe v Abkhaziia', *KS*, XIII (1889), p. 129.
153. Ukaz, 20-X-1821, *PSZ*, Series I, 37 (1821), pp. 871–2.
154. Lang, op. cit., p. 57.
155. E.G. Veidenbaum, *Putevoditel' po Kavkazu*, Tiflis, 1888, p. 29.
156. Bushuev, op. cit., p. 24.
157. T. Tatlock, 'The Ubykhs', *Caucasian Review*, No. 7 (1958), p. 100.
158. In the first three years of Gagra's existence its 650-man garrison was reduced to 100 men by illness. Vianor Pandzhovich Pachulia, *Po Istoricheskim Mestam Abkhazii*, Sukhumi, 1958, p. 57.
159. 'Ocherk Kavkazskoi voiny', op. cit., pp. 293–4.
160. Gordon–Aberdeen, 22-IX-1830, enclosing Brant–Gordon, 25-VIII-1830, FO 195–86.
161. Ukaz 15-VI-1831, *PSZ*, Series II, Vol. 6(1) (1831), op. cit., pp. 435–43; *ZMT*, July 1831, pp. 77–127.
162. Rodolfinkin–Rozen, 8-XI-1831, in *ASKAK*, op. cit., Vol. 8, pp. 845–6.
163. Rodolfinkin–Rozen, 21-XI-1831, in *ASKAK*, op. cit., Vol. 8, p. 846.

164. 'Zamechaniia o reide pri Sukhum-Kale, Leitenanta Romanova', in *Zapiski Uchenogo Komiteta Glavnogo Morskogo Shtaba, Chast' III* (1830), pp. 164–74.
165. A. Khramtsov, 'Gidrograficheskie raboty, proizvedenye v tsarstvovanii Imperatora Nikolaia', *MS*, August 1854, pp. 223–35.
166. Wellington–Crocker, 30-IX-1833, BM. ADD. MSS. 38078.
167. John Gurwood (ed.), *The Speeches of the Duke of Wellington in Parliament*, London, 1854, 2 vols; Vol. 1, pp. 340–44.
168. William Peter Kaldis, *John Capodistrias and the Modern Greek State*, Madison, Wisconsin, 1963, p. 51.
169. Douglas Dakin, 'Lord Cochrane's Greek steam fleet', *MM*, Vol. 39, no. 3 (1953), pp. 212, 217.
170. Charles Callwell, *The Effect of Maritime Command on Land Campaigns since Waterloo*, Edinburgh, 1897, p. 83.
171. Barker–Malcolm, 31-VIII-1830, enclosure in Malcolm–Dawkins, 4-X-1830, FO 286–6.
172. Barker–Malcolm, 17-IX-1830, FO 286–6.
173. Barker–Gordon, 18-IX-1830, FO 286–6.
174. *The Times*, 17-V-1834, p. 2.
175. Malcolm–Dawkins, 4-X-1830, FO 32–14: Malcolm–Dawkins, 7-X-1830; Malcolm–Dawkins, 9-X-1830; Malcolm–Yorke, 9-X-1830, FO 286–6.
176. Yorke–Malcolm, 24-X-1830, FO 32–14.
177. Dawkins–Aberdeen, 19-XI-1830, 1-XII-1830, FO 32–14.
178. Dawkins–Aberdeen, 11-XII-1830, FO 32–14.
179. Grech, op. cit., p. 43.
180. 'Rasporiazheniia po upravleniiu general-gidrografa', *ZGD*, Part 2 (1844), pp. ii–iii.
181. N.G., 'Vospominanie...Geidena', op. cit., p. 18.
182. Hankey–Ball, 27-VIII-1831, CO 714-91; Grech, op. cit., pp. 36–8; John Anthony Petroulos, *Politics and Statecraft in the Kingdom of Greece 1833–1843*, Princeton, 1968, p. 124; W. Alison Phillips, *The War of Greek Independence 1821–1833*, London, 1897, pp. 350–56: *LMU*, 15-IX-1831, p. 1582; 26-IX-1831, p. 1683.
183. E. Chevalier, *Histoire de la Marine Française de 1815 à 1870*, Paris, 1900, pp. 61–2.
184. Damas–Hussein, 28-II-1827, in Eugène Plantet, *Correspondence des Deys d'Alger avec la Cour de France 1579–1833*, Paris, 1889, 2 vols; Vol. 2, pp. 558–62.
185. 'Project sur Alger et des Barbaresques par M. Drovetti', 1-IX-1829, in Georges Drovetti, *Mohammad Ali et l'Expédition d'Alger (1829–1830)*, Cairo, 1930, pp. 1–4.
186. Memoire of 24-IX-1829, in Drovetti, *Mohammad...*, op. cit., pp. 5–7.
187. Barker–Aberdeen, 22-VI-1830 'Secret', FO 142–3.
188. Gordon–Aberdeen, 7-I-1830, FO 195–85.
189. Pezzoni–Ribeaupierre, 24-VI-1830, in Cattaui, *Le Règne...*, op. cit., Vol. 1, p. 375.
190. Claude Martin, *Histoire de l'Algérie Française 1830–1962*, Paris, 1963, p. 58.

191. F. Charles-Roux, *France et Afrique du Nord avant 1830*, Paris, 1932, p. 585.

192. Martin, op. cit., p. 51. In 1827 the Algerian fleet numbered sixteen ships totalling 398 cannons, which included the two frigates *Miftah-el-Jihad*-62 and *Rehber Iskandar*-40, later interned in Alexandria. Albert Devolux, 'La marine de la régence d'Alger', *Revue Africaine*, January 1869, p. 419.

193. J. H. Blofeld, *Algeria Past and Present*, London, 1844, pp. 217–20, 231. Among the tributes annually collected by the Dey were 4000 piastres' worth of ammunition and naval stores from Sweden and Denmark. *The Times*, 16-VII-1830, p. 2.

194. Algiers consulate diary, 14-IX, 1-X-1829, FO 3–31.

195. St John–Murray 14-III-1830, 4-IV-1830, 21-IV-1830, 30-IV-1830, 18-V-1830, FO 3–31.

196. St John–Murray, 4-III-1830, FO 3–31.

197. St John–Murray, 4-IV-1830, FO 3–31.

198. Gordon–Aberdeen, 2-III-1830, FO 195–85.

199. Barker–Aberdeen, 8-III-1830, FO 142–3.

200. Lieven-Cowper, 14-IV-1830, Lord Sudley (ed.), *The Lieven-Palmerston Correspondence*, London, 1943, p. 17.

201. Blofeld, op. cit., p. 222; 'Relation de l'arrivée dans la rade d'Alger, le 30 Juillet 1829, du vaisseau de S.M. la Provence...', *AMEC*, 1830, partie non officielle, Vol. 1, p. 731.

202. Durand-Viel, op. cit., Vol. 2, pp. 39–40.

203. Consular diary, 8-VIII-1830, ff. 215a-215b, FO 3–31; De Lesseps–de Laferronays 10-II-1829, De Lesseps–Portalis 27-VI-1829, De Lesseps–Polignac 20-III-1830, Polignac–De Lesseps 13-IV-1830, De Lesseps–Polignac 27-IV-1830; Eugène Plantet, *Corréspondence des Beys de Tunis et des Consuls de France avec la Cour 1577–1830*, Paris, 1893–1899, 3 vols; Vol. 3, pp. 676, 681–2, 688, 694–5, 697–9; Leon Carl Brown, *The Tunisia of Ahmad Bey 1837–1855*, Princeton, 1974, pp. 62–3.

204. Grenville T. Temple, *Excursions in the Mediterranean*, London, 1835, 2 vols; Vol. 1, pp. 242–3.

205. *The Times*, 16-VII-1830, p. 2.

206. Constantin Grunwald, *Tsar Nicholas I*, London, 1954, p. 105.

207. Heytesbury–Aberdeen, 28-IV-1830, BM. ADD. MSS. 41559.

208. St John–Murray, 1-VI-1830, FO 3–31. The two unfortunate ships were the *Sylène* and *Aventure*. *The Times* 15-VII-1830, p. 4.

209. Plantet, *Corréspondence...d'Alger*, op. cit.; Vol. 2, p. 568. A Royal Navy officer who sailed past the expeditionary force stated that it contained eleven line ships, twenty-five frigates, thirty-three brigs, eighty-seven feluccas, nine smaller vessels and 'about one hundred' square-rigged merchantmen. Hastings-Malcolm, 10-VI-1830, enclosure in Malcolm–Adm., 1-VII-1830, ADM. 1-453. For a detailed breakdown of the fleet's composition see Prince Sixte de Bourbon, *La Dernière Conquête du Roi: Alger 1830*, Paris, 1930, 2 vols; Vol. 1, pp. 216–22.

210. Duperré–Hussein, 5-VII-1830, in Plantet, *Corréspondence...d'Alger*, op. cit., Vol. 2, pp. 567–8.

211. *LMU*, 10-VII-1830, p. 750; Sarlat, capitaine du Sphinx 'Sommaire des operations...', *AMEC*, 1830, partie non officielle, Vol. 2, p. 183; *The*

Times, 12-VII-1830, p. 2. In addition to the twelve operational warships, the French captured one frigate building on the slips. Of the twelve warships, only one belonged to the government; the others paid a percentage of their share to the Dey, but were privately owned and operated. W.H. Smyth, 'A general description of Algiers', *USJ*, 1830, Pt. 2, p. 8; *The Times*, 8-VII-1830, p. 5.

212. *The Times*, 14-VII-1830, p. 2.
213. Martin, op. cit., p. 72.
214. Barker–Aberdeen, 22-VI-1830, 'Separate and secret', FO 142–3.
215. Clot-Bey, *Aperçu Général sur l'Égypte*, Paris, 1840, 2 vols; Vol. 2, p. 246.
216. Barker–Prudhoe, 10-II-1831, in Barker, op. cit., Vol. 2, pp. 154–6; 'Extrait d'une lettre écrite d'Alexandrie (Égypte) le 9 decembre, 1831, au ministre de la marine', *AMEC*, 1832, partie non officielle, Vol. 1, pp. 281–2; Lavison–Ruckman 28-III-1831, Lavison–Ricord, 6-IV-1831, in Cattaui, *Le Règne . . .*, op. cit., Vol. 1, pp. 412–14.
217. Durand–Viel, op. cit., Vol. 2, pp. 24, 56.
218. Colonel Light had been a Captain in the British Army, and had served as a Colonel in the Spanish army. Mehmet used him to recruit officers for his armed forces.
219. Barker–Palmerston, 11-VIII-1831, FO 142–3.

3 The Empire Strikes Back: the First Egyptian Revolt, and Muslim Revolt in the Caucasus

1. Robert William Seton-Watson, *Britain in Europe, 1789–1914*, Cambridge, 1937, p. 61.
2. M.A. Tsimmerman, *Bosfor i Dardanelli*, Sanktpetrburg, 1912, p. 25.
3. Barker–Palmerston, 10-VIII-1831, 15-VIII-1833, FO 142–3.
4. Barker–Palmerston, 23-VIII-1831, FO 142–3.
5. Wood–Ponsonby 'Summary report on Syria' [August] 1834 in Allan Black Cunningham (ed.), *Early Correspondence of Richard Wood, 1831–1841*, London, 1966, pp. 53–4.
6. Durand–Viel, op. cit., Vol. 2, pp. 62–3.
7. Bey, op. cit., p. 55.
8. John Marlowe, *Perfidious Albion*, London, 1971, p. 171.
9. 'Composition de la flotte egyptienne', *AMEC*, partie non officielle, Vol. 2, 1831, pp. 281–2.
10. Cérisy-Beaucousin, 3-I-1832, in Durand–Viel, op. cit., Vol. 2, p. 68.
11. See private letter to Livorno, Livorno, Archivo storico cittadino, Corrispondenza dei Consoli toscani all'Èstero, anno 1831, in Angelo Sammarco (ed.), *La Marina Egiziana sotto Mohammad Ali*, Cairo, 1931, pp. 164–7.
12. Bogoslavskii, op. cit., p. 19.
13. S. Ogorodnikov, *Istoriia Arkhangel'skogo Porta* Sanktpetrburg, 1875, pp. 59–71.
14. Barker–Palmerston, 11-VIII-1831, FO 142–3.
15. Alain Silvera, 'The first Egyptian student mission to France under Muhammed Ali', *Middle Eastern Studies*, 16 (1980), p. 66.

16. 'Voyages de Hassan-Effendi, oficier de la marine Égyptienne, à bord des vaisseaux français', *AMEC*, partie non officielle, Vol. 2, 1834, pp. 724–52.
17. 'Forces navales de Mohamed-Ali, pacha d'Égypte', *AMEC*, partie non officielle, Vol. 2, 1833, p. 211.
18. 'Sketches of a year's service in the Egyptian Marine in 1832 and 1833' *USJ*, Nov. 1833, pp. 316–17.
19. 'Guerre de Mohammed-Ali en Syrie contre la Porte Ottomane, de 1831 à 1833', *LSM*, Oct. 1834, p. 13.
20. Durand–Viel, op. cit., Vol. 2, p. 82.
21. Richardson FO Confidential Print No. 137, p. 19; Temple, op. cit., Vol. 1, p. 242.
22. Lander–Mandeville, 5-X-1831, FO 195–95.
23. 'Guerre...Syrie', op. cit., p. 23.
24. Durand–Viel, op. cit., Vol. 2, pp. 64–5.
25. 'Constantinople in 1831, from the journal of an officer', *USJ*, 1832, Pt II, pp. 222–3.
26. 'Guerre...Syrie', op. cit., pp. 8–9.
27. Durand–Viel, op. cit., Vol. 2, pp. 64–5.
28. J. Mitchell, 'On the expediency of immediately occupying Egypt and Candia', *USJ*, Jan. 1834, p. 34.
29. 'Guerre...Syrie', op. cit., pp. 24–5.
30. M., 'The siege...', op. cit., p. 224.
31. Letters of Commodore Porter, 26-II, 8-IV-1832, in David Porter, *Constantinople and its Environs*, New York, 1835, 2 vols; Vol. 1, pp. 117–18, 158.
32. De Kay, op. cit., pp. 311–12.
33. Porter–Livingston, 12-IV-1832, in Wheelock, op. cit., p. 192.
34. Hotham–Canning, 13-IV-1832, FO 195–83.
35. Lander–Canning, 27-III-1832, 28-III-1832, 31-III-1832, 5-IV-1832, 16-V-1832, FO 195–95.
36. Lander–Canning, 5-IV-1832, FO 195–95.
37. Prikaz Menshikov, 29-II-1832, in *Lazarev*, op. cit., Vol. 2, p. 3.
38. Lazarev–Greig, 9-III-1832, in *Lazarev*, op. cit., Vol. 2, pp. 3–4.
39. Serebriakov–Menshikov, 1-XII-1832, in *Lazarev*, op. cit., Vol. 2, pp. 8–9.
40. Sokolov, op. cit., p. 151.
41. Borovskii–Berkhman, 27-IV-1832, in Felitsin, op. cit., No. 1, p. 1.
42. 'Sekoum-kalleh, Mingrelia, and Goomri', *USJ*, December 1855, p. 548.
43. *Lazarev*, op. cit., Vol. 3, p. 510.
44. Lazarev–Shestakov, 23-VII-1832, *MS*, nos 2-3, 1918, pp. 110–12.
45. Novikov, op. cit., p. 213; Shavrov, 'Vostochnii bereg Chernogo moria i ego znachenie dlia razvitiia russkogo moreplavaniia', *MS*, September 1862, pp. 34–5.
46. G. A. Dzidzariia, *Prisoedinenie Abkhazii k Rossii i ego istoricheskoe znachenie*, Sukhumi, 1960, p. 15.
47. S. Bronevskii, *Noveishie Geograficheskie i Istoricheskie Izvestiia o Kavkaze*, Moskva, 1823, Pt 1, p. 295.
48. Frédéric Dubois de Montpéreux, *Voyage autour du Caucase, chez les Tcherkesses, et les Abkhases, en Georgie, en Armenie et en Crimée*, Paris, 1835–43, 6 vols; Vol. 1, p. 8.

49. Lazarev–Shestakov, 23-VII-1832, 'Pis'ma M. P. Lazareva k Alekseiu Antipovichu Shestakovu v g. Krasnyi, Smolenskoi gubernii', *MS*, nos 2-3, 1918, pp. 110–12.
50. The lack of cruising must have rankled with the sailors, as they received double pay while at sea. *USJ*, 1833, Pt I, p. 238.
51. Ostrovskii, op. cit., p. 131. The differences between the two men did not stop with their deaths – when in 1862 it was proposed to erect a monument to Greig, the naval journals resounded to arguments between the 'Lazarevsty' and 'Greigovsty'. For a pro-Greig viewpoint, see P. B.'s 'Neskol'ko slov o pokoinom admirale A. S. Greige', in *Kronshtadtskii Vestnik*, no. 71, 1862, pp. 299–300; a more balanced view is represented by D. Afanas'ev's Po povodu stat'i ob Admirale A. S. Greig, pomeshchennoi v ianvar'skoi knizhe Morskogo Sbornika sego goda', in *Kronshtadtskii Vestnik*, no. 20, 1864, pp. 77–8.
52. Barker–Bidwell, 25-IV-1832, FO 142–3.
53. Kennedy–Gordon, 29-IV-1832, BM. ADD. MSS. 43218.
54. Lander–Canning, 10-V-1832; Lander–Canning, 16-V-1832, FO 195–95. The Dardanelles were under the direct control of the Kapudan Pasha along with several Aegean islands and coastal areas. See 'Çanak-Kalé Boghazı' in, *EI*, new ed., Vol. II, p. 12.
55. Barker–Palmerston, 3-VI-1832, FO 142–3.
56. 'Campaigns of Ibrahim Pacha in Syria and Karamania', *USJ*, February 1834, p. 166.
57. Barker–Palmerston, 4-VI-1832, FO 142–3.
58. Barker–Palmerston, 13-VI-1832, FO 142–3.
59. Barker–Palmerston, 21-VI-1832, FO 142–3.
60. Lander–Canning, 24-VI-1832, FO 195–95.
61. Durand–Viel, op. cit., Vol. 2, p. 79.
62. 'Guerre . . . Syrie', op. cit., pp. 21–2.
63. Elizabeth Francis Malcolm-Smith, *Stratford Canning, Lord Strangford de Redcliffe*, London, 1933, p. 139.
64. Chesney–Canning, 28-VIII-1832, BM. ADD. MSS. 43218.
65. Sokovnin, op. cit., pp. 189–90.
66. 'Sketches . . .', op. cit., March 1834, p. 336.
67. Durand–Viel, op. cit., Vol. 2, p. 99.
68. Palmerston–Grey, 6-IX-1832, in Kenneth Bourne, *Palmerston: the Early Years 1784–1841*, London, 1982, p. 376.
69. Lander–Mandeville, 23-XII-1832, FO 195–95.
70. Durand–Viel, op. cit., Vol. 2, pp. 100–103.
71. Hobbs, op. cit., pp. 3, 21.
72. Maunsell–Mandeville, 20-X-1832, FO 195–83.
73. Ibid.
74. 'Sketches . . .', op. cit., March 1834, p. 74.
75. Porter–Washington, 16-XII-1832, in Wheelock, op. cit., p. 134.
76. Vogoridis–Mavroyenis (copy, dated 22-I-1833), BM. ADD. MSS. 32302.
77. Mavroyenis–Palmerston, 13-I-1833, enclosing Imperial letter [n.d.] in Theodore Blancard, *Les Mavroyéni*, Paris, 1909, 2 vols, Vol. 2, pp. 192–4.
78. Maunsell–Mandeville, 3-XI-1832, FO 195–83.

79. George Edmundson, *History of Holland*, Cambridge, 1922, p. 401.
80. *The Times*, 5-XI-1832, p. 2.
81. *The Times*, 12-XI-1832, p. 3.
82. *The Times*, 5-XI-1832, p. 2; 12-XI-1832, p. 3.
83. *The Times*, 16-XI-1832, p. 2.
84. Verstolk de Soele–Zuylen de Nyevelt, 16-XI-1833, in *PP*, Vol. XLII.1 (1833), pp. 190–91.
85. *The Times*, 19-VIII-1833, p. 2.
86. *The Times*, 18-I-1833, p. 4.
87. Sir William Laird Clowes, *The Royal Navy*, London, 1897–1903, 7 vols; Vol. 6, p. 266.
88. *The Times*, 1-IV-1833, p. 2.
89. *The Times*, 15-XI-1832, p. 2.
90. *The Navy List, Corrected to December 20, 1832*, London, 1833, pp. 60–84.
91. Palmerston–Hopnner 'private', 2-XI-1832, BM. Egerton MSS. 2343.
92. McCullogh, op. cit., Vol. 2, p. 294.
93. *RI*, 11-VI-1833, p. 543.
94. N. A Shavrov, 'Vostochnyi bereg Chernogo moriia i ego znachenie dlia razvitiia russkogo moreplavaniia', *MS*, nos. 9–10, 1862, pp. 34–5.
95. Visheslavtsev–Malinovskii, 27-I-1832, in Felitsin, op. cit., no. 1, p. 1.
96. Nesselrode–Vorontsov, 25-XII-1832, in *Vorontsov*, op. cit., Vol. 40, pp. 78–9.
97. Menshikov–Greig, 27-XI-1832, in *Lazarev*, op. cit., Vol. 2, pp. 7–8.
98. Greig–Lazarev, 4-XII-1832, in *Lazarev*, op. cit., Vol. 2, p. 9.
99. *The Times*, 2-III-1833, p. 5.
100. Palmerston–Granville, 4-XII-1832, in M. Vereté, 'Palmerston and the Levant Crisis, 1832', *Journal of Modern History*, XXIV, No. 2 (June 1952), p. 148.
101. Palmerston–Mandeville, 5-XII-1832, BM. ADD. MSS. 48492.
102. Ibid.
103. Menshikov–Greig, 6-XII-1832, in *Lazarev*, op. cit., Vol. 2, pp. 34–6.
104. Nikul'chenkov, op. cit., pp. 118–23.
105. 'Rélation de la bataille de Konieh', *LSM*, December 1836, pp. 241–59.
106. 'Sketch of the rise and progress of Mehemet Ali, with a view of the affairs of Turkey and Egypt to the present time', *USJ*, July 1839, p. 299.
107. Sir Charles Edmund Callwell, *Military Operations and Maritime Preponderance, their Relations and Interdependence*, Edinburgh, 1905, p. 262.
108. Nesselrode–Vorontsov, 25-XII-1832, in *Vorontsov*, op. cit., Vol. 40, p. 81.
109. Matthew S. Anderson, *The Eastern Question*, London, 1966, p. 81.
110. 'Prikaz M.P. Lazareva No. 1', 13-I-1833, in Afanase'ev, 'K istorii ... 1853 god', op. cit., pp. 396–9.
111. Lazarev–Menshikov, 26-I-1833, in *Lazarev*, op. cit., Vol. 2, p. 40.
112. Lazarev–Shestakov, 27-I-1833, in 'Pis'ma ...', op. cit., nos. 2-3, 1918, pp. 117–19.
113. Palmerston–Granville, 29-I-1833, in Vereté, op. cit., p. 150.
114. Palmerston–Campbell, 4-II-1833, BM. ADD. MSS. 48451.
115. Lazarev–Menshikov, 22-II-1833, in Afanas'ev, 'K istorii ... 1853 god', op. cit., p. 399.
116. Lazarev–Greig, 13-II-1833, in *Lazarev*, op. cit., Vol. 2, pp. 48–9.

117. Reis Efendi-Butenev, Butenev-Reis Efendi, 17-II-1833, *RI*, 9-IV-1833, pp. 315–16.
118. Letter of Fiquelmont, 25-II-1833, quoted in Temperley, op. cit., p. 412.
119. Mikhail Ivanovich Stavraki, 'Russkie na Bosfor v 1833 godu', *Russkaia Starina*, August 1884, pp. 364–5.
120. Karl Marx, *Secret Diplomatic History of the 18th Century and the Story of Lord Palmerston*, London, 1969, p. 195.
121. De Kay, op. cit., pp. 313–14.
122. Rozen–Chernyshev, 21-II-1833, in *Lazarev*, op. cit., Vol. 2, pp. 51–2.
123. Menshikov–Greig, 24-II-1833, in *Lazarev*, op. cit., Vol. 2, pp. 58–9.
124. *RI*, 17-III-1833, pp. 226–7.
125. Lazarev–Menshikov, 2-III-1833, in *Lazarev*, op. cit., Vol. 2, pp. 59–60.
126. *RI*, 27-III-1833, p. 267; Korguev, op. cit., Pt II, pp. 22–3.
127. Brooke, op. cit., p. 129.
128. Wellington–Aberdeen, 19-III-1833, BM. ADD. MSS. 43060.
129. *The Times*, 25-III-1833, p. 2.
130. *Procès-Verbaux des Séances de la Chambre des Députés: Session de 1832*, Paris, 1833, Vol. 4, p. 2.
131. *RI*, 22-IV-1833, p. 356.
132. Prikaz Lazareva [n.d.] in *Lazarev*, op. cit., Vol. 2, pp. 72–3.
133. *RI*, 11-IV-1833, p. 323.
134. Aslanbegov, op. cit., pp. 136–7.
135. Grand Vizier/Sultan–Grey/Palmerston, enclosure in Palmerston–Mandeville 30-III-1833, BM. ADD. MSS. 48492.
136. 'Zapiska o Turtsii, po dannaia grafa A.Kh. Benkendorfa v 1833 godu', *RA*, 1895, Pt 3, pp. 417–22.
137. Campbell–Palmerston, 31-III-1833, BM. ADD. MSS. 48452.
138. Lazarev–Menshikov, 1-IV-1833, in Afanas'ev, 'K istorii...1853 god', op. cit., p. 405.
139. Palmerston–Mandeville, 3-IV-1833, BM. ADD. MSS. 48492.
140. *RI*, 29-IV-1833, p. 384.
141. Chernyshev-Murav'ev, 12-IV-1833, in Afanas'ev, 'K istorii . . . 1853 god', op. cit., p. 408.
142. Lazarev–Menshikov, 5-V-1833, in Afanas'ev, 'K istorii . . . 1853 god', op. cit., pp. 410–11.
143. Lazarev–Putiatin, 12-IV-1833, in Afanas'ev, 'K istorii . . . 1853 god', op. cit., pp. 405–6; 13-IV/20-V-1833 . . . zhurnal fregata "Erivan". . .' in N. V. Novikov (ed.), *Russkie Flotovodtsy: Vitse-Admiral Kornilov*, Moskva, 1947 (hereafter referred to as *Kornilov*), pp. 28–9; Lane–Wellington, 21-V-1833, in Brooke, op. cit., p. 228; *Gentleman's Magazine*, June 1833, p. 556.
144. Lazarev–Menshikov, 25-II-1834, in *Kornilov*, op. cit., pp. 29–30.
145. 'Bibliographie militaire: cartes, plans, livres etc. publiés au Depôt topograhie militaire de Saint-Pétersbourg', *LSM*, March 1835, pp. 692–3.
146. Lander–Ponsonby, 21-IV-1833; Lander–Mandeville 21-IV-1833; FO 195–95.
147. *OMS*, op. cit., Vol. 10, p. 54.
148. Campbell–Palmerston, 16-IV-1833, BM. ADD. MSS. 48452.

149. *RI*, 11-V-1833, pp. 455–6.
150. *RI*, 12/20-V-1833, pp. 457–65.
151. Stozhevskii's squadron consisted of the line ships *Parizh*-110 (flagship), *Pimen*-84, *Ioann Zlatoust*-74, bombships *Uspekh* and *Podobnyi*, the transport *Redut-Kale* and eleven chartered vessels, carrying the 2nd Brigade of the 26th Infantry Division and the 2nd Company of the 26th Artillery Brigade. Lazarev–Menshikov 24-IV-1833 in Afanas'ev, 'K istorii . . . 1853 god', op. cit., p. 407.
152. *RI*, 21-V-1833, pp. 466–8.
153. *RI*, 8-V-1833, pp. 427–8.
154. Novikov, op. cit., p. 213.
155. *RI*, 11-VI-1833, pp. 543–4.
156. Novikov, op. cit., p. 213.
157. Novikov, op. cit., pp. 213–15.
158. Lander–Ponsonby, 2-V-1833, 11-V-1833, 18-V-1833, FO 195–95.
159. Palmerston–Temple, 7-V-1833, in Sir Henry Bulwer, *Life of Henry John Temple, Viscount Palmerston*, London, 1870–74, 3 vols; Vol. 2, p. 158.
160. Nikolai N. Murav'ev, *Russkie na Bosfore v 1833 Godu, iz Zapisok N. N. Murav'eva*, Moskva, 1869, pp. 329–31. Of the Black Sea Fleet's total operational strength in line ships and frigates, only the *Enos*-60 and *Burgas*-60 frigates were absent from the Hünkâr Iskelessi squadron. Aslanbegov, op. cit., pp. 135–7.
161. *Hansard's Debates*, London, 3rd series, XVII (1833), pp. 1101–3.
162. Palmerston–Ponsonby, 10-V-1832, BM. ADD. MSS. 48492.
163. Adm.–Malcolm, 10-V-1833, BM. ADD. MSS. 48492.
164. 'The crisis of Turkey', *USJ*, May 1833, p. 15.
165. McCullough, op. cit., Vol. 2, p. 249; Zolotov, op. cit., p. 47.
166. *PP*, XLVII, 1837–8 [137], pp. 185–6.
167. Palmerston–Campbell, 10-V-1833, BM. ADD. MSS. 48451.
168. Palmerston–Campbell, 1-VI-1833, BM. ADD. MSS. 48451.
169. 'Sketches . . .', op. cit., Nov. 1833, Pt III, p. 318.
170. Lander–Ponsonby, 26-V-1833, FO 195–95.
171. Ibid.
172. *Rapport Fait au Nom du la Commission Chargeé de l'Examen du Budget de Ministère de la Marine et des Colonies, pour l'Exercice 1834; Séance du 30 Mai 1833*, Paris, 1833, p. 166. The report commented on the growth of Egyptian seapower: 'En 1814 . . . l'Égypte n'avait pas de marine; des aujourd'hui la sienne équivaut à la moitié des forces navales developpées par les États-Unis; elle va l'accroître encore ses forêts nouvellement conquises'.
173. Henri Pirenne, *Histoire de Belgique*, Brussels, 1929–32, 7 vols; Vol. 7, p. 40.
174. *RI*, 1-VIII-1833, p. 724.
175. *RI*, 12/20-V-1833, op. cit., pp. 457–65.
176. Lander–Ponsonby, 29-V-1833, FO 195–95.
177. *RI*, 21-VI-1833, p. 579.
178. *RI*, 12-V/21-VI-1833, op. cit., pp. 457–578.
179. Ibid.

180. Orlov–Nicholas, 6-VI-1833, in Theodor Schiemann, *Geschichte Russlands unter Kaiser Nikolaus I*, Berlin, 1904–19, 4 vols; Vol. III, p. 432.
181. Lander–Ponsonby, 8-VI-1833, FO 195–95.
182. Malcolm–Ponsonby, 'Confidential', 10-VI-1833, FO 195–83; Dawkins–Briggs, 4-V-1833, FO 286–6.
183. Lander–Ponsonby, 23-VI-1833, FO 195–95.
184. Lander–Ponsonby, 24-VI-1833, FO 195–95.
185. Lander–Ponsonby, 29-VI-1833, FO 195–95.
186. *OMS*, op. cit., Vol. 7, pp. 315.
187. Notes of Graf Benkendorf 20-X-1833, in Ogorodnikov, 'Sobstvennoruchnaia...', op. cit., pp. 17–8. With the exception of Benkendorf's report, the manner of Kazarskii's death is ignored in both Tsarist and Soviet naval historical writings. A monument was erected to him in 1834 in Sevastopol. A trapezoidal stone plinth is surmounted by a bronze altar which supports a stylised Roman galley; the monument is inscribed, 'To Kazarskii, 1834; an example to posterity'. The Soviet Black Sea Fleet has a *Kazarskii* mine-sweeper and a *Pamiat' Merkuriia* hydrographic research vessel.
188. *RI*, 23-VII-1833, pp. 690–91.
189. *The Mirror of Parliament*, III (1833), p. 2942.
190. *RI*, 5-VIII-1833, p. 734.

4 The Hünkâr İskelessi Peace, Russophobia, and a Middle Eastern Arms Race

1. Durham-Gray [n.d., 1836] in Stuart J. Reid, *Life and Letters of the 1st Earl of Durham, 1792–1840*, London, 1906, 2 vols.; Vol. 2, p. 25.
2. Nesselrode–Vorontsov, 1-XI-1836, in *Vorontsov*, op. cit., Vol. 40, p. 193.
3. Lazarev, 1836, in *Lazarev*, op. cit., Vol. 1, p. xxxvi.
4. *Mirror of Parliament*, op. cit., Vol. 1 (1834), p. 787.
5. 'Donesenie Orlova' [n.d.], *Voennyi Zhurnal* 5 (1833), pp. 150–51.
6. Mends, op. cit., pp. 31–2. The misconception that Lazarev was present at Trafalgar has been occasionally cited in British publications. Notes on Lazarev's service in the Royal Navy in 1805 published in *Russkii Arkhiv* stated, 'in May 1803...sent with thirty other students to England for instruction in naval matters. After two years sailing in the Atlantic Ocean on December 27, 1805 (8-I-1806), he received the rank of michman, and only on May 27 (9-VI)-1808 returned to Russia.' A British source published in 1827 after Navarino stated of Lazarev's Royal Navy service, 'Capt. Lazaroff, the flag-captain of the St. *Andrew* [*Azov*-74] was five years in the British navy as a volunteer, under Capt. F. L. Maitland'. According to Maitland's entries in the *DNB* and *O'Byrne's Naval Biography*, in 1805 he commanded HMS *Loire*-46, which in 1805 served off the western coast of France, and the northern coast of Spain. The Trafalgar Roll does not list HMS *Loire*-46 as present at Trafalgar, nor Maitland nor Lazarev. Lazarev's entry in the *RBS* states of the time he spent in the Royal Navy, '...on (British) ships Lazarev sailed for almost five years, visited the West Indies, and acquired extremely strong

grounding in the practice and theory of naval matters'. V. I. (Istomin), 'Mikhail Petrovich Lazarev; Ocherk', *RA*, Pt 2, 1881, p. 348; Litvinov, op. cit., p. 51; *RBS*, Vol. 'Labzina-Liashenko', p. 37; 'Russian Navy', *The Naval and Military Magazine*, December 1827, pp. 607–8; 'Maitland, Sir Frederick Lewis', *DNB*, Vol. 35, pp. 353–5: *O'Bryne's...*, op. cit., Vol. 2, p. 712; Robert Holden MacKenzie (ed.), *The Trafalgar Roll*, London, 1913.

7. Lazarev–Menshikov, 15-VII-1833 in Afanas'ev, op. cit., 'K istorii... 1853 g.', op. cit., pp. 414–15. *Companion to the Newspaper*, 1-I-1834, p. 226; Captain F. W. Grey, 'Remarks on the navigation between... the Dardanelles, and the Sea of Marmora, with the anchorage off Therapia...', *NM*, Sept. 1834, p. 519.

8. Stavraki, op. cit., p. 368.

9. Grech, op. cit., pp. 61–2; K. Mosolov, 'Obozrenie deistvii eskadry pod nachal'stvom Kontr-Admirala Rikorda, v Sredizemnom more', *MS*, November 1855, pp. 59–62; Napoli-di-Romani, 2-VII-1833, No. 8, Napoli-di-Romani, 2-VII-1833, No. 9 'Iz pisem D.V. Polenova vo vremia poezdei v Gretsiiu i sluzhby pri tamoshnem posol'stve 1832–1835', *RA*, Pt 3, 1885, pp. 120–21. Orders for the return of the squadron under Rikord's command had been sent in May and June, before the Treaty was signed. 'Petr Ivanovich Rikord', *RBS*, Vol. 'Reitern-Rol'tsberg', p. 203. Rikord then passed the Straits before the Treaty was ratified. Webster, *The Foreign Policy...*, op. cit., Vol. 1, p. 333. European warships were not the only foreign navies to pass the Straits; in June 1837, the American frigate *Constitution*-44 was allowed through the Straits for the use of its country's embassy. Lander–Ponsonby, 2-II-1834, 11-IV-1834, 6-VII-1834, FO 195–20; Rowley–Ponsonby 'Private', 5-VI-1837, FO 195–104.

10. Lagan–Broglie, 10-VII-1833, in *Documente privitóre la istoria Românilor, culese de Eudoxiu de Hurmuzaki*, Bucureşti, 1876–1922, 19 vols; Vol. 17, p. 297.

11. V.I., 'Mikhail... Ocherk', op. cit., p. 355.

12. Aslanbegov, op. cit., p. 138; 'Marine Russe en 1836', *AMEC*, 1836, partie non officielle, Vol. 2, pp. 319–20.

13. Lander–Ponsonby, 14-VII-1833, FO 195–95.

14. *The Times*, 17-IX-1833, p. 3.

15. Blancard, op. cit., Vol. 2, pp. 196–8.

16. *The Times*, 8-X-1833, p. 5.

17. The discrepancies between the Russian and French treaty texts were a further cause of misunderstanding; see Clive Parry (ed.), *The Consolidated Treaty Series*, Dobbs Ferry, New York 1969– ; Vol. 84, pp. 1–3.

18. Nicholas–Paskevich, 6-VIII-1833, in Prince Aleksandr Shcherbatov, *General-Fel'dmarshal Kniaz Paskevich, ego Zhizn' i Deiatel'nost'*, Sanktpetrburg, 1888–1904, 7 vols; Vol. 5, p. 173.

19. Nesselrode despatch, 17-VIII-1833, in Martens, op. cit., Vol. 12, p. 43.

20. Temperley, op. cit., p. 64; *Quarterly Review*, April–July, 1833, p. 527.

21. *Mirror of Parliament*, London, Vol. IV (1833), p. 4018.

22. Ibid.

23. Martens, op. cit., Vol. 12, p. 45.

24. Palmerston–Campbell, 1-XI-1833, BM. ADD. MSS. 48451.
25. Nesselrode–Vorontsov, 20-XII-1833, in *Vorontsov*, op. cit., Vol. 40, p. 90.
26. 'Mouvements de bâtiments de l'État à la fin de 1832 et pendant l'année 1833', *AMEC*, partie non officielle, Vol. 1 (1834), pp. 17–41; 'Mouvements des bâtiments de l'État pendant les neuf premiers mois de l'année 1834', *AMEC*, partie non officielle, Vol. 2 (1834), pp. 704–19.
27. *The Times*, 13-I-1834, p. 3.
28. The majority of the French squadron had sailed from Smyrna on 17 December for Toulon, with the *Ville de Marseilles*-76 and three brigs remaining under the command of Captain Lalande. Malcolm–Adm., 20-XII-1834, ADM. 1-459; *The Times*, 20-I-1834, p. 3. For Russian deployments, see 'A return of the movements of foreign warships from 22-III to 8-IV-1834', enclosure in Rowley–Adm., 8-IV-1834, ADM. 1-459.
29. Diugamel–Nesselrode, 28-I-1834, in Cattaui, *Le Règne . . .*, op. cit., Vol. 2, p. 7; also Campbell–Palmerston, enclosure in Rowley–Adm., 5-V-1834, ADM. 1-459.
30. C. W. Crawley, 'Anglo-Russian relations 1815–40', *Cambridge Historical Journal*, 1 (1929), pp. 60–61.
31. Nesselrode despatch, 16-I-1834 in Martens, op. cit., Vol. 12, p. 51.
32. Palmerston–Ponsonby, 15-II-1834, BM. ADD. MSS. 48492.
33. Palmerston–Ponsonby, 15-II-1834, BM. ADD. MSS. 48492.
34. Lander–Ponsonby, 10-VI-1834, FO 195–120; Schiemann, op. cit., Vol. 3, p. 279; *The Times*, 21-VII-1834, p. 3; Ivanoff–Diugamel, 24-IV-1834; in Cattaui, *Le Règne . . .*, op. cit., Vol. 2, pp. 104–5.
35. Rowley–Ponsonby, 4-VIII-1834, Ponsonby–Rowley, 4-VIII-1834, FO 195–83.
36. Afanas'ev, 'K istorii . . . 1853 god', op. cit., p. 422. The regular area of cruising was between Sevastopol, Tarkhankut and Feodosiia. Arkas, op. cit., p. 434.
37. M. Bukhteev, 'Torgovoe sudostroenie v Khersone', *ZMT*, August 1843, p. 269.
38. M. Bukhteev, 'Chernomorskoe torgovoe sudostroenie i moreplavanie', *Kommercheskaia Gazeta*, 15-X-1840, no. 119, p. 425; Korguev, op. cit., p. 41; 'Uchilitse torgovogo moreplavaniia v Khersone', *ZMT*, November 1838, pp. 350–52.
39. Grigory Nebol'sin, *Statisticheskie Zapiski o Vneshnei Torgovle Rossii*, Sanktpetrburg, 1835, 2 parts; Pt 1, p. 116.
40. 'Chernomorskoe torgovoe sudostroenie i moreplavanie', *ZMT*, March 1841, pp. 401–40; 'Statisticheskoe opisanie Azovskogo torgovogo moreplavaniia', *ZMT*, June 1839, pp. 433–55.
41. The ukaz was issued on 7-II-1834; sailors had to serve 'not less' than five years in the Black Sea Fleet. 'Postanovleniia i rasporiazheniia pravitel'tsva; vysochaishego poveleniia', *ZMT*, January 1835, pp. 6–7; M. Bukhteev, 'Soslovie vol'nykh matrosov v Novorossiiskom krae', *ZMT*, June 1841, pp. 439–49. Captain Drinkwater in one of his reports on Sevastopol numbered the necessary years of service as six; the term of service 'could not be extended as punishment'. 'Note on the Black Sea Fleet, October, 1835' FO 65–229. In 1838 the scheme was extended to all

coastal areas of New Russia, and included eight towns and twenty-seven villages. By early 1841, 2313 men had been enrolled, and 252 were serving in the Black Sea Fleet. Captain Drinkwater's report numbered the participants in the scheme as 3000; the men were kept 'constantly' at sea. Nebol'sin, op. cit., Pt 1, pp. 112–14. The ideal recruit for the sailor corporations was aged 17–20. 'O pravilakh, na koikh dopuskaetsia obrazovanie v Novorossiiskom krae vol'nykh matrosskikh obshchestv', *ZMT*, December 1839, pp. 345–51.

42. The first batch of 'voluntary sailors' to enter the Black Sea Fleet left for Sevastopol in March 1835. *RI*, 17-IV-1835, p. 344. The scheme was of limited immediate value; by 1841, only 252 men had been supplied to the Black Sea Fleet from the sailors' corporations. Phillip E. Moseley, *Russian Diplomacy and the Opening of the Eastern Question in 1838 and 1839*, Cambridge, 1934, p. 39. In 1841, of the 1329 men in Nikopol', 152 were 'volunteers' serving in the Black Sea Fleet; of Aleshëk's 317 men, 37 were serving in the navy. 'Chernomorskoe...moreplavanie', op. cit., p. 426. The number of sailors began to rise after 1841, however; by 1847, 2100 free sailors were enrolled in the corporations. 'The present strength, condition, and organisation of the Russian Navy', *USJ*, November 1849, p. 327. Of Aleshëk's 4147 inhabitants in 1852, 'about 500' were corporation sailors; in 1833 the town's population had been 'about' 2908. P. Dubrova, 'Gorod Alëshki', *ZOOID*, 3 (1852), pp. 220.

43. *RI*, 24-IX-1834, pp. 818–19.

44. 'Note on the port of Kherson – Black Sea, October, 1835' (Captain Drinkwater), FO 65–229; 'O parokhodstve po Dnepru i Limanu ot porogov do Odessy', *ZMT*, February 1841, p. 279.

45. A. A. Skal'kovskii, 'Torgovaia promyshlennost' v Novorossiiskom Krae', *Zhurnal Ministerstva Vnutrennikh Del*, nos 1–2, 1851, pp. 56–66.

46. 'Chernomorskoe...moreplavanie', op. cit., pp. 403, 416–17, 441.

47. *O Sudakh Chernomorskogo Flota, Postroennykh so Vremeni Vstupleniia na Prestol Gosudaria Imperatora Nikolaia Pavlovicha*, Sanktpetrburg 1844, pp. 7–8, 49.

48. The *Varshava*-120 incorporated a number of design innovations; she was the first ship in the Black Sea Fleet to have a rounded stern. *RI*, 20-IX-1834, p. 903. Things were not well with the *Varshava*-120 after her launching, despite the fact that 'Admiral Lazarev himself presides over their finishing'; according to her captain, the warship 'is likely within five years to be scarcely seaworthy'. See 'A return of movements of foreign ships or vessels, 25-VI to 22-VII-1834', enclosure in Rowley–Adm., 22-VII-1834, ADM. 1-459.

49. *Zhurnal Ministerstva Vnutrennikh Del*, August 1838, p. lxxxvii.

50. M. Bukhteev, 'Torgovoe sudostroenie v Khersone', *ZMT*, August 1843, p. 268.

51. *RI*, 6-II-1834, p. 83, 12-V-1834, pp. 415–16; *The Times*, 17-IX-1833, p. 3; 'Otpusk khlebov iz Odesskogo porta s 1830 po 1863 god', *Trudy Odesskogo Statisticheskogo Komiteta*, Odessa, 1865, Part I, pp. 260–1.

52. *RI*, 16-I-1834, p. 12; *The Times*, 2-VII-1834, p. 5, 3-VII-1834, p. 6; *Trudy...*, op. cit., Part III, 1870, pp. 69–70.

53. In 1835, 2024 ships visited Constantinople, 1213 fewer than two years previously. 'Torgovoe sudokhodstvo v Konstantinople', *ZMT*, May 1842, p. 340.

54. *The Times*, 30-V-1834, p. 5.

55. *The Times*, 3-XII-1833, p. 3.

56. 'Return of the movements of foreign ships 22-VII to 23-VIII-1834', enclosure in Rowley–Adm., 23-VIII-1834, ADM. 1-459; *The Times*, 1-VII-1834, p. 5; 'Return of the movements of foreign ships 23-VIII to 23-IX-1834', enclosure in Rowley–Adm., 23-IX-1834, ADM. 1-459; Grey–Rowley, 3-VI-1834, enclosure in Rowley–Adm., 15-VI-1834, ADM. 1-459.

57. Grey, op. cit., p. 580.

58. 'Avtoviografiia A.V. Diugamelia', *RA*, 1885, Pt 1, p. 510.

59. 'Marine Égyptienne en 1834', *AMEC*, partie non officielle, Vol. 2 (1834), pp. 287–9; *NM* Dec. 1833, p. 748. The *al-Jafariyah*-60 caught fire in early 1834 in Alexandria harbour and was destroyed. After a court-martial, three sailors were shot for negligence. Diugamel–Ruckman, 15-IV-1834, in Cattaui, *Le Règne...*, *op. cit., Vol. 2, p. 7*. Mehmet's *Nile* steamer was launched at Limehouse, London on 7 June 1834; it was 'one of the largest steam-vessels ever built in this country...'. 'Launch of a steam-frigate', *NM*, July 1834, p. 431. 'A return of the movements of foreign ships and vessels, 29-IV to 26-V-1834', enclosure in Rowley–Adm., 26-V-1834, ADM. 1-459. See also Diugamel–Nesselrode 6-VI-1834, enclosure, in Cattaui, *Le Règne...*, op. cit., Vol. 2, pp. 83–94; *The Times*, 28-I-1834, p. 1, 6-II-1834, p. 6; *RI*, 2-I-1835, p. 1296.

60. 'Memorial lui Bois le Comte spre Dunare', 15-V-1834, in *Hurmuzaki*, op. cit., Vol. 17, pp. 371–81; also James Brant 'Journey through a part of Armenia and Asia Minor in 1835', *Journal of the Royal Geographical Society*, 6 (1836), pp. 190–91.

61. Mehmet lost no time in exploiting his new acquisitions for ship-timber; see John Franklin, 'Observations on the coast of Syria', *NM*, January 1835, p. 30.

62. Lander–Ponsonby, 29-IV-1834, FO 195–120, Rowley–Ponsonby, 24-IV-1834, FO 195–104; *The Times*, 26-V-1834, p. 5.

63. 'Return of the movements of foreign ships and vessels of war from 26-V to 2-VI-1834', enclosure in Rowley–Adm., 3-VI-1834, ADM. 1-459; Lander–Ponsonby, 3-V-1834, FO 195–120; *The Times*, 30-V-1834, p. 4; 7-VI-1834, p. 6.

64. Mohammad Cekir–Warrington, 10-X-1834, FO 195–104; Mundy–Briggs, 11-X-1834, FO 195–104; *The Times*, 27-IX-1834, 13-X-1834, p. 2; 'Spisok glavneishikh gosudarei i pravitelei Azii i severnoi Afriki, v 1837 godu' *Zhurnal Ministerstva Narodnogo Prosveshcheniia* (hereafter referred to as ZMNP), August 1837, pp. 268–70.

65. Diugamel–Nesselrode, 29-VIII-1834, in Cattaui, *Le Règne...*, op. cit., Vol. 2, pp. 146–7. Diugamel was convinced that in the event of a conflict, Mehmet would not prove to be the aggressor. Diugamel–Nesselrode, in Cattaui, *Le Règne...*, op. cit., Vol. 2, pp. 156–9.

66. *The Times*, 10-XI-1834, p. 5; Lander–Ponsonby, 12-X-1834, FO 195–120; Diugamel–Nesselrode, 3-XI-1834, in Cattaui, *Le Règne...*, op. cit., Vol. 2, pp. 168–71.

67. 'Return of the movements of foreign warships from 30-X to 17-XI-1834', enclosure in Rowley–Adm., 18-XI-1834, ADM. 1-459.

68. Colonel Franz von Rudtorffer, *Militär-Geographie von Europa*, Prague, 1839, p. 554.

69. 'A month's cruize on the Smyrna station', *USJ*, April 1836, pp. 473–9.

70. James A. Sharp (ed.), *Sharp's Memoirs of the Life and Services of Rear-Admiral Sir William Symonds, Kt., C.B., F.R.S., Surveyor of the Navy from 1832 to 1847...*, London, 1858, p. 272.

71. 'A month's cruise...', op. cit., p. 473; 'A return of movements of foreign ships or vessels from 23-III to 8-IV-1834', enclosure in Rowley–Adm., 8-IV-1834, ADM. 1-459.

72. 'Extrait d'une lettre écrite de Smyrne, le 30 Septembre 1835, écrite par un passager à bord la goelette la Mèsange, commandée par M. Lejeune, lieutenant de vaisseau', *AMEC*, 1835, Vol. 2, partie non officielle, pp. 1014–17.

73. 'O Evropeiskoi torgovle v Turtsii i Persei', *ZMT*, January 1838, p. 78.

74. *LSM*, September 1835, pp. 695–6.

75. *The Times*, 28-VII-1835, p. 4.

76. *Companion to the Newspaper*, August 1835, p. 438; Platana, 'O torgovle Trapezontskoi', *ZMT*, May 1834, pp. 92–8; 'Torgovoe moreplavanie po Bosforu', *ZMVD*, March 1836, p. 741.

77. See also Kostas Antonopoulos, 'Apo tou Proton Atmoploion', quoted in George B. Leon, 'The Greek Merchant Marine (1453–1850)', *The Greek Merchant Marine (1451–1850)*, Athens 1972, pp. 44, 483.

78. 'O torgovle s Cherkesami v Anapskom vremennom karantine v 1833 godu', *ZMT*, April 1834, pp. 97–8; *Chernomorskie Kazaki v Nikh Grazhdanskom i Voennom Bytu*, Sanktpetrburg, 1858, 2 Parts, Part 1, p. 122; *Foreign Quarterly Review*, no. 8 (1829), p. 582.

79. Ibid.

80. 'O putiakh dlia privoza tovarov iz Rossii v Zakavkavskii kraia', *ZMT*, November 1835, p. 20; *RI*, 31-I-1836, p. 67; Platon Zubov, *Kartina Kavkazskogo Kraia*, Sanktpetrburg, 1834–5, 4 pts, pt 4, p. 222; 'Torgovye puti iz vnutrennikh oblastei Imperii v Zakavkazskii krai', *ZMVD*, January 1836, pp. 202–3.

81. Nesselrode–Vorontsov, 3-I-1837, in *Vorontsov*, op. cit., Vol. 40, pp. 204–5.

82. 'Vospominaniia Grigoriia Ivanovicha Filipsona', *RA*, 1883, Book 3, p. 29. The stagnation of Sukhum at this time is clearly reflected in its trade; see *Materialy dlia Statistiki Rossiiskoi Imperii*, Sanktpetrburg, 1839–41, 2 vols; Vol. 2, p. 48.

83. Vorontsov–Kankrin, 30-V-1836, in V.I. Pisarev, 'Metody zavoevaniia adygeiskogo naroda tsarizmom v pervoi polovine XIX v.', *Istoricheskie Zapiski*, September 1940, p. 261.

84. Yeames–Palmerston, 11-VIII-1836, FO 65–227; 'Notice sur les russes de la Crimée et des côtés du Caucause visitées en 1836' *LSM*, May 1837,

pp. 170–71; A. A. Skal'kovskii, *Zapiska o Plavanii Parokhoda k Tavri-cheskim i Vostochnym Beregam Chernogo Moria*, Odessa, 1836, p. 16.

85. Lazarev–Menshikov, 27-V-1834, in *Lazarev*, op. cit., Vol. 3, pp. 6–7; A. L. Bert'e-Delagard, 'Ostatki drevnikh sooruzhenii v okrestnostiakh Sevastopolia i peshchernye goroda Kryma', *ZOOID*, 14 (1886), pp. 166–282.

86. Lazarev–Menshikov, 6-VI-1834, in *Lazarev*, op. cit., Vol. 3, pp. 149–52; 'Return of the movements of foreign ships and vessels of war from 25-VI to 22-VII-1834', enclosure in Rowley–Adm., 22-VII-1834, ADM. 1-459; 'Russia: manning of the navy, &c.', *USJ*, January 1837, p. 98.

87. In another despatch, Lazarev reported that a finished line ship-hull without artillery and other fittings cost 'more than a million rubles'. Lazarev–Menshikov, 10-VIII-1839, 'Perepiska M.P. Lazareva s kn. A.S. Menshikovym', *RA*, 1881, Book 3, p. 378.

88. A lack of suitable timber was a problem that bedevilled the Russian Navy from its inception to the end of the sailing ship era; for an earlier report, see Second Memorial to Her Imperial Majesty about the Duty of the Officers of the Dock Yards, Sir Charles Knowles-Catherine I [n.d.], National Maritime Museum, MSS. 84-075.

89. *Hansard's Parliamentary Debates, Lords*, Vol. 45 (1839), p. 1355.

90. Lazarev–Menshikov, 21-XII-1835, in *Lazarev*, op. cit., Vol. 3, pp. 24–5. Captain Drinkwater had been ordered to accompany the Earl of Durham on his voyage through southern Russia via the Black Sea overland to St Petersburg, when in 1835 he was appointed British ambassador. Drink-water visited the Russian naval establishments on the Black Sea, and sent back a number of reports on the Russian navy. Palmerston–Drinkwater, 25-VII-1835, National Maritime Museum, Drinkwater (Bethune) Papers, Vol. 3; Drinkwater & de Roos–Backhouse, 10-III-1836, FO 65–227.

91. S. Golubov, *Bestuzhev-Marlinskii*, Moskva, 1978, p. 388; Yeames–Palmerston, 31-VIII-1836, FO 65–227.

92. Letter of Bestuzhev–Marlinskii, 5-XI-1834, in 'K istorii pokoreniia Kavkaza', *RA*, 1877, Book 3, pp. 106–9.

93. A. L. Gizetti, *Khronika Kavkazskikh Voisk*, Tiflis, 1896, 2 parts; Part 1, p. 34.

94. 'Vospominania Kavkazskogo ofitsera', *Russkii Vestnik*, September 1864, p. 20.

95. Bolgari, op. cit., p. 33.

96. Rozen–Menshikov, 28-VIII-1834, in *Lazarev*, op. cit., Vol. 2, pp. 222–3; Korguev, op. cit., pp. 35–6.

97. Lazarev–Menshikov, 14-X-1834, in *Lazarev*, op. cit., Vol. 2, pp. 224–5.

98. 'Chernomorskaia Beregovaia Liniia', *Brokgauz Entsiklopedicheskii Slovar'*, Sanktpetrburg, 1890–1904, 41 vols; Vol. 38, pp. 646–7.

99. *The Times*, 3-XI-1834, p. 2, 4-XI-1834, pp. 2–3.

100. *The Times*, 15-XI-1834, p. 4.

101. Arkas, op. cit., p. 434.

102. Butenev–Lazarev, 3-XII-1834, in *Kornilov*, op. cit., pp. 30–1.

103. Lander–Ponsonby, 10-II-1835, FO 195–120.

104. *The Times*, 31-III-1835, p. 3; *The Times*, 6-IV-1835, p. 1.

105. *The Times*, 30-III-1835, p. 3.

106. Minton–Ponsonby, 20-II-18, FO 195–104. The six line ships were HMS *Caledonia*-120, HMS *Edinburgh*-72, HMS *Thunderer*-74, HMS *Canopus*-84, HMS *Malabar*-74, and HMS *Revenge*-76.
107. Crawley, op. cit., p. 61. Palmerston restored Ponsonby's authority to call the fleet on 31-V-1836, providing he received 'an application from the Turkish government'.
108. *The Times*, 14-III-1835, pp. 3–4.
109. Menshikov–Lazarev, 7-VI-1835, in *Lazarev*, op. cit., Vol. 3, pp. 181–2; Korguev, op. cit., pt 1, p. 16.
110. V. I. Pisarev, 'Metody zavoevaniia adygeiskogo naroda tsarismom v pervoi polovine XIX v'., *Istoricheskie Zapiski*, September 1940, p. 171.
111. Yeames–Palmerston, 23-V-1836, FO 65–227.
112. Bestuzhev–Benkendorf, 25-VIII-1836, in P.A. Sidrov (ed.), *A.A. Bestuzhev-Marlinskii; Sochineniia v Dvukh Tomakh*, Moskva, 1958, 2 vols; Vol. 2, pp. 670–71: see also Yeames–Palmerston, 11-VIII-1836, FO 65–227.
113. 'Vospominaniia … Filipsona', op. cit., p. 242.
114. Menshikvo–Lazarev, 'Sekretno', 25-I-1836, in 'Perepiska…', op. cit., *RA*, 1881, Book 2, pp. 361–2.
115. Lazarev–Menshikov, 'Sekretno', 12-II-1836, in 'Perepiska…', op. cit., *RA*, 1881, Book 2, pp. 362–3.
116. Menshikov–Lazarev, 24-II-1836, in 'Perepiska…', op. cit., *RA*, 1881, Book 3, pp. 319–20.
117. Nesselrode–Vorontsov, 31-III-1836, in *Vorontsov*, op. cit., Vol. 40, pp. 126–7; Colonel William Monteith, 'Journal of a tour through Azerbijan and the shores of the Caspian', *Journal of the Royal Geographical Society*, 3 (1833), pp. 34–5.
118. *Odesskii Vestnik*, 1831, no. 37.
119. 28-V-1833, *PSZ*, Series II, Vol. 8.1 (1833), pp. 285–91.
120. *ZMT*, June 1836, p. 132, *RI*, 21-IV-1836, pp. 351–2.
121. A. Uner Turgay, 'Trade and merchants in nineteenth-century Trabzon: elements of ethnic conflict', in Benjamin Braude and Bernard Lewis (eds), *Christians and Jews in the Ottoman Empire*, London, 1982, 2 vols; Vol. 1, p. 291.
122. *The Times*, 4-IX-1835, p. 3.
123. 'Gosudarstvennaia … vidakh', *Sovremennik*, 1836, pp. 268–75, 278–80.
124. 'Notes extrait du mémoire sur le commerce du Bosphor Cimmer à Panticape (maintenant Kertch)', *ZOOID*, 22 (1900), pp. 8–9.
125. McCullough, op. cit., Vol. 2, pp. 248–51, Vol. 3, p. 860; Zolotov, op. cit., pp. 30–31.
126. Aleksei Semenov, *Izuchenie Istoricheskikh Svedenii o Rossiiskoi Vneshnei Torgovle i Promyshlennosti s Poloviny XVII Stoletiia po 1858 God*, Santkpetrburg, 1859, 3 parts; Part 2, pp. 242–3.
127. 'Izvestie o Rossiiskikh korabliakh, prishedshikh iz inostrannykh portov, i otoshedshikh v inostrannye porty, v pervoi polovine 1835 goda', *ZMT*, October 1835, pp. 3–5; 'Svedeniia o torgovle po trem glavneishim portam Imperii za 1835 god', *ZMVD*, March 1836, pp. 711–17.
128. 'Situation de la flotte égyptienne au 18 novembre 1836 (10 chaban 1252)', *AMEC*, 1836, Vol. 2, partie non officielle, p. 171; 'État comparatif des forces de terre et de mer de la Turquie et de l'Égypte', *LSM*, April 1836,

pp. 63–94; 'Suite des notes sur la marine turque en 1836', *AMEC*, 1836, partie non officielle, Vol. 2, pp. 397–8; also, *LMU*, 9-VI-1836, p. 1364.

129. 'Notice nécrologique sur Besson, lieutenant de vaisseau, mort amiral de la flotte égyptienne sous le nom de Besson-Bey', *AMEC*, 1837, Vol. 2, partie non officielle, p. 1224.

130. 'Report on the political and moral state of Syria and the Egyptian government', enclosure in Wood–Ponsonby, 22-IV-1836, in Cunningham, op. cit., pp. 78–88.

131. Samir Khalaf, 'Communal conflict in nineteenth-century Lebanon', in Braude and Lewis, op. cit., Vol. 1, p. 112.

132. 'Russian Men of war in the Black Sea, Sept. 1836', Napier Papers, BM. ADD. MSS. 40020.

133. Lazarev–Menshikov, 7-IV-1836, in 'Perepiska...', op. cit., *RA*, 1881, Book 3, pp. 321–2.

134. A. A. Skal'kovskii, *Zapiska o plavanii parokhoda Petr Velikii k Tavricheskim i vostochnym beregam Chernogo Moria*, Odessa, 1836, p. 12.

135. Romanovskii, op. cit., p. 135; 'Podvig Azovskogo kazachego voiska... na Chernom More', *Voennyi Zhurnal*, 6 (1838), pp. 143–6.

136. On 1 June 1836 Palmerston again authorised Rowley to pass the Straits if necessary. See Palmerston–Adm., 1-VI-1836, FO 78–298; Palmerston–Ponsonby, 20-VI-1836, FO 78–271; Lander–Ponsonby, 16-VII-1836, 21-VII-1836, 27-VIII-1836, FO 195–120.

137. Lander–Ponsonby, 19-VII-1836, FO 195–120.

138. Lander–Ponsonby, 14-IX-1836, FO 195–120.

139. Lander–Ponsonby, 22-IX-1836, FO 195–120.

140. Lander–Ponsonby, 28-X-1836, FO 195–120.

141. Lander–Ponsonby, 22-X-1836, Fo 195–120.

142. Bell–Yeames, 12-XII-1836, FO 65–227.

143. Lazarev–Menshikov, 25-XII-1836, in 'Perepiska...', op. cit., *RA*, 1881, Book 2, p. 377.

144. Lazarev–Raevskii, 2-IX-1838, in B.L. Modzalevskii, ed. *Arkhiv Raevskikh* (hereafter referred to as *Raevskii*), Sanktpetrburg, 1908–15, 5 vols; Vol. 2, pp. 543–5.

145. Nesselrode–Vorontsov, 3-I-1837, in *Vorontsov*, op. cit., Vol. 40, pp. 204–5.

146. 'Notes by Dr. Riach on the state of Georgia and the Caucasian tribes 1-VIII-1837', Report – Frontiers of Russia and Turkey, and Georgia and Caucasus (Capt. Stoddart and Dr. J.P. Riach), *Parliamentary Papers 'Confidential Print' No. 510*, London, 1838, p. 21.

147. Nesselrode–Vorontsov, 10-I-1837, in *Vorontsov*, op. cit., Vol. 40, pp. 206–7.

148. Butenev–Nesselrode, 17-1-1837, in K.A. Bushuev (ed.), 'Anglo-Russkii intsident so shkhunoi "Viksen"', *Krasnyi Arkhiv*, 102 (1940), pp. 202–4.

149. Ibid. See also *LMU*, 30-I-1837, p. 207.

150. Vorontsov–Nesselrode, 24-II-1837, in *Vorontsov*, op. cit., Vol. 40, p. 211.

151. Gertrude Robinson, *David Urquhart*, Oxford, 1920, p. 57.

152. Palmerston–Granville, 3-II-1837, in op. cit., Vol. 2, pp. 248–9.

153. Vorontsov–Nesselrode, 24-II-1837, in *Vorontsov*, op. cit., Vol. 40, pp. 210–11.

154. 'The Caucasian War', *Blackwood's Edinburgh Magazine*, November 1840, p. 622.
155. Lazarev–Menshikov, 24-IV-1839, in *RA*, 1881, Book 3, p. 374.
156. *Hansard's Parliamentary Debates*, London (1837), p. 633.
157. Butenev–Lazarev, 7-III-1837, in Bushuev (ed.), 'Anglo-Russkii intsident...', op. cit., pp. 211–12.
158. Borgo–Nicholas, 2-V-1837, in Martens, op. cit., Vol. 12, pp. 64–5.
159. Webster, *The Foreign Policy...*, op. cit., Vol. 2, p. 574.
160. Gardener–Palmerston, 24-II-1837, FO 78–311; E.D. Tappe, 'Bell and Anderson: a Scottish partnership in Wallachia', *Balkan Studies*, 1971, pp. 480–82.
161. *The Times*, 7-IV-1836, p. 7.
162. Duclos–Molé, 19-XII-1836, in *Hurmuzaki*, op. cit., Vol. 17, pp. 657–8.
163. Lazarev–Menshikov, 2-II-1836, in *Lazarev*, op. cit., Vol. 3, p. 26; W.A. Brooks, 'On the course of the formation of bars at the mouths of rivers', *USJ*, 1864, pp. 202–4; 'Mouth of the Danube', *NM*, May 1836, p. 312.
164. Xavier Hommaire de Hell, *Travels in the Steppes of the Caspian Sea, the Crimea, the Caucasus &c.*, London, 1847, pp. 419–20.
165. Lazarev–Menshikov, 11-VII-1836, in 'Perepiska...', op. cit., *RA*, 1881, Book 3, pp. 328–9; Nikolai Levitskii, 'Zapiski o Khersonskoi gubernii', *ZMVD*, July 1836, pp. 136–9.
166. *Materialy...Imperii*, op. cit., Vol. 2, Section II, p. 33; Lazarev–Menshikov, 10-VIII-1839, in 'Perepiska...', op. cit., *RA*, 1881, Book 3, p. 378.
167. Ukaz, 14-III-1837, *ZMT*, April 1837, pp. 43–4; N. Danilevskii, *Kavkaz i ego Gorskie Zhiteli*, Moskva, 1846, pp. 60–3, 265; Zubov, *Kartina...*, op. cit., Part IV, p. 266.
168. 'Obzor gidrograficheskikh s'emok Chernogo i Azovskogo morei', *ZGD*, 2 (1844), pp. 399–401.
169. Ibid. See also Yeames–Palmerston, 11-VIII-1836, FO 65–227; V. Iakovlev, 'Nekrolog; Mikhail Pavlovich Manganari', *ZOOID*, 15, Part III (1889), pp. 863–4; 'Gidrograficheskie raboty na Chernom i Azovskom moriakh v 1850 i 1851 godakh', *ZGD*, 10 (1852), p. 218.
170. 'O postepennom usovershenstvovanii geograficheskikh i topograficheskikh kart', *Voennyi Zhurnal*, 2 (1836), p. 172.
171. N.M. Kumani, 'Sravnenie prezhnikh kart Chernogo i Azovskogo Morei, s noveisheiu', *ZGD*, 2 (1844), pp. 406–11; N. Murzakevich, 'Atlas Chernogo Moria', *ZOOID*, 1849, pp. 722–5.
172. Bolgari, op. cit., pp. 33, 302; 'Zaniatiia Gidrograficheskogo Depo', *ZGD*, 1 (1842), p. xlii; Murzakevich, op. cit., p. 724; 'Izdannyia ot Gidrograficheskogo departamenta atlasy, karty i knigi s 1827 po 1844 god', *ZGD*, 2 (1844), p. xxxviii; 'Gidrograficheskie raboty na Chernom i Azovskom moriakh, s 1844 po 1850 god', *ZGD*, 8 (1850), p. 217; 'Gidrograficheskie... 1851 godakh', op. cit., pp. 216–20; Archibald Day, *The Admiralty Hydrographic Service 1795–1919*, London, 1967, pp. 48–9.
173. Vel'iaminov-Raevskii, 2-IX-1837, in *Raevskii*, op. cit., Vol. 2, pp. 358–68; A. Iurov, 'Tri goda na Kavkaze. 1837–1839', *KS*, 8 (1884), pp. 118–61.
174. Fedorov, op. cit., pp. 64–100.

175. John Augustus, Longworth, *A Year Among the Circassians*, London, 1840, 2 vols; Vol. 1, pp. 123, 290: Fedorov, op. cit., p. 17.

176. 'Vospominaniia...Filipsona', op. cit., p. 200.

177. Vel'iaminov–Rozen, 3-IX-1837, in 'Obzor voennykh deistvii protiv gorskikh narodov v 1835, 1836 i 1837 godakh', in *ASKAK*, op. cit., Vol. 8, pp. 362–6, 383–91.

178. Rozen–Chernyshev, 16-XI-1837, 21-XII-1837, in *ASKAK*, op. cit., Vol. 8, pp. 368–9, 371–2.

179. Beskrovnyi, *Russkaia...*, op. cit., p. 495.

180. 'O Zakavaze: soobshcheno Manufaktur Sovetnikom K. Tribodino', *ZMT*, October 1837, pp. 10–13.

181. Vel'iaminov-Raevskii, 8-VII-1837, in *Raevskii*, op. cit., Vol. 2, pp. 353–5.

182. Lander–Ponsonby, 8-VIII-1837, FO 195–144.

183. Frederick Stanley Rodkey, 'Lord Palmerston and the rejuvenation of Turkey, 1830–41; Part I, 1830–39', *Journal of Modern History*, December 1929, p. 581; M. Manganari, 'S'emka Marmarnego moria, 1845–1848 goda', *ZGD*, 8 (1850), p. 222; *The Times*, 30-V-1839, p. 5; *LMU*, 8-II-1839, p. 238; 'Voennaia sila Pashi Egipetskogo', *Voennyi Zhurnal*, 4 (1839), pp. 155–7.

184. Menshikov–Nesselrode, 16-I-1838, in Mosely, *Russian Diplomacy...*, op. cit., p. 141. The following table lists all the passages of the Straits made by Russian warships during the years 1837–8:

	Date	Ship	Port of departure	Destination
1837	2 March	*Penderaklii*-24	Constantinople	Athens
	18 April	*Penderaklii*-24	Athens	Constantinople
	7 Sept.	*Akhilles*-18	Athens	Constantinople
	26 Nov.	*Orest*-18	Constantinople	Athens
	3 Dec.	cutter (name unknown)	Constantinople	Athens
1838	7 Jan.	*Themistokl*-18	Athens	Constantinople
	12 Jan.	*Telemak*-20	Constantinople	Athens
	12 Feb.	*Telemak*-20	Athens	Constantinople
	5 Oct.	*Inkerman*-2 (steamer)	London	Constantinople
	19 Oct.	*Ifigeniia*-22	Constantinople	Magaia
	19 Nov.	cutter (name unknown)	Greece	?
	1 Dec.	corvette (name unknown)	Passed Dardanelles but didn't communicate with shore	

Compiled from 'List of Russian Men of War which have passed the Straits of the Dardanelles during the year 1837', enclosure in Ponsonby–Palmerston, 31-XII-1837, enclosed in Backhouse–Adm., 8-II-1838, ADM. 1-4270; 'List of Russian Men of War which passed by the Straits of the Dardanelles during the year 1838', enclosure in Ponsonby–Palmerston 31-XII-1838, enclosed in Strangways–Adm., 20-II-1839, ADM. 1-4274.

185. Mosely, *Russian Diplomacy...*, op. cit., pp. 141–5; 'A list of the foreign ships of war at anchor in the Piraeus, and Salamis Bay, the 28th of March, 1838', enclosure in Stopford–Adm., 19-IV-1838, ADM. 1-465.
186. Novikov, op. cit., p. 214.
187. 'Ocherk polozheniia voennykh del na Kavkaze s nachala 1838 do kontsa 1842 god'', *KS*, Vol. 2, 1877–8, p. 9.
188. L.S. Lichkov, *Ocherki iz Proshlogo Nastoiashchego Chernomorskogo Poberezh'ia Kavkaza*, Kiev, 1904, p. 138; 'Kratkoe izvlechenie iz Vysochaishego utverzhdennogo polozheniia o voennom poselenii na Kavkaze', *Voennyi Zhurnal*, 6 (1838), pp. 141–3.
189. Lazarev–Menshikov, 30-VI-1837, in 'Perepiska...', op. cit., *RA*, 1881, Book 3, pp. 335–6; Yeames–Palmerston, 24-XII-1836, FO 65–227; Fedorov, op. cit., p. 127; Simborskii–Golovin, 4-VII-1838, in P.P. Korolenko, 'Zapiski po istorii Severo-vostochnogo poberezh'ia Cherno-go Moria', *ZOOID*, 29 (1911), p. 7; Millbank–Palmerston, 25-VII-1838, enclosure in Strangways–Adm., 4-VIII-1838, ADM. 1-4272.
190. Lazarev–Raevskii, 20-VIII-1838, in *Raevskii*, op. cit., Vol. 2, pp. 524–5; Lazarev–Menshikov, 21-VIII-1838, in 'Perepiska...', op. cit., Part 3, pp. 359–61.
191. 'Ocherk...polozhenie...1842 god', op. cit., p. 10.
192. Filipson, op. cit., p. 241.
193. 'Don', in *Obozrenie Glavnykh Vodianykh Soobshchenii v Rossii*, Sankt-petrburg, 1841, p. 14.
194. Korolenko, op. cit., p. 10–11.
195. A. P. Denisov and Iu. G. Perechnev, *Russkaia Beregovaia Artilleriia*, Moskva, 1956, pp. 68–70; 'O bombovoi pushke Peksana', *Voennyi Zhurnal*, 6 (1833), p. 170.
196. Beskrovnyi, *Russkaia...Flot v XIX V.*, op. cit., p. 573; *Brokgauz*, op. cit., Vol. 18, 'Lopari-Maloletnie prestupniki', pp. 71–2; Lazarev–Menshikov, 3-IX-1836, in 'Perepiska...', op. cit., *RA*, 1881, Book 2, pp. 369–71; 'O parovykh mashinakh Luganskogo zavoda', *ZMT*, April 1841, pp. 145–6.
197. Report of Menshikov, 25-VII-1838, in Ogorodnikov, 'Sobstvennoruch-naia...', op. cit., p. 14.
198. Menshikov–Lazarev, 31-VIII-1838, in 'Perepiska...', op. cit., *RA*, 1881, Book 3, pp. 357–8.
199. Ibid.
200. Menshikov–Lazarev, 19-VIII-1838, in 'Perepiska...', op. cit., *RA*, 1881, Book 3, p. 358.
201. Lamb–Palmerston, 8-IX-1838, FO 7–272.
202. Major-General Edward Napier, *The Life and Correspondence of Admiral Sir Charles Napier*, London, 1862, 2 vols; Vol. 1, pp. 351–4: *The Times*, 12-IV-1838, p. 6.
203. 'Vnutrennee sudokhodstvo v Rossii v 1838 godu', *ZMT*, September 1839, pp. 380–86; 'Vidy vnutrennego sudokhodstva v Rossii, v 1839 godu', *ZMNP*, January 1841, pp. 132–5.
204. 'Vnutrennee sudokhodstvo v Rossii v 1837 godu', *ZMT*, October 1838, pp. 138–44.
205. 'Svedenie o torgovle v Konstaninopple', *ZMT*, April 1842, pp. 95–164.

206. Iu. Gagemeister, 'O torgovykh snosheniiakh Rossii s Arkhipelagom i Gretsiei', *ZMT*, February 1839, pp. 304–5; 'Torgovlia Rossii s Gretsiei', *ZMT*, May 1836, p. 31; McCullough, op. cit., Vol. 2, p. 249.

207. 'O torgovle ostrova Sira', *ZMT*, April 1838, pp. 137–40.

208. 'O vneshnei torgovle Rossii 1838 goda', *ZMT*, August 1838, pp. 239–43; 'Don', *Obozrenie...*, op. cit., p. 16.

209. *LMU*, 19-II-1839, p. 283, 25-IV-1842, p. 892, 2-I-1839, p. 8; 'Oboroty vneshnei torgovli Odesskogo porta so vremeni zakliucheniia Adrianopol'skogo mira', *Trudy Odesskogo Staticheskogo Komiteta*, Odessa, 1865, Section 2, p. 259; Patricia Herlihy, 'Russian wheat and the port of Livorno, 1794–1861', *Journal of European Economic History*, Spring 1976, pp. 45–68; Lewis Siegelbaum, 'The Odessa grain trade; a case study in urban growth and development in Tsarist Russia', *Journal of European Economic History*, Summer 1980, p. 117; *The Times*, 14-V-1838, p. 5.

210. *LMU*, 6-VI-1838, p. 1890.

211. M. Vol'skii, *Ocherk istorii torgovli Novorossiiskogo kraia s drevneishikh vremen do 1852 goda*, Odessa, 1854, pp. 110, 133.

212. Wood–Ponsonby, 2-III-1838, in Cunningham, op. cit., p. 129.

213. *The Times*, 11-V-1838, p. 6.

214. *The Times*, 2-IV-1838, p. 5; *LMU*, 5-I-1839, p. 11.

215. *The Times*, 19-IV-1838, p. 3, 2-VI-1838, p. 5.

216. *Mirror of Parliament*, London, 3 (1838), p. 2382.

217. *The Times*, 26-VII-1838, p. 5, 9-VI-1838, p. 2, 23-IV-1838, p. 5; *LMU*, 1-IX-1838, p. 2141.

218. Medem–Nesselrode, 28-VII-1838, in Cattaui, *Le Règne...*, op. cit., Vol. 3, pp. 147–51; *The Times*, 3-IX-1838, p. 5.

219. Lazarev–Menshikov, 9-IX-1838, in 'Perepiska...', *RA*, 1881, Book 3, op. cit., pp. 361–4.

220. Adm.–Massie, 29-X-1838; Adm.–Massie, 16-XI-1838, National Maritime Museum, Massie Papers MAS 16. The Turks were not alone in their high regard for British specialists; for materials on the career of John Upton in Sevastopol, see 'Note on Black Sea Fleet October 1835 – Drinkwater', 'Note on the Port of Sevastopol – Black Sea', November 1835 (Drinkwater), FO 65–227; Thomas Milner, *The Crimea, its Ancient and Modern History*, London, 1855, pp. 297–9.

221. Adm.–Massie, 15-XII-1838, National Maritime Museum, Massie Papers, MAS 16.

222. Ponsonby–Walker, 21-III-1839; Ponsonby–Stopford, 23-III-1839, FO 195–104; *LMU*, 8-V-1837, p. 1111.

223. Palmerston–Clanricarde, 29-XII-1838, FO 65–243, in Phillip E. Mosely, 'Englisch–Russische Flottenrivalität', *Jahrbücher für Geschichte Osteuropas*, 4 (1936), pp. 556–7.

224. Ibid. The following table gives a comparative breakdown of the relative naval strength of various countries during 1839.

	Line (no. guns)			Frigates (no. guns)			Steamers		P.O.
	100+	80–100	70–80	52–60	50–52	36–50	war	– foreign stations	
Britain									
I	4	4	12	1	1	7	5	13	28
II	12	13	33	10	7	57	2	–	–
III	3	7	2	–	2	8	5	–	–
IV	19	24	47	11	10	72	12*	13	28
France									
I	2	5	3	5	5	6	22	–	–
II	4	2	4	8	7	7	6	–	–
III	16	11	2	9	8	5	9	–	–
IV	22	18	9	22	20	18	37*	–	–
Russia									
I	5	16	19	4	–	20	8	–	–
II	–	2	1	–	–	–	–	–	–
III	2	5	–	–	–	1	–	–	–
IV	7	23	20	4	–	21	8	–	–
Egypt									
I	6	2	1	7	–	–	1	–	–
II	2	–	–	–	–	–	–	–	–
III	1	–	–	–	–	–	–	–	–
IV	9	2	1	7	–	–	–	–	–
Turkey									
I	2	5	3	4	3	3	1	–	–
II	1	1	3	1	2	1	–	–	–
III	–	–	–	1	–	–	2	–	–
IV	3	6	6	6	5	4	3	–	–
United States									
I	2	–	–	6	–	–	1	–	–
II	–	2	3	9	–	2	–	–	–
III	–	8	–	18	–	–	9	–	–
IV	2	10	3	33	–	2	10	–	–

I = Ships in commission; II = ships in ordinary; III = ships building;
IV = Total

* French packet steamers armed with 80-pdr cannon are included here; unarmed British packets are not. John Barrow, *Life of Anson*, London, 1838, supplementary chapter, pp. 423–4. An Admiralty document lists the Black Sea Fleet in December 1837 as having twelve line ships, eight frigates, three corvettes, six brigs and sixteen schooners. Orders had been received at Nikolaev to build 'no less than 11 Sail of the Line and Frigates, and 25 Sloops of War and Brigs'. 'Return of the Russian Forces in the Black Sea, December 31, 1837', enclosure with Yeames–Palmerston, 15-VIII-1838, in Strangways–Adm., 1-X-1838, ADM. 1-4273.

225. Palmerston–Clanricarde, 29-XII-1838, FO 65–243 in Mosely, 'Englisch...', op. cit., pp. 557–9. The reduction that Palmerston was

proposing that Russia unilaterally make in her naval force can be gauged by comparing the size of the reduced armament with the naval forces of Holland, which at this time consisted of eight line ships and twenty-two frigates. 'Statisticheskia svedeniia o Gollendii', *ZMNP*, March 1841, pp. 41–2. 'The Russians have not a single ship-of-the-line in the Baltic, nor in the Black Sea more than they had 15 years ago, except those now on the stocks, intended to replace the old ones; so little has Russia replaced her fleet'. 'Navies of Great Britain, France &c.', *The Times*, 18-I-1839, p. 6. In contrast to Palmerston's attempt to restrict the size of Russia's naval force was the contrast afforded by France, then Europe's second-largest naval power; a government decree in 1837 stated that the French navy was to be maintained at a level of forty line ships (of which ten were to mount 120 guns), fifty frigates, and 220 smaller vessels (which would include forty steamers). Of this number, twenty line and twenty-five frigates were to be constantly maintained, the others 'resteront au chantiers...', until required. *BFSP 1837–1838*, 26 (1855), pp. 1088–90; *LMU*, 28-VII-1838, p. 2000.

226. Clanricarde–Palmerston, 4-II-1839, FO 65–251 in Mosely, 'Englisch...', op. cit., pp. 565–6.
227. Lander–Ponsonby, 16-II-1839, FO 195–120.

5 The Second Egyptian Revolt and an Uneasy Peace

1. Durand–Vieul, op. cit., Vol. 2, p. 26.
2. Précis of despatch of Lord Stuart, 28-XII-1841, BM. ADD. MSS. 43178.
3. A. F. Mackintosh, 'On the military importance of Syria', *USJ*, November 1840, p. 381.
4. Campbell–Palmerston, 11-III-1839, FO 78–373. As a precaution against surprise attack, half of every ship's crew was to sleep aboard their vessel each night. *The Times*, 8-V-1839, p. 5.
5. Clanricarde–Palmerston, 1-IV-1839, FO 65–251.
6. Granville–Palmerston, 8-IV-1839, FO 27–581.
7. Ponsonby–Palmerston, 6-IX-1839, enclosure in Stopford–Adm., 15-IV-1839, ADM. 1-466.
8. Campbell–Palmerston, 4-V-1839, FO 78–373. Francis Stanley Rodkey, *The Turco-Egyptian Question in the Relations of England, France, and Russia 1832–1841*, Urbana, Illinois, 1923, 2 parts; Part 2, p. 83; *The Times*, 8-V-1839, p. 5.
9. Napier memo on Syria [n.d.], BM. ADD. MSS. 40039.
10. Reşit–Palmerston, 26-IV-1839, 27-V-1839, Palmerston–Reşit, 6-V-1839, in *Parliamentary Papers relative to the Affairs of the Levant*, London, 1841, 3 vols (hereafter referred to as *Levant*); Vol. I, pp. 9–15. Draft treaty enclosed in Ponsonby–Palmerston, 22-IV-1839, FO 78–355.
11. Jochmus–Backhouse, 3-II-1839, BM. ADD. MSS. 42808.
12. Lazarev–Verevkin, 28-VI-1839, in F.M. Sukhotin, 'Iz pisem M.P. Lazareva k A.I. Verevkinu (1837–1842)', *RA*, 1883, Book 3, pp. 386–7.
13. Lazarev–Menshikov, 17-V-1839, in *Kornilov*, op. cit., pp. 35–7.

14. Fedorov, op. cit., pp. 157–8; 'Ocherk...do 1842 goda', op. cit., p. 17; *The Times*, 24-V-1839, p. 5.
15. Ponsonby–Palmerston, 22-V-1839, FO 78–356.
16. 'Nyneshnee sostoianie flota ottomanskoi imperii i vitse-korolevstva egipetskogo', *Sin Otechestva*, October 1839, pp. 82–6.
17. T. J. Newbold, 'Present state of the military and naval strength of Egypt', *USJ*, October 1840, pp. 225–32. The *Shems*-100 had earlier burnt in Alexandria. Mehmet suspected arson, and was so angry that he had considered shooting every tenth Arsenal labourer, 'mais il s'est contente de faire fusiller treize hommes qui étaient de garde et un officer'. *LMU*, 31-VII-1838, p. 2006.
18. Prince 'Umar Tusun, *al-Jaish al-Misr al-Barri wa al-Bahr*, Cairo, 1940, pp. 135–50.
19. Stopford–Adm., 30-V-1839, enclosing 'List of the Egyptian fleet ready for sea', ADM. 1-466.
20. Alain Silvera, 'Edme-François Jomard and Egyptian reforms in 1829', *Middle Eastern Studies*, 7 (October 1971), pp. 301–17.
21. Ibid.
22. French Consul-President of Council of Ministers, 18-VI-1839, Ponsonby–Palmerston, 12-VI-1839, FO 78–356. The Ottoman Fleet had a total of twenty-nine ships. *LMU*, 4-VII-1839, p. 1218, 5-VII-1839, p. 1288. Steamers were used to tow the Ottoman Fleet out into the channel. *The Times*, 14-VI-1839, p. 6.
23. Campbell–Palmerston, 16-VI-1839, FO 78–374.
24. Granville–Palmerston, 17-VI-1839, FO 27–583.
25. Dalmatie–Bourquency, 17-V-1839, in *Levant*, op. cit., Vol. I, pp. 77–9.
26. *Archives Parliament*, 124, Paris, (1939), p. 666.
27. Palmerston–Granville, 19-VI-1839, enclosing 'Substance of proposed instructions to Sir Robert Stopford', FO 27–575.
28. 'A return of the movements of foreign ships and vessels of war, 16-IV/27-VI-1839', enclosed in Stopford–Adm., 27-VI-1839, ADM. 1-466.
29. M. Thomas, 'Relation de la bataille de Nezib', *LSM*, May 1840, pp. 154–62.
30. Ibid.; Soliman Pasha (Sève)-Guys, 25-VI- 27-VI-1839; *The Times*, 8-VIII-1839, p. 4.
31. Stopford–Adm., 12-VII-1839, ADM. 1-466.
32. Walker–Ponsonby, 4-VIII-1839, enclosure in Strangways–Adm., 30-IX-1839, ADM. 1-4376.
33. In an interview with the Reale Bey Osman (second in command) Lalande was told that Mahmut had been poisoned. The Kapudan Pasha had intended to go to Crete, but Lalande persuaded him to set sail for Rhodes; the Kapudan Pasha then wanted the French fleet to accompany him. Lalande declined, but he did send the *Bougainville*-24 to escort the Turks while he retired to Smyrna. Lalande–Roussin, 5-VII-1839, in Alfred Stern, 'Documents relatifs à la défection de la flotte turque en 1839', in *Revue Historique*, May–August 1911, pp. 325–6.
34. Mazoillier–Medem, 16-VIII-1839, in Cattaui, *Le Règne...*, op. cit., Vol. 3, pp. 320–21.
35. Palmerston–Ponsonby, 5-VII-1839, FO 78–353.

36. Beauvale–Palmerston, 30-VI-1839, 1-VII-1839, FO 7–281; Palmerston–Beauvale, 13-VII-1839, FO 7–279.
37. Roussin–Ponsonby, 7-VII-1839; Ponsonby–Campbell, 7-VII-1839, enclosed in Ponsonby–Palmerston, 8-VIII-1839, FO 78–353.
38. Telegraphic despatch, Marseilles, 25-VII-1839, enclosure in Granville–Palmerston, 26-VII-1839, FO 27–584.
39. Telegraphic Agent of Foreign Affairs–President of Council, enclosure in Granville–Palmerston, 26-VII-1839, FO 27–584.
40. Campbell–Palmerston, 11-VII-1839, FO 78–374.
41. Tossizza–Ministre, 6-VII-1839, in Athanase G. Politis, *Le Conflict Turco-Égyptien de 1838–1841 et les Derniers Années du Règne de Mohammed Aly d'après les Documents Diplomatiques Grecs*, Cairo, 1931, p. 71.
42. Walker–Ponsonby, 4-VIII-1839, enclosure in Strangways–Adm., 30-IX-1839, ADM. 1-4276.
43. *LMU*, 6-VIII-1839, p. 1601; 'The Turkish Fleet', op. cit., p. 162. With the defection of the Fleet, the only ships remaining were five line ships, four frigates, three corvettes, four brigs, and three steamers. The five line had deserted from the Fleet off Rhodes. *LMU*, 9-IX-1839, p. 1784. In addition, the Sultan had one line ship and a large frigate building at Sinop, and a 110-gun line and a 50-gun frigate building at İzmit.
44. Louis–Adm., 25-VII-1839, ADM. 1-466.
45. *LMU*, 7-VIII-1839, p. 1606; 'Flotte Turque à Alexandrie', *AMEC*, 1839, Vol. 2, partie non officielle, pp. 186–7.
46. *The Times*, 19-VIII-1839, p. 5.
47. *LMU*, 18-VIII-1839, p. 1650.
48. *LMU*, 19-VIII-1839, p. 1653. Mehmet now put the Turkish fleet under the formal control of an Egyptian officer.
49. *LMU*, 1-VIII-1839, p. 1638.
50. Palmerston–Beauvale, 13-VII-1839, FO 7–279.
51. Palmerston–Adm., 13-VII-1839, ADM. 1-4276.
52. Jochmus–Adm., 10-VII-1839, enclosure in Strangways–Adm., 3-VIII-1839, ADM. 1-4276.
53. Napier, *The Life...*, op. cit., Vol. 2, p. 208.
54. Palmerston–Admiralty 18-VII-1839, ADM. 1-4276.
55. Clanricarde–Palmerston, 8-VII-1839, FO 65–252.
56. Beauvale–Palmerston, 11-VII-1839, FO 7–281.
57. Palmerston–Beauvale, 1-VIII-1839, FO 7–279.
58. Pisani–Ponsonby, 19-VII-1839, enclosure in Ponsonby–Palmerston, 20-VII-1839, FO 78–357.
59. Hamilton–Palmerston, 31-VII-1839, FO 64–222.
60. Major-General Edward Napier, *Excursions along the Shores of the Mediterranean*, London, 1842, 2 vols; Vol. 2, pp. 154–5.
61. *LMU*, 18-VIII-1839, p. 1652. Lalande had been severely reprimanded for his failure to deal forcefully with the Turkish fleet's defection. Duperré–Lalande, 27-VII-1839, in Stern, op. cit., pp. 327–8.
62. Napier Memorandum, Besika Bay, Aug. 1839, in Napier, *The Life...*, op. cit., Vol. I, pp. 385–7. Napier could draw on additional resources; an Austrian squadron of six frigates and corvettes was at Smyrna, ready to

cooperate. Major-General Edward Napier, 'A cruise to the Levant in the summer of 1839', *USJ*, September 1840, p. 44.

63. Nesselrode–Medem, 6-VIII-1839, in *Levant*, op. cit., Vol. I, pp. 304–6.
64. Lazarev–Menshikov, 9-VIII-1839, in '*Perepiska...*', op. cit., *RA*, 1881, Book 3, pp. 377–9.
65. Captain Jesse, *Notes of a Half-pay in Search of Health*, London, 1841, 2 vols; Vol. 2, pp. 17–20.
66. 'Statisticheskoe obozrenie voenno-portovogo goroda Sevastopolia, za 1839 god', *ZMVD*, August 1840, pp. 242–50.
67. Clanricarde–Palmerston, 10-VIII-1839, FO 65–252.
68. Menshikov–Lazarev, 3-VIII-1839, in '*Perepiska...*', op. cit., *RA*, 1881, Book 3, pp. 379–80.
69. Granville–Palmerston, 19-VIII-1839, FO 27–585.
70. Palmerston–Admiralty, 23-VIII-1839, ADM. 1-4276.
71. Palmerston–Admiralty, 24-VIII-1839, ADM. 1-4276.
72. *LMU*, 9-IX-1839, p. 1742.
73. Palmerston–Beauvale, 25-VIII-1839, FO 7–279.
74. Clanricarde–Palmerston, 31-VIII-1839, FO 65–253.
75. Bulwer–Palmerston, 6-IX-1839, FO 27–577.
76. Yeames–Palmerston, 6-IX-1839, enclosure in Strangways–Adm., 27-IX-1839, ADM. 1-4276.
77. Lazarev–Menshikov, 18-IX-1839, in '*Perepiska...*', op. cit., *RA*, 1881, Book 3, p. 380.
78. The British line ships were: HMS *Princess Charlotte*-104, HMS *Rodney*-92, HMS *Asia*-84, HMS *Vanguard*-80, HMS *Ganges*-84, HMS *Bellerophon*-80, HMS *Minden*-74, HMS *Implacable*-74, HMS *Powerful*-84, and HMS *Pembroke*-72; the French ships were *Iéna*-90, *Montebello*-120, *Hercule*-100, *Jupiter*-86, *Santi-Petri*-86, *Diadème*-86, *Généreux*-80, *Triton*-80, and *Trident*-80. 'État des forces navales de France et Angleterre en Orient, au 15 septembre 1839', *AMEC*, partie non officielle, 1839, Vol. 2, pp. 1120–21.
79. Campbell–Palmerston, 15-VIII-1839, enclosure in Strangways–Adm., 9-IX-1839, ADM. 1-4276.
80. Palmerston–Bulwer, 10-IX-1839, FO 27–577.
81. Stopford–Ponsonby, 11-IX-1839, enclosure in Ponsonby–Palmerston, 22-IX-1839, FO 78–353.
82. Pisani–Ponsonby, 29-IX-1839, enclosure in Ponsonby–Palmerston, 30-IX-1839, FO 78–353.
83. *LMU*, 9-X-1839, p. 1865.
84. Stopford–Ponsonby, 21-X-1839, ADM. 1-466.
85. *LMU*, 16-XI-1839, p. 2023.
86. Napier, *The Life...*, op. cit., Vol. I, p. 393; *LMU*, 22-XI-1839, p. 2047.
87. Brown, op. cit., p. 144; M. de Pradal de Lamase, 'La station navale français de Tunis au milieu de XIX siècle' in *Revue Internationale d'Histoire Militaire*, 4 (1956), p. 352; A. Mortal, 'L'Armée d'Ahmed Bey d'après un instructeur français, in *Revue Internationale d'Histoire Militaire*, 4 (1956), pp. 382–3.
88. Stopford–Adm., 8-XI-1839, 20-XI-1839, ADM. 1-466.
89. Brunnov–Nesselrode, 8-X-1840, in *Levant*, op. cit., Vol. I, pp. 442–6.

90. Palmerston–Clanricarde, 25-X-1839, FO 65–250.
91. The three-mile limit delineating national sovereignty over coastal waters had only recently come into British usage; Continental jurists continued to use the 'cannon-shot' doctrine during this period without reference to a specific three-mile limit. D.P. O'Connell, *The International Law of the Sea; Volume 1*, Oxford 1982, pp. 124–35, 151–7.
92. Granville–Palmerston, 18-XI-1839, FO 27–588.
93. Nesselrode–Kiselev, 22-XI-1839, in *Levant*, op. cit., Vol. I, pp. 504–5.
94. Stopford–Adm., 20-XI-1839, ADM. 1-466.
95. Palmerston–Granville, 10-XII-1839, FO 27–578.
96. Medem–Nesselrode (Decembre 1839), in Cattaui, *Le Règne...*, op. cit., Vol. 3, p. 353.
97. *LMU*, 13-I-1840, p. 74; 12-II-1840, p. 296.
98. Hodges–Palmerston, 30-XII-1839, FO 78–377.
99. Napier–Hodges, 12-I-1840, in Napier, *The Life...*, op. cit., Vol. I, p. 398. Russia actually had less than $\frac{2}{3}$ this number of line ships in the Black Sea.
100. Napier–Hodges, 14-I-1840, in Napier, *The Life...*, op. cit., Vol. I, p. 399.
101. 'Measures suggested by Baron Brunnow... January 1840', in *Levant*, op. cit., Vol. I, pp. 529–31.
102. Granville–Palmerston, 13-I-1840, FO 27–601.
103. Napier–Palmerston, 17-I-1840, in Napier, *The Life...*, op. cit., Vol. I, p. 400–401.
104. Werry–Bidwell, 9-III-1840, in *Levant*, op. cit., Vol. I, p. 594.
105. Golovin, *Ocherk...*, op. cit., pp. 44–5; 'Obozrenie Vysochaishego prednachertannogo plana k obshchemu usmireniiu Kavkazskikh gorskikh plemen, ot 12 marta 1840', 'Sekretno', in *ASKAK*, op. cit., Vol. 9, pp. 244–7; *LMU*, 29-I-1841, p. 197.
106. Dzidzariia, *Prisoedinenie...*, op. cit., pp. 36–7; 'Predpolozheniia po Kavkazskomu kraiu na 1840 g'., 'Sekretno' [n.d.], 'Arkhiv kniazia A. I. Chernysheva', *SIRIO*, Vol. 122 (1901), pp. 414–23; 'Sobytiia v nachale 1840 goda', in *ASKAK*, op. cit., Vol. 9, pp. 289–92.
107. 'Chernomorskaia beregovaia liniia', in *Brokgauz...*, op. cit., Vol. 38, p. 647. The fort's entire garrison of 78 men perished in the attack.
108. Chernyshev–Golovin, 5-III-1840, in *ASKAK*, op. cit., Vol. 9, pp. 465–6.
109. Lazarev–Menshikov, 30-III-1840, in '*Perepiska...*', op. cit., *RA*, 1882, Book 2, pp. 297–8.
110. Raevskii–Golovin, 17-III-1840, in K.V. Sivkov, 'O proetakh okonchaniia Kavkazskoi voiny v seredine XIX v.', *Istorii SSSR*, 3 (May–June 1958); *ASKAK*, op. cit., Vol. 9, pp. 470–75.
111. Iosif Miroslavskii, 'Vzryv Mikhailovskogo ukrepleniia v 1840 godu', *KS* 4 (1879), pp. 1–17.
112. 'Geroiskii podvig riadovogo Arkhipa Osipova', *Voennyi Zhurnal*, VI (1840), pp. 149–51; 'Smert' na slavu ili zashchita Mikhailovskogo ukrepleniia, 22 Marta 1840 goda', *Sbornik Gazety Kavkaz*, 1847, Part 1, pp. 112–27.
113. Moore–Palmerston, 27-III-1840, FO 78–412.
114. Medem–Nesselrode, in Cattaui *Le Règne...*, op. cit., Vol. 3, p. 367.
115. Palmerston–Admiralty, 7-IV-1840, in *Levant*, op. cit., Vol. I, p. 618.

116. Lazarev–Menshikov, 8-IV-1840, in 'Perepiska...', op. cit., RA, 1882, Book 1, p. 298.
117. Fedorov, op. cit., p. 190.
118. Lazarev–Menshikov, 15-IV-1840, in 'Perepiska...', op. cit., RA, 1882, Book 1, pp. 299–300.
119. Menshikov–Lazarev, 18-IV-1840, in 'Perepiska...', op. cit., RA, 1882, Book 1, p. 300. Reports had been received that Pshade and Novotroitskoe had fallen; Lazarev stated that the reports were false.
120. G.A. Dzidzariia, Makhadzhirstvo i Problemy Istorii Abkhazii XIX Stoletiia, Sukhumi, 1975, p. 43.
121. Golovin–Chernyshev, 24-V-1840, in ASKAK, op. cit., Vol. 9, p. 488. Nine thousand troops were used in the operation. The landing was followed twelve days later by a second one at Psezuape.
122. LMU, 6-VII-1840, p. 1625. The mountaineers were capable of producing their own small arms, which were of excellent quality; 'Dagestan was known as the armory forge of the Caucasus...'. E.G. Astvatsaturian, Istoriia Oruzheinogo i Serebrianogo Proizvodstva na Kavkaze v XIX-Nachale XX V. Dagestan i Zakavkaze; Chast' l, Moskva, 1977, pp. 27, 137.
123. LMU, 11-VIII-1840, p. 1822.
124. Shavrov, op. cit., pp. 18–19. Russia was not the only country interested in the timber of the eastern Black Sea coast; in 1836, Gurians exchanged contracts with foreigners to supply them with oak timber to the value of 40 000 silver rubles. G.V. Khachapuridze and F.E. Makharadze, Ocherki po Istorii Rabochego i Krest'ianskogo Dvizheniia v Gruzii, Moskva, 1932, p. 35.
125. Ibid.
126. Wood–Ponsonby, 3-VII-1840, enclosure in Ponsonby–Palmerston, 14-VII-1840, FO 78–395.
127. Hodges–Palmerston, 6-VI-1840, FO 78–404.
128. Hodges–Palmerston, 16-VI-1840, FO 78–404. Mehmet could now put twenty-one line ships to sea. 'Return of the forces of Mehemet Al', enclosure in Ponsonby–Palmerston, 7-VI-1840, FO 78–404.
129. Medem–Nesselrode (November 1839), (May 1840), in Cattaui, Le Règne..., op. cit., Vol. 3, pp. 348, 370.
130. Palmerston–Hodges, 18-VII-1840, FO 78–403.
131. Napier–Stopford, 25-VII-1840, in Napier, The Life..., op. cit., Vol. I, p. 430.
132. Napier–Palmerston, 3-VIII-1840, BM. ADD. MSS. 40038.
133. Menshikov–Lazarev, 4-VIII-1840, in 'Perepiska...', op. cit., RA, 1882, Book 1, pp. 305–6.
134. Stopford–Napier, 8-VIII-1840, BM. ADD. MSS. 40038.
135. The twelve line ships were HMS Princess Charlotte-104, HMS Asia-84, HMS Ganges-84, HMS Powerful-84, HMS Thunderer-84, HMS Bellerophon-80, HMS Implacable-74, HMS Hastings-78, HMS Benbow-72, HMS Edinburgh-72, HMS Belleisle-72 and HMS Revenge-76. 'List of ships composing the Mediterranean Squadron'; enclosure in Palmerston–Brunnow, 15-VII-1840 in Levant, op. cit., Vol. II, p. 703.
136. Menshikov–Lazarev, 11-VII-1840, in 'Perepiska...', op. cit., RA, 1882, Book 1, p. 307.

137. Menshikov–Lazarev, 'Sekretno', 11-VIII-1840, in *'Perepiska...'*, op. cit., *RA*, 1882, Book 1, pp. 307–8.
138. Stopford–Napier, 19-VIII-1840, BM. ADD. MSS. 40028.
139. Napier–Collier, 'Secret', 16-VIII-1840, BM. ADD. MSS. 40038.
140. Napier–Soliman Pasha, 18-VIII-1840, BM. ADD. MSS. 40036.
141. Soliman–Napier, 19-VIII-1840, BM. ADD. MSS. 40036.
142. Napier–Hodges, 21-VIII-1840, BM. ADD. MSS. 40038.
143. Napier–Stopford, 21-VIII-1840, BM. ADD. MSS. 40036.
144. Medem–Nesselrode, 25-VIII-1840, in Cattaui, *Le Règne...*, op. cit., Vol. 3, pp. 428–9.
145. Hodges–Palmerston, 24-VIII-1840, FO 78–406; Alison–Ponsonby, 26-VIII-1840, in *Levant*, op. cit., Vol. II, pp. 218–19.
146. De Laurin–Sturmer, 26-VI-1840, enclosure in Ponsonby–Palmerston, 8-VII-1840, FO 78–395.
147. Hodges–Napier, 18-VIII-1840, BM. ADD. MSS. 40028.
148. Lazarev–Menshikov, 27-VIII-1840, in *'Perepiska...'*, op. cit., *RA*, 1882, Book 1, pp. 309–10.
149. Lazarev–Verevkin, 2-IX-1840, in Sukhotin, op. cit., p. 388.
150. Lazarev–Menshikov, 28-X-1840, in *'Perepiska...'*, op. cit., *RA*, 1882, Book 1, pp. 311–12.
151. Ponsonby–Wood, 6-IX-1840, in Cunningham, op. cit., pp. 159–61.
152. W. Patterson Hunter, 'Syria; during the campaign against Mehemet Ali', *USJ*, 1841, Part 2, pp. 474–5.
153. Ibid. Napier–Stopford, 29-VIII-1840, BM. ADD. MSS. 40038 lists fifteen merchantmen.
154. Ponsonby–Palmerston in *Levant*, op. cit., Vol. II, p. 265.
155. Bloomfield–Palmerston, 12-IX-1840, FO 65–261; Bloomfield–Palmerston, 2-X-1840, FO 65–262. The advantage of sending the ships to Sveaborg was that they could leave the Baltic both later in the autumn (if needed), or weeks earlier in the spring. The ships had already been winterised and laid up. The ships were to be at the 'disposal' of Her Majesty's Government; and were 'the best ships of the Baltic Fleet'. The squadron was to contain the line ships *Fershampenuaz*-74, *Finland*-74, *Gangut*-84, *Ostrolenka*-74, *Aleksandr Nevskii*-74, *Tsar Konstantin*-74, *Leipzig*-74, *Lefort*-74, and *Retvizan*-74; the frigates *Pallas*-44, *Avrora*-44, *Prince d'Orange*[sic]-44, *Mel'pomena*-44, *Ekaterina*-44, *Venus*-44; the brigs *Agamennon*-20, *Nestor*-20, *Polinur*-20, and *Autinor*-20; transports *Amerika* and *Msta*. 'Division de la Flotte Impériale prête à sortir de la Baltique', enclosure in Bloomfield–Palmerston, 24-X-1840, FO 65–262.
156. Napier–Ponsonby, 17-IX-1840, BM. ADD. MSS. 40038.
157. Stopford–Napier, 19-IX-1840, BM. ADD. MSS. 40038.
158. Stopford–Napier, 23-IX-1840, BM. ADD. MSS. 40038.
159. Stopford–O'Ferrall, 20-IX-1840, *USJ*, November 1840, p. 403.
160. Larking–Palmerston, 6-X-1840, 16-X-1840, FO 78–414.
161. Palmerston–Napier, 23-X-1840, BM. ADD. MSS. 40021.
162. Ponsonby–Stopford, 25-X-1840, BM. ADD. MSS. 40028.
163. Medem–Nesselrode. 8-X-1840, in Cattaui, *Le Règne...*, op. cit., Vol. 3, p. 516.
164. Palmerston–Ponsonby, 27-X-1840, FO 78–391.

165. *USJ*, 1841, Pt 1, p. 116.
166. B. Dichter, *The Maps of Acre: an Historical Cartography*, Acre, 1973, p. 118.
167. *USJ*, 1841, Pt 1, op. cit., p. 116.
168. Hunter, op. cit., 1841, Pt 3, pp. 166–7.
169. Stopford–Adm., 4-XI-1840, 'Theatre of War – Operations of the Allies off the coast of Syria', *NM*, no. 1, 1841, pp. 4–5, 8. Precision in surveying was essential to success; when the *Mukhuddinay-i Hive*-74 took up her appointed position, she was five hundred yards from the fortress with 'not more than seven inches water under her hull'. Hunter, *Syria...*, op. cit., p. 176.
170. *USJ*, 1841, Pt 1, op. cit., pp. 116–17.
171. Heinrich von Bayer and Arthur von Khuepach, *Geschichte der K.K. Kriegsmarine während der Jahre 1814–1847*, Graz-Köln, 1966, pp. 116–25, 243–68.
172. 'Lt. Eliot's account, November 4', in Napier, '*The Life...*, op. cit., Vol. 2, pp. 95–6. Stopford remarked, 'it is generally supposed that shells from the *Gorgon* occasioned the destruction of the powder magazine...'. Stopford–Adm., 31-XI-1840, *USJ*, January 1841, pp. 119–20.
173. Smith–Palmerston, 5-XI-1840, in *Levant*, op. cit., Vol. III, pp. 56–7.
174. *USJ*, 1841, Pt I, op. cit., pp. 116–17.
175. Stopford–Adm., 8-XI-1840, *USJ*, January 1841, pp. 120–21.
176. Stopford–O'Ferrall, 8-XI-1840, *USJ*, January 1841, p. 121.
177. Ibrahim–Mehmet Ali [n.d.], enclosure in Ponsonby–Palmerston, 25-XI-1840, FO 78–399.
178. Stopford–Adm., 4-XI-1840, op. cit., *NM*, No. 1, 1841, pp. 4–5.
179. 'Letter from Alexandria 6/7-XI-1840', in *Levant*, op. cit., Vol. III, pp. 67–8.
180. Ponsonby–Napier, 15-XI-1840, BM. ADD. MSS. 40021.
181. Napier–Minto, 14-XI-1840, BM. ADD. MSS. 40038.
182. Napier, *The Life...*, op. cit., Vol. 2, p. 103.
183. Napier, *The Life...*, op. cit., Vol. 2, p. 115.
184. Wood–Ponsonby, 19-XI-1840, enclosing 'Approximate estimate of Egyptian forces in Syria, 19-XI-1840', in *Levant*, op. cit., Vol. III, pp. 109–11.
185. Napier–Boghos, 24-XI-1840, BM. ADD. MSS. 40036.
186. The convention was signed 27-XI-1840. Napier–Ponsonby, 14-XII-1840; Napier–Stopford, 14-XII-1840, BM. ADD. MSS. 40036.
187. Ponsonby–Napier, 7-XII-1840, BM. ADD. MSS. 40028.
188. Palmerston–Adm., 15-XII-1840, BM. ADD. MSS. 40028.
189. Reshid–Ponsonby, 2-XII-1840, enclosure in Ponsonby–Palmerston, 9-XII-1840, FO 78–399.
190. Londonderry–Peel, 4-XII-1840, BM. ADD. MSS. 40428.
191. Fanshawe–Stopford, 12-XII-1840, BM. ADD. MSS. 40028.
192. 'Alexandria is not a very safe place to Blockade during the winter – you are exposed to two lee shores, one running East and West and another running North and South; and I do not think it safe for a squadron to remain there during the winter'. Napier–Stopford, 10-XII-1840, BM. ADD. MSS. 40036.

193. *NM*, No. 1, 1841, pp. 92–5.
194. Palmerston–Clanricarde, 11-I-1841, FO 65–269.
195. Larking–Palmerston, 22-I-1841, FO 78–452.
196. Napier–Adm., 21-I-1841, BM. ADD. MSS. 40036.
197. Stopford–O'Ferrall, 14-I-1841, enclosure in Barrow–Backhouse, 1-II-1841, in *Levant*, op. cit., Vol. III, pp. 174–5.
198. *LMU*, 21-II-1841, p. 438.
199. Ferman, 12-II-1841, in *BFSP*, 59 (1868–9), pp. 571–6.
200. Ferman, 1-VI-1841, in *BFSP*, 59 (1868–9), op. cit., pp. 578–80.
201. Mehmet Ali–Grand Vizier [n.d.], enclosure in Ponsonby–Palmerston, 9-III-1841, FO 78–432.
202. *LMU*, 6-IV-1841, p. 902, 8-IV-1841, p. 926.
203. *LMU*, 16-IV-1841, p. 1001.
204. Palmerston–Bulwer, 12-VI-1841, FO 27–620.
205. Letter from Alexandria, 16-VI-1841, enclosure in Ponsonby–Palmerston, 2-VI-1841, FO 78–434.
206. Menshikov–Lazarev, 'Sekretno', 6-V-1841, in '*Perepiska. . .*', op. cit., *RA*, 1882, Book 1, p. 317.
207. 'In general here we are in extreme need of steamers, not to mention already the larger ones of three or four hundred horsepower, which, God knows when we will ever have them. . . . The two steamers suggested . . . would completely secure our communications not only in the Black Sea, but wherever they are vital; and their price seems extremely moderate, for building them here would be extremely expensive'. Lazarev–Menshikov, 28-II-1841, in '*Perepiska. . .*', op. cit., *RA*, 1882, Book 1, pp. 315–16.
208. Lazarev–Menshikov, 18-V-1841, in '*Perepiska. . .*', op. cit., *RA*, 1882, Book 1, p. 31.
209. *LMU*, 17-V-1842, p. 1131.
210. G. Wright, 'The Bosphorus – anchorages of Therapia and Tophana', *NM*, no. 12, 1841, p. 796. Russia also expanded her Black Sea steam packet-service; Bloomfield reported a decision to buy four steamers in Britain for use in an Odessa–Constantinople passenger-trade route. Précis of a despatch from Bloomfield, 27-X-1841, BM. ADD. MSS. 43178.
211. 'Convention between Austria, France, Great Britain, Prussia, Russia, and Turkey respecting the Dardanelles and Bosphorus – signed at London, July 13, 1841', in *BFSP*, 29 (1840–41), p. 705.
212. *ZMT*, July 1841, p. 16.
213. *USJ*, August 1841, pp. 554–5.
214. Lord Aberdeen, 'Memorandum on proposed reduction of Mediterranean Fleet', 22-X-1841, BM. ADD. MSS. 43238.
215. '*Torgovoe sudokhodstvo. . .*', op. cit., pp. 17–42.
216. 'Extracts from my Remark Book', in Sharp, op. cit., p. 265.
217. Sharp, op. cit., p. 280.
218. Sharp, op. cit., p. 286.
219. Lazarev–Menshikov, 7-IX-1841, in '*Perepiska. . .*', op. cit., *RA*, 1882, Book 1, p. 319.

Conclusions

1. The first translation of Mahan's *Influence of Sea Power upon History 1660–1783* into Russian was done in 1895, five years after its initial publication. The Marine Ministry followed this with a second edition in 1896. The Soviets produced their own translation in 1941. Mahan's *The Influence of Sea Power upon the French Revolution and Empire, 1793–1812* appeared in Russian in 1897, with a Soviet edition appearing in 1940. See John B. and Lynn C. Hattendorff, comps. *A Bibliography of the Works of Alfred Thayer Mahan*, Newport, Rhode Island, 1986. Current Soviet assessment of Mahan is harsh; his entry in the *Sovetskaiia Voennaiia Entsikhlopediia* notes, 'From 1883 to 1913 he published a series of works which founded the politics of American imperialism and justified the USA's aggressive wars... The theory of "sea power" in expressing the interests of American imperialism, exerted a great influence on the development of naval theory in the USA and other imperialist powers.'

2. While Gorskhov's historical comments are quite terse, other Soviet commentators are more expansive. 'The reasons for this decline are the following; first, in the beginning of the 19th century the leadership lost...interest in the fleet as a consequence of a lack of understanding of its important meaning for Russia. Then the Russian navy in the course of the entire first half of the 19th century did not fight and accumulate military experience as in earlier times, but gradually sank into soulless routine. Finally, and this is the most important, in the course of the 19th century occurred the evolution from a sail to a steam fleet...'. A. D. Bubnov, 'Voenno-morskoe iskusstvo v russkom flote', *Morskie Zapiski*, XX, nos. 3–4 (1962), p. 25.

3. S. G. Gorshkov, 'Voenno-morskie floty v voinakh i v mirnoe vremia', *Morskoi Sbornik*, March 1972, p. 21. A superb account placing Gorshkov's theories within the context of earlier Russian naval strategists is Jacob W. Kipp's 'Sergei Gorshkov and Naval Advocacy; the Tsarist Heritage' in the *Soviet Armed Forces Review Annual*, Vol. 3, Gulf Breeze, Fl 1979, pp. 225–39.

4. Gorshkov, 'Voenno-...', op. cit., p. 20.

5. Mahan, *Influence...*, op. cit., pp. 28–9. While Mahan is the best-known naval theorist of his time, other authors, in particular Captain Sir John Colomb were also searching for an analytical basis on which to formulate naval policy. For a discussion of John and Phillip Colomb, John Laughton, Herbert Richmond and Julian Corbett and their relationships to Mahan, see Donald M. Shurman's *The Education of a Navy; the Development of British Naval Strategic Thought, 1867–1914*, Chicago, 1965.

6. Gorshkov, 'Voenno-...', op. cit., p. 22.

7. Robert J. Hanks, *The Unnoticed Challenge; Soviet Maritime Strategy and the Global Choke Points*, Washington, D.C., 1980. It is interesting to note that Hanks in his discussion of Mediterranean 'choke points' omits the Straits, concentrating on Gibraltar and Aden-Somalia as the critical

pressure points. See the Map 'World Shipping Routes and Choke Points' between pages 4–5.

8. Gorshkov, 'Voenno...', op. cit., p. 31.
9. Mahan, *Influence...*, op. cit., p. 13.
10. Gorshkov, ,'Voenno...', op. cit., p. 31.
11. Alfred Thayer Mahan, *Naval Strategy compared and contrasted with the Principles and Practice of Military Operations on Land*, Boston, 1911, p. 309. While Mahan was regarded by many naval officers of his time as profoundly insightful, a radically different geopolitical interpretation was being developed by Sir Halford Mackinder. As expressed in his essay, 'The Geographical Pivot of History', a Central Asian "heartland" would rise to a position of unparalleled economic and industrial power, due to advances in land communications allied to its population and raw resources. A discussion comparing these theories can be found in Paul Kennedy's essay 'Mahan *versus* Mackinder; Two Interpretations of British Sea Power' in his *Strategy and Diplomacy 1870–1945*, London, 1983, pp. 43–85. For an essay which places Mahan in the context of his time, see Kenneth J. Hagan's 'Alfred Thayer Mahan: Turning America Back to the Sea' in Frank J. Merli and Theodore A. Wilson (eds), *Makers of American Diplomacy*, New York 1974, pp. 279–304. For many historians, many of Mahan's ideas remain relevant; for an application of Mahan's logistic principles to the American naval presence in the Persian Gulf, see William H. Russell's 'Foundations of Military Thought; Has Mahan's Time Arrived?' in *Marine Corps Gazette*, May 1988, pp. 84–6. The standard source work on the genesis of Mahan's writing remains Doris D. Macquire and Robert Seager *Letters and Papers of Alfred Thayer Mahan*, Annapolis, 1975, 3 vols. For an insightful view of Mahan's relevance to the modern world, see Chapters 14–5 of William E. Livezey's *Mahan on Sea Power*, Norman, Oklahoma, 1947.
12. Gorshkov, 'Voenno-...', op. cit., p. 20.
13. Mahan, *Naval Strategy...*, op. cit., p. 55.
14. Marx Leva, 'Barring the door to the Med', *United States Naval Institute Proceedings*, August 1987, p. 88.
15. S. G. Gorshkov, *Morskaia Moshch' Gosudarstva*, Moskva, 1979, p. 342.
16. 'Iz pis'ma V. A. Kornilova A. S. Menshikovu o vmeshatel'stve sukho-putnogo komandovaniia v voprosy podgotovki Chernomorskogo flota k voine i slavom rukovodstve flotom so storony admirala M. B. Berkha', in *Kornilov*, op. cit., pp. 172–3. Once war broke out, technology relegated the Black Sea Fleet to the defensive. Gorshkov notes, 'with the entry of the Anglo-French fleet into the Black Sea, the technical backwardness and weakness of the Black Sea Fleet was not fated to continue the battle at sea'. Gorshkov, *Morskaia...*, op. cit., p. 122.
17. While the Crimean War was fought primarily in the Black Sea, the proximity of a large Russian Baltic Fleet only "several days sail" from Britain produced spasmodic alarms in the British press and politics in the 1830s and 1840s. While the British expedition sent to the Baltic during the Crimean War failed in its attacks on Sveaborg and Kronstadt, the Russian Baltic Fleet was effectively neutralised. For a thorough

treatment of this little-known campaign, see Basil Greenhill and Ann Gifford's superb study, *The British Assault on Finland*, London, 1988.

18. Mahan, *The Influence*..., op. cit., p. 59.
19. Mahan, *The Influence*..., op. cit., p. 50.
20. This is in direct opposition to Gorshkov's criteria for a powerful maritime state; 'Naval states with great economic means, have widely used their naval fleets in peacetime for exerting pressure on their potential enemies, as a sort of military demonstration, threatening the breaking of maritime communications, and preventing marine trade'. Gorshkov, 'Voenno-...', op. cit., p. 29.
21. Sun Tzu, 'On the Art of War' in T.R. Phillips (ed.), *Roots of Strategy*, Harrisburg, PA, 1940, p. 27.
22. B. Mitchell Simpson (ed.), *The Development of Naval Thought: Essays by Herbert Rosinski*, Newport, RI, 1977, pp. xix–xx.
23. Gorshkov, *Morskaiia*..., op. cit., p. 120.
24. Gorshkov, *Morskaiia*..., op. cit., p. 53.
26. Palmerston–Clanricarde, 29-XII-1838, FO 65–243.

Bibliography

MANUSCRIPT SOURCES

Public Record Office

Admiralty MSS

ADM. 1 In-Letters; Vols 447, 448, 449, 450, 451, 452, 453, 459, 465, 466, 467, 468, 469, 478, 855, 1338, 1340, 3860, 4270, 4272, 4273, 4274, 4276.
ADM. 2 Out-Letters, Vols. 244, 246, 254, 270.
ADM. 12 Indexes, Series II, Vols 244, 246, 254, 270.
ADM. 106 Navy Board Records, Vol. 2050.

Foreign Office MSS

FO 3 (Algiers), Vol. 31.
FO 7 (Austria), Vols 272, 279, 281.
FO 27 (France), Vols 395, 396, 397, 575, 577, 578, 581, 583, 584, 585, 588, 601, 603, 620.
FO 32 (Greece), Vol. 14.
FO 60 (Persia), Vol. 31.
FO 64 (Prussia), Vols 220, 221, 222.
FO 65 (Russia), Vols 227, 229, 243, 250, 251, 252, 253, 259, 261, 262, 269.
FO 78 (Turkey), Vols 160, 182, 192, 271, 298, 311, 353, 355, 356, 357, 373, 374, 377, 391, 395, 396, 399, 403, 404, 405, 306, 412, 414, 432, 434, 452.
FO 97 (Supplementary: Turkey), Vol. 402.
FO 142 (Egypt: Letter-books), Vols 2, 3.
FO 195 (Turkey: Correspondence), Vols 20, 65, 82, 83, 85, 86, 93, 104, 120, 144, 647.
FO 257 (Russia: Odessa; Correspondence), Vol. 3.
FO 286 (Greece; Correspondence), Vol. 6.
FO 360 (Howard de Walden Papers; Original Correspondence), Vol. 5.
FO Confidential Print No. 137.

Colonial Office MSS

CO 158 (Malta; Original Correspondence), Vol. 56.
CO 714 (Index), Vol. 91.

British Library MSS

BM. ADD. MSS. 32290. Deciphers of despatches: Russia, Vol. III, 1828–37.
BM. ADD. MSS. 41557, BM. ADD. MSS. 41558, BM. ADD. MSS. 41559,
BM. ADD. MSS. 41560, BM. ADD. MSS. 41562. Heytesbury Papers.
BM. ADD. MSS. 42808. Rose Papers.
BM. ADD. MSS. 43060, BM. ADD. MSS. 43089. BM. ADD. MSS. 43178.
BM. ADD. MSS. 43218. BM. ADD. MSS. 43231. BM. ADD. MSS. 43232.
BM. ADD. MSS. 43238. Aberdeen Papers.
BM. ADD. MSS. 47248, BM. ADD. MSS. 47249. BM. ADD. MSS. 47262.
Lieven Papers.
BM. ADD. MSS. 48451, BM. ADD. MSS. 48452. BM. ADD. MSS. 48492.
Palmerston Papers.
BM. ADD. MSS. 40020, BM. ADD. MSS. 40021, BM. ADD. MSS. 40028,
BM. ADD. MSS. 40036, BM. ADD. MSS. 40038, BM. ADD. MSS. 40039.
Napier Papers.
BM. EGERTON MSS. 2343. Palmerston–Hoppner Correspondence.
BM. EGERTON MSS. 3168. Jomini–Onou Papers.

National Maritime Museum MSS

Drinkwater (Bethune) Papers, Vol. 3.
Massie Papers, Vol. 16.
Sir Charles Knowles MSS 84-075.

NEWSPAPERS AND PERIODICALS

American Historical Review
Annales Maritimes et Coloniales
Archivum Ottomanicum
Army Quarterly Defence Journal
Artilleriiskii Zhurnal
Balkan Studies
Belletin
Biblioteka dlia Chteniia
Blackwood's Magazine
British and Foreign Review
Bulletin of the History of Medicine
Bulletin of the Institute of Historical Research
Cahier Monde Russe et Soviétique
Cahiers d'Histoire Égyptienne
Cambridge Historical Journal
Canadian Slavic Papers
Caucasian Review
Colburns New Monthly Magazine
Drevniaia i Novaia Rossiia
English Historical Review
Études Balkaniques

Études Slaves et Est-Européens
Foreign Quarterly Review
Foreign Review and Continental Miscellany
Fortnightly Review
Fraser's Magazine
Gentleman's Magazine
The Geographical Journal
History
Iakhty
Index Islamicus
International Journal of Middle East Studies
International Review
Istoriia SSR
Istoricheskii Vestnik
Istoricheskii Zhurnal
Istoricheskie Zapiski
Jahrbücher für Geschichte Osteuropas
Journal of the American Oriental Society
Journal of Asian and African Studies
Journal of Asian History
Journal Asiatique
Journal of Central European Affairs
Journal of European Economic History
Journal of Modern History
Journal of Near Eastern Studies
Journal of Oriental and African Studies
Journal of the Royal Geographical Society
Journal des Sciences Militaires des Armées de Terre et de Mer
Journal of the Royal Asiatic Society
Kavkazskii Sbornik
Krasnyi Arkhiv
Kronshatadtskii Vestnik
Kubanskie Vedomosti
Le Moniteur Universel
Le Spectateur Militaire
Mariners Mirror
Middle Eastern Studies
Middle East Journal
Morskoi Sbornik
Nautical Magazine
Nautical and Maritime Magazine
Odesskii Vestnik
Quarterly Review
Revue Africaine
Revue des Deux Mondes
Revue Historique
Revue Internationale d'Histoire Militaire
Russkaia Starina
Russkii Arkhiv

Russkii Invalid
Russkii Vestnik
Sanktpeterburgskiia Vedomosti
Sin Otechestva
Sovremennik
Sudostroenie
The Times
United Service Journal and Naval and Military Magazine
Vestnik Leningradskogo Gosudarstvennogo Universiteta
Voennyi Zhurnal
Zapiski Gidrograficheskogo Departamenta Morskoi Ministerstva
Zapiski Odesskogo Obshchestva Istorii i Drevnosti
Zhurnal Manufaktur i Torgovli
Zhurnal Ministerstva Narodnogo Prosveshcheniia
Zhurnal Ministerstva Vnutrennikh Del

BOOKS AND ARTICLES

Abaza, K. K., *Obshchedostupnaia Voenno-istoricheskaia Khrestomatiia*, Sankt-petrburg, 1887, 2 vols.
Abhazian, T., 'Liberation in Abhazia and the Abkhazian-Abhazaians', *Caucasian Review*, No. 7 (1958).
Abbot, G. F., *Greece in Evolution*, London, 1909.
——, *Turkey, Greece and the Great Powers*, London, 1916.
Abir, M., 'Modernisation, Reaction and Muhammad Ali's 'Empire', *Middle Eastern Studies*, 13 (1977).
'Abkhaz', *Encyclopedia of Islam*, Series I, London, 1913–38, 5 vols; Vol. 1.
Adair, Sir Robert, *Negociations For the Peace of the Dardanelles*, London, 1845, 2 vols.
'Administrative system and policy-making process', *Military–Naval Encyclopedia of Russia and the Soviet Union*, Gulf Breeze, Fl. 1978- ; Vol. 2.
Afanas'ev, D., 'Po povodu stat'i ob Admirale A.S. Greig, pomeshchennoi v ianvar'skoi knizhe Morskogo Sbornika sego goda', *Kronshtadtskii Vestnik*, no. 20, 1864.
Afans'ev, D. M., 'K istorii Chernomorskogo Flota, 1768–1816 gg.', *Russkii Arkhiv*, No. 2 (1902).
——, 'K istorii Chernomorskago Flota s 1816 po 1853 god', *Russkii Arkhiv*, nos. 1–7 (1902).
Akiner, Shirin, *Islamic Peoples of the Soviet Union*, London, 1983.
Akty Sobranie Kavkazskoiu Arkheograficheskogo Kommissieiu, Tiflis, 1866–1904, 12 vols.
Albion, Robert Greenhalgh, *Naval and Maritime History; an Annotated Bibliography*, Mystic, Conn. 1963, 3rd ed.
——, *Forests and Sea Power; the Timber Problem of the Royal Navy 1652–1862*, Cambridge, Mass. 1926.
Alexander, James Edward, *Travels To the Seat of the War in the East...*, London, 1830, 2 vols.

Allen, William Edward David, *The Caucasus*, London, 1923.

——, Muratoff, Paul Paulovich, *Caucasian Battlefields; A History of the Wars on the Turc-Caucasian Border, 1828–1921*, Cambridge, 1953.

Altindağ, Şinasi, *Kavalalı Ali Paşa İsyani; Mısır Meselesi, 1831–1841*, Ankara, 1945.

Ami Boué, *La Turquie d'Europe ou Observation sur la Géographie de cet Empire*, Paris, 1840, 4 vols.

'A month's cruize on the Smyrna station', *United Service Journal*, April 1836.

'A naval sketch', *Nautical and Maritime Magazine*, December 1827.

Ancel, J., 'Les Bases Géographiques de la Question des Détroits', *Monde Slav* (1–6), 1928.

Anchabadze, Zurab Vianorovich, *Ocherki Ekonomicheskoi Istorii Gruzii Pervoi Poloviny XIX Veka*, Tiflis, 1966.

Anderson, M. S., *The Eastern Question, 1774–1923*, London, 1966.

Anderson, Roger Charles, *Naval Wars in the Levant 1559–1853*, Liverpool, 1952.

Andreevskaia, V. P. (ed.), *O Podvigakh Russkikh Moriakov, Navarinskii Boi*, Sanktpertburg, 1911, 3rd ed.

Antonopoulos, Kostas, 'Apo tou Proton Atmoploion', in George B. Leon, 'The Greek Merchant Marine (1453–1850)', *The Greek Merchant Marine (1451–1850)*, Athens, 1972.

Aptsimovich, A., 'Admiral Dmitri Nikolaevich Seniavin', *Morskoi Sbornik*, December 1855.

Apushkin, V. A.; fon-Shvarts, A. V.; fon-Shvarts, G. K.; Noviyskii, V. Th. (eds), *Voennaia Entsiklopediia*, Sanktpetrburg, 1911–16, 18 vols.

Archives Parliament, 124, Paris (1839).

Arens, E. I., *Morskaia Sila i Istoriia*, Sanktpetrburg, 1912.

——, *Russkii Flot, Istoricheskii Ocherk*, Sanktpetrburg, 1904.

Arkas, Z., 'Prodolzhenie Deistvii Chernomorskogo Flota s 1806 po 1856 god', *Zapiski Odesskogo Obshchestva Istorii i Drevnosti*, Odessa, vol. 6, (1867).

'Arkhiv Kniazia A. I. Chernysheva', *Sbornik Imperatorskogo Russkogo Istoricheskogo Obshchestva*, Sanktpetrburg, Vol. 122 (1901).

Armstrong, T. B., *Journal of Travels to the Seat of War During the Two Campaigns of Russia and Turkey*, London, 1831.

Aslanbegov, Avramii, *Admiral Aleksei Samuilovich Greig*, Sanktpetrburg, 1873.

Astvatsaturian, E. G., *Istoriia Oruzheingo i Serebrianago Proizvodstva na Kavkaze v XIX-Nachale XX V. Dagestan i Zakavkaze; Part 1*, Moskva, 1977.

Atak, M. Sadik, *Türkiyenin Kapisi Boğaz*, Ankara, 1947.

'Avtobiografiia A. V. Diugamelia', *Russkii Arkhiv*, 1885, Books 1–3.

Ayverdi, Samiha, *Boğazici'nde Tarih*, Istanbul, 1966.

Badawi, M. A. Zaki, *The Reformers of Egypt*, London, 1978.

Bailey, F. E., 'The Economics of British Foreign Policy, 1825–50', *Journal of Modern History*, XII (Dec. 1940).

Baker, R. L., 'Palmerston on the Treaty of Unkiar Skelessi', *English Historical Review*, 43 (1928).

Barbier, E. and Prévost, L., *Sur la Conquête d'Alger*, Rouen, 1930.

Barker, John, *Turkey and Egypt under the Last Five Sultans of Turkey*, London, 1876, 2 vols.

Barrault, E. and Cadalvène, E., *Histoire de la Guerre de Mehéméd-Ali contre la Porte Ottomane en Syrie et en Asie-Mineure*, Paris, 1837.

Barrow, John, *Life of Anson*, London, 1838.

Bartenev, P. I. (ed.), *Arkhiv Kniazia Vorontsova...bumagi Grafa M. L. Vorontsova*, Moskva, 1870–95, 40 vols.

Bartlett, C. J., *Great Britain and Sea Power 1815–1853*, Oxford, 1963.

Bayer, Heinrich von; Khuepach, Arthur von, *Geschichte der K. K. Kriegsmarine während der Jahre 1814–1847*, Graz–Köln, 1966.

Baynham, Henry (ed.), *From the Lower Deck*, London, 1972.

——, *The Royal Navy 1780–1840*, Barre, Mass. 1970.

Bazili, Konstantin, *Arkhipelag i Gretsiia v 1830 i 1831 Godakh*, Sanktpetrburg, 1834, 2 vols.

Beaujour, Louis Auguste Félix de, *Voyage Militaire dans l'Empire Othoman où Description de ses Frontières et de ses Principales Défenses, soit Naturelles soit Artificielles*, Paris, 1829, 2 vols.

Belavenets, Petr Ivanovich, *Admiral Pavel Stepanovich Nakhimov*, Sevastopol, 1902.

Bengescu, George, *Essai d'une Notice Bibliographie sur la Question d'Orient*, Paris, 1897.

Benis, A. G. *Une Mission Militaire Polonaise en Égypte*, Cairo, 1938, 2 vols.

Benkendorf, A. Kh., 'Imperator Nikolai v 1828–1829 i v 1830–1831 gg. (iz Zapisok Grafa A. Kh. Benkendorfa)', *Russkaia Starina*, Vol. 87, (1896–7).

——, 'Imperator Nikolai v 1828–1829 i v 1830–1831 gg. (iz Zapisok Grafa A. Kh. Benkendorfa), *Russkaia Starina*, Vol. 87, nos. 6–7 (1896); Vol. 88, no. 10 (1896).

——, 'Iz Zapisok Grafa A. Kh. Benkendorfa', *Istoricheskii Vestnik*, Vol. 41 (1903).

——, 'O Rossii v 1827–1830 gg.', *Krasnyi Arkhiv*, Vol. 37 (1929).

Berger, Morroe, *The Military Elite and Social Change in Egypt since Napoleon*, Princeton, NJ, 1960.

Berkes, Niyasi, *The Development of Secularism in Turkey*, Montreal, 1964.

Bert'e-Delagard, A. L., 'Ostatki drevnikh sooruzhenii v okrestnostiakh Sevastopolia i peshchernye goroda Kryma', *Zapiski Odesskogo Obshchestva Istorii i Drevnosti*, Vol. 14 (1886).

Berzhe, A., *Istoriia Adygeiskogo Naroda*, Tiflis, 1861.

——, *Kratkii Obzor Gorskikh Plemen na Kavkaze*, Tiflis, 1858.

Beskrovnyi, Liubomir G., *Ocherki po Istochnikovedeniiu Vooennoi Istorii Rossii*, Moskva, 1957.

——, *Ocherki Voennoi Istoriografii Rossii*, Moskva, 1962.

——, *Russkaia Armiia i Flot v XIX V.*, Moskva, 1973.

——, *Russkoe Voennoe Iskusstvo XIX V.*, Moskva, 1974.

Bétant, E.A. (ed.), *Correspondence du Comte Capodistrias 20 Avril 1827 jusqu'au 9 Octobre 1831*, Geneva, 1839, 4 vols.

Bey, M. Rifaat, *The Awakening of Modern Egypt*, Lahore, 1964.

'Bibliographie militaire: cartes, plans, livres etc. publiés au Dépot topographie militaire de Saint-Pétersbourg', *Le Spectateur Militaire*, March 1835.

Bil'basov, V.A. (ed.), *Arkhiv Grafov Mordvinov*, Sanktpetrburg, 1901–3, 10 vols.

Birdeanu, Nicolae; Nicolaescu, Dan, *Contribuții la Istoria Marinei Române, Vol. 1*, București, 1979.

Blackwell, William L. *The Beginnings of Russian Industrialization 1800–1860*, Princeton, NJ, 1968.

Blancard, Theodore, *Les Mavroyéni*, Paris, 1909, 2 vols.

Blofeld, J. H., *Algeria Past and Present*, London, 1844.

Bogdanovich, Eugene, *La Bataille de Navarin*, Moskva, 1877.

Bogoslavskii, P. A., *O Kupecheskom Sudostroenii v Rossii, Rechnom i Pribrezhnom*, Sanktpetrburg, 1859.

Bolsover, G. H., 'Aspects of Russian Foreign Policy, 1815–1914', Pares, R. and Taylor, A. J. P. (eds), *Essays Presented to Sir Louis Namier*, London, 1956.

——, 'David Urquhart and the Eastern Question, 1833–37; A Study in Publicity and Diplomacy', *Journal of Modern History*, 8 (1936).

——, 'Lord Ponsonby and the Eastern Question;, *Slavonic Review*, 13 (1934–5).

——, 'Nicholas I and the Partition of Turkey', *Slavonic and East European Review*, 27 (1948).

Bostashvili, Nevi Ivanovna, *Bibliografiia Turtsii*, Tbilisi, 1971.

Bot'ianov, 'Prebivanie Imperatora Nikolaia Pavlovicha na Chernomorskom flote, v 1828 godu', *Morskoi Sbornik*, August 1869.

Boukharow, Dmitri de, *La Russie et la Turquie depuis le Commencement de leurs Rélations Politiques jusqu'à nos Jours*, Amsterdam, 1877.

Bourchier, Lady (ed.), *Memoirs of the Life of Admiral Sir Edward Codrington*, London, 1873, 2 vols.

Bourbon, Prince Sixte de, *La Dernière Conquête du Roi: Alger 1830*, Paris, 1930, 2 vols.

Bourne, Kenneth, *Palmerston; the Early Years 1784–1841*, London, 1982.

——, *The Foreign Policy of Victorian England 1830–1902*, Oxford, 1970.

Bowring, John, *Report on Egypt*, London, 1840.

——, *Report on the Commercial Statistics of Syria*, London, 1840.

Brant, James, 'Journey through a part of Armenia and Asia Minor in 1835', *Journal of the Royal Geographical Society*, 6 (1836).

Bronevskii, S., *Noveishie Geograficheskie i Istoricheskie Izvestiia o Kavkaze*, Moskva, 1823.

Brooks, W. A., 'On the course of the formation of bars at the mouths of rivers', *United Service Journal*, 1864.

Broughton, Lord, *Recollections of a Long Life*, London, 1909–11, 6 vols.

Brown, Leon Carl, *The Tunisia of Ahmad Bey 1837–1855*, Princeton, 1974.

Bruce, W. N., *Life of Sir Charles Napier*, London, 1885.

Brzozowski, Marie, 'Notice sur la ville de Constantinople, et sur ses moyens de défense', *Le Spectateur Militaire*, December 1837.

Bubnov, A. D., 'Voenno-morskoe iskusstvo v russkom flote', *Morskie Zapiski* XX, nos. 3–4 (1962).

Bukhteev, M., 'Chernomorskoe torgovoe sudostroenie i moreplavanie', *Kommercheskaia Gazeta*, 15-X-1840, No. 119.

——, 'Soslovie vol'nykh matrosov v Novorossiisom krai', *Zhurnal Manufaktur i Torgovli*, June 1841.

——, 'Torgovoe sudostroenie v Khersone', *Zhurnal Manufaktur i Torgovli*, August 1843.

Bulwer, Sir Henry Lytton, *The Life of Henry John Temple, Viscount Palmerston*, London, 1870–74, 3 vols.

Burçak, Rifki Salim, *Türk-Rus-İngiliz Münasebetleri 1791–1941*, Istanbul, 1946.

Bushuev, K. A. (ed.), 'Anglo-Russkii intsident so shkhunoi "Viksen"', *Krasnyi Arkhiv*, Vol. 102 (1940).

Bushuev, S., *Iz Istoriia Vneshnepoliticheskikh Otnoshenii v Period Prisoedineniia Kavkaza k Rossii*, Moskva, 1955.

Butakhov, A., *Slovar' Morskikh Slov i Rechenii*, Sanktpetrburg, 1832.

Buxton, Noel E. and Phillipson, Coleman, *The Question of the Bosphorus and Dardanelles*, London, 1917.

Büyüktuğrul, Admiral Afif, *Osmanlı Deniz Harp Tarihi*, Istanbul, 1970, 2 vols.

Callwell, E. E., *The Dardanelles*, London, 1919.

——, *The Effect of Maritime Command on Land Campaigns Since Waterloo*, Edinburgh, 1897.

——, *Military Operations and Maritime Preponderance, Their Relation and Interdependence*, Edinburgh, 1905.

'Campaigns of Ibrahim Pacha in Syria and Karamania', *United Service Journal*, February 1834.

'Çanak-Kale Boghazı', *Encyclopedia of Islam*, new ed., London, 1954– , Vol. 2.

Castille, Hippolyte, *Rechid-Pasha*, Paris, 1858.

Cattaui, Joseph E., *Coup d'Oeil sur la Chronologie de la Nation Égyptienne*, Paris, 1931.

——, *Histoire des Rapports de L'Égypte avec la Sublime Porte (du XVIIIe a 1841)*, Paris, 1919.

Cattaui, René, *Le Règne de Mohammad-Ali d'après les archives russes en Égypte*, Cairo, 1931–5, 3 vols. in 2.

'The Caucasian War', *Blackwood's Edinburgh Magazine*, November 1840.

Chamberlain, Muriel, *British Foreign Policy in the Age of Palmerston*, London, 1980.

Charles-Roux, F., *France et Afrique du Nord avant 1830*, Paris, 1932.

Chassériau, Fréderic Victor Charles, *État Maritime de la France*, Paris, 1845.

Cherman, Timofei Pavlovich; Sverchevskaia, Antonina Karlovna, *Bibliografiia Turtsii (1713–1917)*, Moskva, 1961.

'Chernomorskaia Beregovaia Liniia', *Brokgauz Entsikhlopedicheskii Slovar'*, Sanktpetrburg, 1890–1904, 41 vols; Vol. 38.

Chernomorskie Kazaki v Nikh Grazhdanskom i Voennom Bytu, Sanktpetrburg, 1858, 2 parts.

'Chernomorskoe torgovoe sudostroenie i moreplavanie', *Zhurnal Manufaktur i Torgovli*, March 1841.

Chernyshev, A.I., 'Vsepoddanneishii Doklad Grafa Chernysheva-Imperatora Nikolaia I', *Sbornik Imperatorskogo Russkogo Istoricheskogo Obshchestva*, 122 (1905).

Chesney, Francis Rawdon, *The Russo-Turkish Campaigns of 1828 and 1829; 'With a View of the Present State of Affairs in the East*, London, 1854, 2nd ed.

Chetverukhin, G. N., *Istoriia Razvitiia Korablenei i Beregovoi Artillerii*, Leningrad, 1942.

Chevalier, E., *Histoire de la Marine Française de 1815 à 1870*, Paris, 1900.
Chichagov, M. N., *Shamil na Kavkaze i v Rossii*, Sanktpetrburg, 1889.
Chikachev, Petr Aleksandrovich, *Le Bosphore et Constantinople*, Paris, 1864.
Chubinskii, V., *Istoricheskoe Obozrenie Ustroistva Upravleniia Morskim Vedomstvom v Rossii*, Sanktpetrburg, 1869.
Cipolla, Carlo Maria (ed.), *The Economic Decline of Empires*, London, 1970.
Clark, Edward C., 'The Ottoman Industrial Revolution', *International Journal of Middle Eastern Studies*, 5 (1974).
Clark, J. J., 'Merchant Marine and the Navy: A Note on The Mahan Hypothesis', *Royal United Service Institution Journal*, 122 (May 1967).
Clarke, Sir George Sydenham, *Russia's Sea Power*, London, 1898.
Clot-Bey, *Aperçu Général sur L'Égypte*, Paris, 1840, 2 vols.
Clayton, G. D., *Britain and the Eastern Question: Missolonghi to Gallipoli*, London, 1971.
Clowes, Sir William Laird, *The Royal Navy*, London, 1897–1903, 7 vols.
Cochrane, Thomas B., *The Life of Thomas Lord Cochrane*, London, 1869, 2 vols.
Colomb, Phillip Howard, *Naval Warfare; Its Ruling Principles and Practice Historically Treated*, London, 1891.
'Composition de la flotte égyptienne', *Annales Maritimes et Coloniales*, 1832, partie non officielle, Vol. 2.
'Constantinople in 1831, from the journal of an officer', *United Service Journal*, 1832, Pt II.
'Convention between Austria, France, Great Britain, Prussia, Russia, and Turkey respecting the Dardanelles and Bosphorus – signed at London, July 13, 1841', *British and Foreign State Papers*, 29 (1840–41).
Coolidge, Archibald C., 'The European Reconquest of North Africa', *American Historical Review*, 17 (July 1912).
Corbett, Sir Julian Stafford, *England in the Mediterranean*, London, 1904.
Crawley, C. W., 'Anglo-Russian relations 1815–40', *Cambridge Historical Journal*, 1 (1929).
Creswell, John, *Generals and Admirals; the Story of Amphibious Command*, London, 1952.
'The crisis of Turkey', *United Service Journal*, May 1833.
Cunningham, Allan Black (ed.), *Early Correspondence of Richard Wood, 1831–1841*, London, 1966.
Curtiss, John Shelton, *The Russian Army under Nicholas I*, Durham, NC, 1965.
'Daghistan', *Encyclopedia of Islam*, new edition, Vol. 2.
Dakin, Douglas, *The Greek Struggle for Independence 1821–1833*, London, 1973.
——, 'Lord Cochrane's Greek Steam Fleet', *Mariners Mirror*, 39 (1953).
Daly, Robert Welter, 'Russia's Maritime Past', *The Soviet Navy*, edited by M. G. Saunders, London, 1959.
Damiani, Anita, *British Travellers to the Near East 1715–1850*, Beirut, 1979.
Danilevskii, N., *Kavkaz i ego Gorskie Zhiteli*, Moskva, 1846.
Danişman, Zuhuri, *Osmanlı İmparatorluğu Tarihi*, Istanbul, 1964- , vols 1–14.
Danişmend, İsmail Hâmil, *İzahli Osmanlı Tarihi Kronolojisi*, Istanbul, 1947–55, 4 vols.
Dantsig, Boris Moissevich, *Russkie Puteshestvenniki na Blizhnem Vostoke*, Moskva, 1965.

Dascovici, Nicholas, *La Question du Bosphore et des Dardanelles*, Geneva, 1915.

Davydov, Iuri Vladimirovich, *Nakhimov*, Moskva, 1970.

——, *Seniavin*, Moskva, 1972.

Day, Archibald, *The Admiralty Hydrographic Service 1795–1919*, London, 1967.

Debu, Iosif, *O Kavkazskoi Linii*, Sanktpetrburg, 1829.

'Deiatel'nost', Admiralteistva v tsarstvovanie Imperatora Nikolaia I', *Morskoi Sbornik*, November 1859.

De Kay, James E., *Sketches of Turkey in 1831 and 1832*, New York, 1833.

Denisov, A. P.; Perechnev, Iu. G., *Russkaia Beregovaia Artilleriia*, Moskva, 1956.

Despatches, Correspondence and Memorandum of H.M. the Duke of Wellington, London, 1837–9, 13 vols.

Devolux, Albert, 'La marine de la régence d'Alger', *Revue Africaine*, January 1869.

D'iachkov-Tarasov, A. N., 'Abhaziia i Sukhum v XIX Stoletii', *Izvestiia Kavkazskogo Otdela Imperatorskogo Russkogo Geograficheskogo Obshchestva*, Tiflis, 20 (1909–10).

Dichter, B., *The Maps of Acre: an Historical Cartography*, Acre, 1973.

Djevad Bey, Colonel Ahmad, *État Militaire Ottoman, depuis la Fondation de l'Empire jusqu'à nos Jours*, Paris, 1882.

Djuvara, Trandafir G., *Cent Projects de Partage de la Turquie 1281–1913*, Paris, 1914.

Dmitriev, N. I.; Kolpichev, V.V., *Sudostroitel'nye Zavody i Sudostroenie v Rossii i za Granitsii*, Sanktpetrburg, 1909.

Dobrotvorskii, L., *Kakoi Flot Neobkhodim Rossii?*, Sanktpetrburg, 1904.

——, *Uroki Morskoi Voiny*, Sanktpetrburg, 1902.

Documente privitóre la istoria Românilor, culese de Eudoxiu de Hurmuzaki, Bucureşti, 1876–1922, 19 vols.

Dodwell, Henry Herbert, *The Founder of Modern Egypt: a Study of Mohammed Ali*, Cambridge, 1931.

'Don', *Obozrenie Glavnikh Vodianikh Soobshchenii v Rossii*, Sanktpetrburg, 1841.

'Donesenie Orlova', [n.d.], *Voennyi Zhurnal*, V (1833).

Dontas, Domna N., *The Last Phase of the Greek War of Independence*, Thessaloniki, 1966.

'Dopolnitel'nyia svedeniia no vnutrennei Rossiiskoi torgovle za 1829 god', *Zhurnal Manufaktur i Torgovli*, February 1830.

Dostyan, Irina Stepanovna, *Rossiia i Balkanskii Vopros*, Moskva, 1972.

Douin, Georges *L'Égypte de 1828 à 1830*, Cairo, 1935.

——, *La Première Guerre de Syrie; la Conquête de Syrie (1831–1832)*, Cairo, 1931.

——, *La Mission du Baron de Boislecomte; L'Égypte et la Syrie en 1833*, Cairo, 1927.

——, *Navarin (6 Juillet–20 Octobre 1827)*, Cairo, 1927.

——, *Les Premières Frégates de Mohamed Aly (1824–1827)*, Cairo, 1924.

Dranov, B. A., *Chernomorskoe Prolivy*, Moskva, 1948.

Driault, Edouard, *L'Égypte de l'Europe; la Crise de 1839–1841*, Rome, 1903–4, 5 vols.

——, *L'Expédition de Crète et de Morée (1823–1828)*, Cairo, 1930.

Drovetti, Georges, *Mohammad Ali et l'Expédition d'Alger (1829–1830)*, Cairo, 1930.

Dubois de Montpéreux, Frédéric, *Voyage Autour de Caucase chez les Tcherkesses, et les Abkhases, en Géorgie, en Arménie et en Crimée*, Paris, 1839, 6 vols in 3.

P. Dubrova, 'Gorod Alëskhi', *Zapiski Odesskogo Obshchestva Istorii i Drevnosti*, 3 (1852).

Dubrovin, N. F., *Istoriia Voiny i Vladychestva Russkikh na Kavkaze*, Sanktpetrburg, 1871–86, 6 vols in 8.

——, (ed.), 'Materialy i Cherty k Biografii Imperatora Nikolaia I i k Istorii ego Tsarstvovaniia', *Sbornik Imperatorskogo Russkogo Istoricheskogo Obshchestva*, 98 (1896).

——, 'Voini Rossii s Turtsiei (Kratkii Voenno-politicheskii Ocherk)', *Voennyi Sbornik*, nos. 1–3, 5–6 (1877).

Duggin, Stephane Pierce Hayden, *The Eastern Question; a Study of Diplomacy*, New York, 1970.

Duhamel, A. O., 'Avtobiografiia', *Russkii Arkhiv*, 1885, pts 1–3.

Durand-Viel, G., *Les Campagnes Navales de Mohammad Aly et d'Ibrahim*, Paris, 1935, 2 vols.

Dzidzariia, G. A., *Makhadzhirstvo i Problemy Istorii Abkhazii XIX Stoletiia*, Sukhumi, 1982.

——, *Prisoedinenie Abkhazii k Rossii i ego Istoricheskoe Znachenie*, Sukhumi, 1975.

Eardley-Wilmot, S. M., *Life of Vice-Admiral Edmund, Lord Lyons*, London, 1898.

Edmundson, George, *History of Holland*, Cambridge, 1922.

Edwardes, Michael, *Playing the Great Game; A Victorian Cold War*, London, 1975.

Edwards, H. Sutherland, *Russian Projects against India, From the Czar Peter to General Skobeleff*, London, 1855.

Elagin, Sergei I., 'Poiavlenie Turetskogo Flota na Chernom More v 1829 Godu', *Morskoi Sbornik*, October 1850.

Ellenborough, Lord, *A Political Diary 1828–1829*, London, 1881, 2 vols.

Enegol'm, Il'ya Ivanovich, *Zapiski o Gorodakh Zabalkanskikh Zaniatykh Rossii Voiskami v Dostopamiatnoi Kampanii 1829-go Goda*, Sanktpetrburg, 1830.

Enkiri, Gabriel, *Ibrahim Pacha*, Cairo 1948.

Epanchin, N. A. and N. N., *Tri Admirala, iz Semeinoi Kroniki 1787–1913*, New York 1946.

Epanchin, Nikolai Aleksievich, *Ocherk Pokhoda 1829 G. v Evropeiskoi Turtsii*, Sanktpetrburg, 1905–7, 3 vols.

——; Epanchin, M. N., *Tri Admirala*, Moskva, 1946.

Esquer, Gabriel, *La Prise d'Alger (1830)*, Alger, 1923.

'État comparatif des forces de terre et de mer de la Turquie et de l'Égypte', *Le Spectateur Militaire*, April 1836.

'État des forces navales de France et Angleterre en Orient, au 15 septembre 1839', *Annales Maritimes et Coloniales*, partie non officielle, 1829, Vol. 2.

Evans, Lt-General Sir George de Lacy, *On the Designs of Russia*, London, 1828.

'Extrait d'une lettre écrite d'Alexandrie (Égypte) le 9 decembre, 1831, au ministre de la marine', *Annales Maritimes et Coloniales*, 1832, partie non officielle, Vol. 1.

'Extrait d'une lettre écrite de Smyrne, le Septembre 1835, écrite par un passager à bord la goelette la Mèsange, commandée par M. Lejeune, lieutenant de vaisseau', *Annales Maritimes et Coloniales*, 1835, partie non officielle, Vol. 2.

Fadeev, A., *Kratkii ocherk istorii Abhazii; chast' pervaia*, Skuhum, 1934.

Fadeev, A., 'Miuridizm kak orudie agressivnoi politiki Turtsii i Anglii na Severo-Zapadnom Kavkaze v XIX stoletti', *Voprosy Istorii*, September 1951.

Fadeev, A.V., *Rossiia i Kavkaz Pervoi Treti XIX V.*, Moskva, 1960.

Fadeev, R.A., ''O miuridizm', *Sobranie Sochinenii R.A. Fadeeva*, Sankpetrburg, 1889–90, 3 vols, Vol. 1, Part 1.

Fadeeva, R., *Shest'desiat' Let Kavkazskoi Voiny*, Tiflis, 1860.

Fairlie, Susan 'Shipping in the Anglo-Russian grain trade, to 1870', *Maritime History*, 1 (1971).

'Fel'dmarshal Paskevich i Diplomatiia v 1827–1829 Godakh', *Istoricheskii Vestnik* 4, (1892)

Felitsin, E.D., 'Deistviia Russkikh Kreiserov u Kavkazskikh beregov Chernogo Moria v 1830–1840 gg.', *Kubanskie Vedomosti*, nos. 1–2, 4–5, 7–8 (1890).

Field, James A., *America and the Mediterranean World, 1776–1832*, Princeton, 1969.

Finlay, George, *History of the Greek Revolution*, London, 1861.

Finnie, David H., *Pioneers; the Early American Experience in the Middle East*, Cambridge, Mass., 1967.

Fleming, D.C., *John Capodistrias and the Conference of London 1828–1831*, Tessaloniki, 1971.

Fleuriot de Langle, Vicomte P., *L'Affaire de Navarin*, Paris, 1939.

Florescu, Radu R., 'British Reaction to the Russian Regime in the Danubian Principalities', *Journal of Central European Affairs*, April 1962.

'Flotte Ottomane', *Annales Maritimes et Coloniales*, 1832, partie non officielle, Vol. 1.

'Flotte Turque à Alexandrie', *Annales Maritimes et Coloniales*, 1839, partie non officielle, Vol. 2.

Fonton, Feliks Petrovich, *La Russie dans L'Asie Mineure ou Campagnes du Maréchal Paskevich en 1828 et 1829*, Paris, 1840.

'Forces navales de Mohamed-Ali, pacha d'Égypte', *Annales Maritimes et Coloniales*, partie non officielle, Vol. 2, 1833.

Frankland, Charles Colville, *Travels to and from Constantinople in the Years 1827 and 1828*, London, 1829, 2 vols.

Franklin, John, 'Observations on the coast of Syria', *Nautical Magazine*, January 1835.

Gabriel, Albert, *Châteaux Turcs du Bosphore*, Paris, 1943.

Gabriel, Guemard, *Les Réformes en Égypte d'Ali-Bey el Kébir à Méhémet-Ali, 1760–1848*, Cairo, 1936.

Gagameister, Iu., *O Evropeiskoi Torgovle v Turtsii i Persii*, Sanktpetrburg, 1838.

———, 'O torgovykh snosheniiakh Rossii s Arkhipelagom i Gretsiei', *Zhurnal Manufaktur i Torgovli*, February 1839.

Georgiev, Vladimir Anatol'evich, *Vneshnaia Politika Rossii na Blizhnem Vostoke v Kontse 30-Nachale 40-kh XIX V.*, Moskva, 1975.

Gerby Komandira i Ofitsera Briga Merkuriia, Petrograd, 1915.

'Geroiskii podvig riadovogo Arkhipa Osipova', *Voennyi Zhurnal*, VI (1840).

Gessen, S. Ia., *Kholernye Bunty (1830–1832 Gg.)*, Moskva, 1932.

Ghorbal, Shafik, *The Beginnings of the Egyptian Question, and the Rise of Mehemet Ali*, London, 1928.

'Gidrograficheskie raboty na Chernom i Azovskom moriakh, s 1844 po 1850 god', *Zapiski Gidrograficheskogo Departamenta*, 8 (1850).

'Gidrograficheskie raboty na Chernom i Azovskom moriakh, v 1850 i 1851 godakh', *Zapiski Gidrograficheskogo Departamenta*, 10 (1852).

Gifford, Ann and Greenhill, Basil, *The British Assault on Finland*, London, 1988.

Gillard, David, *The Struggle For Asia 1828–1914: a Study in British and Russian Imperialism*, London, 1977.

Gizetti, A. I., *Bibliograficheskii Ukazatel' Pechatannyi na Russkom Iazike Sochineniiam i Stat'iam o Voennykh Deistviiakh Russkikh Voisk na Kavkaze*, Sanktpetrburg, 1901.

———, *Khronika Kavkazskikh Voisk*, Tiflis, 1896, 2 vols.

———, *Sbornik Svedeniia o Poteriakh Kavkazskikh Voisk*, Tiflis, 1896.

Gleason, John Howes, *The Genesis of Russophobia in Great Britain*, Cambridge, Mass., 1950.

Gökçe, Cemal, *Kafkasya ve Osmanlı Imparatorluğunun Kafkasya Siyaseti*, Istanbul, 1979.

Golovachev, V. F., *Istoriia Sevastopolia kak Russkogo Porta*, Sanktpetrburg, 1872.

Golovin, E. A., *Ocherki Polozheniia Voennykh Del na Kavkaze s Nachala 1838 po Konets Godu*, Riga, 1847.

Goloviznin, K., *Russkii Flot na Chernom More*, Sanktpetrburg, 1885.

Golubov, S., *Bestuzhev-Marlinskii*, Moskva, 1978.

Gooch, Brison, 'A Century of Historiography on the Originas of the Crimean War', *American Historical Review*, 62 (Oct. 1956).

Goodenough, Edward, 'Memoir on the voyage of his Majesty's ship Blonde in the Black Sea', *Journal of the Royal Geographical Society*, 1 (1831).

Gorshkov, Sergei G., *Morskoi Moshch' Gosudarstva*, Moskva, 1977.

———, 'Voenno-morskie floty v voinakh i v mirnoe vremia', *Morskoi Sbornjk*, March 1972, pp. 20–32.

Goryainov, Serge, *Le Bosphore et Les Dardanelles*, Paris, 1910.

'Gosudarstvennaia...vidakh', *Sovremennik*, 1836.

Graham, Gerald Sandford, *The Politics of Naval Supremacy*, Cambridge, 1964.

———, 'The Transition from Paddle Wheel to Screw Propeller', *Mariners Mirror*, 44 (1958).

Graves, Phillip Percival, *The Question of the Straits*, London, 1931.

Grech, N., 'Obozrenie deistvii eskadry pod nachal'stvom Kontr-Admirala Rikorda v Sredizemnom more', *Morskoi Sbornik*, November 1855.

Grechko, A. A. (gen. ed.), *Sovetskaiia Voennaiia Entsikhlopediia*, Moskva, 1976–80, 8 vols.

Grey, Captain F. W., 'Remarks on the navigation between...the Dardanelles, and the Sea of Marmora, with the anchorage off Therapia...', *Nautical Magazine*, Sept. 1834.

Grunwald, Constantin, *Tsar Nicholas I*, London, 1954.

Grzhegorzhevskii, I., 'Ocherk Voennykh Deistvii i Sobytii na Kavkaze, 1835–1838 Gg.', *Russkaia Starina*, 15 (1876).

'Guerre de Mohammed-Ali en Syrie contre la Porte Ottomane, de 1831 à 1833', *Le Spectateur Militaire*, Oct. 1834.

Guichen, Comte Eugène de, *La Crise d'Orient de 1839–1841 et l'Europe*, Paris, 1921.

Gulia, D. I., *Istoriia Abkhazii; Tom 1*, Tiflis, 1925.

Gulishambarov, S. O., *Vsemirnaia Torgovlia v XIX V. i Uchastie v Nei Rossii*, Sanktpetrburg, 1898.

Gurwood, John (ed.), *The Speeches of the Duke of Wellington in Parliament*, London, 1854, 2 vols.

Hagan, Kenneth J., 'Alfred Thayer Mahan: Turning America Back to the Sea' in Frank J. Merli and Theodore A. Wilson (eds), *Makers of American Diplomacy*, New York, 1974.

Halleck, Fitz-Greene, *Outline of the Life of George C. De Kay*, New York, 1847.

Hamilton, Richard Vesey (ed.), *Letters and Papers of Admiral of the Fleet Sir Thos. Byam Martin, Vol. 1*, London, 1898.

Hamilton-Gordon, Sir Arthur, *The Earl of Aberdeen*, London, 1893.

Hamont, Pierre N., *L'Égypte sous Mehemet-Aly*, Paris, 1843, 2 vols.

Hanks, Robert J., *The Unnoticed Challenge: Soviet Maritime Strategy and Global Choke Points*, Washington, DC, 1980.

Hansard's Debates, London, 3rd Series, Vol. XVII (1833)

Hansard's Parliamentary Debates, London, (1837).

Hansard's Parliamentary Debates, Lords, Vol. 45, London, (1839).

Hansen, Lieutenant-General H.V., *Zwei Kreigsjahre. Erinnerungen eines alten Soldaten an den Feldzug der Russen gegen die Türken 1828 und den Polinischen Aufstand 1831*, Berlin, 1881.

Hastings, Frank Abney, *Memoir on the Use of Shells, Hot Shot, and Carcass*, London, 1828.

Hattendorff, John B. and Lynn C. (comps), *A Bibliography of the Works of Alfred Thayer Mahan*, Newport, Rhode Island, 1986.

Haxthausen, August Von, *Transcaucasia*, London, 1854.

Hell, Xavier Hommaire de, *Travels in the Steppes of the Caspian Sea, the Crimea, the Caucasus &c.*, London, 1847.

Herlihy, Patricia, 'Russian wheat and the port of Livorno, 1794–1861', *Journal of European Economic History*, Spring 1976.

Herman, G. F., 'The defences of the Dardanelles and Bosphorus', *United Service Journal*, May 1843.

Hertslet, Sir Edward, *Treaties, Etc., between Turkey and Foreign Powers, 1535–1855*, London, 1855.

——, *Map of Europe by Treaty, Showing the Various Political and Territorial Changes which have taken Place since the General Peace of 1814*, London, 1875–91, 4 vols.

Heyd, W., *Histoire du Commerce du Levant*, Paris, 1885–6, 2 vols.

Hobbs, J. S., *Sailing Directions for the Black Sea* [n.p.], 1857.

Hoegg, H. R. Anhegger, *Türken burgen an Bosphorus und Hellespont*, Dresden, 1932.

Horsetzky Von Hornthal, Feldzugmeister Adolf von, *Kriegsgeschichtliche Uebersicht (der Krieg 1828–1829 in der europäischen Türkei)*, Vienna, 1905.

Hunter, W. Patison, *Narrative of the Late Expedition to Syria under the Command of Admiral Sir Robert Stopford*, London, 1842, 2 vols.

——, 'Syria; during the campaign against Mehemet Ali', *United Service Journal*, 1841, pt 2,.

Hurewitz, Jacob Coleman, *Diplomacy in the Near and Middle East; a Documentary Record*, Princeton, 1956, 2 vols.

——, *The Middle East and North Africa in World Politics*, New Haven, Connecticut, 1975, 2 vols.

——, 'Russia and the Turkish Straits; A Re-evaluation of the Origins of the Problem', *World Politics*, 14 (1962).

Iakovlev, V., 'Nekrolog; Mikhail Pavlovich Manganarii', *Zapiski Odesskogo Obshchestva Istorii i Drevnosti*, Vol. 15, Part II (1889).

Il'in, Kap. Korp. Mors. Art., *Nauka Morskoi Artillerii*, Sanktpetrburg, 1846.

Ingle, Harold N., *Nesselrode and the Russian Rapproachment with Britain 1836–1844*, Berkeley, 1976.

Ireland, J. de Courcy, 'The cruisers of North Africa', *Mariners Mirror*, 1976, no. 3.

Issawi, Charles (ed.), *The Economic History of the Middle East 1800–1914*, Chicago, 1966.

——, *The Economic History of Turkey, 1800–1914*, London, 1980.

(Istomin), V.I., 'Mikhail Petrovich Lazarev; Ocherk', *Russkii Arkhiv*, 1881, pt 2.

Istomin, V. K., 'Kontre-Admiral Istomin', *Russkii Arkhiv*, 1877, pt 1

'Istreblenie pozharom korablia Fershampenuaz', *Morskoi Sbornik*, April 1855.

Iurov, A., 'Tri goda na Kavkaze. 1837–1839', *Kavkazskii Sbornik*, 8 (1884).

Ivashintsov, N., 'Russkie krugosvetnye puteshestviia', *Zapiski Gidrograficheskogo Departamenta*, 7 (1849).

'Izdannyia ot Gidrograficheskogo departamenta atlasy, karty i knigi s 1827 po 1844 god', *Zapiski Gidrograficheskogo Departamenta*, 2 (1844).

'Izvestie o Rossiiskikh korabliakh, preshedskikh iz inostrannykh portov, i otoshedshikh v inostrannye porty, v pervoi polovine 1835 goda', *Zhurnal Manufaktur i Torgovli*, October 1835.

Iz Pisem D.V. Polenova vo Vremia Poezdki v Gretsiiu i Sluzhby pri Tamoshnem Posol'stve 1832–1835', *Russkii Arkhiv*, 1885, Pt 3.

Jane, Frederick Thomas, *The Imperial Russian Navy: Its Past, Present, and Future*, London, 1899.

Jeffries, William Worthington, *Geography and National Power*, Annapolis, Maryland, 1967, 4th ed.

Jelavich, Barbara, 'British Means of Defence Against Russia in the Nineteenth Century', *Russian History*, 1 (1974).

——, *A Century of Russian Foreign Policy 1814–1914*, Philadelphia, 1964.

Jesse, Captain, *Notes of a Half-pay in Search of Health*, London, 1841, 2 vols.

Jordan, K., *Der ägyptisch-tüerkishche Krieg*, Freburg, 1923.

Jouannin, Joseph Marie, *Status Quo d'Orient, Revue des Événéments qui se sont Passés en Turquie Pendant l'Année 1838*, Paris, 1839.

Jovanic, Vojislav M., *An English Bibliography of The Eastern Question*, Belgrade, 1909.

Kaldis, William Peter, *John Capodistrias and the Modern Greek State*, Madison, Wisconsin, 1963.

Kallistov, D., 'Grecheskii vopros,... Eskadra Rikorda', Grishinskii, A.S.; Klado, N. L.; Nikol'skii, V.A.(eds), *Istoriia Russkoi Armii i Flota*, Moskva, 1911–15, 12 vols; Vol. 9.

'Kap. Bellinsgauzen i Leit. Lazarev shliupy Vostok i Mirnyi 1819–1821, *Zapiski Gidrograficheskogo Departamenta*, 7 (1849).

Karadağ, Raif, *Şark Meselesi, Rusya, İngiltere, Fransa, Almanya, Avusturya ve Osmanlı İmparatorlukarinin Tarihi Şark Siyasetleri ve Bügün Sartaki Hadiselerin Gerçek Sebebleri*, Istanbul, 1971.

Karal, E. Z., *Osmanlı Tarihi: V. Cilt; Nizamı Cedit ve Tanzimat Devirleri 1789–1856*, Ankara, 1947.

'Kavkaz Nikolaevskogo Vremeni v Pis'makh Voinskikh Deiatelei'. *Russkii Arkhiv*, 1904, Part 1.

'Kavkazshaia voina', *Voennaia Entsiklopediia*, Vol. 11.

'Kazi-Mulla (Gazi Magomet) – iz zapisok pokoinogo Kapitana Pruzhanovskogo', *Sbornik Gazety Kavkaz*, 1847, Part 2.

Kennedy, Paul, 'Mahan *versus* Mackinder; two Interpretations of British Sea Power', *Strategy and Diplomacy 1870–1945*, London, 1983.

——, *The Rise and Fall of British Naval Supremacy*, London, 1976.

Kerner, Robert Joseph, 'Russia's New Policy in the Near East After The Peace of Adrianople', *Cambridge Historical Journal*, 5 (1937).

——, *The Urge to the Sea; the Course of Russian History*, Los Angeles, 1942.

Khachapuridze, G.V., *K istorii Gruzii Pervoi Poloviny XIX Veka*, Tbilisi, 1950.

——; Makharadze, F. E., *Ocherki po Istorii Rabochego i Krest'ianskogo Dvizheniia v Gruzii*, Moskva, 1932.

Samir Khalaf, 'Communal conflict in nineteenth-century Lebanon', Braude, Benjamin and Lewis, Bernard (eds), *Christians and Jews in the Ottoman Empire*, London, 1982, 2 vols.

Khanykov, N., 'O miuridakh i miuridizm', *Sbornik Gazety Kavkaz*, 1847, Pt 1.

Khramtsov, A., 'Gidrograficheskie raboty, proizvednye v tsarstvovanii Imperatora Nikolaia', *Morskoi Sbornik*, August 1854.

Khartakhai, F., 'Zhenskii bunt v Sevastopole', *Sovremennik*, no. 10 (1865).

Khripkov, Aleksandr, 'Rasskazy ob Admoriale M.P. Lazareve', *Russkii Arkhiv*, August 1877, Parts 1–3.

Kiniapina, N. S. (ed.), *Vostochnyi Vopros vo Vneshnei Politike Rossii, Konets XVIII-Nachale XX V.*, Moskva, 1978.

Kipp, Jacob W., 'Sergei Gorshkov and Naval Advocacy; the Tsarist Heritage', *Soviet Armed Forces Review Annual*, Vol. 3, Gulf Breeze, Fla., 1979, pp. 225–39.

Kirilov, S. I., 'Zarozhdenie sudostroeniia na severe', *Sudostroenie*, March 1966.

'K istorii pokoreniia Kavkaza', *Russkii Arkhiv*, 1877, Part 3.

Koch, C., *Die Kaukasische Militärstrasse*, Leipzig, 1851.

Konkevich, Lt, *Letopis Krushenii i Drugikh Bedstvennikh Sluchaev Voennykh Sudov Russkogo Flota*, Sanktpetrburg, 1874.

Koray, Enver, *Türkiye Tarih Yayanları Bibliografyasi 1729–1955*, Istanbul, 1959–70, 2 vols.

Korguev, N., 'Russkii Flot v Tsarstvovanii Imperatora Nikolaia I-go', *Morskoi Sbornik*, July 1896.

Korolenko P. P., 'Zapiski po istorii Severo-vostochnogo poberezh'ia Chernogo Moria', *Zapiski Odesskogo Obshchestva Istorii i Drevnosti*, 29 (1911).

'K Portretu Admirala Grafa Logina Petrovicha Geidena', *Severnaia Pchela*, no. 48, 1851.

Kornrumpf, H.- J., *Osmanische Bibliographie. Mit besonderer Berücksichtigung der Türkei in Europa*, Leiden, 1973.

'Kratkoe izvlechenie iz Vysochaishego utverzhdennogo polozheniia o voennom poselenii na Kavkaze', *Voennyi Zhurnal*, 6 (1938).

Krotkov, Gen.-Major A., *Morskoi Kadetskii Korpus. Kratkii Istoricheskii Ocherk*, Sanktpetrburg, 1901.

Kruglov, A., 'Razvitie Russkoi Morskoi Artillerii', *Morskoi Sbornik*, May 1940.

Kumani N. M., 'Sravnenie prezhnikh kart Chernogo 1 Azovskogo Morei, s noveisheiu', *Zapiski Gidrograficheskogo Departamenta*, 2 (1844).

Kurat, Akdeş Nimet, *Türkiye ve Rusya; Yüzyil Sonundan Kürtülüş Savaşina Kadar Türk-Rus İliskileri (1798–1919)*, Ankara, 1970.

Kurtoğlu, Fevzi, *Türklerin Deniz Muharebeleri*, Istanbul, 1935–40, 2 vols.

La Croix, Paul, *Histoire de la Vie du Règne de Nicholas Ier*, Paris, 1864–71, 6 vols.

Lamase, M. de Pradal de, 'La station navale français de Tunis au milieu de XIX siècle', *Revue Internationale d'Histoire Militaire*, 4 (1956).

Lambin, Boris and Petr Petrovich, *Russkaia Istoricheskaia Bibliografiia*, Sanktpetrburg, 1861–84, 10 vols.

Landau, J. M., 'Russian Travel Accounts of the Middle East', *Middle Eastern Studies*, 13 (1977).

Lane-Poole, Stanley, *The Life of the Right Hon. Stratford Canning, Viscount de Redcliffe*, London, 1888, 2 vols.

Lang, David Marshall, *A Modern History of Georgia*, London, 1962.

Lapeyrouse, Bonfils Le Comte, *Histoire de la Marine Française*, Paris, 1845, 3 vols.

Lapinski, Oberst Theophil, *Die Bergvölker des Kaukasus und ihr Freiheitskampf gegen die Russen*, Hamburg, 1863, 2 vols.

'Launch of a steam-frigate', *Nautical Magazine*, July 1834.

Laurie, Major G. B., *The French Conquest of Algeria*, London, 1927.

Leaf, Walter, 'Forts of the Dardanelles', *Country Life*, 17 April 1915.

Lebedev, A. I., 'Il. Voennye deistviia na Chernom more v voine s Turtsiei v 1828–1829 gg.', Grishinskii, A. S.; Klaod, N. L.' Nikol'skii, V.A. (eds), *Istoriia Russkoi Armii i Flota*, Moskva, 1911–15, 12 vols; Vol. 9.

Lecomte, Jules Girard Fulgence, *Chronique de la Marine Française 1789 à 1830*, Paris, 1836–7, 5 vols.

Leer, Genrikh Antonovich, *Entsiklopediia Voennikh i Morskikh Nauk*, Sanktpetrburg, 1883–97, 8 vols.

Lefroy, Brigadier J. H., 'An Account of the Great Cannon of Muhammud II', *Proceedings of the Royal Artillery Institution*, 6 (1868).

'Leit. Lazarev R. A. K., korabl' Suvorov 1813–1816', *Zapiski Gidrograficheskogo Departamenta*, 7 (1849).

Leon, G. B. (ed.), *The Greek Merchant Marine*, Athens, 1972.

Leva, Marx, 'Barring the door to the Med', *United States Naval Institute Proceedings*, August 1987, pp. 83–8.

Levasheva, Z. P., *Bibliografiia Russkoi Voennoi Bibliografii*, Cambridge, 1972.

Kevitskii, Nikolai, 'Zapiski o Khersonskoi gubernii', *Zhurnal Ministerstva Vnutrennikh Del*, July 1836.

Lewis, Michael, *The Navy in Transition 1814–1864*, London, 1965.

Liakhov, V. A., *Russkaia Armiia i Flot v Voine s Ottomanskoi Turtsiei v 1828–1829 Godakh*, Iaroslavl, 1972.

Lichkov, L. S., *Ocherk Iz Proshlogo i Nastoiashchego Chernomorskogo Poberezh'ia Kavkaza*, Kiev, 1904.

Lichtenstadt, J. R. von, *Die asiatische Cholera in Russland in den Jahren 1829–30. Nach Russischen amtlichen Quellen bearbeitet*, Berlin, 1831.

Litvinov M., *Chernoe More; Moria v Raznykh Istoricheskikh Epokhakh*, Sanktpetrburg, 1881.

Livezey, William K., *Mahan on Sea Power*, Norma, Okla., 1947.

Lloyd, Christopher, *The Nation and the Navy*, London, 1961

Longworth, John Augustus, *A Year Among the Circassians*, London, 1840, 2 vols.

Lord, Walter Frewen, *England and France in the Mediterranean 1660–1830*, London, 1901.

Lotsiia Chernogo Moria, Nikolaev, 1851.

Luk'ianovich, Nikolai, *Opisanie Turetskoi Voiny 1828–1829 Gg.*, Sanktpetrburg, 1844–7, 4 vols.

MacDermott, A., 'Guns and gunners of olden times', *Mariners Mirror*, No. 2, 1958.

MacFarlane, Charles, *Constantinople in 1828; a Residence of Sixteen Months in the Turkish Capital and Provinces*, London, 1829, 2 vols.

Robert Holden MacKenzie (ed.), *The Trafalgar Roll*, London, 1913.

Mackintosh, A. F., 'On the military importance of Syria', *United Service Journal*, November 1840.

Mahan, Alfred Thayer, *Armaments and Arbitration; or the Place of Force in the International Relations of States*, London, 1912.

——, *The Influence of Sea Power upon History, 1660–1783*, Boston, 1890.

——, *The Influence of Sea Power upon the French Revolution and Empire, 1793–1812, Boston, 1894.*

——, *Naval Administration and Warfare; Some General Principles*, London ,1908.

——, *Naval Strategy, Compared and Contrasted with the Principles of Military Operations on Land*, Boston, 1911.

——, *Retrospect and Prospect: Studies in International Relations, Naval and Political*, London, 1902.

——, *Some Neglected Aspects of War*, London, 1907.

'Maitland, Sir Frederick Lewis', *Dictionary of National Biography*, Vol. 35.

Malcolm-Smith, Elizabeth Francis, *Palmerston*, London, 1935.

——, *Stratford Canning, Lord Strangford de Redcliffe*, London, 1933.

Mamuishev, Vsevolod, *Admiral P. S. Nakhimov*, Sanktpetrburg, 1904.

Manganari, M., 'S'emka Marmarnego moria, 1845–1848 goda', *Zapiski Gidrograficheskago Departamenta*, 8, (1850).

Manwaring, G. E., *A Bibliography of British Naval History*, London, 1930.

'Marine Égyptienne en 1834', *Annales Maritimes et Coloniales*, 1834, partie non officielle, Vol. 2.

'Marine Russe en 1836', *Annales Maritimes et Coloniales*, 1836, partie non officielle, Vol. 2.

Marlowe, John, *Perfidious Albion*, London, 1971.

Marriot, Sir John Arthur Ransome, *The Eastern Question*, Oxford, 1940, 4th ed.

Martens, F., *Sobranie Traktatov i Konventsii zakliuchennykh Rossieiu s Inostrannymi Derzhavami*, Sanktpetrburg, 1874–1905, 15 vols.

Martin, Claude, *Histoire de l'Algérie Française 1830–1962*, Paris, 1963.

Marston, Thomas Ewart, *Britain's Imperial Role in the Red Sea Area 1800–1870*, Hamden, Conn., 1961.

Marx, Karl, *Secret Diplomatic History of the 18th Century and the Story of Lord Palmerston*, London, 1969.

Materialy dlia Statistiki Rossiiskoi Imperii, Sanktpetrburg, 1839–41, 2 vols.

McCullough, John Ramsey, *A Dictionary Practical, Theoretical, and Historical of Commerce and Commercial Navigation*, London, 1834–5, 3 vols.

McGrew, Roderick Erle, 'The first cholera epidemic and social history', *Bulletin of the History of Medicine*, 34 (January–February 1960).

——, *Russia and the Cholera 1823–1832*, Madison, Wisc., 1965.

Melikhov, V. I., 'Opisanie deistvii Chernomorskogo flota v prodolzhenii voiny s Turtsiei, v 1828 i 1829 godakh', *Morskoi Sbornik*, January–September 1850, January 1851.

Mel'nitskii, Vsevolod Petrovich, *P. I. Rikord i Ego Sovremenniki*, Sanktpetrburg, 1856, Part 1.

——, 'Tri glavy iz ocherki deistvii russkogo flota pri osvobozhdenii Gretsii', *Morskoi Sbornik*, February 1861.

'Mémoire (extrait du) sur les affaires de Circassie, présenté en 1816 par M. de Scassi', *Zapiski Odesskogo Obshchestva Istorii i Drevnosti*, 22 (1900), Pt II.

Mends, Bowen Stilton, *Life of Admiral William Robert Mends*, London, 1899.

Miansarov, M. M., *Bibliographia Caucasia et Transcaucasia*, St Pétersburg, 1874–6, 2 vols.

Miazgovskii, E. A., *Istoriia Chernomorskogo Flota 1696–1912*, Sanktpetrburg, 1914.

Middleton, R. D., 'Observations on the navigation of the Black Sea', *Nautical Magazine*, April 1833.

Mignan, R., *A Winter Journey Through Russia, the Caucasian Alps, and Georgia, thence into Koordistan*, London, 1839, 2 vols.

The Military–Naval Encyclopedia of Russia and the Soviet Union, Gulf Breeze, Fla., 1978– .

'Military reforms of Turkey and Egypt', *United Service Journal*, 1832, Pt 1.

Miller, Hunter (ed.), *Treaties and Other International Acts of the United States of America*, Washington, DC, 1931–48, 8 vols.

Milner, Thomas, *The Crimea, its Ancient and Modern History*, London, 1855.

Minorsky, Vladimir Fedorovich, *Studies in Caucasian History*, London, 1953.
Miroshevskii, Vasilii, *Vospominanie o Russkom Flote*, Sanktpetrburg, 1833.
Miroslavskii, Iosif, 'Vzryv Mikhailovskogo ukrepleniia v 1840 godu', *Kavkazskii Sbornik*, 4 (1879).
The Mirror of Parliament, London, Vols. III–IV (1833), Vol. III (1838).
Mischef, P. H., *La Mer Noire et Les Détroits de Constantionople*, Paris, 1899.
Mitchell, J., 'On the expediency of immediately occupying Egypt and Candia', *United Service Journal*, January 1834.
Mitchell, John, *Thoughts on Tactics and Military Organization; together with an Enquiry into the Power and Position of Russia*, London, 1838.
Mitchell, Mairin, *The Maritime History of Russia 1848–1948*, London, 1949.
B. L. Modzalevskii (ed.), *Arkhiv Raevskikh*, Sanktpetrburg, 1908–15, 5 vols.
Moltke, Helmuth von, *Der russisch–türkische Feldzug in der europäischen Türkei, 1828 und 1829*, Berlin, 1845.
——, *The Russians in Bulgaria and Rumelia in 1828 and 1829*, London, 1854.
Monasterev, N. and Tereshchenko Serge, *Histoire de la Marine Russe*, Paris, 1932.
Montandon, C., *Guide du Voyageur en Crimée*, Odessa, 1834.
Monteith, Colonel William, *Kars and Erzeroum; with the Campaigns of Prince Paskevich in 1828 and 1829*, London, 1856.
——, 'Journal of a tour through Azerbijan and the shores of the Caspian', *Journal of the Royal Geographical Society*, 3 (1833).
Mortal, A., 'L'Armée d'Ahmed Bey d'après un instructeur français', *Revue Internationale d'Histoire Militaire*, 4 (1956).
Mosely, Phillip E., 'Englisch–Russische Flottenrivalität', *Jahrbücher für Geschichte Osteuropas*, 4 (1936).
——, *Russian Diplomacy and the Opening of The Eastern Question in 1838 and 1839*, Cambridge, Mass., 1934.
Mosolov, K., 'Obozrenie Deistvii Eskadry Pod Nachalstvom K. A. Rikorda v Sredizemnom More', *Morskoi Sbornik*, November 1855.
Mouriez, Paul, *Histoire de Mehemet Ali, Viceroi d'Égypte*, Paris, 1858, 4 vols.
'Mouth of the Danube', *Nautical Magazine*, May 1836.
'Mouvements des bâtiments de l'État à la fin de 1832 et pendant l'année 1833', *Annales Maritimes et Coloniales* 1834, partie non officielle, Vol. 1.
'Mouvements des bâtiments de l'État pendant les neuf premiers mois de l'année 1834', *Annales Maritimes et Coloniales* 1834, partie non officielle, Vol. 2.
'Mouvements des bâtiments du Roi', *Annales Maritimes et Coloniales*, 1830, partie non officielle, Vol. 1.
Mowat, R. B., *History of European Diplomacy*, London, 1928–33, 3 vols.
Muench, Ernst Joseph Hermann von, *Mahmud II, Padischah des Osmanen: sein Leben, seine Begierung und seine Reformen*, Stuttgart, 1839.
Mufti (Habjoka), Shaukeit, *Heroes and Emperors in Circassian History*, Beirut, 1972.
Murav'ev, Andrei, *Puteshestvie ko Sviatym Mestam v 1830 Godu*, Sanktpetrburg, 1835, 2 vols.
Murav'ev, Nikolai N., *Russkie na Bosfore v 1833 Godu, iz Zapisok Nikolaia Nikolaevicha Murave'eva*, Moskva, 1869.

Murzakevich, N., 'Atlas Chernogo Moria', *Zapiski Odesskogo Obshchestva Istori i Drevnosti*, 4–5, (1849).

——, 'Ofitserskii klass i akademicheskii kurs morskikh nauk', *Iakhty*, January 1877.

Nadvoskii, V. E., 'Slavnaia pobeda', *Sudostroenie*, October 1967.

Napier, Sir Charles, *The War in Syria*, London, 1842.

Napier, Major-General Edward, 'A cruise to the Levant in the summer of 1839', *United Service Journal*, September 1840.

——, *Excursions along the Shores of the Mediterranean*, London, 1842, 2 vols.

——, *The Life and Correspondence of Admiral Sir Charles Napier*, London, 1862, 2 vols.

——, *Memoirs and Correspondence of Admiral Sir Charles Napier*, K.C.B., London, 1862.

'Navies of Great Britain, France &c.', *The Times*, 18-I-1839.

The Navy List, Corrected to December 20, 1832, London, 1833.

Nebol'sin, Grigory, *Statisticheskie Zapiski o Vneshnei Torgovle Rossii*, Sanktpetrburg, 1835, 2 Parts.

'Nekrolog Admirala Mikhaila Petorvicha Lazareva', *Morskoi Sbornik*, July 1851.

'Neskol'ko slov o pozhare na korable Fershampenuaz', *Morskoi Sbornik*, May 1855.

'Neskol'ko ukazanii o desantakh', *Morskoi Sbornik*, February 1865.

Nesselrode, A. D. (ed.), *Lettres et Papiers du Chancelier Comte de Nesselrode 1760–1856*, Paris, 1904–12, 11 vols.

Newbold, T. J., 'Present state of the military and naval strength of Egypt', *United Service Journal*, October 1840.

N. G., 'Vospominaniia o zhizni i sluzhbe Admirala Grafa Logina Petrovicha Geidena', *Morskoi Sbornik*, December 1850.

Nikul'chenkov, K. I. (ed.), *M.P. Lazarev: Dokumenty*, Moskva, 1956–61, 3 vols.

N. N., 'Pis'mo k Izdatel'iam S. Pch., s Rosiiskoi Eskadry, blokiriushchei Dardanelli', *Severnaia Pchela*, 6-X-1829.

Noradounghian, Gabriel Effendi, *Recueil d'Actes Internationaux de L'Empire Ottoman*, Paris, 1897–1903, 4 vols.

'Notes by Dr. Riach on the state of Georgia and the Caucasian tribes 1-VIII-1837', Report – Frontiers of Russia and Turkey, and Georgia and Caucasus (Capt. Stoddart and Dr. J. P. Riach), *Parliamentary Papers, 'Confidential Print', no. 510*, London, 1838.

'Notes extrait du mémoire sur le commerce du Bosphor Cimmer à Panticape (maintenant Kertch)', *Zapiski Odesskogo Obshchestva Istorii i Drevnosti*, 22 (1900).

'Notice nécrologique sur Besson, lieutenant de vaisseau, mort amiral de la flotte égyptienne sous le nom de Besson-Bey', *Annales Maritimes et Coloniales*, 1837, partie non officielle, Vol. 2.

'Notice sur les russes de la Crimée et des côtes du Caucase visitées en 1836', *Le Spectateur Militaire*, May 1837.

Novikov, N.V. (ed.), *Boevaia Letopis' Russkogo Flota*, Moskva, 1948.

——, (ed.), *Russkie Flotovodtsy; Vitse-Admiral Kornilov*, Moskva, 1947.

Novosil'skii, A. P., *Opisanie Krushenii i Drugikh Bedstvennykh Sluchaev Voennykh Sudov Inostrannykh Flotov*, Sanktpetrburg, 1874.

'Nyneshnee chislitel'noe sostoianie voisk Evropeiskikh derzhav', *Voennyi Zhurnal*, 1835, No. 1.

'Nyneshnee sostoianie flota ottomanskoi imperii i vitse-korolevstva egipetskogo', *Sin Otechestva*, October 1839.

'O bombovoi pushke Peksana', *Voennyi Zhurnal*, 1833, no. 6.

'Oboroty vneshnei torgovli Odesskogo porta so vremeni zakliucheniia Adrianopol'skogo mira', *Trudy Odesskogo Staticheskogo Komiteta*, Odessa, 1865, Part 2.

Obozrenie Glavnykh Vodianykh Soobshchenii v Rossii, Sanktpetrburg, 1841.

Obozrenie Rossiiskikh Vladenii Zakavkazom v Statisticheskom Etnograficheskom, Topograficheskom i Finansovom Otnosheniakh, Proizvedennoe i Izd. po Vysochaishemu Soizvoleniiu, Sanktpetrburg, 1836, 4 vols.

'Obozrenie Vysochaishego prednachertannogo plana k obshchemu usmireniiu Kavkazskikh gorskikh plemen, ot 12 marta 1840', 'Sekretno', *Akty Sobranie Kavkazskoiu Arkheograficheskogo Kommissieiu*, Vol. 9.

'Observations on the navigation of the Dardanelles, Bosphorus and Black Sea ... by R. D. Middleton...', *Nautical Magazine*, March 1833.

O'Byrne, William R., *A Naval Biographical Dictionary: Comprising the Life and Services of Every Living Officer in Her Majesty's Navy, from the Rank of Admiral to the Fleet to that of Lieutenant, Inclusive*, London, 1845–9, 2 vols.

Obzor Deiatel'nosti Morskogo Upravleniia v Rossii (1855–1880) Chast' I, Sanktpetrburg, 1880.

'Obzor gidrograficheskikh s'emok Chernogo i Azovskogo morei', *Zapiski Gidrograficheskogo Departamenta*, 2 (1844).

'Obzor voennykh deistvii protiv gorskikh narodov v 1835, 1836 i 1837 godakh', *Akty Sobranie Kavkazskoiu Arkheograficheskogo Kommissieiu*, Vol. 8.

'Ocherk polozheniia voennykh del na Kavkaze s nachala 1838 do kontsa 1842 god', *Kavkazskii Sbornik*, 2 (1877).

'O chumnom vozmushchenii v Sevastopole 1830 goda', *Russkii Arkhiv*, August 1867.

O'Connell, D. P., *The International Law of the Sea; Volume 1*, Oxford, 1982.

Odessa 1794–1894, Odessa, 1895.

'O Evropeiskoi torgovle v Turtsii i Persei', *Zhurnal Manufacktur i Torgovli*, January 1838.

Ogorodnikov, S. Th. *Istoriia Arkhangel'skogo Porta*, Sanktpetrburg, 1875.

——, *Istoricheskii Obzor Razvitiia i deiatel'nosti Morskogo Ministerstva 1802–1902*, Sanktpetrburg, 1902.

——, 'Sobtvennoruchnaia rezoliutsii Imperatora Nikolaia I po morskomu vedomstvu', *Morskoi Sbornik*, December 1907.

'On the commerce of Russia', *Nautical Magazine*, December 1832.

'O parokhodstve po Dnepru i Limanu ot porogov do Odessy', *Zhurnal Manufaktur i Torgovli*, February 1841.

'O parovnykh mashinakh Luganskogo zavoda', *Zhurnal Manufaktur i Torgovli*, April 1841.

'O postepennom usovershenstvovenii geograficheskikh i topograficheskikh kart', *Voennyi Zhurnal*, 2 (1836).

'O pravilakh, na koikh dopuskaetsia obrazovanie v Novorossiiskom krae vol'nikh matrosskikh obshchestve', *Zhurnal Manufaktur i Torgovli*, December 1839.

'O putiakh dlia privoza tovarov iz Rossii v Zakavkazskii kraia', *Zhurnal Manufaktur i Torgovli*, November 1835.

Orlik, O.V., *Rossiia i Frantsuzskaia Revoliutsiia 1830 G.*, Moskva, 1968.

Ostrovskii, Boris Genrikhovich, *Lazarev*, Moskva, 1966.

O Sudakh Chernomorskogo Flota, Postroennykh so Vremeni Vstupleniia na Prestol Gosudaria Imperatora Nikolaia Pavlovicha, Sanktpetrburg, 1844.

'O torgovle ostrova Sira', *Zhurnal Manufaktur i Torgovli*, April 1838.

'Otpusk khlebov iz Odesskogo porta a 1830 po 1863 god', *Trudy Odesskogo Statisticheskogo Komiteta*, 1864, Part I.

'O torgovle s Cherkesami v Anapskom vremennom karantine v 1833 godu', *Zhurnal Manufaktur i Torgovli*, April 1834.

'O vneshnei torgovle Rossii 1838 goda', *Zhurnal Maufaktur i Torgovli*, August 1838.

Owen, R.J., *Cotton and the Egyptian Economy 1820–1914: a Study in Trade and Development*, Oxford, 1969.

Owen, Roger, *The Middle East in the World Economy, 1800–1914*, London, 1981.

'O Zakavaze: soobshcheno Manufaktur Sovetnikom K. Tribodino', *Zhurnal Manufaktur i Torgovli*, October 1837.

Pachulia, Vianor Pandzhovich, *Abkhaziia; Istoriko-kul'turnyi Ocherk*, Sukhumi, 1976.

——, *Po Istoricheskim Mestam Abkhazii*, Sukhumi, 1958.

Paleolog, G.; Sivinis, M., *Istoricheskii Ocherk Narodnoi Voiny za Nezavisimost' v Gretsii*, Sanktpetrburg, 1867.

Platana, 'O torgovle Trapezontskoi', *Zhurnal Maufaktur i Torgovli*, May 1834.

Parliamentary Papers, London, 1829 (XVII); 1830 (XXVII); 1831–2 (XXIV); 1833 (XLII.1); 1837–8 [137] (XLVIII).

Parliamentary Papers relative to the Affairs of the Levant, London, 1841, 3 vols.

Parry, Clive (ed.), *The Consolidated Treaty Series*, Dobbs Ferry, New York, 1969– .

Parry, V.J.; Yapp, M.E., *War, Technology, and Society in the Middle East*, London, 1975.

Pasternatskii, F.I.; Sergeev, N.V.; Voeikov, A.I., *Chernomorskoe Poberezh'e*, Sanktpetrburg, 1898.

Paullin, Charles Oscar, *Diplomatic Negociations of American Naval Officers 1778–1883*, Baltimore, 1912.

P.B., 'Neskol'ko slov o pokoinom admirale A.S. Greige', *Kronshtadtskii Vestnik*, 1862, no. 71.

Pekina, Z.M., *Russkaia Bibliografiia Morskogo Dela za 1701–1882 God Vkliuchitel'no*, Sanktpetrburg, 1885.

Pel'chinskii, V., *O Sostoianii Promishlennykh Sil Rossii do 1832 Goda*, Sanktpetrburg, 1833.

'Perepiska M.P. Lazareva s Kn. A.S. Menshikovym', *Russkii Arkhiv*, 1881, pt 3.

Perrier, Ferdinand, *La Syrie sous le Gouvernement de Méhmet-Ali jusqu'en 1840*, Paris, 1842.

Petran, Tabitha, *Syria, a Modern History*, London, 1978.

'Petr Ivanovich Rikord', *Russkii Biografischeskii Slovar'*, vol. 'Reitern-Rol'tsberg'.

Petroulos, John Anthony, *Politics and Statecraft in the Kingdom of Greece 1833–1843*, Princeton, 1968.

Phillips, W. Alison, *The War of Greek Independence 1821–1833*, London, 1897.

Pinter, Walter McKenzie, *Russian Economic Policy under Nicholas I*, Ithaca, 1967.

Pirenne, Henri, *Histoire de Belgique*, Brussels, 1929–32, 7 vols.

Pisarev, V. I., 'Metody zavoevaniia adygeiskogo naroda tsarizmom v pervoi polovine XIX v.', *Istoricheskie Zapiski*, September 1940.

'Pis'ma Admirala Lazareva', *Morskoi Sbornik*, January 1918.

Pitcairn-Jones, C. G., *Piracy in the Levant*, London, 1934.

Plantet, Eugène, *Correspondence des Beys de Tunis et des Consuls de France avec la Cour 1577–1830*, Paris, 1893–9, 3 vols.

——, *Correspondence des Deys d'Alger avec la Cour de France 1579–1833*, Paris, 1889, 2 vols.

'Plavanie voennykh sudov iz Arkhangel'ska v Kronshtadt s 1801–1842 god', *Zapiski Gidrograficheskogo Departamenta*, 2 (1844).

'Podvig Azovskogo kazach'ego voiska...na Chernom More', *Voennyi Zhurnal*, no. VI (1838).

Pohler, Dr John, *Bibliotheca Historico-Militaris*, Cassel, 1887, 4 vols.

Pokrovskii, M., 'Sbornik svedenii po istorii i statistike vneshnoi torgovli Rossii', *Khrrestomatiia po Istorii SSSR*, Moskva, 1949–53, 3 vols; Vol. 2.

Politis, Athanase, G. *Le Conflict Turco-Égyptien de 1838–1841 et les Derniers Années du Règne de Mohammed Aly d'après les Documents Diplomatiques Grecs*, Cairo, 1931.

Polkanov, A. I., *Sevastopol'skoe Vosstanie 1830 G.*, Simferopol', 1936.

'Politicheskoe i Torgovoe Polozhenie Beregov Chernogo Moria', *Severnaia Pchela*, no. 31, 21-II-1843.

Polnoe Sobranie Zakonov, Sanktpetrburg, Series I, 45 vols; Vol. 37 (1821); Series II, Vol. 4 (1829), Vol. 5(1), (1830), Vol. 6(1) (1831), Vol. 7 (1832), Vol. 8.1 (1833).

Porter, David, *Constantinople and its Environs*, New York, 1835. 2 vols.

'Postanovleniia i rasporiazheniia pravitel'tsva; vysochaishego poveleniia', *Zhurnal Manufaktur i Torgovli*, January 1835.

Post, Henry A.V., *A Visit to Greece and Constantinople in 1827–1828*, New York, 1830.

'The present strength, condition, and organisation of the Russian Navy', *United Service Journal*, November 1849.

Presniakov, Aleksandr Evgen'evich, *Emperor Nicholas I of Russia: the Apogee of Autocracy, 1825–1855*, Gulf Breeze, Fla., 1974.

Proces-Verbaux des Séances de la Chambre des Députés: Session de 1832, Paris, Vol. 4, 1833.

Prokesch-Osten, Count Anton, *Mehmed-Ali, Vize-König von Aegypten*, Vienna, 1877.

Przhetslavskii, Pavel, 'Vospominanie o blokade Derbenta, v 1831 godu (Kazymulloiu, s istorich. vedeniem)', *Kavkazskii Sbornik*, February 1864.
Psomiades, Harry J., *The Eastern Question; the Last Phase*, Thessaloniki, 1968.
Pückler-Muskau, Hermann Ludwig Heinrich von, *Aus Mehmet-Alis Reich*, Stuttgart, 1844, 3 vols.
Puryear, Vernon John, *England, Russia and the Straits Question 1844–1856*, Hamden, Conn. 1965.
——, *France and the Levant from the Bourbon Restoration to The Peace of Kutiah*, Los Angeles, 1941.
——, *International Economics and Diplomacy in the Near East*, Stanford, 1935.
——, *Napoleon and the Dardanelles*, Los Angeles, 1951.
——, 'Odessa: its rise and importance, 1815–1850', *Pacific Historical Review*, 3 (1934).
Putiatin, N.V., 'Adrianopol v 1829 Godu', *Russkii Arkhiv*, 1877, pt 2.
Rapport Fait au Nom du la Commission Chargée de L'Examen du Budget de Ministère de la Marine et des Colonies, pour l'Exercice 1834; Séance du 30 Mai 1833, Paris, 1833.
'Rasporiazheniia po upravleniiu general-gidrografa', *Zapiski Gidrograficheskago Departamenta*, 2 (1844).
Reid, Stuart J., *Life and Letters of the 1st Earl of Durham, 1792–1840*, London, 1906, 2 vols.
'Rélation de l'arrivée dans la rade d'Alger, le 30 Juillet 1829, du vaisseau de S.M. la Provence...', *Annales Maritimes et Coloniales*, 1830, partie non officielle, Vol. 1.
'Rélation de la bâtaille de Konieh', *Le Spectateur Militaire*, December 1836.
Resad, Ekren Kocu, *Yeniçeriler*, Istanbul, 1964.
Reynolds, Clark G., *Command of the Sea; the History and Strategy of Maritime Empires*, New York, 1974.
Rhinelander, L. Hamilton, 'Russia's Imperial Policy; the Administration of the Caucasus the First Half of the Nineteenth Century', *Canadian Slavic Papers*, 17, nos. 2–3 (1975).
Riboper, Aleksandr Ivanovich 'Zapiski', *Russkii Arkhiv*, May 1877.
Richmond, Sir Herbert, *Amphibious Warfare in British History*, Exeter, 1941.
——, *Statesmen and Sea Power*, Oxford, 1946.
Robertson, Frederick Leslie, *The Evolution of Naval Armament*, London, 1921.
Robinson, Gertrude, *David Urquhart*, Oxford, 1920.
Robinson, L.G. (ed.), *Letters of Princess Dorothea Lieven During her Residence in London 1812–1834*, New York, 1902.
Rodkey, Frederick Stanley, 'Anglo-Russian Negotiations About a "Permanent" Quadruple Alliance', *American Historical Review*, 35 (1930–31).
——, 'Colonel Campbell's Report on Egypt 1840 With Lord Palmerston's Comments', *Cambridge Historical Journal*, 3 (1929–31).
——, 'Conversations on Anglo-Russian Relations in 1828', *English Historical Review*, 50 (1935).
——, 'Lord Palmerston and the rejuvenation of Turkey, 1830–41; Part I, 1830–39', *Journal of Modern History*, December 1929.
——, *The Turko-Egyptian Question in the Relations of England, France and Russia 1832–1841*, Urbana, Ill., 1924, 2 Parts.

Romanovskii, D. I., *Kavkaz i Kavkazskaia Voina*, Sanktpetrburg, 1860.

Roncière, Charles de la, *Histoire de la Marine Française*, Paris, 1899, 4 vols.

Rose, John Holland, *The Indecisiveness of War and Other Essays*, London, 1927.

Roskill, Captain Stephan Wentworth, *The Strategy of Sea Power; its Development and Application*, London, 1962.

Rottiers, Bernaid Eugène Antoine, *Itinéraire de Tiflis à Constantinople*, Brussels, 1829.

Rowbottom, Commander W. B., 'Naval Operations on the Coast of Syria in 1840', *Royal United Service Institution Journal*, November 1952.

Rozhkova, M.K., *Ekonomicheskaiia Politika Tsarskogo Pravitel'stva na Srednem Vostoke vo Vtoroi Cherte XIX Veka i Russkaia Burzhuaziia*, Moskva, 1949.

Rudtorffer, Colonel Franz von, *Militär-Geograhie von Europa*, Prague, 1839.

Russell, William H., 'Foundations of Military Thought; Has Mahan's Time Arrived?' *Marine Corps Gazette*, May 1988, pp. 84–6.

Russell, Frank S., *Russian Wars with Turkey*, London, 1877.

Russkii Biograficheskii Slovar', Moskva, 1897–1916, 21 vols.

Russia; Manning of the navy, &c.', *United Service Journal*, January 1837.

'Russian Navy', *The Navy and Military Magazine*, December 1827.

Rustum, Assad, *Notes on Akka and Its Defences under Ibrahim Pasha*, Beirut, 1926.

Rykachev, Mikhail Aleksanrovich, *God Navarinskoi Kampanii*, Sanktpetrburg, 1977.

Sabry, M., *L'Empire Égyptiean sous Mohamed Ali et la Question d'Orient 1811–1849*, Paris, 1930.

Sammarco, Angelo (ed), *La Marina Egiziana sotto Mohammad Ali*, Cairo, 1931.

Sarlat, capitaine du Sphinx, 'Sommaire des operations...', *Annales Maritimes et Coloniales*, 1830, parie non officielle, Vol. 2.

Schiemann, Theodor, *Geschichte Russlands unter Kaiser Nikolaus I*, Berlin, 1904, 4 vols.

'Sekoum-kalleh, Mingrelia, and Goomri', *United Service Journal*, December 1855.

Semenov, Aleksei, *Izuchenie Istoricheskikh Svedenii o Rossiiskoi Vneshnei Torgovle i Promyshlennosti*, Sanktpetrburg, 1859, 3 vols.

A. Sergeev (ed.), 'Gr. A. Kh. Benkendorf o Rossii v 1827–1830 gg.', *Krasnyi Arkhiv*, Vol. 37 (1929).

——, 'Gr. A. Kh. Benkendorf o Rossii v 1831–32 Gg.', *Krasnyi Arkhiv*, Vol. 46 (1931).

Seton-Watson, Robert William, *Britain in Europe, 1789–1914*, Cambridge, 1937.

Sharp, James A. (ed.), *Memoirs of the Life and Services of Rear-Admiral Sir William Symonds, Kt., C.B., F.R.S., Surveyor of the Navy from 1832 to 1847...*, London, 1858.

Shavrov, 'Vostochnyi bereg Chernogo moria i ego znachenie dlia razvitiia russkogo moreplavaniia', *Morskoi Sbornik*, September 1862.

Shavrov, N. A., *Doklad Obshchestvu Sodeistviia Russkomu Torgovomu Moreplavaniiu o Chernom More i ego Vazhnosti dlia Russkogo Morekhodstva*, Sanktpetrburg, 1874.

Shaw, Stanford J., *History of the Ottoman Empire and Modern Turkey*, Cambridge, 1976–7, 2 vols.

Shcherbatov, Prince Aleksandr, *General-Fel'dmarshal Paskevich, ego Zhizn' i Deiatel'nost'*, Sanktpetrburg, 1889–1904, 6 vols.

Sheremet, V. I., *Turtsiia i Adrianopol'skii Mir 1829 God*, Moskva, 1976.

——, 'Turtsiia i Rotshilda v 1828–1830 gg.', *Vestnik Leningradskogo Gosudarstvennogo Universiteta (Istorii)*, 1967, No. 2.

Shershov, A. P., *K istorii Voennogo Korablestroeniia*, Moskva, 1959.

Shil'der, N. K., *Adrianopol'skii Mir 1829 Goda; iz Perepiska Grafa Dibicha*, Sanktpetrburg, 1879.

——, 'Adrianopol'skii mir. Po rasskazu Mikhailovskogo Danilevskogo', *Khrestomatiia po Istorii SSSR*, Moskva, 1949–53, 3 vols; Vol 2, (1682–1856).

Shipov, 'Ocherk zhizni i gosudarstvenno deiatel'nosti gr. Kankrina', *Biblioteka dlia Chteniia*, 1864.

Shotwell, James T., *Turkey at the Straits*, New York, 1940.

Shparo, O., *Osvobozhdenie Gretsii i Rossiia 1821–1829*, Moskva, 1965.

Sidrov, P. A. (ed.), *A. A. Bestuzhev-Marlinskii; Sochineniia v Dvukh Tomakh*, Moskva, 1958.

Shurman, Donald M., *The Education of a Navy; the Development of British Naval Strategic Thought, 1867–1914*, Chicago, 1965.

Siegelbaum, Lewis, 'The Odessa grain trade; a case study in urban growth and development in Tsarist Russia', *Journal of European Economic History*, Summer 1980.

Silvera, Alain, 'Edme-François Jomard and Egyptian reforms in 1839', *Middle Eastern Studies*, 7 (1971).

——, 'The first Egyptian student mission to France under Muhammed Ali', *Middle Eastern Studies*, 16 (1980).

Simpson, B. Mitchell (ed.), *The Development of Naval Thought; Essays by Herbert Rosinski*, Newport, 1977.

'Situation de la flotte égyptienne au 18 novembre 1836 (10 chaban 1252)', *Annales Maritimes et Coloniales*, partie non officielle, 1836, Vol. 2.

K.V. Sivkov, 'O protekh okonchaniia Kavkazskoi voiny v seredine XIX v.', *Istorii SSSR*, No. 3, (May–June 1958).

Sk., Al., 'Astrakhanskii port s 1783 po 1827 god', *Morskoi Sbornik*, January 1851.

Skal'kovskii, A. A., 'Torgovaia promyshlennost'' v Novorossiiskom Krae, *Zhurnal Ministerstva Vnutrennikh Del*, nos. 1–2, 1851.

——, *Zapiska o Plavanii Parokhoda k Tavricheskim i Vostochnym Beregam Chernogo Moria*, Odessa, 1836.

——, *Zapiski o Torgovykh i Promyshlennykh Silakh Odessi*, Sanktpetrburg, 1859.

'Sketches of a year's service in the Egyptian Marine in 1832 and 1833', *United Service Journal*, November 1833.

'Sketch of the rise and progress of Mehemet Ali, with a view of the affairs of Turkey and Egypt to the present time', *United Service Journal*, July 1839.

Slade, Sir Adolphus, *Maritime States and Military Navies*, London, 1859.

——, *Records of Travels in Turkey, Greece, &c. and of a Cruize in the Black Sea with the Captain Pacha in the Years 1829, 1830, and 1831*, London, 1833, 2 vols.

——, *Travels in Germany and Russia, including a Steam Voyage by the Danube and Euxine from Vienna to Constantinople in 1838, 39*, London, 1840.

——, *Turkey and the Crimean War, a Narrative of Historical Events*, London, 1867.

——, *Turkey, Greece, and Malta*, London, 1837, 2 vols.

'Smert' na slavu ili zashchita Mikhailovskogo ukrepleniia, 22 Marta 1840 goda', *Sbornik Gazety Kavkaza*, 1847, Part 1.

Smirnov, N. A., *Miuridizm na Kavkaze*, Moskva, 1963.

Smyth, W. H., 'A general description of Algiers', *United Service Journal*, 1830, Pt 2.

'Sobytiia v nachale 1840 goda', *Akty Sobranie Kavkazskoiu Arkheograficheskogo Kommissieiu*, Vol. 9.

Sokolov, Kapt.-Leit. Aleksandr, *Letopis' Krushenii i Pozharov Sudov Russkogo Flota, ot Nachala ego po 1854 God*, Sanktpetrburg, 1855.

Solov'ev, S. M., 'Vostochnyi Vopros v 1827, 1828 i 1829 Godakh', *Drevniaia i Novaia Rossiia*, October 1877.

Spencer, Edward, *Travels in Circassia, Krim Tartary &c., including a Steam Voyage Down the Danube from Vienna to Constantinople and Round the Black Sea in 1836*, London, 1837, 2 vols.

——, *Travels in the Western Caucasus, Including a Tour through Imeritia, Turkey, Moldavia, Galicia, Silesia and Moravia in 1836*, London, 1838, 2 vols.

'Spisok glavneishikh gosudarei i pravitelei Azii i severnoi Afriki, v 1937 godu', *Zhurnal Ministerstva Narodnogo Prosveshcheniia*, August 1837.

Stanislavskaia, A. M., *Russko-Angliiskie Otnosheniia i Problemy Sredizemnomoriia*, Moskva 1962.

'Statisticheskie svedeniia o Gollendii', *Zhurnal Ministerstva Narodnago Prosvecheniia*, March 1841.

'Statisticheskoe obozrenie voenno-portovogo goroda Sevastopolia, za 1839 god', *Zhurnal Ministerstva Vnutrennikh Del*, August 1840.

'Statisticheskoe opisanie Azovskogo torgovogo moreplavaniia', *Zhurnal Manufaktur i Torgovli*, June 1839.

Stavraki, Mikhail Ivanovich, 'Russkie na Bosfor v 1833 godu', *Russkaia Starina*, August 1884.

Stavrianos, Leften S., *The Balkans Since 1453*, New York, 1958.

Stern, Alfred, 'Documents relatifs a la défection de la flotte turque en 1839', *Revue Historique*, May–August 1911.

Strachen, P. L., *On the Oriental Question and the Balance of Power*, Paris, 1841.

Sudley, Lord (ed.), *The Lieven–Palmerston Correspondence*, London, 1943.

'Suite des notes sur la marine turque en 1836', *Annales Maritimes et Coloniales*, 1836, partie non officielle, Vol. 2.

Sukhotin, F. M., 'Iz Pisem M. P. Lazareva k A. I. Verevkinu (1837–1842)', *Russkii Arkhiv*, 1883, Pt 3.

'Sur les châteaux forts de l'Hellespont', *Le Spectateur Militaire*, May 1828.

'Svedeniia o torgovle po trem glavneishim portam Imperii za 1835 god', *Zhurnal Ministerstva Vnutrennikh Del*, March 1836.

'Svedenie o torgovle v Konstaninople', *Zhurnal Manufaktur i Torgovli*, April 1842.

Tagher, Jacques, *Mémoires de A. B. Clot Bey*, Cairo, 1945.

Tal'berg, N. D., *Imperator Nikolai I v Svete Istoricheskoi Pravdi 1826–1829 (1830, 1831, 1832–34) Gg.*, Jordanville, NY, 1954–57, 4 Parts.

Tappe, E. D., 'Bell and Anderson: a Scottish partnership in Wallachia', *Balkan Studies*, 1971.

Tatlock, T., 'The Ubykhs', *Caucasian Review*, no. 7 (1958).

Temperley, Harold William Vazeille, *England and the Near East; the Crimea*, London, reprinted 1964.

Temple, Grenville T., *Excursions in the Mediterranean*, London, 1835, 2 vols.

Thomas, M., 'Rélation de la bâtaille de Nezib', *Le Spectateur Militaire*, May 1840.

Tillet, Lowell R., 'Shamil and Muridism in Recent Soviet historiography', *Slavonic and East European Review*, 20 (April 1961).

'Torgovliia Rossii s Gretsiei', *Zhurnal Manufaktur i Torgovli*, May 1836.

'Torgovoe moreplavanie po Bosforu', *Zhurnal Ministerstva Vnutrennikh Del*, March 1836.

'Torgovoe sudokhodstvo v Konstantinople', *Zhurnal Manufaktur i Torgovli*, May 1842.

'Torgovye puti iz vnutrennikh oblastei Imperii v Zakavkazskii krai', *Zhurnal Ministerstva Vnutrennikh Del*, January 1836.

Toy, Sidney, *The Castles of the Bosphorus*, Oxford, 1930.

Traho, Ramazan, 'Literature on Circassia and the Circassians', *Caucasian Review*, no. 1 (1955).

Troude, O., *Bâtailles Navales de France*, Paris, 1867, 4 vols.

Trudy Odesskogo Staticheskogo Komiteta, Odessa, 1865–70, 4 vols.

Tsimmerman, M. A., *Bosfor i Dardanelli*, Sanktpetrburg, 1912.

Tuleja, T. V., 'The Historic Pattern of Russian Naval Policy', *U.S. Naval Institute Proceedings*, September 1961.

Turgay, A. Uner, 'Trade and merchants in nineteenth-century Trabzon: elements of ethnic conflict', Braude, Benjamin and Lewis, Bernard (eds), *Christians and Jews in the Ottoman Empire*, London, 1982, 2 vols.

Tusun, Prince, *'Umar Al-Jaish al-Misr al-Barri wa al-Bahr'*, Cairo, 1940.

Tzamitzis, A. I., 'Ships, ports, and sailors', Stelius A. Papadopoulos (ed.), *The Greek Merchant Marine (1453–1850)*, Athens, 1972.

Tzu, Sun, 'On the Art of War' T. R. Phillips (ed.), *Roots of Strategy*, Harrisburg, PA, 1940.

'Uchilishch torgovogo moreplavaniia v Khersone', *Zhurnal Manufaktur i Torgovli*, November 1838.

Urquhart, David, *Turkey and Its Resources*, London, 1833.

Ushakov, A., *Istoriia Voennykh Deistvii v Aziatskoi Turtsii v 1828 i 1829 Godakh*, Varshava, 1843, 2 vols.

Ustrialov, Nikolai Gerasimovich, *Istoricheskoe Obozrevanie Tsarstvovaniia Gosudaria Nikolaia I*, Sanktpetrburg, 1847.

'Utverzhdenie nashe v Abkhaziia', *Kavkazskii Sbornik*, Vol. 13 (1889).

Valentini, General F.W. Baron de, *Description of the Seat of the War in European Turkey*, London, 1854.

Váli, Ferenc Algert, *The Turkish Straits and NATO*, Stanford, 1972.

Veidenbaum, E. G. *Putevoditel' po Kavkazu*, Tiflis, 1888.

Vereté, M., 'Palmerston and the Levant Crisis, 1832', *Journal of Modern History*, 24 (June 1952).

Verigin, A., *Voennoe Obozrenie Pokhoda Rossiiskikh Voisk v Evropeiskoi Turtsii v 1829 Godu*, Sanktpetrburg, 1846.

Veselago, F. F., *Kratkaia Svedeniia o Russkikh Morskikh Srazheniiakh za Dva Stoletiia s 1656 po 1856 God*, Sanktpetrburg, 1871.

——, *Ocherk Istoriia Morskogo Kadetskogo Korpusa s Prilozheniem Spiska Vospitannikov za 100 Let*, Sanktpetrburg, 1852.

——, *Spisok Russkikh Voennyh Sudov s 1668 po 1860 God*, Sanktpetrburg, 1872.

'Vidy vnutrenniago sudokhodstva v Rossii, v 1839 godu', *Zhurnal Ministerstva Narodnago Prosveshcheniia*, January 1841.

Viesse de Marmont, Auguste Frédéric Louis, *The Present State of the Turkish Empire*, London, 1839.

Viskovatov, A., 'Soiuz Rossii s Turetsiei i Russkii Flot v Konstantinople', *Severnaia Pchela*, nos 46–8, 1833.

'Vnutrennee sudokhodstvo v Rossii v 1837 godu', *Zhurnal Manufaktur i Torgovli*, October 1838.

'Vnutrennee sudokhodstvo v Rossii v 1838 godu', *Zhurnal Manufaktur i Torgovli*, September 1839.

'Voennaia sila Pashi Egipetskogo', *Voennyi Zhurnal*, April 1839.

Volkonskii, N. A., 'Voina na vostochnom Kavkaze s 1824 po 1834 g. v sviazi s miuridizm (prodolzhenie), *Kavkazskii Sbornik*, 11 (1857).

Vol'skii, Mikhail, *Ocherk Istorii Khlebnoi Torgovli Novorossiikogo Kraia s drevneiskikh Vremen Do 1852 Godu*, Odessa, 1854.

'Vospominaniia Grigoriia Ivanovicha Filipsona', *Russkii Arkhiv*, 1883, Pt 3.

'Vospominaniia Kavkazskogo ofitsera', *Russkii Vestnik*, September 1864.

'Vospominanie o zhizni i sluzhbe Admirala Aleksandra Pavlovicha Avinova', *Morskoi Sbornik*, January 1855.

'Vostochnaia Politika Imperatora Nikolaia I-go', *Istoricheskii Vestnik*, 46 (1891).

'Voyages de Hassan-Effendi, oficier de la marine Égyptienne, à bord des vaisseaux français', *Annales Maritimes et Coloniales*, partie non officielle, 1834, Vol. 2.

Vronchenko, Mikhail Pavlovich, *Obozrenie Maloi Azii v Nyneshnem eia Sostoianii*, Sanktpetrburg, 1839, 2 vols.

Webster, C. K., *The Foreign Policy of Palmerston 1830–44*, London, 1951, 2 vols.

——, 'Palmerston, Metternich, and the European System 1830–1841', *Proceedings of the British Academy*, 10 (1934).

——, 'Urquhart, Ponsonby, and Palmerston', *English Historical Review*, 62 (1947).

Westcott, Allan, *Mahan on Naval Warfare: Selections on the Writings of Rear Admiral Alfred Thayer Mahan*, London, 1919.

Wheelock, Patricia DeKay, 'Henry Eckford (1775–1832), an American shipbuilder', *American Neptune*, 7 (1947).

Wilbrahim, Sir Richard, 'Asia in Europe and A Sketch of The Russo-Turkish Campaigns of 1828–29, with Maps', *Royal United Service Institution Journal*, 20 (1876).

——, *Travels in the Trans-Caucasian Provinces of Russia . . . in the Autumn and Winter of 1837*, London, 1839.

Williams, H. Noel, *Life and Letters of Admiral Sir Charles Napier, K.C.B. (1766–1860)*, London, 1917.

Wilmot, Sir Sydney Marrow Eardley, *Life of Vice-Admiral Edmund, Lord Lyons*, London, 1898.

Woodhouse, Christopher Montague, *The Battle of Navarino*, London, 1965.

——, *Capodistrias*, London, 1973.

——, *The Greek War of Independence; its Historical Setting*, London, 1952.

Wright, G., 'The Bosphorus – anchorages of Therapia and Tophana', *Nautical Magazine*, December 1841.

Yovanovitch, Vojislav M., *An English Bibliography on the Near Eastern Question 1481–1906*, Belgrade, 1909.

Zaionchkovskii, A. M., *Vostochnaia Voina 1853–1856*, Sanktpetrburg, 1908, 2 vols.

Zakrevskii, 'Fregat "Shtandart" 1830 god', *Morskoi Sbornik*, June 1861.

——, 'Korabl "Erivan" 1833 god', *Morskoi Sbornik*, March 1861.

——, 'Na beregu v Sevatopole', *Morskoi Sbornik*, April 1861.

'Zamechaniia o reide pri Sukhum-Kale, Leitenanta Romanova, Zaniatiia Gidrografiskogo Depo', *Zapiski Gidrograficheskogo Departamenta*, Vol. 1 (1842).

'Zapiska o Turtsii, po dannaia grafa A. Kh. Benkendorfa v 1833 godu', *Russkii Arkhiv*, 1895, Pt 3.

Zapiski Uchenogo Komiteta Glavnogo Morskogo Shtaba Chast' III (1830).

Zhigarev, S. A., *Russkaia Politika v Vostochnom Voprose*, Moskva, 1896, 2 vols.

Zolotov, V. A., *Vneshnaia Torgovlia Iuzhnoi Rossii v Pervoi Polovine XIX Veka*, Rostov, 1963.

Zotov, R. M., *Voennaia Istoriia Rossiiskogo Gosudarstva*, Sanktpetrburg, 1839, 5 pts.

Zubov, Platon, *Kartina Kavkazskogo Kraia*, Sanktpetrburg, 1834–5, 4 pts.

——, *Podvigi Russkikh Voinov v Stranakh Kavkazskikh s 1800 po 1834 G.*, Sanktpetrburg, 1835, 2 vols.

——, *Shest' Pisem Gruzii i Kavkaze Pisannyia v 1833 Godu*, Moskva, 1834.

Index

292